Individual therapy:
a handbook

Open University Press
Psychotherapy Handbooks Series
Series editor: Windy Dryden

TITLES IN THE SERIES

Published titles:

Individual Therapy: A Handbook
Windy Dryden (ed.)

Integrative and Eclectic Therapy: A Handbook
Windy Dryden (ed.)

Hypnotherapy: A Handbook
Michael Heap and Windy Dryden (eds)

Couple Therapy: A Handbook
Douglas Hooper and Windy Dryden (eds)

Child and Adolescent Therapy: A Handbook
David A Lane and Andrew Miller (eds)

Art Therapy: A Handbook
Diane Waller and Andrea Gilroy (eds)

Individual therapy: a handbook

Edited by
WINDY DRYDEN

Open University Press
Milton Keynes · Philadelphia

Open University Press
Celtic Court
22 Ballmoor
Buckingham MK18 1XW

and
1900 Frost Road, Suite 101
Bristol, PA 19007, USA

First Published 1990
Reprinted 1991, 1992, 1993, 1994, 1995

British Library Cataloguing in publication data

Individual therapy.—Rev. ed
  1. Medicine. Psychotherapy
  I. Dryden, Windy   II. Individual therapy in Britain.
  III. Psychotherapy handbooks series
  616.8914

  ISBN 0–335–09446–5
  ISBN 0–335–09445–7 (pbk)

Library of Congress Cataloging-in-Publication Data

Individual therapy / edited by Windy Dryden.
    p. cm.
    ISBN 0–335–09446–5. — ISBN 0–335–09445–7 (pbk.)
    1. Psychotherapy.   I. Dryden, Windy.
  RCX 480.I497   1990
  616.89'dc20   89–78212
                                                CIP

Typeset by Colset Private Ltd, Singapore
Printed and bound in Great Britain by
Biddles Ltd, Guildford and King's Lynn

This book is dedicated to current and future students on the MSc Counselling course in the Department of Psychology at Goldsmiths' College, University of London, and to the memory of Laurence Collinson and Kenneth Lambert

Contents

Preface

The preceding edition of this handbook, *Individual Therapy in Britain* (Dryden 1984), attempted to fill a gap in the market by having British authors write on well-established approaches to individual psychotherapy for a British readership. Judging by the feedback received (and the sales figures!) the book was successful in its aims.

In this handbook edition the most successful elements of the previous book have been retained. Contributors* to this volume were asked to keep firmly to a common structure (see Appendix 1) in writing their chapters. This structure has been expanded from the first edition to include (1) the approach's views on how psychological change *outside* the therapeutic situation is deemed to occur; (2) the selection criteria that are used by practitioners of the approach in question to determine whether or not clients will benefit from the approach in its *individual format* (the inclusion of this item enabled me to omit the chapter on 'Therapeutic arenas' which appeared in the first edition); and (3) the limitations of each approach (again the inclusion of this item permitted the omission of the separate chapter on limitations that appeared in the first edition).

With respect to the therapies covered, a chapter on Adlerian therapy has been added here and a chapter on cognitive therapy replaces that on rational-emotive therapy (RET) which appeared in the first edition. This was done to acknowledge the fact that cognitive therapy is currently practised more widely in Britain than RET. Unfortunately there was not enough room for both of these cognitive-behaviour therapies to be included.

Greater emphasis has been placed in this volume on purity of approach. This is particularly true in the chapters on 'Psychodynamic therapy: the Freudian approach' and on 'Behaviour therapy', which are more 'pure' than the corresponding chapters in the first edition. The feedback I received from readers indicated that greater 'purity' would be welcomed in this new edition.

A number of other changes have also been made. New to this edition are (1) a chapter which places psychotherapy in its British social context; (2) one which

---

*It should be noted that contributors who were updating their chapters were asked to include a new case example.

considers the major research findings on individual therapy; and (3) one which deals with the issues of the training and supervision of individual therapists. Gone are the chapters on eclectic approaches to individual therapy (a separate planned volume in this series entitled *Integrative and Eclectic Therapy: A Handbook* will be devoted to this increasingly important area of psychotherapy). Finally, I have used a different and, I hope, less confusing format for the comparative chapter.

The book ends as did the first edition with information on clinical services and training opportunities offered by every approach (see Appendix 2).

Once again I welcome feedback on this, the first in the *Psychotherapy Handbooks* series, and hope that after reading the book readers will join me in thanking all the contributors for a job very well done.

Reference

Dryden, W. (ed.) (1984) *Individual Therapy in Britain*, Milton Keynes: Open University Press.

Windy Dryden
Goldsmiths' College
University of London

The editor and contributors

WINDY DRYDEN is Senior Lecturer in Psychology at Goldsmiths' College, University of London, and has edited or written thirty books in the area of counselling and psychotherapy. He edits two series for the Open University Press, *Psychotherapy Handbooks* and *Therapeutically Speaking*, and three for Sage Publications, *Counselling in Action*, *Counselling in Practice* (with E. Thomas Dowd) and *Key Figures in Counselling and Psychotherapy*. He is a Fellow of the British Psychological Society.

MARK AVELINE, MD FRC Psych., is Consultant Psychotherapist for the Nottingham Health Authority and Clinical Teacher in the Medical School. His research and clinical publications are on teaching individual and group psychotherapy with an interpersonal focus, forming the membership examination of the Royal College of Psychiatrists, group therapy, action techniques, psychodrama, diabetes, and the use of questionnaires in assessment for psychotherapy. He is senior editor with Windy Dryden of *Group Therapy in Britain* (Milton Keynes: Open University, 1988).

MICHAEL BARKHAM is a Research Clinical Psychologist in the MRC/ESRC Social and Applied Psychology Unit, University of Sheffield. He is actively engaged in several comparative studies investigating the process of outcome in psychotherapy and has a particular interest in the evaluation of very brief psychotherapeutic interventions. He has published in clinical psychology, counselling, and psychotherapy journals, and is an active member within the UK chapter of the Society for Psychotherapy Research (SPR).

RICHARD CARVALHO is a psychiatrist and a Jungian analyst. He is in analytic practice and a psychotherapist at St Mary's Hospital, London. He has published several papers on Jungian psychotherapy, including two in the *Journal of Analytical Psychology*.

PETRŪSKA CLARKSON is a clinical psychologist, a psychotherapist, a Clinical Teaching and Supervising Transactional Analyst – ITAA and a past member of the ITAA Board of Trustees. She founded metanoia Psychotherapy Training Institute in London. Petrūska has published numerous articles on Transactional Analysis and other psychotherapies and is currently working on an advanced TA book to be published by Routledge. She is the Co-ordinator of the British branch of the Society for the Exploration of Psychotherapy Integration.

JENNY CLIFFORD is an Adlerian Counsellor Trainer and Supervisor and Chairman of the Adlerian Society for Individual Psychology. She is a speech therapist and has a psychology degree. She co-authored a chapter on 'Family counselling with children who stutter: an Adlerian approach', in Celia Levy (ed.) *Stuttering Therapies: Practical Approaches* (London: Croom Helm, 1987), and is co-author, with Charlotte Padfield and Elizabeth Smith, of an article on using the Adlerian approach with adults who stammer, in *Speech Therapy in Practice*, 4, 6, 1989.

CASSIE COOPER is a psychotherapist/psychologist who is Head of the Student Counselling and Welfare Services at the Harrow College of Higher Education, London. She is the author of many papers on psychotherapy and counselling published in learned journals, and has contributed chapters in V.J. Varma (ed.) *Psychotherapy Today* (London: Constable, 1974) and in H. Cooper (ed.) *Soul Searching* (London: SCM Press, 1988). She is, at present, working on a chapter for *The Secret Life of Vulnerable Children* (London: Routledge) to be published in September 1991. She is currently Editor of the Newsletter of the Psychotherapy Section of the British Psychological Society.

EMMY VAN DEURZEN-SMITH is Director of the Regent's College Psychology Programmes, including the Antioch University MA in the Psychology of Therapy and Counselling. She is author of *Existential Counselling in Practice* (London: Sage, 1988) and is the founder and first Chair of the Society for Existential Analysis.

FAY FRANSELLA is Founder and Director of the Centre for Personal Construct Psychology in London. She has written or edited ten books, mainly in the areas of the theory and applications of personal construct psychology. She is currently co-authoring a book on personal construct counselling, with Peggy Dalton, in the *Counselling in Action* series (Sage Publications) edited by Windy Dryden.

MARIA GILBERT is a clinical psychologist, a psychotherapist, a Clinical Teaching and Supervising Transactional Analyst – ITAA and a past member of the ITAA Board of Trustees. She heads a major training programme in Transactional Analysis at metanoia Psychotherapy Training Institute in London. She has co-authored several articles on Transactional Analysis and is currently involved in research on supervision.

STIRLING MOOREY is Lecturer in Psychological Medicine at the Royal Marsden Hospital, London. He has written on the clinical application of cognitive therapy in depression and drug abuse and is currently engaged in research into the effectiveness of cognitive therapy in distressed cancer patients. He is co-author with Dr Steven Greer of *Psychological Therapy for Cancer Patients: A New Approach* (Oxford: Heinemann Medical Books, 1989).

GERALDINE O'SULLIVAN is a Lecturer/Research Worker in Experimental Psycho-pathology, Department of Psychiatry, Institute of Psychiatry, London. She is currently involved in research into the treatment of agoraphobics. She has written five articles on the area of efficacy of various treatments in anxiety disorders, both in the short term and long term. In addition, she has published articles on diverse topics such as arsonists and self-immolators, mental illness in doctors and lycanthropy.

FAYE PAGE is a Principal Clinical Psychologist working part-time in a NHS psychiatric hospital in Worcester and has a growing private practice. She facilitates ongoing residential Gestalt therapy groups and is a freelance consultant and trainer in England and Wales for various organizations. She is an Associate Fellow of the British Psychological Society, chartered clinical psychologist and an honorary tutor for the Clinical Psychology Department in the University of Birmingham. Her interest and training in Gestalt therapy began about fifteen years ago in the USA and is continuous.

MALCOLM PARLETT is a chartered psychologist, Gestalt psychotherapist and trainer, and organizational consultant in Bristol. He is General Secretary of the Gestalt Psychotherapy Training Institute in the United Kingdom, and is also associated with the Gestalt Centre, London, and the metanoia Psychotherapy Training Institute. He is a member of the Gestalt Institute of Cleveland, USA, where he trained in 1977–8. He is editor of a forthcoming publication, *The British Gestalt Journal*.

DAVID PILGRIM is Senior Lecturer in Psychology at Roehampton Institute. His interests are currently in mental health policy and in the history of psychology and psychotherapy.

DAVID L. SMITH is Associate Director of the Psychology Programme, Regent's College, London. He has published numerous papers on psychoanalysis and related subjects in professional journals. He is a specialist in communicative psychoanalysis; his forthcoming book on this subject is *Hidden Conversations* (London: Routledge).

BRIAN THORNE is Director of Student Counselling at the University of East Anglia, Norwich, and a founding partner of the Norwich Centre. He has published widely in the fields of counselling and education; he is currently associate editor of the *Person-Centred Review*. He is co-author with Dave Mearns of *Person-Centred Counselling in Action* (London: Sage, 1988).

British psychotherapy in context

DAVID PILGRIM

This chapter will be about a form of psychological practice (psychotherapy) but will not be written from a psychological perspective. That is, some attempt will be made to go outside the boundaries of academic and therapeutic psychology and draw upon other bodies of knowledge, notably sociology, social history and economics, in order to offer some account of the way in which British psychotherapy has been shaped by its social context. Attempts at developing a sociology of psychological knowledge have produced some fruitful and provocative ideas but, by and large, they have not captured the sustained attention of psychotherapists (see e.g. Holland 1977; Ingleby 1985). I hope to build upon these, and other undervalued works, in order to re-focus the attention of therapists on the social origins of their own practice. This social perspective is necessary in order to correct some patterns of faulty reasoning evident within writings in the field. In particular, there is a tendency to view the history of ideas and practices associated with psychotherapy as a history of great people or, less speciously, a history of great ideas. Within these inadequate accounts, it is assumed that a single variable, e.g. genius, or brilliance of theory, or scientific credibility, can account for why this, rather than that, version of theory and practice took root and flourished, while others were marginalized or superseded.

In the first edition of this book (Dryden 1984) authors, to various degrees, cited biographical details of innovators or the persuasiveness of new arguments, e.g. the irresistible thoughts of Meichenbaum in relation to 'cognitive-behaviourism', when placing their topic in its British context. To be clear about this, I am not arguing that clever people have no role in history nor that the cogency of particular theoretical innovations have no relevance. What I am emphasizing is that these are weak rationales, *in themselves*, to account for socio-historical developments in the field of psychotherapy, unless they are placed into a wider socio-economic context.

The tendency on the part of these authors to offer incomplete accounts of their therapy in context may be a function of the subdivision of intellectual labour (Braverman 1974). Because of the compartmentalization of academic skills and knowledge, psychologists and psychotherapists not surprisingly, in the main, reason psychologically. Psychological models, no matter how reflexive they are at the individual level (e.g. Kelly 1955), cannot account for their own existence as *social* phenomena (Holland 1981). Having introduced these cautions, I want to begin to focus on those factors which need to be invoked in order to build up a picture of psychotherapy in its British social context. The factors include the following:

1 *Politics* e.g. the politics of mental health professionalism; the relationship between professional structures in the field of mental health and the development of individual psychotherapy; the sociology of the mental health professions, with particular emphasis on professional dominance.
2 *Economics* e.g. variations over time in socio-economic conditions and their influence on policies concerning the social control of psychological distress; the role of the mental hospital in the past and its absence in the future; the link between war and peace economies and psychotherapy.
3 *British culture* e.g. the role of cultural traditions in Britain in influencing the legitimacy of particular psychotherapeutic forms of knowledge; philosophical continuities in British intellectual life; and the role of foreign intellectual labour in Britain.

It can be seen that even in this summarized form, the complex of social variables noted is extensive. Before moving on to explore some of this complexity, within the constraints of space in this chapter, a particular assumption needs to be declared. Human systems, which are the context for the emergence of knowledge forms including psychotherapy, are open systems. As such, they defy complete description as they are in dynamic flux over time. Consequently, descriptions and, sometimes, explanations can be offered about the past but predictions about the future are precarious. As with Freud's emphasis on learning after the event within, and about, individuals, I assume that the past is easier to make sense of than the future in relation to the social world. Now that these assumptions have been outlined, psychotherapy in Britain will be explored in relation to political, economic and cultural factors in its history.

Victorian roots

Britain is a favoured focus for social historians of psychiatric practice (e.g. Scull 1979; Donnelly 1983). The reasons for this are not exactly clear but one explanation could be that as the oldest capitalist country, its forms of social organization represented prototypes for elsewhere. As far as the early signs of psychotherapy are concerned, moral therapy emerged within the expanding state asylum system in the nineteenth century, and descriptions of the events in England and France are described by Scull (1979) and Castel (1985) respectively. Moral therapy can be viewed as an early attempt to operate psychological rather than physical methods to correct mental disorder. Its roots in the charity sector at the Quaker Retreat in York, at the beginning of the nineteenth century, led to it being commonplace in the rhetoric of social reformers, but it transferred poorly to the state asylum system (Digby 1985). Whether it represented a more humane form of intervention than chains and sedation is a moot point.

While it emphasized the inhuman tendency within early biological psychiatry (Bynum 1974), Castel (1985) describes it as 'authoritarian pedagogy', with the tyranny of social conformity replacing the tyranny of physical interference. However it is evaluated, it is certainly true that its utility for the state was linked closely to its value in re-socializing deviants. As its name suggests, this was done within an overall moral regime, which depended on a mixture of benign and authoritarian paternalism, in order to reverse deviant conduct.

As far as future trends were concerned, what was important about moral treatment was that it offered *both* individual and collective rationales for changing conduct. Falret, reviewing the scene in the mid-nineteenth century (cited by Castel 1985), considered that the blanket application of the rules of moral therapy within an institution were necessary because of the inexact state of the science or art of this brand of medicine at the time. He hoped that refinements of moral therapy as it developed would allow *each patient to be treated individually*.

Ultimately moral therapy failed to become the dominant rationale within Victorian psychiatry not because of its inadequacy as a version of social control for the state, but because of the offence it created to the profession of medicine (Scull 1979). The primary need of the state was that mental disorder was segregated in order to leave the economic system free to operate uncontaminated by the unemployed or unemployable (Barham 1984). The success or otherwise of particular treatment methods were a secondary political consideration. To this day all rationales for changing mental disorder (as opposed to containing or controlling it) have proved to fall well short of ideal; this is as true for biological as for psychological models.

Mainstream medicine in the nineteenth century, and for a long time to come, was characterized by a biological rather than psychological or social model of aetiology and treatment. Consequently, moral therapy constituted, *inter alia*, an ideological opposition to bio-determinism and physical treatment methods. According to Scull and Bynum, a strategic error of Tuke, the patriarch of moral therapy at York, was his terminology ('treatment', 'illness', and so on, which were medical terms although Tuke was not a physician) along with a deliberate emphasis on the ordinary non-expert features of his approach (such as paternalism and kindness, which were not peculiar to experts). This error made Tuke's approach vulnerable to attack from biological psychiatrists, who could thereby protect their status and salaries. The use of medical terminology poses problems to this day when non-physicians use it in relation to a client group over which they hope to have some jurisdiction (Pilgrim 1987b). Thus today the term 'psychotherapy' remains problematic for non-medical practitioners, in terms of their claiming autonomous status within health care contexts.

What is implicit to this description which needs to be considered in itself now is the dominant role of medicine (Freidson 1970). The position argued by most social historians of British psychiatry is that in the mid-nineteenth century, the medical profession as a whole (Parry and Parry 1976) and in its psychiatric specialization (Scull 1979; Baruch and Treacher 1978) succeeded in gaining a legal mandate on behalf of the state to have sole jurisdiction over deviance-as-illness. As far as Victorian psychiatry was concerned, the profession established a position of dominance in three ways. First, it established a legal monopoly of jurisdiction over forms of deviance which could be framed as illness (in the Lunacy Act 1842 and the General Medical Act 1858). Second, it secured a territorial base to control and to work from, the mental hospital. Third, it offered a conceptual framework of mental disorder which would guarantee that medicine would be in permanent control of knowledge about mental disorder (bio-determinism). Thus moral therapy or any *subsequent* psychological model would need to be warded off, as would any move towards de-carceration. Although medicine exploited moral therapy for rhetorical purposes at times, emphasizing its humanitarianism, in practice, this prototype of psychotherapy was marginalized in the Victorian asylum system.

Warfare and British psychotherapy

Following the demise of moral therapy, asylum-based, biological psychiatry began to consolidate its position at the turn of this century. Despite the seminal developments surrounding psychoanalysis and its derivatives at this time, depth psychology merely provoked vociferous antipathy from the medical profession. It is true that it commanded some version of allegiance from a very small number of physicians, some of whom were quite prestigious (Glover, Murray, Ernest Jones, Forsyth, Eder, Trotter, Hart and Stanford Read). However, the bulk of the profession were ignorant of, or indifferent or hostile to, the 'new psychology'. Developments in the latter were barely reported or cited in medical journals. Leaders of the medical profession such as Mercier led a campaign to boycott psychoanalysis as a morally corrupting influence. Stone (1985) reports a meeting held at the BMA (Neurological Section) in which the audience stood up and left the room before the beginning of a discussion on a paper presented by Jones and Eder. As Stone notes, the status of psychoanalysis and its psychotherapeutic derivatives was dramatically changed by the outbreak of the First World War.

Until this event, the great bulk of interest on the part of asylum doctors had been in madness. After all, during times of a peace economy it is the disruptive influence of the mad (and other pauper deviants such as criminals and handicapped people) that stands out as being of political importance to the state. Warfare brings a different set of problems as far as managing the population is concerned. Before 1914, neurologists, not 'mad-doctors', were more likely to take a psychological interest in the lesser disturbed (neurotic) part of the population. This interest was intensified during the war years. Not only were biological psychiatrists displaced by neurologists and psychologists for practical reasons when shell-shock was being described and treated, but also the whole edifice of Kraepelinian psychiatry, which gave self-congratulatory accounts of its own performance in peacetime (Doerner 1970), was being shaken. Bio-determinism in Victorian psychiatry largely depended on the unproven, elitist assumption that mental disorder was a result of genetically inherited degeneracy. What the war spawned was a large number of stalwart British soldiers (volunteers in the lower ranks and commissioned officers and gentlemen) who were mentally breaking down. It was out of the question to tolerate the unpatriotic notion that these men were in any sense degenerate. Environmentalist and psychological ideas could thus find a new type of legitimacy on the mental health scene.

Hence, the war had vital consequences. It helped legitimize the role of verbal psychotherapy within medicine. For a while it undermined the power of asylum doctors and their bio-deterministic ideas. As Stone notes about this time 'If psychotherapists had been the hero of the piece, the asylum doctors had been its villains' (Stone 1985: 236). Also, the war contributed to the emergence of a psychological discourse in Britain. Psychoanalytical and other psychological ideas about shell-shock flourished in the immediate post-war period. In 1919 the first Section in the British Psychological Society to be established within this current was the Medical Section. Along with the Medico-Psychological Association (later the Royal College of Psychiatrists) the BPS was becoming a forum for psychological ideas.

Asylum doctors were so out of favour with the government after the First World War that none were appointed to the Royal Commission on Lunacy and Mental Disorder in 1924 (Armstrong 1980). This led to a gap between policy and practice during the inter-war periods. In 1930 the Mental Treatment Act was passed which was a relatively liberal piece of legislation encouraging both voluntary patients, and outpatient, rather than inpatient, treatment. Following on the 1924 Commission, such legislation took the form it did because of the temporary marginalization of asylum doctors at the level of mental health policy formation. However, their practical authority was gradually being re-established in the asylum system. The outpatient clinics set up to mop up after the war, responding to neuroses psychotherapeutically, were competing with business as usual in the hospitals, which were returning to their traditional peacetime role of segregating the disruptive mad. Whatever the 1930 Act said, old-fashioned inpatient psychiatry was returning to an ascendant position.

During this period, Klein and the Freuds came and settled in Britain. This had the effect of importing a crucial developing tension within psychoanalysis about the role of very early infantile experience, which dated back to a dispute between Anna Freud and Klein at the Innsbruck Conference in 1927 (Roazen 1974). However, a vital point to make here is that the existence in England of such esteemed psychoanalytical mentors did not, in the inter-war period, produce an impact on mainstream psychiatry. None the less, the scene was set for some crucial developments after the defeat of Nazism. Although the practical impact of psychoanalysis was warded off by asylum doctors, theoretical creativity in the inter-war period was not stymied. Moreover, within this creativity were elaborate psychoanalytical debates about warfare itself, which were available to military authorities (Richards 1986b). Following on from this first point, the anticipation of problems of the First World War recurring led military authorities to seek to pre-empt, where possible, psychological difficulties. Not surprisingly, psychoanalysts found themselves to be favoured advisers on military selection, morale and psychotherapy during the course of the war and its aftermath. These included Rees, Bion, Rickman, Main and Foulkes. This grouping, as with the psychotherapists of the First World War, temporarily displaced asylum doctors as far as state-recognized psychiatric leadership was concerned.

Another implication emerging from the Second World War was that the previous emphasis on individual psychotherapy was altered. The pressure to see more 'soldier-patients' led to the military psychoanalysts experimenting with both group therapy and ward democracy as an enabling process (the beginnings of the therapeutic community movement in Britain). Bion's seminal work on group dynamics, *Experiences in Groups* (Bion 1959) is characterized at times by the genuine humility of an individual therapist trying to make sense of fresh psychological data (group processes).

These shifts, from an individual to a group model, were to have important implications for post-war developments in NHS mental health services, as group rather than individual work could be offered as being more cost-effective, and therapeutic community regimes could paradoxically be cited in defence of institutional psychiatry. Maxwell Jones, who, as well as Main, developed the work of the military psychoanalysts in the NHS during the 1950s, comments wryly that his medical colleagues would 'wheel me out' whenever a benign picture of psychiatry was required (Jones 1984). (This has echoes of the Victorian times when moral treatment was used for purposes of humanitarian rhetoric.)

Welfarism and psychotherapy

As with the First World War, the Second World War led to a period of optimism about psychotherapeutic developments in Britain. Returning from the war Tavistock Clinic practitioners hoped that through their 'Operation Phoenix' they could spread the psychoanalytical word to mental health services throughout the newly formed NHS (Dicks 1970). However, this was not to be. Most psychoanalytical practice remained ghettoized around Hampstead, with the important exceptions of Main's development at the Cassel in south London and Sutherland exporting a version of the Tavistock to Edinburgh. Although, in principle, the NHS held out the possibility of psychotherapy (both group and individual) being offered, like other interventions, free at the time of need, history was to repeat itself as far as a post-war decline in psychotherapy was concerned.

In the 1950s psychodynamic psychotherapy was opposed on two fronts. The first, and most predictable, was once more from biological psychiatry. The invention of major tranquillizers strengthened the claims being made about chemotherapy facilitating the 'open door' policy in mental hospitals and enabling patients to stay in the community. This myth, since still colluded with by all but the most honest academic psychiatrists, does not tally with what is known about the changing psychiatric population. Inpatient numbers began to drop *before* the introduction of major tranquillizers (Scull 1977; Busfield 1986). None the less, the authoritative claims of biological psychiatry with its chemical solutions to personal problems went, once more, into the ascendancy during a post-war period.

Psychotherapy was facing opposition on another front though, this time from a non-medical, nascent profession. A pre-condition of clinical psychology being established, as a profession separate from medicine, was that it could appeal to a set of cultural values deeply embedded in British life (positivism and empiricism). By contrast, the high status of psychoanalysis in Britain, during two historical wartime epochs, was a cultural aberration. The latter was possible because psychoanalysis was imported into *medicine*. With the exception of the odd 'lay' (non-medical) analyst, British psychoanalysis, as elsewhere, was one of several *medical* clubs. Once it was incorporated, albeit under conditions of initial vilification, into the dominant profession of medicine, psychoanalysis gained substantial protection from hostile intellectual currents traditional to Britain.

Psychoanalysis is a case *par excellence* of a European style of thought. It goes beyond the given, common-sense view of reality favoured by the British. It is not rationalistic but a psychology of the *irrational*. Though sternly intellectual as a form of therapeutic practice in one sense, it is at the end of the day a profound psychology of the emotions (primitive anxiety, sexual desire, murderous hatred, and so on). It is not surprising that when the first substantial history was written of British psychology it revealed that outside its medical enclave, psychoanalysis did not find favour with mainstream academic psychology between the wars, any more than did behaviourism (Hearnshaw 1964). At the risk of over-generalizing about my own culture, the British tend to treat emotionality *and* elaborate intellectual theorizing with equal suspicion.

In the context of these anomalies surrounding psychoanalysis in Britain, a new profession, clinical psychology, emerged in the 1950s. There is an irony in the beginnings of the profession in Britain. While, as has been argued above, psychoanalysis was, metaphorically, an enemy alien in British intellectual life, gaining sanctuary within the prestigious boundaries of the mature profession of medicine, this was also true in a more direct personal sense of the man inheriting a leadership role within British differential psychology. The irony is compounded when we can now reflect that this man was to gain notoriety for, among other things, championing the vilification of psychoanalysis. Eysenck, a German in England during the war years, gained the protection of Aubrey Lewis at Mill Hill from 1942 and later the Institute of Psychiatry (Gibson 1981). This psychiatric paternalism was to provide another irony, in the light of Eysenck's later moves to subvert the therapeutic monopoly held by medicine, and thus initiate clinical psychology's boundary disputes with psychiatry (Eysenck 1958).

In the early 1950s, Eysenck began to rehearse the strategic considerations needed for the emergence of clinical psychology. One aspect of his strategy was to make a bid for legitimacy for the new profession based upon challenging the other major psychological model operating in a health context (psychoanalysis) (Eysenck 1952). It cannot be a coincidence that a preoccupation with the denigration of psychoanalysis, and its psychotherapeutic derivatives, has gone hand-in-glove with clinical psychology differentiating itself from medicine and marking out an area of separate epistemological validity. This post-war challenge to the dominance of psychoanalysis was one reason, amongst others, why therapeutic psychology was to develop into an eclectic mixture of theoretical positions. However, en route to this eclecticism were other vital stages of maturation.

Initially, British clinical psychology was not characterized by therapy of any description. Until the late 1950s the scientific (or 'scientistic' depending on one's ideology) approach to psychology was mainly represented by the British psychometric tradition. Eysenck was the most recent trustee of the latter which dates back to Galton via Burt, Spearman and Pearson (Hearnshaw 1964). As

Anderson (1969) points out, Eysenck was part of a wider movement of cultural renewal in Britain, entailing a number of white émigrés (exemplified by Karl Popper) who were faithful to British empiricism. Émigrés not in a position to champion the latter were passed over, in terms of academic status, or failed to settle in Britain. Immigrant intellectual workers willing to work hard at systematizing British traditions were welcomed and well rewarded.

Thus, Eysenck's importance cannot be underestimated but it should be emphasized that his leadership role was established as a result of the British intellectual values he championed. His host culture incorporated him, amongst others, to re-energize the flagging empiricist discourse in Britain. Eysenck and Popper joined with native defenders of the faith, like Russell and Ayer, to define what types of knowledge claim could be legitimately made about mental life. As Holland (1977) has noted, this British climate of naive positivism and empiricism in the main could resist the penetration of grander 'continental' idealist and materialist theoretical systems, derived from, say, Husserl, Marx, Freud, Levi-Strauss or Lacan. (The term 'continental' in English usage, to mean mainland Europe, itself reveals the Anglo-centrism epitomized by the classic headline 'Channel fogbound – Europe isolated'.)

Clinical psychology, although a new profession, was thus being built upon old conservative foundations. When it came to the second phase of its development, during the 1960s, the scientific model of psychological change advocated was based on long-established assumptions. Behaviour therapy was a sort of atavistic return to the innovations of Scottish physiology, where Whytt discovered the conditioned reflex 150 years before Pavlov (Millenson 1969), and philosophical notions associated with Hobbes, Locke, Hume, the Mills and Spencer. Hobbes provided a blueprint for both associationism and behaviourism in his work *Leviathan* (1651) and 50 years later Locke even gave a cognitive-behavioural account of the aetiology of phobias (see Woodworth and Sheehan 1964: 62).

Indeed, the shaping of their views abroad, in revolutionary Russia by Pavlov and Kornilov and frontier-expanding America by Thorndike and Watson, marks another irony about the logical consequences of British empiricism. The latter leads to a preoccupation with methodological rigour at the expense of theorizing, which is disvalued and so falls into disuse. It is no exaggeration to claim that every major theoretical debate within the human sciences has taken place between positions shaped into coherent forms in countries outside of Britain. However, Britain has been the *host* to these debates in and between both behavioural and psycho-dynamic psychology, since the Second World War.

As Hearnshaw (1964) notes, in relation to British psychology, theoretical systems-building has not been popular during its academic maturation this century. Moreover, because philosophers retarded the academic differentiation of psychology (from philosophy on one side and medicine on the other) British psychology severed its attachments eventually from the philosophical roots of its own traditions, by developing more applied than theoretical interests. Conse-quently, empiricism manifested in both psychometrics and behaviour therapy was expressed in ways which were naive. In particular, this took the form of *methodological* behaviourism associated with the Maudsley training course in clinical psychology and the efforts made by psychiatrists (Marks and Gelder) there to claw back therapeutic authority from the newer profession. The courses on nurse therapy at the Maudsley have their roots in the confluence of methodological behaviourism and medical power. As well as being technique oriented (directed in the main at symptom reduction rather than elaborate functional analysis) they emphasize the traditional division of labour between doctors and nurses, with the former diagnosing and the latter being delegated therapeutic tasks. This situation prompted Blackman, a British academic advocate of American radical be-haviourism, to comment:

> British psychology appears to have an unduly crude and ill-formulated view of contemporary behaviourism, and this must be a source of concern when one sees the *techniques* of behaviour modification being enthusiastically advocated by clinical psychologists who have little respect for, or facility in, the functional analysis of behaviour. It is probably inevitable that members of other professions may turn to behaviour modification merely as a set of effective techniques.
>
> (Blackman 1979: 39)

The problem with Blackman's lament is that it is essentially moralistic and does not go any way to account for *why* the situation he describes exists. British psychologists failed to 'respect' functional analysis because they are acculturated generally not to theorize too much. Likewise, nurses carry out prescribed techniques because their profession has been in this type of structural relationship with medicine for a hundred years. Having no knowledge base of its own, nursing traditionally follows the epistemological contours and professional directives of medicine. (Of course this is now changing, with nursing studies being integrated more into *higher* rather than further education in Britain, but the changes are very recent and still quite slow.)

The hey-day of behaviour therapy in British clinical psychology during the late 1960s and early 1970s gave way to a period of eclecticism (Richards 1983). In academic psychology the popularity of behaviourism was replaced by cognitivism, which culminated in a peculiar and arguably paradoxical trend towards 'cognitive-behaviour therapy'. Mackay (1984) notes a certain inertia within Britain concerning this trend compared to other countries. However, it should also be noted that, as would be expected, given our poor track record on theorizing, philosophical concerns about the contradictions of integrating cognitivism with behaviourism, rather than practitioner inertia, emerged abroad rather than here.

By 1980, British clinical psychology had become eclectic to a point where even verbal psychotherapy was now being integrated. Although Eysenck retained his intense hostility towards psychoanalysis and verbal psychotherapy during the 1980s, the bulk of the profession no longer had need for this old debate. After all, with the publication of the Trethowan Report on the role of psychologists in the health service (DHSS 1977), structural autonomy from medicine was becoming a possibility, which no longer depended on the posturing of 1952. During this phase, clinical psychologists were keen to boast the advantages of eclecticism and in a thorough-going debate in the *British Journal of Clinical Psychology* (1983: 22, 2), which gave over rare space to theoretical rather than empirical issues, only a

British expatriate in Australia, Yates (1983), tried to defend the faults of integration. A series of contributors from both sides of the Atlantic (Murray, Wachtel, Messer and Davis) queued up to point out the errors of his ways.

As far as psychotherapy was concerned, then, eclecticism eventually predominated within clinical psychology, with neophytes in the profession demonstrating theoretical agnosticism and ambivalence. Smail (1982) noted ironically in this period that clinical psychology had become 'homogenised and sterilised'. Consistent with this trend, no fewer than three full chapters of this book's first edition (Dryden 1984) contained lengthy pleas for eclecticism. My concern here is not to evaluate whether eclecticism is a good or bad thing; rather it is to highlight its over-determined emergence in a certain historical context in Britain.

Whatever its merits and de-merits eclecticism was, in Britain, an inevitability brought about by five main factors. First, as already mentioned, the lack of thoroughgoing theorizing in British academic psychology meant that no coherent model existed. Second, linked to this, both psychoanalysis, as a powerful cultural aberration, and methodological behaviourism, as an expression of British empiricist orthodoxy, were here to stay. Both, in some form or other, had to find a place within professional structures. Thus in all of the main mental health professions, both traditions began to co-exist. Third, this co-existence was facilitated by a breakdown during the 1960s in the hegemony of what Anderson (1969) describes as 'aggressive scientism', represented by the Maudsley School. Britain amongst others during this period had witnessed a wider cultural upheaval and became noteworthy for a particular brand of anti-psychiatry. British anti-psychiatry was predicated on a variety of European traditions though which were antithetical to naive empiricism: psychoanalysis; phenomenology; existentialism; Marxism; and post-structuralism. When eastern mysticism is added to this list, it can be seen that this new and alternative form of eclecticism was at odds with older British intellectual currents.

Not only could methodological behaviourism not hold sway under these conditions of criticism and cultural turmoil, but also the two-horse race between behaviour therapy and psychodynamic psychotherapy recruited new runners. While humanistic psychology associated in the USA since the 1940s with Maslow, May, Rogers, Kelly and others had found little place in British culture, the libertarian ethos of the 1960s (*c.* 1966–75) now allowed this third force in. Caution needs to be applied at this point about the impact of this American humanistic genre. To this day, derivatives of behaviourism and psychoanalysis have a greater presence inside the statutory mental health services than do humanistic derivatives, which have been contained more in the voluntary sector (Samaritans, Marriage Guidance Council, now Relate, and so on) or in education (student and youth counselling). Moreover, as Neimeyer (1985) points out in his study of Personal Construct Theory, British culture mainly incorporated the methodological prowess of the 'grid', rather than the therapeutic emphasis of Kelly.

The fourth critical factor needed to account for the eventual integration of discrepant therapeutic psychologies is economics. The sheer power of economics, at times, to shape ideological forms is evident when similarities are observed between different cultures in similar economic phases of development. For instance, notwithstanding any of the cultural differences acknowledged between the USA and Britain, it is true that integrations of psychotherapeutic practice did take place at similar times on both sides of the Atlantic. (The former is associated with theoretical pluralism and a greater emphasis on the matrix of humanistic therapies than the latter, which is more associated with practical eclecticism.)

The aftermath of the Second World War for both countries was associated with welfare capitalism. The relationship between welfarism and therapy is summarized well here by Richards:

> The emergence of psychological practices is . . . coincident with welfare capital. By and large those practices have developed within the apparatuses of the welfare state, and we might therefore expect that they are deeply implicated in the principal business of those apparatuses, which is the containment and appropriate management of the economic and social tensions generated by the capitalist market. Amongst the main sites of psychological intervention are . . . the education and health services: through these vast and socially porous sectors permeate all the conflicts and tensions of society as a whole, along class, gender, ethnicity and party lines; between national and local government; between occupational groups and so on. They are above all scenes of contradiction and of resolution attempted sometimes falteringly and sometimes with a confidence born of traditional authority and/or technological power. This is the modality of power which may be referred to as 'social democracy': a sociopolitical strategy for moderating market relations . . . through mitigatory provision and conciliatory practice.
>
> (Richards 1986a: 115–16)

As Richards goes on to point out, this general process associated with post-war rebuilding culminated in an integrative ideology, manifested in consensus politics and 'social democracy'. Eclecticism within welfarism (including the psychological therapies) is one aspect for Richards, which, by the 1970s, is described as 'scientific humanism' (the integration of the opposing currents of scientism and humanism). Space was found now not only for the one-sided 'aggressive scientism' of Eysenck but also for the softer elements within psychotherapy derived from phenomenology, psychoanalysis and humanistic psychology. When after 1979, Thatcherism disturbed the balance of social democracy by applying one side of the consensus equation (market forces) and attacking the other (individual dependency on the state for the amelioration of physical and psychological distress) the middle way, so characteristic of post-war welfarism, broke down, with consequences for the social organization of psychological practices.

As Offe (1984), a member of the late Frankfurt School, emphasizes, the welfare state is a 'de-commodifying' tendency. That is, publicly funded and owned welfare bureaucracies though protecting (via conciliation and pacification of the population) the stability of the capitalist system, drain finance from the profit-making private sector. This eventually creates a fiscal crisis, one solution for which is the 're-commodification' of the welfare state. Welfare structures themselves are encouraged to fall victim to market forces and thus are relocated in the private profit-making area of the economy. All of this is now very familiar with

Thatcherism, although elements of this can be found with Labour administrations of the 1960s and 1970s. Offe notes that 'administrative re-commodification' is a solution for fiscal crisis in the capitalist state, which can be traced back to the 1960s. It is against this economic backdrop that certain aspects of mental health service reorganization impinging on psychotherapy can be appreciated.

Probably the most contentious aspect of mental health service reform since the Second World War is the run-down of mental hospital services. The fiscal crisis of the welfare state noted here is the major factor promoting this, though it is debatable precisely *when* this pressure led to dramatic hospital run-down consequences (Scull 1977; cf. Busfield 1986). What is certain is that the role and legitimacy of psychotherapy is altered according to where it is physically sited. Authoritarian hospitals sabotage psychotherapy (Pilgrim 1988). By contrast, community facilities may at least come nearer to offering the architectural conditions of what Tuke called an 'ordinary household' (Donnelly 1983; cf. Winnicott 1958 in relation to the importance of setting in psychotherapy).

The fifth factor which needs to be borne in mind, when considering the over-determination of eclecticism within therapeutic psychology, is that of professionalism. Because of its ambiguous epistemological status (is it a psychological practice or medical treatment?) as far as ownership is concerned, psychotherapy has been at the centre of important boundary disputes and conflicts between professional groups inside the mental health services over the past twenty years (Goldie 1974; Baruch and Treacher 1978). Moreover, because verbal psychotherapy ideologically offends both biological psychiatry and methodological behaviourism within clinical psychology, it has also been the focus at times of intra-professional conflicts (Pilgrim 1986). During the 1970s before the full impact of the Trethowan Report (the DHSS review of the role of psychologists in the health service) psychotherapy often was the focus of disputes between psychologists and psychiatrists, along the lines noted earlier, when behaviour therapists strayed from their hand-maiden, psychometric-tester role. Since then even where NHS sites of work have an inter-professional consensus on the multidisciplinary delivery of psychotherapy, resentments accrue surrounding salary differentials, managerial authority and the rights of staff other than psychiatrists and psychologists to accept direct referrals from GPs (Pilgrim 1986). (Note with reference to the maintenance of medical dominance inside mental health services, that the Royal College of Psychiatrists, which was formed in 1971 out of the old Royal Medico-Psychological Association, advised the DHSS about the importance of medically managed NHS psychotherapy services – Royal College of Psychiatrists 1975.)

In a context wider than the NHS alone, disputes also continue surrounding *which* professional groupings should be entrusted with the regulation of psychotherapeutic practice. This debate became formalized in the 1970s following government concern over Scientology (Foster 1971). Subsequently, the British Psycho-Analytic Society contacted the Department of Health and Social Security to discuss the regulation of psychotherapy. The DHSS took no immediate action but encouraged the formation of a Joint Working Party in 1975 by five analytically oriented groups plus representatives from the Royal College of Psychiatrists and the British Association of Behavioural Psychotherapy. They produced a report three years later (Seighart 1978).

At that time, the British Psychological Society would send only an observer and subsequently the other main statutory representative bodies (the Royal College of Nurses, the Central Council for Education and Training in Social Work and the Royal College of Psychiatrists) disagreed with the need for a register of practitioners on the grounds that the standards of their profession provided any necessary protection for the public. Later, the Royal College of Psychiatrists changed its stance, taking a new interest in registration provided that it had a central role in establishing and policing the register. However, there was sufficient dissent amongst the mental health professions groupings, that by 1981 the Secretary of State for Health refused parliamentary time for the matter. Since then, the Working Group has continued to facilitate regular annual meetings on the topic (the Rugby Conference).

As with the parallel debates going on during this period concerning the registration of psychologists, effected in 1987, those arguing for the need for regulation emphasized the protection of the public and underplayed the issue of professional self-interest (protectionism, kudos, status, salary improvements, etc.). Such is the way of professionalization exemplified in the maturer professions like law and medicine, that public interest not self-interest tends to be the hallmark of official statements and rhetoric. These professional processes have tended to push psychological practices in a more eclectic direction with inter- and intra-professional compromises being worked out from faltering conflict resolution. The siting of multidisciplinary contact in smaller groupings outside hospitals has undoubtedly facilitated these compromises, as have the distractions of the consequences of attacks on welfare funding noted above.

Turning now to some tentative conclusions about the future of British psychotherapy based upon the discussion of the five factors above concerning the overdetermination of eclecticism, the following implications arise:

1 In the near future, some new opportunities will be afforded to therapists to work in settings more conducive to their work than the old 'asylum' system. Moreover, the dominance of biological psychiatry associated with the territorial base of the hospital will break down to some degree, allowing in alternative (psychological and social) interventions.
2 There will be some further relocation of psychiatric services to acute units within District General Hospitals, which actually *amplifies* processes associated with the medicalization of personal problems (Baruch and Treacher 1978).
3 Because of the wider deterioration of funding for the NHS and Social Services, positive opportunities will be offset by crises in staffing levels, and access to psychotherapy will be more and more limited to those able to pay privately. Consequently, morale is likely to deteriorate within state-funded groups of therapists.
4 Psychological distress will increase in the population and thereby put greater pressure on existing resources. On this point it is important to note that monetarism and re-commodification have solved a problem at one level (by stabilizing the economy) but generated another problem at a second level (by amplifying distress and deviance due to higher levels of unemployment and its associated poverty and greater levels of anxiety in those remaining in work).

5 Eclecticism within psychological therapy delivery will be strengthened as a
  result of practical questions of working in the community within cash limits,
  taking precedence over finer points of dispute about particular models of
  intervention.
6 Eclecticism will be strengthened further by market forces generating pluralism
  in the private sector, where counsellors and therapists continue to proliferate,
  offering virtually any variant of therapy imaginable, for those able to pay for the
  services on offer.

Discussion

In this chapter I have attempted to sketch out some of the main considerations
which need to be made when understanding how the British social context has
shaped psychotherapy. In the main, these considerations are a function of shifts in
economic factors and the tensions and contradictions set up by foreign theoretical
systems offending conservative empiricist traditions. Together these have
culminated in a contemporary picture of fluid eclecticism within both the mental
health services in the statutory and voluntary sectors and the burgeoning private
practice sector. I hope that I have gone beyond the inadequate accounts associated
with the 'great men' view of history, and the view that somehow the cogency and
intellectual appeal of therapeutic styles defines their degree of predominance in a
particular time and place.

Nowhere is this more evident than in the history of the strongest British
therapeutic current, namely behaviour therapy. As Yates (1970) noted, many
important case studies of behaviour therapy were on record dating back to the
1920s. Both Pavlovian and Skinnerian psychology were well-established areas of
academic discourse before the salad days of behaviour therapy. It was only when
post-war welfarism emerged that social conditions were right for behaviour
therapy to be effected. And it entered the arena of welfarism offering itself as a
short, simple and rational solution for mass distress (cf. the pre-war elitism of
lengthy private psychoanalysis) (Holland 1977; Portes 1971). It is these economic
and ideological advantages which account for its growth, not its intrinsic
'scientific' validity (cf. Eysenck 1971). Likewise, the softening of scientism by
humanism meant that the former could not remain predominant even within the
British cultural context which highly favours its maintenance.

My personal evaluation of the picture I describe is rather depressing. To start
with the past, it is evident that Britain has no track record of setting the world
alight as far as theorizing within psychotherapy is concerned. This statement of
course demands an immediate caveat. Britain has certainly been the *host* to vital
debates and its strong tradition of developing or reworking foreign materials into
finished products customized for native consumption is evident within both
psychoanalysis and behaviourism. In psychoanalysis, British object-relations
theory and creative tensions between Kleinians and Freudians have spawned
developments of international proportions. Likewise, with regard to applied
methodological behaviourism (behaviour therapy) the Maudsley School certainly
took bits from Russian reflexology and American learning theory and produced a

credible therapeutic technology. However, in both cases, these developments were essentially derivative rather than original. The same can be said of the intelligent reworking of French existentialism by the British anti-psychiatrists. This re-shaping of foreign material is more telling in relation to behaviourism than any other therapeutically linked area of knowledge. The great paradox here is that American and Russian behaviourism were derived *themselves* from British empiricist philosophy and experimental physiology.

Despite the eventual eclectic integration of psychotherapy into the mainstream workings of the British mental health industry, I fear that it can no longer claim the role of the radical humanistic conscience of that industry. This is a result of the energy dissipated in intra- and inter-professional disputes about ownership and regulation and in the obsessive desire to acquire the trappings of professional accreditation. The role of therapists as the 'conscience' of the mental health professions was tenable only when psychotherapy was on the margins, where it could snipe at scientism in psychology and biological reductionism in psychiatry. Once professional self-interest took over, client-interest inevitably suffered. Consequently, those of radical consciousness in the field have dealt with the role-strain this created by questioning self-critically the limits of therapy as a commodity and instead advocating the cause of self-help (Smail 1987).

Whereas some possibility exists in other fields of welfare for consumers to act as quality controllers of the professions ostensibly serving them, people with mental health problems, because of their psychological disabilities, are less prone to organizing critical feedback. This is confounded by reductionism in psychotherapy actually tending to discredit the political demands of clients (which can be psychologized as 'resistance' or inadequacy of character). It is hardly surprising in this context that the radical consumers of mental health services in the 1980s have often pressed for being *left alone* by therapists of *any* type of persuasion and emphasized instead social demands (jobs and accommodation). In my view, these types of demands are eminently sensible given that biological psychiatrists have objectified their clientele in a protracted Titanic biochemical experiment and psychotherapists, by and large, have evaded their responsibilities to the more disturbed, poorer or chronically disabled client. Moreover, the evidence from epidemiological longitudinal studies within psychiatry suggest that it is *social opportunities*, not the ministrations of professional therapists, which predict improvements in those with severe mental health problems (e.g. Ciompi 1980). If psychotherapy in Britain is to regain its old reputation as a more humane version of mental health care, it must attend to its responsibilities to clients which to date have been avoided in the main. To say the least, the edge is taken off the humanitarian advantages of psychotherapy if these are selectively awarded to richer and lesser disturbed members of society.

References

Anderson, P. (1969) Components of the national culture, *New Left Review* 50, July/August.
Armstrong, D. (1980) Madness and coping, *Sociology of Health and Illness* 2, 2: 296.
Barham, P. (1984) *Schizophrenia and Human Value*, Oxford: Basil Blackwell.

Baruch, G. and Treacher, A. (1978) *Psychiatry Observed*, London: Routledge & Kegan Paul.

Bion, W.R. (1959) *Experiences in Groups*, New York: Basic Books.

Blackman, D. (1979) Behaviour modification: control and counter-control, *Behaviour Analysis* 1, 2: 37–50.

Braverman, H. (1974) *Labour and Monopoly Capital*, London: Monthly Review Press.

Busfield, J. (1986) *Managing Madness*, London: Hutchinson.

Bynum, W.F. (1974) Rationales for therapy in British psychiatry, *Medical History* 18: 39–45.

Castel, R. (1985) Moral treatment: mental therapy and social control in the nineteenth century, in S. Cohen and A. Scull (eds) *Social Control and the State*, Oxford: Basil Blackwell.

Ciompi, L. (1980) The natural history of schizophrenia in the long term, *British Journal of Psychiatry* 136: 413–20.

DHSS (Department of Health and Social Security) (1977) *The Role of Psychologists in the Health Service*, Trethowan Report, London: HMSO.

Dicks, H. (1970) *Fifty Years of the Tavistock*, London: Routledge & Kegan Paul.

Digby, A. (1985) Moral treatment at the Retreat, 1796–1846, in W.F. Bynum, R. Porter and M. Shepherd (eds) *The Anatomy of Madness*, Vol. II, London: Tavistock.

Doerner, K. (1970) *Madmen and the Bourgeoisie*, Oxford: Basil Blackwell.

Donnelly, M. (1983) *Managing the Mind*, London: Tavistock.

Dryden, W. (ed.) (1984) *Individual Therapy in Britain*, Milton Keynes: Open University Press.

Eysenck, H.J. (1952) The effects of psychotherapy: an evaluation, *Journal of Consulting Psychology* 16: 319–24.

—— (1958) Learning theory and behaviour therapy. Paper presented to the Royal Medico-Psychological Association, 3 July.

—— (1971) Behavior therapy as a scientific discipline, *Journal of Consulting and Clinical Psychology* 36: 314–19.

Foster, J.G. (1971) *Enquiry into the Practice and Effects of Scientology*, London: HMSO.

Freidson, E. (1970) *Profession of Medicine*, New York: Dodd Mead.

Gibson, H.B. (1981) *Hans Eysenck*, London: Peter Owen.

Goldie, N. (1974) Professional processes among three occupational groups within the mental health field, unpublished PhD thesis, City University, London.

Hearnshaw, L.S. (1964) *A Short History of British Psychology 1840–1940*, London: Methuen.

Holland, R. (1977) *Self and Social Context*, London: Macmillan.

—— (1981) From perspectives to reflexivity, in J.C.J. Bonarius, R. Holland and S. Rosenberg (eds) *Personal Construct Psychology*, New York: Macmillan.

Ingleby, D. (1985) Mental health and social order, in S. Cohen and A. Scull (eds) *Social Control and the State*, Oxford: Basil Blackwell.

Jones, M. (1984) Interview in *Guardian*, 1 August.

Kelly, G.A. (1955) *The Psychology of Personal Constructs*, New York: Norton.

Mackay, D. (1984) Behavioural psychotherapy, in W. Dryden (ed.) *Individual Therapy in Britain*, London: Harper & Row.

Millenson, J.R. (1969) *Principles of Behavioural Analysis*, London: Macmillan.

Neimeyer, R.A. (1985) *The Development of Personal Construct Theory*, London: University of Nebraska.

Offe, C. (1984) *Contradictions of the Welfare State*, London: Hutchinson.

Parry, N. and Parry, J. (1976) *The Rise of the Medical Profession*, London: Croom Helm.

Pilgrim, D. (1986) NHS psychotherapy: personal accounts, unpublished PhD thesis, University of Nottingham.

—— (1987a) Past, present and . . . an interview with Miller Mair, *Changes* 4, 3: 225–9.

—— (1987b) Psychologists and psychopathy, *Bulletin of the British Psychological Society* 40: 168–71.

—— (1988) Psychotherapy in special hospitals: a case of failure to thrive, *Free Associations* 7: 11–26.

—— (1989) The rise and rise of clinical psychology, *Changes* 7, 2: 44–6.

Portes, A. (1971) On the emergence of behavior therapy in modern society, *Journal of Consulting and Clinical Psychology* 36: 303–13.

Richards, B. (1983) Clinical psychology, the individual and the state, unpublished PhD thesis, North East London Polytechnic.

—— (1986a) Psychological practice and social democracy, *Free Associations* 5: 105–36.

—— (1986b) Military mobilisations of the unconscious, *Free Associations* 7: 11–26.

Roazen, P. (1974) *Freud and his Followers*, London: Allen Lane.

Royal College of Psychiatrists (1975) Norms for medical staffing of a psychotherapy service for a population of 200,000, *Bulletin of the Royal College of Psychiatrists* October: 4–9.

Scull, A. (1977) *Decarceration*, Englewood Cliffs, NJ: Prentice-Hall.

—— (1979) *Museums of Madness*, London: Allen Lane.

Seighart, P. (1978) *Statutory Registration of Psychotherapists: A Report of a Professions Joint Working Party*, Cambridge: Plumridge.

Smail, D. (1982) Clinical psychology – homogenised and sterilised, *Bulletin of the British Psychological Society* 35: 345–6.

—— (1987) *Taking Care*, London: Dent.

Stone, M. (1985) Shellshock and the psychologists, in W.F. Bynum, R. Porter and M. Shepherd (eds) *The Anatomy of Madness*, Vol. II, London: Tavistock.

Winnicott, D.W. (1958) Metapsychological and clinical aspects of regression in the psychoanalytical set-up, in D.W. Winnicott, *Collected Works*, London: Hogarth.

Woodworth, R.S. and Sheehan, M.S. (1964) *Contemporary Schools of Psychology*, London: Methuen.

Yates, A. (1970) *Behavior Therapy*, New York: Wiley.

—— (1983) Behaviour therapy and psychodynamic psychotherapy: basic conflict or re-conciliation and integration?, *British Journal of Clinical Psychology* 22, 2: 107–26.

Psychodynamic therapy: the Freudian approach

DAVID L. SMITH

Historical context and development in Britain

Historical context

Freudian psychotherapy originated in the work of Sigmund Freud (1856–1939), who developed it as the therapeutic application of the science of the human mind, which he called *psychoanalysis*.

Originally trained as a research biologist and neurologist, Freud became interested in hypnosis and the emotional basis of mental illness as a result of his studies with Jean-Martin Charcot in 1885–6. Charcot was able to demonstrate that certain neurotic symptoms could be replicated by the use of hypnosis.

Upon returning to Vienna, Freud initiated a professional collaboration with Joseph Breuer (1842–1925), a distinguished physician, who had several years earlier stumbled upon a form of psychotherapy which he came to call the *cathartic method*. Freud experimented with and refined Breuer's approach and in 1895 they jointly published *Studies on Hysteria*, which summarized their methods and findings.

By 1897 Freud had moved beyond the cathartic method and had begun to develop psychoanalytic therapy. Among his chief intellectual influences were Ernst von Brücke (1819–92) and Johann Wolfgang von Goethe (1749–1832). Brücke had been Freud's mentor at the University of Vienna. He had earlier joined forces with Emil du Bois-Reymond, Hermann von Helmholtz and Karl Ludwig to revolutionize biology through a programmatic insistence on a purely physico-chemical theory of biological processes, in opposition to 'vitalist' theorists. Freud felt that the polymath Goethe displayed a deep understanding of the human soul in his writings (especially *Faust*, which Freud frequently quoted in his psychological writings). Goethe advocated the notion of the unity of soul and nature over and against the prevailing Cartesian idea of their radical separation (Kaufmann 1980).

Freud began to attract followers in 1902, and by 1910 psychoanalysis had become an international scientific movement. The Freudian approach continued to expand in continental Europe until the Nazis came to power. Hitler branded psychoanalysis as *zersetzend* (corrosive), and Freud's books were consigned to the flames. Carl Jung, the editor of the official German psychotherapy journal, described psychoanalysis as a 'Jewish' as opposed to an 'Aryan' science.

These developments caused the virtual collapse of psychoanalysis in continental Europe. Most analysts fled to Britain and the Americas, where a strong psychoanalytic culture was already flourishing. Freud himself emigrated to London in 1938, where he died of cancer in 1939.

During the years following the Second World War, the Anglo-American world became the centre of psychoanalytic research and practice. Since that time psychoanalysis has re-established itself throughout Europe and, indeed, all over the world.

Development in Britain

The British Psycho-Analytic Society was established in 1913 by Ernest Jones. Original members included David Eder, the first practising analyst in Britain. Jones dissolved and reconstituted the original Society in 1919, and in the same year began publishing the *International Journal of Psycho-Analysis*, which remains the official organ of the International Psycho-Analytic Association to this day. By 1923 the British Society included among its membership such luminaries as Sylvia Payne, Edward Glover, John Rickman and James and Alix Strachey. James Strachey became general editor and translator of the twenty-four volumes of *The Complete Psychological Works of Sigmund Freud*.

By the time that the Freuds arrived in London after the *Anschluss* of Austria, Sigmund's daughter Anna had become a distinguished psychoanalytic theorist and practitioner herself. There was considerable tension between the group of analysts affiliated with Anna Freud and the Kleinians, a rival school of psychoanalysis founded by Melanie Klein which had become firmly established in Britain through Jones's sponsorship. British psychoanalysis became split between the continental Freudians, the Kleinians, and a rather heterogenous group consisting mainly of indigenous British Freudians who became known as the 'Independents' or the 'Middle Group'. This situation gave rise to a good deal of intellectual ferment which produced a distinctive, creative and influential British psychoanalytic culture.

Although psychoanalytic therapy is difficult to obtain within the National Health Service, there are numerous groups which offer training and/or private psychoanalytic therapy. Those centred in London include the British Association of Psychotherapists, the London Centre for Psychotherapy, the Association for Group and Individual Psychotherapy, the Centre for Analytical Psychotherapy, the Guild of Psychotherapists, the Lincoln Centre and Institute for Psychotherapy, the Society of Psycho-Analytical Psychotherapists, the Tavistock Clinic and the British Psycho-Analytic Society. Groups centred outside London include the Guildford Centre and Society for Psychotherapy, the Northern Association for Analytical Psychotherapy, the North West Regional Psychotherapy Association, the Severnside Institute for Psychotherapy, the West Midlands Institute of Psychotherapy and the Yorkshire Association for Psychodynamic Psychotherapy.

Theoretical assumptions

Image of the person

Psychoanalysis has been in existence now for practically a century and has, over the years, developed numerous models of the person and conceptions of human nature. Within the broad Freudian tradition there are various fundamental disagreements regarding these matters. Given the relatively heterogenous nature of Freudian theory today, the reader should bear in mind that the account to follow is but one description among many.

Fundamental to the Freudian image of the person is the theory of *psychical determinism*, which asserts that the human mind is part of the same causal web that governs the physical universe. The theory of psychical determinism opposes the theory of 'agent causation' (Dennett 1984): the view that people cause their own behaviour through autonomous acts of choice. Freud would have approved of Spinoza's hypothesis that if a stone rolling down an incline was capable of thought, it would think that it was causing itself to roll down the incline. The theory of psychical determinism suggests that the human mind is regulated by *laws* which can be scientifically identified and studied.

The Freudian approach also affirms that the bulk of mental processes and contents, including those with the most crucial impact on human behaviour, remain outside awareness. Freud rejected the Cartesian identification of mind with consciousness, and suggested that we are all in a very basic sense alienated and divided beings. Some of our thoughts (e.g. recent memories) may be temporarily out of awareness but easily retrievable. Freud described these as *preconscious*. Other contents of our minds cannot under normal circumstances be brought to consciousness. Freud referred to these as *unconscious* (the popular term 'subconscious' has no place in Freudian theory). The process of keeping ideas out of conscious awareness is called *defence*. Ideas that are defended against – kept out of consciousness – are invariably terrifying. Although such unconscious ideas are kept out of mind, they influence the person indirectly through their derivatives. Derivatives are conscious or preconscious ideas that are associatively linked with unconscious ideas and function as substitutes for unconscious ideas. For example, a man with an unconscious wish to harm his father might express this indirectly by means of an intense hatred directed towards men in positions of authority.

Freud (1900) described the unconscious and preconscious mental systems in *The Interpretation of Dreams* and extended the model in an important paper entitled 'The unconscious' (Freud 1915). However, because of limitations which he felt were inherent in the model, Freud proposed a new model of the mind in 1923 (Freud 1923). This 'structural' model described the human personality in terms of three fields of force: the id, the ego and the superego.

The id (in German, *das Es*, 'the it') is the biological bedrock of motivation. It is a system of biological needs: needs for physical gratification. Unlike other animals, whose needs are regulated by complex inbuilt instinctual patterns, the id of human beings is totally out of touch with external reality. It is focused entirely on its own gratification. The id is regarded as the 'motor' of the human being: the ultimate source of human motivation.

The ego (in German *das Ich*, 'the I') includes what people ordinarily mean when they say 'I', but also much more. It is the part of the personality responsible for adaptation to external reality. Its main function is to secure the gratification of the id while keeping the person out of danger. Because the ego is adapted to external reality, it must often suppress the desires of the id when their expression would be disadvantageous.

The id is innate, and therefore present from birth. The ego begins to develop during the first year. Later, as the child becomes socialized, the values of society become internalized. This sets up the third 'force-field' in the person termed the superego (in German *das Uber-Ich*, 'the Above-I'). The superego can be imagined as a part of the mind that rewards one for being 'good' and punishes one for being 'bad'. The feeling of guilt is evoked when the values of the superego have been violated.

Because of the completely asocial and passionate nature of the id, it is in a state of more or less incessant conflict with the superego. The ego, caught in the middle and attempting to adapt to external reality as well, must find ways of skilfully effecting compromises between these uncompromising contenders. When conflict is severe this can be virtually impossible. This provides a powerful motive for the ego to defend against conflict by rendering it unconscious.

Conceptualization of psychological disturbance and health

In the Freudian scheme, psychological disturbance can be equated with the inability of the ego to manage severe states of conflict. I have already remarked on how the process of making emotionally charged ideas unconscious is a result of unmanageably distressing conflict. Through defending against inner conflict, the person treats an internal state in the same manner as an external danger: he flees from it.

Defence, however, is not useful as a long-term solution. The distressing ideas disappear only from *conscious awareness*: they do not go out of existence. They live on in the unconscious part of the mind and exert continual pressure because of their roots in the unextinguishable biological drives of the id. Unconscious ideas then find disguised expression through dreams, irrational behaviour, etc. When the ego becomes overloaded and consequently unable to handle the pressures engendered by defence, the unconscious ideas erupt and find expression in psychological symptoms. The *form* that symptoms then take will be determined by numerous factors such as the nature of the warded-off ideas and impulses, the type of defence mechanisms used and the unique hereditary strengths and vulnerabilities of the individual. Freudian writers such as Fenichel (1980) show how these factors interact for different diagnostic categories.

The Freudian approach sees psychological illness as an inability to manage rationally inner states of intense conflict and anguish. Psychological health is therefore equated with the ability to handle inner conflict rationally and crea-tively. It must be emphasized here that Freud was opposed to any hard and fast demarcation between 'health' and 'illness'. We are all ill; we are all somewhat mad. This is seen as an inevitable consequence of the contradictions inherent in human existence.

Acquisition of psychological disturbance

Severe psychological conflict is a necessary condition for the outbreak of psychological disturbance. A second necessary condition is the deployment of defence. We must examine both of these elements more carefully in order to understand the emergence of psychological symptoms.

Freud came to the conclusion, after years of psychotherapeutic work with adults, that the conflicts powerful enough to produce symptoms inevitably stem from infancy. This led him to an intensive study of the psychological development of children. He attempted to *reconstruct* important aspects of child psychology through his psychoanalytic investigations of adults. Freud eventually settled on a group of interrelated emotions, aspirations and fantasies which he came to believe were the universal root of neurotic conflict. He called this the *Oedipus complex.*

The term 'Oedipus complex' derives from the ancient Greek legend of Oedipus. Oedipus was the son of King Laius and Queen Jocasta of Thebes. Because it had been foretold that Laius would spawn a son who would murder him, Oedipus is mutilated (a spike is thrust through his feet) and sent away to be killed. Oedipus manages to escape this fate and is brought up by the King and Queen of the city-state of Corinth. As an adult, Oedipus consults the Oracle of Delphi who informs him that he is fated to kill his father and marry his mother. Mistakenly believing that the King and Queen of Corinth are his natural parents, Oedipus decides – in an effort to avert this fate – to banish himself from Corinth. Oedipus travels throughout Greece and on one occasion engages an older man in a dispute about right of way at a crossroads. The disputants come to blows, and Oedipus kills the stranger without realizing that he has in fact killed Laius, his natural father. Oedipus proceeds to Thebes, which is being ravaged by a hideous monster called the Sphinx. Whoever is unable to answer correctly a riddle posed by the Sphinx would be destroyed by her. Oedipus correctly answers the riddle, freeing Thebes from her grip. In reward, Oedipus is given the hand of the recently widowed Jocasta in marriage and becomes the new King of Thebes. Many years later Oedipus mounts an investigation into the death of King Laius, only to discover he himself to be the murderer. He blinds himself and Queen Jocasta takes her own life.

Freud termed his discovery the 'Oedipus complex' because of the twin themes of incest and patricide found in the Oedipus legend. Freud came to believe that not only adults but also children experience erotic yearnings. Infantile sexuality is of a different order from adult sexuality. Some of its chief distinguishing characteristics are (1) that it does not aim at sexual *intercourse*, (2) that it is *incestuous* and (3) that it is expressed in *bizarre fantasies and anxieties*. During babyhood, infantile sexuality is focused on sensations in the mouth, which is why Freud called this the *oral stage* of development. During the toddler or *anal stage* sexuality becomes focused on the anal region. The *phallic stage*, so named because during it children of both sexes come to be preoccupied with the phallus, lasts from about the age of 3 until about the age of 7. During the *latency period* (Freud called this a *Periode*, 'period', rather than a *Stufe*, 'stage') sexuality becomes somewhat suppressed and undergoes no new developments. This continues until puberty, which marks the onset of the *genital stage* of mature, non-incestuous genital sexuality.

The Oedipus complex reaches its height during the phallic stage. This phase is often erroneously described as a period when children entertain sexual desires directed towards the parent of the opposite sex. Freud, however, made it quite explicit that the Oedipal longings possess a homosexual as well as a heterosexual character (Freud 1923).

Freud believed that the little boy is usually most intensely focused on his mother during this stage. He wishes to possess her completely and is fiercely jealous of all rivals, especially his father who appears to have a special status for his mother. His most intense erotic sensations are localized in his penis:

> Attached to the excitation are impulsions which the child cannot account for – obscure urges to do something violent, to press in, to knock to pieces, to tear open a hole somewhere.
>
> (Freud 1908: 218)

Because of his passionate jealousy the little boy wishes that his father were out of the way and, as is typical of infantile psychology, consequently imagines that his father wishes to retaliate. A common fantasy during this period is that the boy's father will castrate him (*castration anxiety*). The young boy's observation that females do not possess a penis lends credibility to these ideas. Under the pressure of castration anxiety the boy renounces his incestuous claims and enters the latency period. Freud was more tentative in his account of female development, believing that his theory was not altogether satisfactory. The issue of the nature of female sexual development is still largely unresolved and continues to be researched and debated by psychoanalysts.

Freud describes the little girl as entering the phallic phase like the little boy with a powerful incestuous attachment to her mother. Like the boy, she feels her father to be a rival and, also like the boy, thinks that her father will punish her for her rivalrous attitude. At this point the observation that males have penises takes on an emotional significance. Freud believed that the little girl comes to regard her clitoris as a stunted or inferior phallus, and begins to envy the male genitals (*penis envy*). Freud (in Mitchell and Rose 1982) was puzzled about why this should be the case, and suggested that the importance of the penis might derive from it representing a link with the desired mother (Freud 1926). Paradoxically penis envy is seen as a force propelling the girl towards a heterosexual, feminine stance. Feeling that she cannot compete with her father, she blames her mother for not having equipped her with a penis and despises her mother for not possessing a penis herself. The loving attachment to the mother thus becomes replaced by a largely hostile one. Simultaneously the girl unconsciously transforms her wish for a penis into a wish for a baby from her father and finally into an incestuous wish for her father. She now enters the heterosexual Oedipal position, desiring her father and rivalling with her mother. Freud felt that girls have greater difficulty abandoning the incestuous attachment to the parent of the opposite sex than do boys because of the absence of castration anxiety as a motivating factor.

The collapse of the Oedipus complex coincides with the establishment of the superego, which opposes the now repressed incestuous and rivalrous wishes. The core of neurotic conflict is seen to lie in the tension between these unconscious desires and the watchful, punitive superego.

Oedipal conflicts are a necessary condition for the occurrence of psychological disturbance. However, because they are universal these conflicts cannot be seen as a sufficient condition for psychological disturbances. Psychological symptoms emerge when the ego can no longer *cope* with these conflicts. It becomes overloaded and breaks down – usually in response to a specific precipitating trigger, and the desires of the id surge towards expression. These are then defended against desperately, and appear in disguised forms as symptoms. Because symptoms are encoded representations of unconscious concerns there will be some symbolic, thematic or associative link between the form or content of the symptom and the specific content of the unconscious idea that is its source. A repressed desire, say, to observe one's parents enjoying sexual intercourse might, for example, appear as the symptom of psychogenic blindness. Usually, though, the link between a symptom and its corresponding unconscious idea is considerably more convoluted than this because of the intervening defensive processes.

Perpetuation of psychological disturbance

Freud (1926) believed that symptoms persist because of the advantages that the patient accrues from them. He used the terms *primary* and *secondary gain* to designate these advantages. Primary gain is the main 'reinforcer' of neurotic symptoms, and is entirely intrapsychic. It can be best understood with reference to the Freudian theory that neurotic symptoms are substitutes for repressed ideas pressing towards expression. The discomfort of psychological symptoms is felt to be more tolerable than the anguish that would be engendered by such ideas entering consciousness. The primary gain provided by symptoms is just this function of preventing unconscious conflicts from becoming conscious.

Secondary gain is less causally significant. It is mainly if not entirely interpersonally based. Once a symptom becomes established it may be used by the ego to provide other advantages. The disturbed person might, for example, use his symptom as an excuse for evading burdensome responsibilities or as a means for obtaining special privileges. It must be stressed, however, that secondary gain is of minimal significance in comparison with primary gain.

As defensive processes are essential for the perpetuation of emotional disturbances, it seems appropriate to explore them a little more fully. Defence processes or 'mechanisms' are unconscious cognitive strategies for keeping disturbing, emotionally charged ideas at a distance from consciousness. Some of the main defences are

1 *Repression*   This is the process of dealing with disturbing memories by actively forgetting them. For example, one might 'forget' one's incestuous longing for one's mother, one's fear of castration, etc.
2 *Disavowal*   Sometimes called *denial*, this defence bars a *perception* rather than a memory from consciousness (Dorpat 1985). For example, a person might attempt to deal with unconscious fears of his father through forming the irrational idea that he does not really have a father.
3 *Projection*   Projection is the process of attributing an aspect of oneself to someone else. For example, aggressive impulses towards others might be

transformed by means of projection into the belief that one is being persecuted by others.

4 *Introjection*   Introjection is the process of unconsciously emulating someone else. A child whose masturbatory activities are severely curtailed by her parents might, for example, begin to suppress and condemn these desires herself.

5 *Reversal*   Reversal is the process of detaching an attitude from its proper object and directing it towards oneself instead. For example, the desire to harm one's father might be transformed by means of reversal into a self-destructive tendency.

6 *Displacement*   In displacement an attitude is detached from its original object and directed towards someone else instead. For example, an Oedipal desire for one's mother might become a desire for women of the same general physical type.

7 *Isolation*   In isolation the appropriate emotion is detached from an idea in order to deprive that idea of real significance. For example, one might recall being neglected or abused as a child in an entirely detached way with no affect of rage, grief, etc.

8 *Reaction formation*   Reaction formation is the process of turning an attitude into its opposite. For example, an unconscious attitude of contempt towards one's mother might become transformed into feelings of veneration for her.

9 *Negation*   Often confused with denial, this defence entails negating a disturbing attitude. For example, the desire to get rid of a sibling might give rise to the idea that one would *not* ever want to be separated from that sibling. Negation is clearly closely related to reaction formation.

10 *Rationalization*   In rationalization false reasons are found to justify unacceptable attitudes. For example, the sadistic desire to hurt someone might be rationalized by means of the false belief that the person to be hurt is bad and therefore deserves punishment.

11 *Conversion*   Conversion is the process of transforming a psychological disturbance into a physical disorder. The unconscious feeling of dependency ('not being able to stand on one's own two feet') might give rise to incapacitating leg pains.

Defence mechanisms are essential for the perpetuation of psychological disturbance because they keep conflicts outside consciousness. Defence mechanisms may work singly or in combination. Specific defences are linked with specific psychological disorders: for example, paranoia always involves the extensive use of projection, depression thrives on introjection and reversal while obsessional neurosis deploys reaction formation, negation and isolation extensively.

Generally speaking, apart from the concept of secondary gain the Freudian approach has little to say about the role of interpersonal mechanisms in the perpetuation of psychological disturbances. Interpersonal processes are mainly seen as important only in so far as they augment either the underlying conflicts or the ego's ability to deal with them. Mounting sexual tension caused by the lack of an ongoing sexual relationship might, for example, aggravate underlying sexual conflicts. Interpersonal events are seen as significant only to the extent that they induce a shift in the purely intrapsychic sphere.

Change

According to the Freudian theory the disturbed personality can be seen as a tenuously stable system. The price paid for this stability is the existence of psychological symptoms. These symptoms are the product of unconscious ideas pressing towards expression and unconscious defences keeping them at bay. In ordinary life, then, symptoms might be modified in two ways: the lessening of the intensity of unconscious urges pressing towards consciousness or the strengthening of the defences against those urges.

The lessening of unconscious urges might come about through the effects of ageing. A change in life circumstances might also play a role here: for example, leaving a job in which aggressive urges were continually being aroused by an excessively oppressive boss. It is also possible that the sufferer from neurotic symptoms might find channels for 'sublimating' unconscious urges, that is symbolically expressing them in more adaptive ways. For example, an individual troubled by infantile anal urges might take up a pastime like pottery which may symbolically represent faecal play.

The reinforcement of defences might come about through a change in life circumstances. For example, one's ego might be taxed by the fatigue stemming from over-work. A change to employment which is less demanding might make more energy available to the ego for purposes of defence.

Practice

Goals of therapy

Freudian therapists do not strive to turn 'disturbed' people into 'normal' people. 'Normal' people are simply those who have been able to suppress their inner conflicts to such an extent that they are quite unaware of them. 'Disturbed' people are less psychologically complacent. They are unable to manage their inner turmoil and hence cannot ignore its existence, but the real nature of these inner concerns remains unconscious. Disturbed people know that they are disturbed but do not know what, at bottom, is disturbing them. The normal person is not conscious of any inner disturbance. The Freudian therapist seeks to help a person become more self-aware than those who are normal and more able to cope with this awareness than those who are disturbed. Schneiderman makes the point that

> People who present themselves for psychoanalysis are said to be alienated from the norm. Perhaps this is true, but that does not justify attempting to reinsert them back in that norm. They are alienated because they have had a taste of something else, and once they have had that experience the norm does not seem to be worth the bother.
>
> (Schneiderman 1983: 112)

Winnicott (1960: 43) puts this pithily: 'We are poor indeed if we are only sane.'

Freudian therapists concentrate on helping their patients to come to an understanding of previously unconscious aspects of themselves. Freudian therapists accordingly do not work just to eliminate symptoms, but try to turn symptoms into insights. The gap left by a successfully analysed symptom is filled by a deepened understanding of one's own inner life. This goal is incompatible with irrational, manipulative or authoritarian modes of treatment.

Freud believed that all psychotherapy works through one of two incompatible modes: insight or suggestion. In cures through suggestion, the patient is influenced by a therapist who is seen as an idealized parental figure. The therapist, often without realizing it, manipulates this relationship by using the power invested in him or her by the patient. The therapist finds a way to convince the patient through seduction or intimidation to make the desired changes. In contrast to this type of procedure, Freudian therapists attempt to eliminate the element of suggestion as completely as possible. To stick doggedly to the path of insight and avoid the more reassuring sidestreets of suggestion makes great demands on both therapists and patients. Complete candour is expected of patients, who are invited to confront all of those things in themselves which they have spent their life attempting to evade because of the anguish that they evoke. Therapists are required to refrain from all suggestive measures and to singular-mindedly pursue their patients' inner truth wherever it may lead.

One further point ought to be made in this context. Because of the emphasis on insight and self-knowledge, many individuals enter Freudian psychotherapy because they wish to understand themselves better and have a richer inner life, rather than because they suffer from psychological symptoms. The psychoanalytic therapy of such people does not differ in any essentials from the treatment of those who complain of 'disturbances'.

Selection criteria

Freudian therapy is essentially a one-to-one therapeutic modality. Although some therapists have attempted to do Freudian therapy in a group setting, this alteration of the fundamental boundary conditions of treatment (total privacy and confidentiality) sets such efforts apart from classical Freudian therapy. It is perhaps more accurate to speak of group and couple therapy that is psychoanalytically *informed* than to speak of psychoanalytic therapy in groups or couples.

There is a second rather problematic distinction to consider here: the distinction between 'psychoanalytic therapy' and 'psychoanalysis'. Of course, in the broad sense psychoanalytic therapy is just the application of psychoanalysis (a theory of the mind) to psychotherapy. However, the term 'psychoanalysis' is also used to designate a form of intensive psychotherapy which is in some way distinguishable from psychoanalytic therapy as well. It is difficult if not impossible to discover substantive differences between psychoanalytic treatment and psychoanalytic psychotherapy. Opinion has it that psychoanalytic therapy is the less intensive and less rigorous of the two. Psychoanalytic therapists are said to see their patients less frequently than their strictly psychoanalytic colleagues, and are said to place their patients on a chair rather than the traditional Freudian couch. Psychoanalytic therapists are also often described as alloying the pure gold of analysis with the copper of suggestive measures. These generalizations, however, do not survive scrutiny of the actual work of practitioners, as some Freudian analysts work in a rather 'loose' way while some Freudian therapists are quite disciplined and rigorous. The designations of 'psychoanalyst' and 'psychoanalytic therapist' are more useful as guides to the type of training that a practitioner has received than as reliable indications of the type of therapy on offer. In this chapter I shall describe psychoanalytic therapy as a rigorous and disciplined form of treatment which does not differ in any essential respect from 'psychoanalysis'. The terms 'psychoanalysis' and 'psychoanalytic therapy' will therefore be used interchangeably.

Freud regarded the indications for psychoanalytic therapy as a reasonable degree of education, a reliable character and a non-psychotic personality (Freud 1905). Later writers such as Karush (1960) and Kuiper (1968) describe the tolerance of frustration, anxiety, depression and passivity; a capacity for insight, adequate reality testing, meaningful interpersonal relations and positive motivation as favourable attributes of patients seeking out this form of therapy.

Bachrach and Leaf (1978) concluded, after a careful study of the literature, that the better the pre-treatment level of functioning the more favourable would be the outcome after psychoanalysis.

Outcome research has cast doubt on all of these criteria by showing that there is little relationship between how well patients do in psychoanalysis and predictions made on the basis of pre-treatment assessments (Wallerstein 1987). One important factor which has not been studied is the 'fit' between patient and therapist (Wallerstein 1987). Chiefetz (1984) has effectively refuted Freud's view that a 'reasonable degree of education' is an important factor and has pointed to the conditions of treatment (the provision of an adequate therapeutic environment: privacy, confidentiality, set fee, etc.) as a more important variable.

Generally speaking, Freudian therapy is not indicated for persons suffering from psychotic disorders (Freud 1905), although forms of the approach have been developed for the treatment of the 'borderline' syndrome (Kernberg 1980). The Freudian approach is best suited for the treatment of neurotic symptoms, inhibitions and character traits.

Qualities of effective therapists

Because the Freudian approach precludes any attempt to cure the patient through force of personality or 'charisma', one of the most important qualities of the competent practitioner is the ability to subordinate his or her personality to the 'analytic attitude'.

The Freudian adherence to the ethical commitment of cure through insight must suffuse every aspect of the therapist's work. This is expressed in the three main professional values of Freudian therapy (Dorpat 1979): a caring commitment to the patient, a respect for the patient's autonomy and a devotion to the pursuit of truth. These attitudes are collectively referred to as the *rule of neutrality*.

Because the Freudian approach is rooted in the attitude of 'finding out' about human beings rather than the attitude of 'already knowing', the therapist should be a naturally inquisitive person (Schafer 1983). The arduous and often lengthy nature of psychoanalytic treatment demands patience as well as emotional stamina. As Freudian therapy focuses on the unknown (unconscious) dimension of mental life, the therapist must be able to tolerate or perhaps even enjoy long periods during which he or she does not really understand what is going on. Bion quotes Keats, who called this attitude 'negative capability':

> Negative Capability, that is, when a man is capable of being in uncertainties, mysteries, doubts, without any irritable reaching after fact and reason.
>
> (John Keats, quoted in Bion 1970: 125)

Finally, the Freudian therapist must be capable of enduring extended periods of outward passivity. Because psychoanalysis is rooted in understanding rather than manipulation it eschews an active, conversational or interventionist approach. In order to begin to understand something of another person's unconscious mental life, it is necessary to spend long periods of time quietly listening.

Therapeutic style

Many aspects of the Freudian therapeutic style are entailed by the rule of neutrality and have already been touched on in the foregoing discussion. Therapists are outwardly passive because they spend most of their time listening to their patients and attempting to formulate the deeper implications of what has been said. This type of therapy has a somewhat formal or mannered quality because of the therapist's strict, self-imposed discipline. In their efforts to pursue unconscious meaning, therapists must one-pointedly focus on patients' communications. They must avoid interfering with patients' autonomy in any way. Freudian therapists must abandon naturalistic attitudes and conventional social modes of interaction. Because of the exclusive focus on their patients' inner world, therapists are non-self-disclosing (this is called the *rule of anonymity*).

Freudian therapists break their silence in order to speak only infrequently. When they speak it is almost always in order to share with their patients their ideas about what is going on in their patients' unconscious mind (this is called *interpretation*). Freudian therapists never strive to persuade their patients of anything, never reproach their patients, never praise their patients and never reassure their patients. Apart from an initial handshake, therapists do not engage their patients in any physical contact. The seeming austerity of these restrictions on therapists' behaviour is offset by the fact that they are designed to create an 'atmosphere of safety' (Schafer 1983) in which patients can authentically be themselves without fear of censure or interference.

Major therapeutic strategies and techniques

According to Freudian theory, emotionally charged ideas can produce symptoms only in so far as they are unconscious. For this reason the main therapeutic strategy employed by Freudian therapists is to 'make the unconscious conscious'. This process, if successfully carried out, does not necessarily *solve* the underlying problem. It does not automatically render a person content or happy. Rather, it enables people to confront their own deep concerns more directly, and undermines symptoms which make adaptive solutions impossible. As Freud ironically put it, it is not the therapist's task to solve all of the patient's problems, but rather to replace neurotic misery with ordinary unhappiness (Freud 1895).

The Freudian therapist strives to insightfully remove psychological obstacles against the recognition of disturbing inner truths. The therapeutic environment is an important component of this process. The Freudian therapist attempts to create an environment in which their patients can feel safely contained. Therapists behave in a non-intrusive 'neutral' manner. They secure total privacy and confidentiality for their patients. Sessions are of set duration and frequency; there is a set fee. Many therapists provide a couch on which the patient can recline, with the therapist seated unobtrusively outside the patient's visual field. This arrangement encourages unconscious expression. Other therapists place two chairs at a ninety-degree angle for the therapist and patient to sit on.

Patients are expected to *free-associate* during sessions. 'Free-association' is a rather pallid translation of Freud's *freier Einfall*; *freier* means 'free', but *Einfall* has no precise English equivalent. It could be literally rendered as 'falling in'. Free-association is the process of allowing things to come to mind while making no conscious effort to shape or control one's own mental processes and products. Patients are asked to enter this meditative state of mind and to describe frankly to their therapists what occurs. In an early publication, Freud described free-association thus:

> He [Freud] asks the patient to 'let himself go' in what he says, 'as you would do in a conversation in which you were rambling on quite disconnectedly and at random'. . . . He insists that they must include in it whatever comes into their heads, even if they think it unimportant or irrelevant or nonsensical; he lays special stress in their not omitting any thought or idea . . . because to relate it would be embarrassing or distressing to them.
>
> (Freud 1904: 251)

What is the purpose of free-association? Freud believed in the principle of *psychical determinism*, which states that the human mind is part and parcel of the great causal web that governs the physical universe. He accordingly felt that all mental events are causally determined. It follows from this that when mental processes are no longer controlled consciously, they must be guided by some other influence. By abandoning conscious control, the unconscious influences become more apparent.

When one attempts to free-associate with complete candour one finds that at certain points there is a powerful tendency to 'break the rules': to discount certain images appearing before the mind's eye or to refrain from reporting them. One may even go so far as to convince oneself that one's mind is a complete 'blank' (an impossibility) or to abandon free-association in favour of consciously structured thought. Freudian therapists refer to this phenomenon as *resistance*. Resistance occurs whenever disturbing unconscious ideas are close to becoming conscious. Resistance is therefore an unconscious attempt to 'block' free-association and thereby re-entrench a defensive attitude.

Resistance is important because its presence points to 'chinks' in patients' defensive armour. It is accordingly very important for therapists to be able to detect the presence of resistance. Resistance is a signal that something is unconsciously causing a patient anguish.

When listening to their patients, Freudian therapists enter a frame of mind which makes them particularly sensitive to the presence of resistance. This is called the attitude of *free-floating attention*.

Free-floating attention is quite similar to free-association. Therapists silently let themselves go, refraining from conscious reflection on or analysis of their patients' discourse. Theoretical beliefs are allowed to sink into the background, and no attempt is made to fix information in memory. Therapists listen to their patients as though they were listening to music or poetry. When one is in this state of mind any obstruction to the flow of patients' free-associations becomes readily noticeable.

The aim of psychoanalytic intervention is to make the unconscious conscious through the dissolution of resistances. There is a good deal of disagreement in the field over just what constitutes an acceptable psychoanalytic intervention. Some Freudian therapists believe that the rule of neutrality is consistent with a wide variety of interventions, including questions and 'confrontations'. Others believe that the rule of neutrality when taken quite seriously permits only a very restricted range of interventions. Using the strict interpretation of the rule of neutrality there are only three types of interventions available to the Freudian therapist: silence, management of the environment and interpretation.

A Japanese riddle poses the question 'What is the most important part of a rice bowl?' The correct answer is 'The space inside'. Silence, the most frequently used Freudian intervention, creates a 'space inside' the therapeutic encounter: a space to be filled by patients' freely associating and resisting, and by therapists' listening and detecting resistance. Silence is clearly an intervention of fundamental importance. It is therefore regarded as something that therapists actively *do* rather than as a mere absence of speech.

Management of the environment entails the creation and perpetuation of a therapeutic environment that reliably safeguards and encourages the therapeutic process. As the environment determines the basic conditions of therapy, its management must be regarded as of great importance. Like silence, management is a non-verbal intervention. These two non-verbal interventions are the most important activities of Freudian therapists. By creating an atmosphere of safety in which patients can readily communicate derivatively and therapists can listen, these two forms of intervention create the preconditions for the interpretation of unconscious meanings.

While listening to patients' free-associations, Freudian therapists will at some point detect the presence of resistance. They will then move *out* of the state of free-floating attention and reflect upon this observation, attempting to reach an understanding of *how* the resistance is operating, *why* it is being deployed (i.e. its motive) and *what* the resistance is barring from consciousness. A hypothesis of this kind is called an *interpretation* (Freud 1913). At the appropriate moment the interpretation is offered as an intervention. Strictly speaking, this is called 'voicing an interpretation' but it has come to be called 'interpretation' for short.

To summarize, interpreting is just offering to patients an idea about the unconscious basis of a resistance that has come into play. Interpretations are given in simple, straightforward, non-theoretical language and Freudian therapists explain to their patients how it is that they have come to their hypotheses. The correctness or incorrectness of interpretations can be determined only on the basis of patients' reactions (see Smith 1987). An accurate and timely interpretation of a resistance should diminish resistance and allow unconscious concerns freer play.

During the course of psychoanalytic therapy patients often develop powerful preoccupations with their therapists, often experiencing strong feelings about them and having intense fantasies about them. These feelings and fantasies are believed to be caused by an unconscious process called *transference*. In states of transference patients unconsciously treat their therapists as a surrogate for a significant figure from their past: typically mother, father or sibling. Aspects of relationships from childhood that have been repressed are enacted in the 'playground' of the therapeutic setting. This lends the relationship between therapist and patient a unique aura of emotional intensity.

Because of the emotional immediacy of transference phenomena, and because everything that occurs in the therapeutic situation will be coloured by patients' attitudes towards their therapists, Freudian therapists try to interpret their patients' resistances within the context of transference. Patients may be inhibited when free-associating because they believe that the therapist will despise and ridicule them if they mention certain topics. In Freudian therapy the relationship between patient and therapist quickly becomes and remains the central focus of the therapy. Transference becomes the stage on which the long-forgotten dramas of childhood are repeated and reintegrated.

The term 'counter-transference' is often mentioned in the same breath as 'transference'. In spite of appearances, 'counter-transference' is quite a different sort of concept. It can be defined most economically as any disruption of the analytic attitude of neutrality. Counter-transference springs mainly from therapists' own unresolved emotional difficulties, but it can also be prompted by pressures exerted by patients. For example, a patient tells his therapist that he is refraining from mentioning something important, and goes on to talk about trivial matters. This evokes a state of intense curiosity in the therapist. The patient uses a good deal of body-language while discussing the unimportant matters. Because the therapist is in a state of heightened curiosity, she pays disproportionate attention to the patient's body. Here the patient has unconsciously yet skilfully induced his therapist to gaze intensely at his body. Through recognizing and silently analysing her lapse, the therapist might draw valid conclusions about this patient's repressed need to exhibit himself. So, in some instance counter-transference reactions may be used to reveal important information about patients.

The change process in therapy

The only thing that Freudian therapists try directly to change is their patients' level of self-awareness. From beginning to end the process is characterized by the gradual, careful and systematic analysis of resistance, with an increasing focus on transference issues. The analysis of resistance alters the structure of patients' defences, bringing unconscious material to light and eliminating symptoms. The course of treatment can be divided into an opening phase, a middle phase and a termination phase. The opening phase begins with the establishment of a verbal contract and includes the identification and beginning analysis of patients' resistances. This phase not infrequently includes a 'honeymoon period' of rapid improvement which, however, is unstable and not rooted in real insight. The middle phase is marked by a deepening of the transference and the intensive analysis of resistance. Gains made during the middle phase may be temporarily lost during the termination phase, and important death- and separation-related issues may be explored. A good deal of important work also goes on *after* termination.

The elimination of symptoms is not the sole measure of therapeutic progress and is perhaps not the most important indicator. The insights gleaned through a Freudian therapeutic experience should, in the end, influence patients in the direction of greater 'soulfulness', tolerance, passion, and independence of spirit. Patients develop an acute awareness of the complexity and contradictoriness of human existence. They come to feel more at home with their own and others' bodily yearnings.

Failure to progress in therapy may be due to therapist, to patient or to both. There is always a price to be paid for the resolution of symptoms. In suggestion-based therapies the price is a rigidification of the defences and the consolidation of self-deception. Such patients are implicitly given the model of 'cure' through the submission to the manipulations of an external authority, which will influence their mode of conduct in the world. The price paid in Freudian therapy is the experience of a good deal of previously buried anguish. For many this is too high a price to pay: neurotic suffering is more tolerable than the suffering attendant on making the unconscious conscious. This may stem from the sheer magnitude of a person's distress and/or the lack of consolations and compensations elsewhere in life. To some extent this is true of all of us. Each of us can tolerate only so much insight. No therapist has the right to presume that such natural barriers must be crossed: it is the patient who draws the line.

More frequently the lack of progress can be attributed to therapist's errors. Such is the complexity of the analytic process that even successful treatments may include therapist errors of considerable magnitude. The opportunities for error are endless. The maintenance of strict analytic self-discipline together with some form of ongoing supervision are the best and most extensively used safeguards. In the face of an impasse it is best first to consider that one has been missing something important and consequently to redouble efforts at understanding. As Freud was fond of saying, the best way to shorten an analysis is to do it correctly!

Limitations of the approach

The limitations of the Freudian approach are manifold. Freud believed that he had created a science of the human mind. With the benefit of hindsight it is obvious that he did not succeed in creating a science, but it is arguable that he created a *potential science*. Isolated from the scientific and philosophical communities, psychoanalysis since Freud has not made good its founder's challenge to create a science concerned with the inner life of human beings: a science embracing passion, conflict and anguish within its domain. The upshot of this is that psychoanalytic therapy remains a rather vague, intuitive and unvalidated procedure: an art or craft rather than an applied science. This is no mere academic matter. It is known that sometimes Freudian treatment 'works' and sometimes it 'doesn't work'. Psychoanalysis lacks the clarity and intellectual resources to determine (non-speculatively) why this should be the case. There is no objective method for studying basic problems of technique and refining the approach. Psychoanalysis must therefore achieve greater scientific and philosophical clarity in order to advance beyond its present position. The work of Adolf Grünbaum (1984) has explicitly and meticulously demonstrated just how weak the scientific claims of psychoanalysis are, and has inspired numerous analysts to rethink their position. New methods of empirical research are now being developed for the analysis and mathematical modelling of psychoanalytic interactions (Albanese 1988; Langs 1988b) which promise to put psychoanalysis on a more secure footing. It is already clear that this will involve discarding some of the older, unfounded notions, many of which continue to be widely held by contemporary Freudian practitioners.

On a more prosaic note, Freudian therapy has a limited range of applicability (as described on pp. 27–8). It is lengthy and uncertain, and is therefore not widely regarded as a cost-effective approach. It is difficult to obtain on the NHS. Although forms of short-term 'psychodynamic' therapy have been developed, these are only marginally Freudian, departing from the classical spirit and technique in numerous respects. The vast majority of those seeking Freudian therapy must obtain it privately, and this places the method beyond the reach of those not sufficiently well-off.

Case example

The client

The patient, whom I shall call Mr T, was 37 years old when he began the once-a-week psychotherapy that was to continue for the next six years. He had been in psychotherapy twice before: once with a Freudian psychoanalyst and at a later stage with a bio-energetic therapist. His presenting problem was psychosomatic: he suffered from severe neck pains which his physician attributed to 'stress'. Mr T was an architect. He had been born and raised in the North of England and settled in London shortly after graduating from university.

The therapy

After a few weeks of therapy Mr T's neck pains disappeared, never to return. Only then did Mr T reveal his deeper reasons for coming to therapy. He suffered from outbursts of extreme rage and suspiciousness, often with racist overtones, which he feared would one day get out of hand and lead him to kill someone. He was also prone to periods of depression and profound despair. In addition to all of this, Mr T was sexually troubled. He was unhappily homosexual, and felt that there was something inauthentic about his attraction to dark, swarthy boys.

During the first year of therapy most sessions were taken up with the patient's two passionate interests: English literature and tennis. He was deeply interested in the personalities of the (male) authors and tennis champions. Very little significant interpretative work could be done during this period, but two crucially important themes emerged: the theme of admired men who have achieved immortality through their progeny and the theme of men locked in intense heated competition.

During the first year of therapy Mr T blamed virtually all of his problems on his mother, who was described as a sinister witch-like figure. His father was presented in glowing terms as a friend and protector. In the years of therapy that followed this picture was substantially revised. An important step in this direction came about when the patient noticed that he would invariably arrive at my office in a depressed mood if his previous session had been particularly productive. Free-associating to this, the patient struck a rich vein of images of male–male competition and memories of his father. He realized himself that the prospect of improvement led him to feel guilty. After many weeks of work it turned out that the patient was deeply frightened of doing better than his father. His depression functioned as a prohibition. It took Mr T much longer to realize that this guilt concealed a potent ambition to 'beat' his father. This was expressed in the transference by his depressively showing me that I was impotent to help him.

Mr T's relationship with his father came more into focus as we explored the nature of his complex sexuality. His attraction to dark boys was multiply determined. Mr T wanted to love a boy like the boy in him wanted to be loved. Through identifying with the boy he could imagine that he was a boy being treated with tender sensuality. It became clear, eventually, that this expressed an unconscious desire for his mother's affection. Also, the essential characteristic of 'darkness' that the attractive boy was required to possess was derived from Mr T's father, who possessed a Mediterranean appearance. The boy therefore also appeared to represent the patient's father. This could not be fully understood until the quality of 'ungenuineness' which the patient attributed to his homosexual fantasies could be analysed. It became evident that Mr T's homosexual love contained a powerful undercurrent of hatred. This 'love' was partly a reaction-formation against aggression. Mr T's sexual preference thus contained the two themes characteristic of the Oedipus complex: the wish for his mother's sensual affection and the hatred of his father.

As these matters were gradually unravelled, Mr T began to revise his portrayal of his parents. His mother now emerged as a caring but rather inhibited woman who lived in fear of her husband. The patient's father appeared to be a very disturbed man who was prone to episodes of violence and paranoid jealousy, as well as hypochondriacal anxieties concerning his testicles. The patient began to feel that he had vilified his mother because of his terror of his father's jealousy, and recalled how his father had attempted to turn him against his mother. These realizations coincided with the disappearance of his depressive and violent episodes which had been based on an introjection of his frightening father.

The patient's fear and hatred of his father explained an important detail of his outbursts of rage and suspiciousness. When these occurred Mr T would frequently form the idea that a black male (e.g. a black employee at his firm) was attempting to take advantage of him in some way. He would then feel a sense of hatred towards black people in general. The theme of 'blackness' here was derived from his father's black hair and dark complexion. When the patient's unconscious attitude towards his father was brought to light his episodes of racial hatred ceased entirely.

During the fourth year of therapy the patient began to experience strong heterosexual desires, and his conscious homosexual tendencies correspondingly diminished. He had one brief heterosexual affair during this period, but was generally too frightened of rejection to approach women who interested him. During times of stress he found himself once again attracted to boys. At around this time the analysis of a dream triggered a memory of a disturbing childhood event. Mr T had, at the age of 4, visited a neighbour in the company of his mother and witnessed her breastfeeding a baby. This evoked an uncanny feeling in the patient and shortly after the experience he was plagued by a dreadful sense that his head was about to explode, which persisted on and off for several years of his childhood. When the feeling came upon him the patient would run to his mother in a state of panic. The analysis of these memories suggested that the observation of the breastfeeding scene had stirred powerful erotic longings in Mr T which, in turn, stimulated fears of his father's violent punishment. The explosion of the patient's head appeared to be a disguised portrayal of castration.

As we approached termination a new symptom emerged. The patient complained of losing all sexual desire and came to believe that his penis was shrinking away. This seemed to be rooted in anxieties surrounding the prospect of becoming more sexually potent than his father. The patient unconsciously introjected his father, who had hypochondriacal ideas about his testicles and suppressed his sexuality for fear of castration, which was expressed in the image of his penis shrinking away.

Therapy was terminated at the patient's behest. He was satisfied with the disappearance of his rages and depressions. His somatic symptoms had gone and he felt generally more self-confident, happy and socially at ease. He was not satisfied with his sexuality. He continued to fear women and the anxieties about his penis had not entirely disappeared. The patient felt, however, that he could fully resolve these problems only when he no longer had me to fall back on.

From a Freudian perspective this therapy has a number of rather obvious weaknesses. One of these was my failure to analyse consistently Mr T's aggression towards his father in the transference. Another was my failure to explore his infantile fantasies about the female genitalia in any depth. Third, I might justifiably be taken to task for not having explored pre-Oedipal psychotic anxieties to any significant extent. All of these factors could be seen as having a strong bearing on the patient's fear of women, which was never eliminated.

Since my work with Mr T I have moved from a classical Freudian to a communicative psychoanalytic approach (see Langs 1988a). I would now refrain from the pursuit of infantile fantasies and memories and concentrate instead on Mr T's subliminal perceptions of the here-and-now. When I worked with Mr T I was relatively unaware of the potent destructive impact of incorrect interventions on the patient's free-associations and behaviour. The neglect of this factor adds to rather than subtracts from the patient's difficulties. Finally, in accordance with Langs's seminal discoveries, I would be considerably more careful about accepting the validity of my own interventions and would be much more sceptical about the real value of many of my therapeutic manoeuvres.

References

SE refers to the *Standard Edition of the Complete Psychological Works of Sigmund Freud*, 24 vols (1955–74), ed. and trans. J. Strachey, London: Hogarth Press and Institute of Psycho-Analysis.

Albanese, R.A. (1988) An increased role for mathematics in research and practice in psychotherapy, *British Journal of Psychotherapy* 5, 2: 213–18.

Bachrach, H.M. and Leaf, L.A. (1978) Analyzability: a systematic review of the clinical and quantitative literature, *Journal of the American Psychoanalytic Association* 26: 881–920.

Bion, W. (1970) *Attention and Interpretation*, London: Tavistock.

Chiefetz, L.G. (1984) Frame work violations in psychotherapy with clinic patients, in J. Raney (ed.) *Listening and Interpreting: The Challenge of the Work of Robert Langs*, New York: Jason Aronson.

Dennett, D. (1984) *Elbow Room: The Varieties of Free Will Worth Wanting*, Oxford: Clarendon Press.

Dorpat, T. (1979) On neutrality, *International Journal of Psychoanalytic Psychotherapy* 6: 39–65.

—— (1985) *Denial and Defense in the Therapeutic Situation*, New York: Jason Aronson.

Fenichel, O. (1980) *The Psychoanalytic Theory of Neurosis*. London: Routledge & Kegan Paul.

Freud, S. (1895) Studies on hysteria, *SE* 2: 1–323.

—— (1900) The interpretation of dreams, *SE* 4 and 5: 1–626.

—— (1904) Freud's psychoanalytic procedure, *SE* 7: 249–57.

—— (1905) On psychotherapy, *SE* 7: 257–68.

—— (1908) On the sexual theories of children, *SE* 9: 205–26.

—— (1913) On beginning the treatment: further recommendation on the technique of psycho-analysis, *SE* 12: 121–45.

—— (1915) The unconscious, *SE* 14: 159–209.

—— (1923) The ego and the id, *SE* 19: 3–63.

—— (1926) Inhibitions, symptoms and anxiety, *SE* 20: 77–175.

—— (1971) Freud and female sexuality: a previously unpublished letter, *Psychiatry* 328–9.

Grünbaum, A. (1984) *The Foundations of Psychoanalysis: A Philosophical Critique*, Berkeley, Calif: University of California Press.

Karush, C.F. (1960) in S.A. Guttman (reporter) Criteria for analyzability: panel reports, *Journal of the American Psychoanalytic Association* 8: 141–51.

Kaufmann, W. (1980) *Discovering the Mind, Volume 3: Freud vs Adler and Jung*, New York: McGraw-Hill.

Kernberg, O. (1980) *Internal World and External Reality: Object Relations Theory Applied*, New York: Jason Aronson.

Kuiper, P.C. (1968) Indications and contraindications for psychoanalytic treatment, *International Journal of Psycho-Analysis* 49: 261–4.

Langs, R. (1988a) *A Primer of Psychotherapy*, New York: Gardner.

—— (1988b) Mathematics for psychoanalysis, *British Journal of Psychotherapy* 5, 2: 204–13.

Mitchell, J. and Rose, C. (eds) (1982) *Feminine Sexuality: Jacques Lacan and the École Freudienne*, London: Macmillan.

Schafer, R. (1983) *The Analytic Attitude*, London: Hogarth.

Schneiderman, S. (1983) *Jacques Lacan: The Death of an Intellectual Hero*, Cambridge, Mass: Harvard University Press.

Smith, D.L. (1987) Formulating and evaluating hypotheses in psychoanalytic psychotherapy, *British Journal of Medical Psychology* 60, 4: 313–17.

Wallerstein, R.S. (1987) The assessment of analyzability and of analytic outcomes, *Yearbook of Psychoanalysis and Psychotherapy* 2: 416–27.
Winnicott, D.W. (1960) The effect of psychosis on family life, in D.W. Winnicott (1965) *The Family and Individual Development*, London: Tavistock.

Suggested further reading

Bettelheim, B. (1982) *Freud and Man's Soul*, New York: Fontana.
Freud, S. (1915–17) *Introductory Lectures on Psycho-Analysis*, Harmondsworth: Penguin (1979).
Kaufmann, W. (1980) *Discovering the Mind, Volume 3: Freud vs. Adler and Jung*, New York: McGraw-Hill.
Lindner, R. (1982) *The Fifty-Minute Hour: A Collection of True Psychoanalytic Tales*, New York: Jason Aronson.
Schafer, R. (1983) *The Analytic Attitude*, London: Hogarth.

3

Psychodynamic therapy:
the Kleinian approach

CASSIE COOPER

Historical context and development in Britain

Historical context

Melanie Klein was born in Vienna in 1882, the youngest of four children. Her family, the Reizes, were well-known members of the local orthodox Jewish community. Her mother was the daughter of a Rabbi and her father a Talmud student. For the Jewish community in Europe this was the heady period of 'emancipation'. Age-old prejudices were receding, and professional barriers crumbling at the onset of new and radical political philosophies. Stimulated by these new opportunities Melanie's father (at the age of 37) left his religious studies to read for a medical career and later still took up practice as a dentist.

Melanie Klein's published recollection of these early years was that her family was a warm, loving and united group. Both parents were intellectuals with an extensive knowledge of literature and the sciences. In particular Melanie had a great admiration for her only brother Emmanuel, a medical student who was five years her senior. At the age of 14 Melanie also wanted to study medicine and with her brother's help and encouragement mastered the Latin and Greek necessary to enter Gymnasium. What happened next can only be surmised. In a surprising change of direction, Melanie returned to the social and religious conventions of the day and, at the age of 17, became engaged to Arthur Klein, an industrial chemist and friend of her brother, seemingly choosing to abandon her plans for a medical career. A year before the marriage in 1903 her beloved brother died, in tragic circumstances, at the youthful age of 25.

Melanie later expressed regret at not having qualified as a doctor and continued her strong interest in the science of medicine. For this reason and others the marriage was not wholly a successful one, although in due course Melanie gave birth to three children, a daughter and two sons. In 1911, prior to the outbreak of the First World War, the Klein family moved to Budapest and it was here in the course of her continued interest in medical matters that Melanie was introduced to the writings of Sigmund Freud, and in particular to his work on dreams. She was both excited and intrigued for she found in his theories of human development some truths that she had always been seeking. Living in Budapest enabled her to meet Sandor Ferenczi, the principal Hungarian analyst of that time and a colleague and correspondent of Freud. She became his patient and during the course of her personal analysis he facilitated her emerging ideas about the application of psychoanalysis to young children. He helped her to develop her techniques in which toys and play are used as the equivalent to the dreams and free association which are part of the analytic process for adults. Melanie was now able to return, albeit in a new form, to her interrupted career and before the end of the First World War had already begun to specialize in the analysis of children and to establish her own practice. Her first published paper, ''The development of a child', was read to the Hungarian Psychoanalytic Society in 1921. The analysis of small children was an unknown area, barely touched upon except by Freud in his work with 'Little Hans', and the paper received a mixed reception from the strictly Freudian group.

Dr Karl Abraham, President of the Berlin Psychoanalytic Society, showed considerable interest in this work, and extended an invitation to Melanie to settle in Berlin and devote herself to further psychoanalytic practice and research. Melanie accepted and went to Berlin, taking the children with her, but this move precipitated the end of an unsuccessful marriage, her husband choosing to live in Sweden where he had extensive business interests. The end was rancorous, with both parties arguing bitterly about custody of the children until their final divorce in 1921.

In Berlin, Melanie continued her personal analysis with Karl Abraham. She was strongly influenced by his ideas and formed a deep and lasting admiration for his work on the early stages of infantile development. Like Ferenczi, Karl Abraham urged her to develop further her innovative techniques for working with children. Soon she was introducing new and startingly bright ideas into the processes of child and adult analysis.

Abraham was her staunch supporter and advocate, but this remarkable relationship was a brief one. After only one year, Abraham developed a fatal illness and died in 1925. Following his death Melanie carried on regular daily self-analysis, a procedure which Freud himself had initiated. All her later works were based on this process, with daily analytic observations of her own and her patients' behaviour compared, examined and interpreted one against the other. Continuing to enlarge and report on new insights into the earliest years of a child's life, Melanie's contributions to the Berlin Society evoked much controversy. In London, Ernest Jones, Freud's biographer, one of his original pupils and the doyen of psychoanalysts in Britain, gave support to her views by inviting her over to give a course of lectures to the British Society and, incidentally, to analyse his own children. This was followed, in 1926, by an invitation for her to stay and work permanently in London. Melanie was pleased to do so and it was in London that her work flourished and her individual clinical and theoretical approach was eventually accepted by other British analysts. She continued to live in London, writing, practising, arguing and teaching until the time of her death in 1960.

Members of the British Psychoanalytic Society are often referred to as the 'English' School. This differentiated the work that was developing in London (under the influence of Melanie Klein) from that of other centres of psychoanalytic learning, notably that of the so-called 'Viennese' School.

Development in Britain

The differences I refer to were accentuated by the view of the British (Kleinian) analysts that the experiences of the first weeks of life were *significant* to the development of the individual. They were also of the opinion that the anxieties, defences, unconscious phantasies, and the development in children of 2 years of age and even younger of a transference relationship could be explored and understood, using the method of free-association. In this case the word 'transference' relates to the development of an evaluative relationship between therapist and patient. This emotional relationship can be interpreted as either 'positive' (good feelings) or 'negative' (rejection and hostility).

In the early 1930s, before the Nazis invaded Europe, an attempt was made in an exchange of lectures (Riviere 1936; Waelder 1937) with the Berlin and Viennese Societies to clarify their different stance on this and other issues. In fact they agreed to be different. From 1933 to 1939 psychoanalysis (the so-called Jewish disease) was persecuted out of existence on the continent. In 1938 many German and Austrian analysts fled from the Nazi persecution in Europe to settle in London. At this point, theoretical and practical conflicts of opinion became emphasized, threatening to cause a split within the established British Society. Melanie Klein continued her work and there grew around her a large group of analysts and psychotherapists, with an increasing number of students who wished to apply to her for training analyses and supervision. Susan Isaacs, D.W. Winnicott, Joan Riviere, Ernest Jones, T.E. Money-Kyrle, Hanna Segal, all supported and developed the theories of Melanie Klein. Unity was preserved in the British Society only by developing two separate streams of training within the main teaching course: the 'Continental' School of Anna Freud and the 'English' School of Melanie Klein, and later on the evolution of the current 'Independent' Group, who are able to develop their own techniques and interpretations without rigid adherence to one 'school' or another.

In old Vienna psychoanalysis was considered a 'fringe' profession which guaranteed only an uncertain income and a distinct lack of the up-market prestige enjoyed by others in the sphere of academic psychiatry. The larger number of psychoanalysts who left Germany and Austria chose to live in the USA, where they are now firmly ensconced, and have become financially and socially members of the upper-middle class. It is not surprising, therefore, that they tend to veer towards conservative Freudian theories. (Kleinian theory did not take on in the USA.) It was left to the English School, which in the early 1920s was substantially non-medical and somewhat amateurish, to be more daring and experimental in its approaches to Freud's original teaching. The fact that psychoanalysis in England can never be considered as intellectually complacent is due in part to the influence of Melanie Klein.

Melanie Klein can be truly described as one of the great innovators in dynamic psychotherapy but she nevertheless accepted as fundamental the common themes of psychoanalytic theory which Farrell (1981) simplified as follows:

1 No item in mental life or in the way we behave is accidental. It is always the outcome of antecedent conditions.
2 Mental activity and behaviour is purposeful or goal-directed.
3 Unconscious determinants mould and affect the way we perceive ourselves and others. These are thoughts of a primitive nature, shaped by impulses and feelings within the individual of which he is unaware.
4 Early childhood experience is overwhelmingly important and pre-eminent over later experience.

In addition to these basic assumptions, Melanie Klein threw new light on the hitherto unexplored regions of the pre-Oedipal stage (i.e. the child's unconscious wish to be sexually united with a parent of the opposite sex and thus eliminate the other parent). She went on to propose

1 that environmental factors are much less important than had previously been believed
2 that the beginnings of the superego can be identified within the first two years of life
3 any analysis which does not investigate the stages of infantile anxiety and aggressiveness in order to confront and understand them is necessarily unfinished
4 that the most important drives of all are the aggressive ones.

Theoretical assumptions

Image of the person

The birth of a baby somewhere in the world during the next few years will signal that the population of the world has reached 10 billion. Every minute 150 babies push their way to or are pulled towards birth, 220,000 per day, 80 million a year, are wrested supine and exhausted from the darkness of the birth canal into the glare of light. Some of these babies will go hungry and their families will starve, they will arrive unwanted, neglected, be abandoned, abused, used; life for them will be the Vale of Tears that is described in Ecclesiastes 2.v.19: 'For some it would have been better not to have been born – only one in a thousand will be so lucky'.

To some extent Kleinian theory shares this bleak point of view. Life is never portrayed as a bowl of cherries but rather as a series of events that have to be endured, experienced, overcome. Psychoanalytic theory holds the view, however, that each human being possesses a unique capacity to tap into resources that lie hidden deep within the psyche waiting to be utilized, which can make their own special contribution to the human condition.

The Kleinian psychoanalytic concepts which surround the mysterious processes of conception, pregnancy and birth endeavour to identify those elements of life which start to evolve in the foetus before it develops into a living person. The parents bring to this situation an already developed capacity for living their own lives in a certain way; while the baby's persona is split, at one moment a clear page waiting to be inscribed, at another a mass of powerful instinctual drives focused on one aim – survival.

We now know that a foetus 8 weeks from conception can move its limbs and in a further 8 weeks it has gained sufficient strength to communicate these movements to its mother through the uterine walls. At approximately 26 weeks, this tiny being can change position at will and if poked or prodded by external examination will attempt to avoid this contact. The baby is sensitive to pain, it winces, opens its mouth in a silent cry and responds to cold and heat. The foetus has been observed drinking amniotic fluid and is able to distinguish the food eaten by its mother; sweetness (which it likes) and bitterness (which is avoided). The foetus responds to stroking of the abdomen and gentle noise, turning its face, opening its mouth and moving its tongue. It can reach forward to obtain comfort by sucking its thumbs, fingers and toes. The ability to see, to hear and to feel are therefore not senses which are magically bestowed at birth and the foetal heart beat resonates rapidly to the external situation of its mother.

The human baby is born prematurely, its instincts are weak and it seems to have poor instinctual notions of how to avoid danger or to get satisfaction for its own needs. The human baby is more helpless and dependent upon others for the satisfaction of its vital needs than even those mammals most closely related to our species. When its caretaker (usually its mother) satisfies the baby's hunger, she is at one with it and hence not felt as separate. When, however, she is unable to satisfy the baby's needs she (or her breast) are experienced as separate from the baby and thereby become its first distinct psychological object. If the mother is thus perceived as missing, two things happen. One is that the loss or removal of the means to satisfy its needs produces an anxiety in the baby. Anxiety is an effectual state that warns the baby of danger. In order to cope with this anxiety, the baby has to re-create a mother for itself. The satisfaction she represented has to be phantasized so that the baby can conjure up in its mind the imagery and feeling of a good feed. This in turn becomes the ego, a separate area within oneself.

It is hard to believe that 'mothering' was not deemed relevant psychologically until the 1920s. In view of the emphasis in this direction by Bowlby, Winnicott, and more recently in the popular writings of Miller, it is easy to forget that the processes of mothering appeared of little interest to psychoanalysis.

Freud's work, and the observations of those who followed him, concentrated upon the divisions that affect the human condition. Human beings are born under one law but bound unremittingly to another. All individuals at birth bring something unique with them, but the divisions of the mind are formed by a headlong incursion into a world which is the arena for the orders, wishes, desires, phantasies and commands of other people and which is racked by the tortured patterns of humankind's laws, prohibitions, aggression and culture.

It was left to Melanie Klein to emphasize the importance of the 'pre-Oedipal layers' of personality development. The relationship between the ego and the impulses, the drives and the body feelings, and the outside world (represented by the touch and feel of its parents' hands) became the two poles of Klein's basic model of the neonate. She maintained that the baby brings into the world two main conflicting impulses, love and hate. Love is the manifestation of the life drive, hate, destructiveness and envy are the emanations of the death drive. These innate feelings are constantly at war with each other. The neonate tries to deal with these conflicts. A tiny body that struggles to cope with various impulses, a body with sensations which are constantly endangered by the need to gratify overwhelming desires, and which has, in a very short space of time, to develop mature mechanisms for dealing with them. The baby meets a world which is both satisfying and frustrating. It exists from the moment it seeks and finds its mother's breast or its substitute, then gradually the world becomes more complicated and it seeks and finds again its father.

During the early months of life it must be supposed that the child can make no distinction between itself as a personal entity, and the bewildering world of light and darkness which surrounds it. The child can only at this stage attribute them to an object. Its mother's nipple, a good feed, a soft cot or the touch of a hand which gives it pleasure are easily regarded as good objects, while something that gives pain, like hunger, cold, discomfort, can easily be converted in terms of something that is bad. To the baby, hunger is a frightening situation; it is not able to understand the meaning of time, of patience, of the tolerance of frustration. It cannot appreciate that these situations are of a temporary nature, and will soon be followed by a feeling of pleasurable relief as the warm milk goes down. A small change in the immediate situation can change feelings of anger and discomfort into blissful gratification. It follows then that the baby is able to love and hate one and the same object in rapid succession. There are no qualifications. It is all or nothing at all, black and white.

Conceptualization of psychological disturbance and health

Introjection and projection
In her paper 'Notes on some schizoid mechanisms', which was read to the British Society, Melanie Klein (1952a) introduced the concepts of ego splitting and projective identification. This was a more complicated process than the theory of projection described by Freud. An understanding of the processes of introjection and projection are of major importance since in therapy we can find parallels for all these situations. Every human being will go through phases in life in which they return to or experience relationships which were unsatisfactory in their past.

Introjection   For every human being the outer world and its impact, the kind of experiences they live through, and the objects they come into contact with are not only dealt with externally, but also taken into the self to become part of their inner world. As we introject these new experiences into our personalities, we take on the concept that we can truly *rely on ourselves*. An enduring self-image and increased self-esteem can be facilitated by this form of introjection. Where this process can go awry relates to the relative strength or weakness of a person's ego. If, for example, we admire someone else to such an extent that we endow this other person with abilities and characteristics (be they good or bad) that we would wish to emulate, and identify with them to such an extent that we endeavour to live as they do, taking into ourselves and taking over the image and behaviour of this other person, we subsequently fail to take responsibility for our own future development.

Projection   This goes on simultaneously and is a manifestation of a person's ability to project on to other people those aggressive and envious feelings (predominantly those of aggression) which by the very nature of their 'badness' must be passed on either by the process of projection or, alternatively, carefully repressed. It is important to understand that although projection is a general term used in other analytical theories, *projective identification* is a strictly Kleinian concept which is held, by Kleinian therapists, to be responsible for severe difficulties in both establishing one's own identity and feeling secure enough to establish other outward looking relationships.

Projective identification   This term covers a complex clinical event: one person not wishing to own to his or her feelings of love and hate manipulatively inducing another into experiencing them, with consequent visible changes of affect in the behaviour of both people concerned. It is a difficult and complicated concept to understand as it deals – in the main – with the subjective experience of a therapist and the use to which the therapist is put in being unwittingly drawn into the patient's phantasy world. For example, patients may deal with the deprived part of their own childhood by idealizing the parenting process in therapy. This can in turn deprive patients of future resourcefulness, but may also trigger off in the therapist a mutual longing for the closeness and dependence of parenthood. This process highlights the internal world built up in the child and the adult alike which is partially a reflection of the external one. This two-way process continues throughout every stage of our lives, zigging and zagging, interacting and modifying itself in the course of maturation but never losing its importance in relation to the world around us. The judgement of reality is never quite free from the influence of the boiling mercury of our internal world.

Meltzer considers the concept of projective identification to be one of Melanie Klein's greatest contributions to psychoanalysis: 'A concrete conception of the inner world . . . a theatre where meaning can be generated' (1979: 18–19). In his view Melanie Klein did not really consider herself to be a theoretician; rather she saw herself as a face worker simply describing these phenomena as and when she observed them.

Splitting   In *Our Adult World and its Roots in Infancy* Melanie Klein (1960) described the situation which arose when the projected bad objects – those representations of the child's own ferocious and aggressive impulses – rebound upon it. The desperate situation of a young mother, who tries to please a baby who is literally biting the hand that feeds it, is a case in point. Children may refuse food and scream even when they are desperately hungry or kick and push when they mostly long for a caress: these stages, which thankfully are largely outgrown in the process of normal development, can be identified with the delusional sense of persecution sometimes found in the paranoid adult. Indeed a residual persecutory element can always be found in the sense of guilt which is central to all civilizations. Since the infant continues to need a good mother – indeed its life depends upon it – by splitting the two aspects and clinging only to the good one like a rubber ring in a swimming pool, it has evolved for the time being a means of staying alive. Without this loving object to keep it buoyant the child would in truth sink beneath the surface of a hostile world which would engulf it.

Melanie Klein's view was that in the early years of life the objects which surrounded the infant were not seen and understood in *visual terms*. This included a wide range of 'objects': parents, siblings, blankets, food, bathing, cots, prams, toys, and so on. These would be construed only as they were *experienced* as good or bad. Klein took this further and became concerned with the splitting of aspects of the ego itself into good and bad parts. In later life, these could become more obsessional, leading to a fragmentation of the self. Klein linked this fragmentation process to the onset of schizophrenia. Here the patient had carried this process of splitting to an extreme, splitting each split yet again into a multifarious and bewildering group of repressions and concessions that in the end became chaos. Klein maintained that this chaotic world was itself a psychotic regression to an earlier childhood fear of annihilation.

Acquisition of psychological disturbance

The paranoid-schizoid position

This combination of mechanisms and anxieties – feelings of great power over the parent, contrasting with a sudden sense of persecution, are very common indeed in the first year of life. Paranoid anxieties and constant splitting into categories of good and bad are characteristic of this stage. These destructive feelings are of great importance developmentally but can also, as has been pointed out in extreme cases, become the basis of later paranoia and schizophrenic illness.

Let us look again at the moment when a baby arrives in this world, in a parlous state, weak, helpless, and at the mercy of the terrifying anxiety of annihilation. Initially, little can be done to confront this anxiety, some parts of which are split off, relegated for the time being to the unconscious, but which remain always on tap and potentially active. Anxieties about murder and madness may remain forever in the mind impoverishing the personality, while others can safely be examined and confronted as the ability to think and act is strengthened.

Some frustration and anxiety is necessary for the growth and development of the personality, for if there is no balance of communication between the real and phantasized parts of the mind there is little opportunity for growth of the self. On this point, Mollon writes

> If the anxiety is firmly split off and deeply repressed then a relative absence of overt psychopathology may result but at the expense of substituting a rigid and shallow 'false-self' type of adjustment in place of the full potential richness of the personality. In view of these considerations we may now define psychopathology as an arrest of personality development due to the presence of anxiety which is felt to be intolerable.
>
> (Mollon 1979: 18–19)

In her paper 'Notes on some schizoid mechanisms' Melanie Klein (1952a) singled out greed and envy as two very disturbing factors, relating them first to the child's dominant relationship with the mother and later to other members of the family and eventually extending to the individual's cycle of life.

Greed is exacerbated by anxiety, the anxiety of being deprived, the need to take all one can from the mother and from the family. A greedy infant may enjoy what it has for the time being, but this feeling is soon replaced by the feeling of being robbed by others of all that it needs for food, love, attention or any other gratification. The baby who is greedy for love and attention is also afraid that it is unable to give out to others and this in its turn exacerbates their own situation. The baby needs everything, it can spare nothing and therefore what can it reasonably expect to receive from others? If an infant is relatively unable to tolerate frustration and anxiety on its own, serious difficulties can arise if the mother is unable, through depression or environmental problems, to provide consolation and mediation. The infant can then experience murderous feelings toward this seemingly un-giving mother. In seeking to destroy that which is needed for its own survival, the infant is experiencing ambivalent feelings, one moment contemplating murder, the next, suicide.

Envy is a spoiling pursuit. If milk, love and attention is being withheld for one reason or another then the loved object must be withholding it and keeping it for their own use. Suspicion is the basis of envy. If the baby cannot have what it desires there is a strong urge to spoil the very object of desire so that no one can enjoy it. This spoiling quality can result in a disturbed relationship with the mother, who cannot now supply an unspoilt satisfaction. It is only when there is such a breakdown of the natural protective forces that one notices how distorted the relationship between mother and child can become, exacerbating the postnatal situation and leading to the depressive illness to which some women are liable.

Melanie Klein enlarged on these problems, stating quite firmly that the aggressive envy experienced in infancy can inhibit the development of good object relations, that is children's ability to develop an intense and personal relationship with other objects (such as toys) which they may treat as alive, lovable, able to give love in return, needing sympathy or producing anger and to develop personalities which could be seen to be alive. This in its turn can affect the growth of the capacity to love.

> Throughout my work I have attributed fundamental importance to the infant's first object relation – the relation to the mother's breast and to the mother – and we have drawn the conclusion that, if this primal object which is introjected, takes root in the ego with relative security the basis for a satisfactory development is laid.
>
> (Klein 1957: 389)

Projective identification

Projective identification illustrates most clearly the links between human instinct, phantasy, and the mechanisms of defence. Sexual desires and aggressive impulses can be satiated by phantasy. Phantasy can be as pleasurable and as explicit as we wish to make it, and it is also a safety net – it contains and holds those bad parts of our inner self. The use of phantasy is obvious: in literature, in science, in art, and in all activities of everyday life.

One aspect of murderous phantasy is the rivalry which results from the male child's desire for the mother, his rivalry with his father and all the sexual phantasies which can be linked to this situation. The Oedipus complex (described in Chapter 2 on Freudian therapy) is rooted in the baby's suspicions of the father, who takes the mother's love and attention away from him. The same applies to the female child for whom the relationship to the mother and to all women is always of supreme importance.

But Klein placed her emphasis on earlier and more primitive stages in terms of precursors of the Oedipus complex. She argued that these Oedipal feelings were identifiable in the baby at the age of 6 months and were the result of the projection of infantile phantasies of rage and aggression on to the parent. While continuing to support Freud's tripartite differentiation of the psychic apparatus into ego, id and superego, she went on to claim that each of these areas of the psyche were identifiable almost from the day of birth.

The depressive position
The depressive position begins when the baby begins to recognize its mother. In the early months of life the baby is concerned with the integration of the sights and sounds and stimuli, both pleasant and unpleasant with which it is surrounded. Out of this dream-like world sufficient integration is achieved for the baby to experience its mother as a whole object, not a succession of parts. She is no longer breasts that can feed, hands that can hold, a voice that can soothe, facial grimaces that either please or frighten, but a complete entity on her own, separate, divided from the baby: someone who can choose to hold it close or stay away, can kiss or neglect or abuse her child. This gradual understanding of the separation process, this gradual awakening to the fact that it is one and the same person who is the container of both good and bad feelings is then transposed internally to the baby. It is as separate from her as she is from it and the infant can both love and hate this mother.

Its previous fears of being the frail objective of destruction extend subtly to an inner knowledge that it too can destroy the one person it loves and needs for survival. The anxiety has changed from a paranoid to a depressive one. In acknowledging the very existence of a separate being, the baby becomes exposed to the fear that it has made the cut. Aggression has destroyed the cord which linked the baby to the mother, leaving the child with feelings of unutterable guilt, sadness and deprivation, a hurt that can never be healed, a pain that can never be assuaged. In the Kleinian view, mental pain *is* pain, it hurts and mere gratification does not make it go away. Separation is painful, is experienced as a kind of death, the death of that which was and can never be again.

This process of separation and the depressive anxieties that it invoked was contained in the paper 'On the theory of anxiety and guilt' (Klein 1952b). This emphasized that depressive anxieties are a part of everyone's normal development and the guilt feelings which have developed are understood as part of the *imagined* harm done to the child's love object. When this is facilitated it can enable the process of reparation to commence. A child can show subtle tenderness to those around it and the anxieties and paranoid fears of early infancy can become modified during this period, although these anxieties may be painfully reawakened in the normal mourning processes of later life. Adult depression is known to involve a reactivation of this stage of infantile depression, so Kleinian psychotherapists consider the actual mourning situation a productive period in therapy. When an adult admits to feeling menaced and persecuted, the recriminations and self-reproaches of the depressed patient are interpreted and hopefully understood as a manifestation of the early persecutory impulses which were directed so savagely to the self.

Perpetuation of psychological disturbance

In preceding paragraphs some developmental models have been explained, in particular those of the impulses of destruction, greed and envy, and illustrating how the persecutory and sadistic anxieties of early life can disturb the child's emotional balance and inhibit his ability to acquire and maintain good social relationships.

Melanie Klein's understanding of what she was later to label 'the depressive position' highlighted the simple truth that human beings feel better when they are labelled as being 'good' than they do when they are made to feel bad.

The world in which we now live has taken its toll of childhood. Alongside the obvious signs of materialistic success comes the urgent need to be seen to be a good and successful parent. Whatever the criteria for this measure of success and in order to make sure of being loved, children have to go along with this creation. If they feel unloved, it must be their fault. They are too slow at school, too ugly, naughty, unacademic, lacking in social graces, poor at sport, should have been a boy or should have been a girl. Their self-esteem is low. Parents have suppressed any recollection of their own, innocent and painful childhood experiences. We are terrified of the possibility that hatred can overpower the love we are expected to profess.

Twenty years on from the death of Melanie Klein, Dr Alice Miller wrote

> Almost everywhere we find the effort, marked by various degrees of intensity and by the use of coercive measures, to rid ourselves as quickly as possible of the child within us – i.e. the weak, helpless, dependent creature – in order to become an independent competent adult deserving of respect. When we encounter this creature in our children we persecute it with the same measures once used on ourselves. And this is what we are accustomed to call child rearing. . . . The methods that can be used to suppress vital spontaneity in the child are: laying traps, lying, duplicity, subterfuge, manipulation, 'scare' tactics, withdrawal of love, isolation, distrust, humiliating and disgracing the child, scorn, ridicule and coercion even to the point of torture.
>
> (Miller 1983: 105)

All human beings, wherever they live, exist only in relationship to other human beings. The physical processes of conception, pregnancy and birth are the same for us all. In the uterus all babies exist in comparative safety; it is only when the baby makes its postnatal appearance, be it head or feet first or precipitately by Caesarian section, that it learns about the reality of solitary existence.

Loss of the parent in any form – breast or hand – gives rise to a primary separation anxiety which gives way to grief and then to the experience of mourning that which is lost. Aggression is also a major part of the mourning process. If the normal processes of childhood are disrupted in some way, if phantasy becomes reality and the loved object dies, leaves, neglects, batters, sexually abuses, reacts too possessively, becomes obsessional, it follows then that these disruptions of a normal interaction are likely to take a pathological course later in life, leading not only to an aggressive stance towards society but also to self-aggression and abuse.

Bowlby (1979) gives the following examples:

> Many of those referred to psychiatrists are anxious, insecure individuals usually described as over-dependent or immature. Under stress they are apt to develop neurotic symptoms, depression or phobia. Research shows them to have been exposed to at least one, and usually more than one, of certain typical patterns of pathogenic parenting, which includes
>
> (a) one or both parents being persistently unresponsive to the child's care-eliciting behaviour and/or actively disparaging and rejecting him;
> (b) discontinuities of parenting, occurring more or less frequently, including periods in hospital or institution;
> (c) persistent threats by parents not to love a child, used as a means of controlling him;
> (d) threats by parents to abandon the family, used either as a method of disciplining the child or as a way of coercing a spouse;
> (e) threats by one parent either to desert or even to kill the other or else to commit suicide (each of them more common than might be supposed);
> (f) inducing a child to feel guilt by claiming that his behaviour is or will be responsible for the parent's illness or death.
>
> (Bowlby 1979: 136–7)

Cooper (1988) writes:

> To be a child and especially to be a 'good' child in today's world is not to be a child at all. Instead these children of the nineties, the children of projection, grow up too quickly to become in their turn the mothers, friends, comforters, translators, advisers, support and sometimes lovers of their own parents. In taking care of other siblings, throwing themselves between parents in order to save a marriage, attempting to provide academic kudos, high earnings, sexual titillation and satisfaction, masochistic or sadistic gratification, the child will do anything, anyhow, for parental love and approval.
>
> (Cooper 1988: 12–13)

It is these anxieties which are the cause, if not confronted, of both childhood psychoses and mental illness in adult life.

Change

As has already been pointed out earlier on in this chapter, Kleinian psychotherapy adheres to the common principles which underlie psychoanalytic theory;

namely, that it is the unconscious mechanisms operating within the human psyche which dominate the process of change for every human being. However, Melanie Klein had more to add to this original concept.

Let us take the well-used analogy that, at birth, every human being is equipped with a *tabula rasa*, a white tablet, a clean slate. The circumstances of one's life are then written on the white surface. To this end human beings learn to live with their history and the alternating vicissitudes and pleasantries of life. What is important here is the emphasis placed by Kleinians on two factors:

1 There is no gain in life without a subsequent loss and the ambivalent feelings that temper any form of progress i.e. the baby gains approval from its parents when it takes its first mouthful of solid food – but the breast is then lost to it forever. The pride a baby will experience when learning to walk diminishes when acknowledging that the intimacy of helplessness is relinquished.
2 Survival in a dangerous world depends on one's ability to reconcile oneself to the fact that every 'have' is balanced by a 'have not'.

The well-known game played by children, 'I'm the King of the Castle', is a case in point. The consciousness of the self and the feeling of enjoyment in winning are transient. As children grow up they become more aware of the effect of their behaviour on other people and they learn to compromise and to understand the implications of frustration.

The process of change can never be viewed as a clear and shining goal, rather it is the development of a growing sense of wise detachment towards life. Developing from this detachment comes the sense of personal identity which enables us to go through life with a tolerant irony and strengthens our resistance to the transient temptations of fame, wealth and self-aggrandisement and enables us to take what comes.

Hinshelwood (1989) identifies the change processes within Kleinian theory as

1 the development of the subject's awareness of psychic reality
2 balancing the currents of love and hate which run within the self.

(Hinshelwood 1989: 19)

Practice

Goals of therapy

Melanie Klein never altered the technical principles which were the foundation of her early work, *The Psycho-Analysis of Children* (1932). This work continues to form the basis of the psychodynamic work undertaken by Kleinian psychotherapists and colours their distinctive concepts of mental functioning.

It is important to stress here that the theories of Melanie Klein have never been popular. Freudian and post-Freudian doctrines have had more appeal. It was perhaps easier to accept the hidden agenda of the Oedipal conflict and the 'tidy' processes of oral, anal and later libidinal development than to take on board the confrontation with a life-and-death struggle which lies at the root of Kleinian thinking. To tilt at the precious idealization of the 'loving' mother and to confront instead the infantile struggle for 'survival' are unpleasant and uncomfortable thoughts. In Kleinian therapy we have to take a long, hard look at our phantasies of parental love; if these are removed what bleak prospect of life does the Kleinian therapist provide?

Patients who undertake this kind of psychotherapy are bound to come to the first session full of hopes and fears, with deep-rooted phantasies and phobias about themselves and about their therapist. They present material in the very first session which concern anxieties that are central to them at that moment in time. Predominantly they want to feel 'better', to obtain relief from suffering (Colby 1951), and are seeking, like an infant, immediate gratification of their needs. Wish-fulfilment is not confined to those who seek psychotherapy. Eavesdrop on any everyday conversation and you will conclude that people will always hope to get what they feel they need to make them happy and want to obtain it in the shortest possible time and with a minimum of effort.

The Kleinian psychotherapist maintains that this form of anxiety can act as a spur to development and personal achievement, providing it is not excessive. At the beginning of therapy, the patient tends to seek immediate gratification from the therapist. This behaviour can often be as thoughtless, demanding and extortionate as the infant's relationship with its mother, reflecting the need to exhaust and exploit one's mother and, to experience, yet again, the subsequent feelings of guilt that are associated with such behaviour.

At the beginning of therapy, therefore, the therapist will wish to work with patients' unconscious phantasies about themselves and their relationships with others and the ways in which these phantasies relate to the reality of the outside world in the way it has been experienced both in the past and in the present. Some Kleinian therapists would have it that psychotherapy has more in common with an educational experience than a form of medical treatment. Successful psycho- therapy should begin a process of learning and personal development which moves along at its own pace. The foundation stone of this process must be the relationship between therapist and patient. If this goal is similarly perceived and worked upon by both parties, the outcome will result in the achievement of some mutual satisfaction.

Melanie Klein was quite clear about the efficiency of her method in the treatment of adults. Her primary goal to reduce immediate anxiety, by encour- aging patients to face their inhibitions and to facilitate a more positive relationship with their therapist. This in turn would enable the patients to experience them- selves as real people in a real world and to maintain a balance between the feelings of love and hate which alternate in every psyche. By the end of therapy, therefore, it is hoped that patients will feel able to form full and satisfactory personal relation- ships, that they will have gained insight into their personal situation and feel released from their early fixations and repressions.

They will be less inhibited and more able to enjoy the good things of life while remaining sensitive, open and capable when problems arise. They will be able to assess their internal world, possess a quiet reassurance and ego strength which stems from the knowledge that even in times of great stress, they will survive and perhaps even more importantly that they want to survive.

The means by which true reparation (i.e. growth in the Kleinian sense) takes place are essentially mysterious. It is something which happens when the 'mental atmosphere is conducive to objects repairing one another. The frame of mind of tolerance, of pain, of remorse over one's destructiveness' (Meltzer 1979: 18–19). These reparative mental conditions follow when there is an understanding of one's infantile dependency upon internal objects: your idealized mother and father and the moment of your own creation, so that you can go on in life to accept yourself as a product of what was and is, in an atmosphere of tolerance and acceptance.

Melanie Klein stated

> My criterion for the termination of an analysis is, therefore, as follows: have persecutory and depressive anxieties been sufficiently reduced in the course of analysis, and has the patient's relation to the external world been sufficiently strengthened to enable him to deal satisfactorily with the situation of mourning arising at this point?
>
> (Klein 1950: 78–80)

Selection criteria

There are many patterns to therapy and many different approaches to the relief of psychic pain. Patients have a choice in the kind of treatment they would prefer, and can and do move from individual to group therapy, from group therapy to family therapy, if they so wish, and in whatever sequence seems more beneficial to them at a particular time.

Initially the referral of a patient for psychotherapy would be made by a general practitioner. With luck, would-be patients and their doctors have discussed a preference for one modality or another. There is a need for patients to accept responsibility for their problems and, in seeking for some amelioration of their situation, to participate actively in making the decision, choosing to work on a one-to-one basis in individual therapy or deciding that they would feel greater motivation and strength by the support, modelling and challenge which can be offered in a therapy group or a family group setting.

In selecting patients for individual therapy there are criteria which the Kleinian psychotherapist would seek to fulfil:

1 that the patient has problems which can be clearly defined in psychodynamic terms
2 that the patient appears motivated enough for change and insight into their previous behaviour
3 that the patient will have enough internal strength to cope with the demands and tensions that are to be created by the process of interpretation and confrontation
4 that the patient produces evidence that they are able to accept and sustain a long-standing relationship with the therapist and with significant others in their immediate surroundings.

Patients will arrive with little knowledge of how the Kleinian treatment procedure works and even less knowledge about the outcome of psychotherapy. Initially the psychotherapist will indicate that therapy involves a detailed process of examining and discussing problems. They are told that it could be distressing and painful, that there are no guaranteed 'cures', but patients can be enabled to help themselves to identify the origin of their symptoms, the reaction to these symptoms and the way in which these symptoms constrict their life.

The therapist must have the right to decide if he or she is prepared to work with a specific patient. Personal feelings will obviously affect the outcome of an initial diagnostic interview. Conversely the patient may also decide that he or she will be unable to work with the therapist. It is essential to respect the rights of both parties in such a delicate transaction. What is probably important is that the relationship between therapist and patient can be a relationship where there is mutual respect, the respect of one human being for another and hope for the potentialities of this other person. This is termed the 'therapeutic alliance'.

It is hoped that each patient has the capacity to come out of therapy with the opportunity to love well, to work well, to play well and to have some optimism for the future. The Kleinian psychotherapist finds it most suitable to work with patients whose underlying conflicts are towards the narcissistic side, whose egos have undergone considerable deformation or weakening. These patients will come into therapy expressing inability to love or be loved by others, with conflicts about dealing with other people in a social, sexual or work setting, general intellectual and academic underfunctioning and symptomatic phobias, anxiety states and minor perversions.

For some patients there may be a need to limit the period of treatment. It is useful anyway to indicate that the treatment will not go on indefinitely, that it will end at a certain time. A statement of this kind may not be indicated for all patients, but could be necessary in certain instances. In contrast to psychoanalysis, in Kleinian psychotherapy there is a realistic indication that the treatment will end some day. The therapist will point out that the therapeutic relationship will come to an end and this is an important and necessary factor in working through the attachment process, a process which is repeated throughout life when some aspect of a 'good object' is given up in this way.

Qualities of effective therapists

Freudian and Jungian analysts continue to proliferate but Kleinian psycho-therapists have always been in short supply. As with other modalities, it is an expensive and prolonged training, in most cases a postgraduate training, and in every case a training which involves the student in an extensive commitment both of time and money over many years, tailoring one's life-style to personal therapy four or five times a week.

It is a training which centres itself on the personality of the would-be therapist and it is this understanding of the self which is tuned to perfect pitch like the finest violin. The person of the therapist is encouraged to become an instrument which can interpret, colour and respond to the musical score, resonate and bend beneath the fingers of the musician, constantly changing and developing their diagnostic sensitivities in interpretation and technique. A Kleinian psychotherapist will have experienced this long-term period of personal analysis, followed by a shorter period of training analysis at one of the formal institutes and long-term super-vision of their work with individual clients.

In *The Psycho-Analysis of Children* Melanie Klein wrote:

The analysis of children at puberty demands a thorough knowledge of the technique of adult analysis, I consider a regular training in the analysis of adults as a necessary foundation. . . . No one who has not gained experience adequately and done a fair amount of work on adults should enter upon the technically more difficult field of child analysis. In order to be able to preserve the fundamental principles of analytic treatment in the modified form necessitated by the child's (and the adult's) mechanisms at the various stages of development, the therapist must besides being fully versed in the technique of early analysis, possess complete mastery of the technique employed in analysing adults.

(Klein 1932: 342)

It is the Kleinian view that an analyst or a psychotherapist who dogmatically believes that they and only they, plus a few other chosen spirits who adhere rationally and rigidly to this particular school or this particular form of dogmatism has not, in Kleinian terms, advanced beyond the paranoid-schizoid position, to acquire the capacity for being depressed. Sensitivity to the depression within oneself enables the Kleinian therapist more easily to doubt whether they, or anyone else has the key to understanding the complexity of a human being.

The fundamental concepts of the paranoid-schizoid and depressive positions will naturally affect the ways in which the Kleinian psychotherapist will view their patient's presentations. In dealing with the early anxieties which arise from the relationship between the baby and the breast, faced by the harsher and more persecutory anxieties which lie in the deepest strata of the mind, the more primitive the processes that are mobilized, the more important it is for the Kleinian therapist to remain unaltered in a basic function: to refer the anxiety back to its source and resolve it by systematically analysing the transference situation.

The therapist will need to be sensitive to those embryonic features of emotional problems which are present in all human beings and which can be seen clearly reflected in the patients. The therapist will be aware that possible events in one's life, both in reality and in imagination which did occur and which could have developed, are not denied and repressed. It requires an understanding of the fact that in every person lies the capacity to have been something and someone else. The therapist should be able to encourage the flowering of this inner self in the patient, while remaining for the bulk of professional life in a situation where their own self-expression in this context is forbidden.

The steady, accepting but neutral attitude of the Kleinian psychotherapist differs from the manipulative and role-playing attitudes advocated by certain other strategies of intervention. Power is acknowledged and interpreted. In Kleinian psychotherapy, in the continuing interaction of the process, the therapist allows himself or herself to be used as an *object*; in this way the psychotherapist actually intrudes but does not obtrude.

Making clear the transference manifestations which develop during this process is regarded as the primary means by which the patient is helped towards better health, to be able to maintain continuing psychic functioning. The personality of the therapist – calm, interested, helpful, giving full attention to each minute detail of the patient's behaviour and language – re-creates in the therapeutic alliance an opportunity to correct the infantile distorted view of object relationships that have constricted the patient's life. It provides incentive and reward in a benign relationship that encourages the patient to achieve the tasks that are imposed by the discipline of therapy and provides each one with a model of strength and an identification with a reality, the real live person of the therapist.

At the same time psychotherapists, guided by the ethical goals of treatment and the understanding obtained from their own training and personal psychotherapy, must safeguard against any interference with a professional attitude to the patient based on this prior knowledge which stems from a particular/personal set of ethical values, attitudes and boundaries. For instance if the therapist was in the recent process of mourning the death of a parent it may be too difficult to work with a patient in a similar position. Therapists are not empty husks: they have prejudices, fears and painful trigger spots. It is better for both therapist and patient alike to acknowledge and identify these feelings. This may mean that at times the therapist will decide not to take a particular patient into treatment. This is a serious decision for both patient and therapist alike and must be handled in such a fashion that, in making a referral to another agency or individual, it does not further disturb the patient and cause more pain.

Therapeutic style

A Kleinian therapist is aware that if a patient gains control in psychotherapy difficulties will be perpetuated since the patient will continue to live a life constricted by the paranoid-schizoid symptoms which caused him or her to seek therapy in the first place. It follows then that however neutral and laid back the therapist may contrive to be, successful therapy could be described as a process whereby the therapist maintains control of the kind of relationship that will operate with this patient.

In all forms of psychoanalytic psychotherapy, therapist and patient are confronted with a basic problem: the problem of object need.

> Every patient regards the psychotherapist as real, regards all the manifesta-
> tions of the treatment situation as real and strives to regard the therapist as a
> real object. The therapist too wants to regard the patient as real and to
> respond to the patient as a real object.
>
> (Tarachow 1970: 498–9)

The primary urge in this relationship is the temptation to turn back the clock, to regress, to restore the symbiotic parental relationship that initially occurred with the mother, to lose the boundaries and fuse, to re-create the past as it was before and return to the time of ultimate dependency replete, at one inside the mother.

It is important to point out here that in no way should the therapist confuse the therapeutic function with the parental function. The therapist may give over part of their mind to this experience coming as close as we do to the patient's life experience but in essence the therapist must also remain detached from it, holding on as it were to the anonymity of a professional therapist. The therapist will be aware of the seductive danger of imagining oneself (even for the briefest time) as the ideal parent figure for the patient. The therapist uses these skills of awareness and identification to assess and understand the complexities of the interaction between the patient and the parent parts of the therapist. We may be deeply affected, feel involved but paradoxically this affection and involvement is distilled, detached and separated in a way which is impossible in the true relationship between a parent and child.

The Kleinian psychotherapist works assiduously to develop this therapeutic alliance, the intimate, real and close working together of two minds. For this to come about both the therapist and the patient undertake a controlled ego splitting in the service of the treatment. The therapist and the patient work together in constructing a barrier against the need for a constricted object relationship. The therapist is not a breast, a hand or a voice, but a human being who is complete in every way. The therapist as well as the patient has to struggle constantly against the array of temptations which lead one to believe that you can allow yourself to become closer to your patient, with consequent dissolution and camouflaging of the existing ego boundaries.

Such temptations are further compounded because certain aspects of the therapeutic alliance are real. The therapist behaves in a caring, concerned, real and human way to the patient, and the patient is able to glean over a period of time real things about the therapist: that the therapist may be single or married, the family is away on holiday, that the therapist smokes, prefers one colour to another, that there is a secretary, a family pet, small children, that the therapist may share accommodation with other psychotherapists, and so on.

These realistic aspects of the treatment relationship must be understood by the Kleinian psychotherapist, who uses them *wordlessly* to correct transference distortions and supplies the motivation necessary for the therapeutic work of transference interpretation.

It is important to stress at this point that every interpretation made by a therapist results in a loss or a deprivation for the patient. It can frustrate, denying the patient an opportunity to gratify their phantasy wishes, often placing them in the position of relinquishing some infantile object. 'It is a paradox that the interpretation – the act of the therapist that deprives the patient of the infantile object – also provides him with an adult object in the form of the sympathetic therapist' (Tarachow 1970: 498–9).

Psychoanalytically oriented Kleinian psychotherapy is a method of treatment in which *at the very beginning* it is the therapist's function to help the patient slowly but surely to surrender any hope of receiving gratification from the therapist as an idealized object. This happens even while the patient is encouraged to focus on the therapist as a possible source of other gratifications – gratifications which the patient is able in the real world to perceive and acknowledge.

Major therapeutic strategies and techniques

The role of the psychotherapist is centred entirely on the transference situation and its interpretation. The therapist listens intently to the patient's material and endeavours not to be involved at all in giving practical advice, encouragement, reassurance or offer any active participation in the life of the patient or patient's family.

Transference interpretation
The concept of transference relates not only to an understanding of the 'here and now', the situation which is actually evolving between the psychotherapist and the patient, but also an understanding of the way facts and phantasies which relate to past relationships, especially those of internal figures from the patient's inner world, are transferred on to the therapist.

This lively process takes in current problems and relationships, which are again related to the transference as it develops. The Kleinian psychotherapist is aware of the transference at the very *beginning* of therapy, but in giving interpretations careful attention must be given to the way they are handled, the timing, the order and the language used, and especially the amount of interpretation.

Understanding of the transference and counter-transference and their effect on the process of therapy are the tools which are used to investigate both the positive and negative feelings directed towards the therapist. Interpretation of these feelings should be sparse and succinct, using everyday language suitable for the patient, avoiding the use of technical and analytic terms which may give satisfaction to the therapist but are of little value to the patient. If your patients cannot understand you, they may as well go home. The best initial interpretations are simply re-statements of the problem as presented by the client but relayed back in dynamic terms.

If it is difficult to teach psychotherapy, it is even more difficult to describe the techniques of psychotherapy. In an earlier paragraph I stressed that the Kleinian psychotherapist will have learnt skills through the process of long-term psychoanalysis or psychodynamic psychotherapy, a process not unlike the age-old system of apprenticeship to a master or skilled craftsman of some repute and proven worth. The technique of psychotherapy is not a static process and psychotherapists regularly attend case discussion groups, supervision sessions, seminars and study groups to meet and compare experiences and to learn from each other in a lively fashion.

Contemporary Kleinian technique emphasizes

1 the immediate here and now situation
2 the total of all aspects of the setting
3 the importance of understanding the content of the anxiety.

'The consequence of interpreting the anxiety rather than the defences only (so-called deep interpretation)' (Spillius 1983: 321–2).

In ways that are comparable with other techniques, the therapist keeps expressions of personality and life-style out of the session. Winnicott (1958) humorously remarked 'of course you can acknowledge that there is a war going on', but political statements or discussion of other issues do not belong in the consulting room.

In this way the client is enabled to make contact with an expectation of *others* which relates more closely to the emotions that are experienced as a result of therapy, than they do to what is happening at that moment in the external world. It is important to emphasize here that the past is connected to the present *gradually*. Interpretations are given in a certain sequence. The therapist makes use of preparatory interventions, interpreting the resistances and defences, gauging the patient's readiness to accept later interpretations, wording them carefully and appropriately so that understanding can be facilitated and contained.

In the Kleinian model, interpretations go from the surface to the depths. From what is known or imagined to occur in the present to what exists in the past, which is less well known or unknown. The therapist layers slowly to the earliest mental processes and to the later more specialized types of mental functioning which are the unconscious infantile archaic wishes and phantasies, that is those which focus on the therapist as a possible source of gratification.

The change process in therapy

Atholl Hughes in 'Contributions of Melanie Klein to psychoanalytic technique' (1974) gives a particularly clear definition of the change process in Kleinian therapy:

> As the patient is helped to distinguish good experiences they can identify with the analyst as a person who can care for their own insight and well being and the way is open for the patient to do the same. As the patient's envy lessens it becomes possible to appreciate positive qualities in oneself and others, acknowledged along with destructive qualities. Integration of split off parts of oneself is comparable to a process in the development of the normal infant who begins, at about three months of age, to tolerate loving and hating the same object with less splitting and projection.
>
> On the basis of a repeated satisfying experience, the child is able to introject, that is to take into their own personality ideas and feelings of a good mother with less hostility and idealisation. The child is then in a position to tolerate feelings of concern and responsibility towards the mother in whom the capacity to introject is crippled.
>
> (Hughes 1974: 113–14)

During the treatment process, the patient comes to understand that feelings of aggression and love can be valuable, and so it is possible to value them. Early responses to interpretation which were felt by the patient to be prohibitive, unkind or unduly harsh which tended either to frustrate desire or to punish – permitting, even commanding the patient to enter in fear and trepidation the forbidden areas of primitive and passionate feelings, – these regressive infantile expectations are overcome and replaced by a rationality that can be accepted and understood.

Melanie Klein opened the door to insights which enable us at least to attempt to contend with human behaviour. We are confronted in life with a view of ourselves in a succession of social relationships which are disrupted by hatred, jealousy, rivalry, greed and other destructive feelings. The process of change in therapy enables us at least to establish more constructive relationships.

Patients change as they become more open and free to acknowledge their constant struggle between love and hate. Facilitated by their therapy, knowledge of the destructive elements which are present in the psyche can lead to clearer judgement, increased tolerance of ourselves and others, with the ability to remain in control, and to be less fearful.

This problem of change can be identified as a desire for reconciliation and reparation. The patient can begin to identify with other people in a caring and sensitive way. The patient can let go of the negative aspects of the painful frustrations and suffering of the past, believing once again in their own capacity to love and therefore to expect to be loved in return. In making this reparation for the past the patient can make good the imagined injuries both given and received in infancy and move on to relinquish their guilt.

Limitations of the approach

There is a proliferation of different methods of psychotherapy, many of which do not emphasize self-awareness, and which open wide the question of causation of therapeutic change. They postulate that change is not engendered by the growth of self-awareness.

Any scientific examination of the causes of therapeutic change must involve an examination and description of the variables which, in context, facilitate such change. Experimental methods can then be evolved which will test the hypotheses which are formed. Kleinian psychotherapy, as judged by these contemporary standards, is still unable to provide the scientific evidence which is necessary to meet the basic criteria of dis-confirmability. Moreover, it becomes increasingly evident that it is an oversimplification to look at psychopathology as if it can be isolated from the changing attitudes of the nuclear age.

But what of the Kleinian method both as a focus of inquiry and as a therapy? Some Kleinian therapists find it difficult to acknowledge there is an outside environment that their patients have created and in which they function. In seeking to recreate the patient's internal and phantasized world of childhood the Kleinian is perhaps too eager to divorce patients from their social and cultural background.

We have, after all, moved on considerably from the early 1900s and have come to realize (I hope) that our patients are a specific group of people who have reacted in a specific way to their problems and who come, specifically, to seek help from Kleinian psychotherapy. A human being cannot develop in a sterilized plastic bubble. A baby is conceived at the coming together of its parents who contribute to this act of creation the essence of their own personalities at that given moment in time. The baby is born at a predicted time and season of the year, in a special place and in a particular way, and significant others become involved in its well-being. It depends throughout life on the availability and proximity of other human beings. In the wheatfields of America, someone will sow the wheat that provides bread for this child, and in the sweatshops of Hong Kong another child will labour to cut its clothes.

In the heat of the moment, focusing mainly on early childhood experiences and/or recollections, the broader social context and subjective processes which brought these two human beings together can sometimes get left out of the consulting room, especially as the focus is on manoeuvrability and tactics.

Kleinian psychotherapy holds the view that external events are not of primary importance, but we now know that these events can exacerbate or alleviate certain aspects of the personality.

Inevitably the point of view on what process to use with the patient in effecting change is shaped by one's theoretical approach. However, if the therapist practises therapy all day and every day from only one viewpoint, then there is the real danger of Kleinian therapists becoming subsumed and consumed by their own stance.

This contrasts sharply with other strategies of intervention where the emphasis has shifted from the processes within an individual to those in the context of his or her relationships with others (i.e. family therapy and personal construct psychology).

Again, Farrell (1981) reinforces the limitations imposed by strict adherence to one particular kind of analytic theory and in response to Melanie Klein he makes the point that Kleinian theory was (and still is) innovative. In continuing to extemporize and to employ new and novel forms of psychoanalytic method, the Kleinian therapist may be tempted to seek to obtain affirmation of any novel input from the patients themselves. Melanie Klein's view that the free play of young children can be interpreted psychoanalytically still provides the Kleinian therapist with a wealth of new material and has continued to provoke a considerable revision of analytic theory.

But the question is: when the Kleinian therapist continues to report new case material and new and novel findings, how then is it possible to decide whether the therapist has, in fact, just misinterpreted basic Kleinian theory? If the therapist is positive about challenging results, does this imply that the original theory itself is 'shaky' and in need of amendment? For the Kleinian therapist the nagging doubts must persist. The crucial question remains: what effect does the assumption of this particular theoretical stance have on the behaviour of this therapist? Do interpretations always dictate the therapist's goals for patients? Do Kleinian therapists seek out only what they expect to find? Do therapists, in order to fit their own expectations, distort what information the patient provides?

Kleinian psychotherapists tend to forget that because they see their patients in such a strictly controlled analytic setting, they are felt to be immolated from a view of their patient in the external world. True, patients report on their daily life, but these reports are highly selective and often pertinent only to the failures rather than the successes of life outside the consulting room.

Anxious behaviour by one patient can be interpreted as a repression of unconscious ideas which are threatening to become conscious. The same anxious behaviour in another could be viewed externally as a way of appealing for a sympathetic approach from the therapist. These two interpretations of behaviour represent astonishingly different theoretical systems. In this way the therapist's viewpoint can be distorted.

The reader of this book will note that various theorists have differed considerably on the postulation of central motives or goals for *all* human beings. Why do they differ so much? Is it not that the task of ferreting out the central motives of all human beings is an impossible task? Is it not an unattainable goal to poll every patient on their expectations of life and their private responses to the slings and arrows of outrageous fortune? Would Kleinian psychotherapy suffer if each patient's motives were seen as unique? Psychoanalytical psychotherapy has been defined as a perspective which is essentially pre-theoretical in nature, but perspectives are often constricted by ideological underpinnings whether we are aware of them or not.

It was Huxley who wrote 'Give me good mothers and I shall make a better world', but it is the converse which is true: 'Make me a good world and I shall give you good mothers'. It is hoped that Kleinian therapy could, eventually, be more explicit in stating that the amelioration of at least some areas of maternal deprivation and childhood abuse will be possible only when these intrinsic requirements can be met.

Case example

The client

Frances Ashe has been my patient for five years. She has progressed from twice-weekly psychotherapy sessions to our current arrangement when I see her for one session every three weeks. Frances recently celebrated her 40th birthday, a significant landmark for a woman who had previously made two serious attempts at suicide and has a long history of so-called psychiatric illness beginning in childhood. Between 1967 and 1971 she consulted a psychiatrist on a regular basis and was diagnosed as manic-depressive, a diagnosis which she appeared happy to accept. She continues to receive medication from her GP.

The presenting problem for Frances was 'overwhelming anxiety' about the imminent death of her parents, now in their late 70s. What would she do? Where would she turn to if they died? Anxiety, too, about her ambivalent feelings when contrarily she wished her parents *would* die so that she could be free of their influence and constant invasion of her privacy.

Frances's mother is Jewish from Jewish parents while her father, marrying for the second time, is himself the product of a mixed marriage – a Jewish mother and a Christian father. Mr Ashe's mother became a long-term patient in a psychiatric hospital and, as a result, he was brought up as a practising Christian by his father's family. Later he reverted to Judaism.

Mrs Ashe was told that there was little chance of her carrying a baby to full term, but eventually she did conceive and gave birth to Frances. The birth was normal although the uterus was compressed by large fibroid growths. At the time Mrs Ashe was 37 years of age.

Following surgery to remove the growths, Mrs Ashe was constantly unwell and took to her bed for long periods of time. A mother's help was engaged and this lady became a surrogate mother to Frances, who called both her and her mother 'Mummy'. Mrs Ashe then had a hysterectomy, and the mother's help became resident in the family home. It was she who taught Frances to walk and talk.

At 3 Frances was sent to nursery school 'to relieve the pressure on my mother'. Frances felt 'different'; other children at the school experienced Frances as 'strange', and she wasn't able to make friends. She was a difficult child, grown-up, superior and speaking with a plush accent. Her mother used her as a confidante or a friend. She had nothing in common with other little girls of her own age but could entertain older people and preferred their company. The conversation of children in contrast was boring and a waste of time. Frances had a 'poor' appetite. She could eat only tiny portions of daintily prepared food. She would not swallow her lunchtime sandwiches at school and a teacher would stand over her forcing her to eat.

In primary school there was a continuous saga of unhappiness. The head-mistress found her to be argumentative and impertinent and was asked by her mother to keep her under control as she was 'difficult' at home. Struck across the hands with a ruler, Frances wet her knickers in shame. She was expected to travel home from school on her own. Her mother was still too 'unwell' to collect her. This time – with swollen hands – she could not extricate the money to pay her bus fare home. The parents reluctantly moved Frances to another school.

> Here I was in a new school predominated by Jewish children. No one wanted to play with me and I was left out of games. They would not believe that I was Jewish. I didn't know much about Judaism and could not speak any Hebrew or Yiddish words. Food just stuck in my throat. I started to be sick every time I tried to swallow. I was taken to Great Ormond Street Hospital but they could find nothing physically wrong with me.
>
> My parents' attitude was that I was being awkward, uncooperative. It was deliberate. I behaved badly. I made myself a burden, I was a misery and unhelpful to my mother who was in poor health.

The family then moved house; Frances changed school and the change was for the better – a nice house, a new school. She made some friends and played with the son of her mother's friend. She was regarded as 'clever' and did well. The school had a strong Christian tradition and Frances enjoyed the New Testament teaching, but her parents still insisted that Frances took Hebrew lessons which she hated. She was given a choice by her parents. Continue at this school or go to a prestigious grammar school? Frances chose the former:

> Serve them bloody well right in the end. I decided not to go to the posh school. How they would have liked it. Evidence of my wonderful upbringing! As soon as I could I went to see my headmistress and told her that I wished to convert to Christianity. She was very nervous, assuming that my parents would accuse her of influencing my decision.
>
> My parents were horrified. Again I was labelled disruptive, ungrateful, destructive and of course MAD! Needing psychiatric help. They could think what they liked. I went to church, asking the vicar to help me and I kept to my conviction.

Frances continued to enjoy the school and developed a passionate 'crush' on Susan, a girl of her own age:

> I stayed in love with her until I was 20. She didn't realize the depths and passion of my feelings, and was pleasant to me but we never made the sexual contact I thought about, dreamed of and longed for. I was still being sick when eating. My parents sent me to a psychiatrist and I came home with a

load of tranquillizers. Susan went on to Drama School. I was still in love with
her.

Frances spent a brief time at Art School. Students and staff became concerned
about her eating problem and increasing dependence upon tranquillizers. At the
end of the first year, an alternative place was suggested at a teacher training college
but Frances decided to leave.

After two years of looking for suitable work and trying to find a boyfriend
Frances determined to lose her virginity to a man she met in temporary work. Her
'engagement' lasted only two months. She was still unable to stay in a job,
constantly needing to be absent, trying to obtain some sexual comfort in a series of
short encounters which gave little satisfaction. Her mother continued to confine
herself to bed.

> Even when I was a little girl I would come home from school and let myself
> in. Then I would hear this faint voice calling, 'That you darling? Mummy's
> in bed. Can you be a dear and boil the potatoes/put the oven on, ready for
> Daddy's dinner?' Always something for me to do.

In 1969 Frances took an overdose of tranquillizers. She was still a patient of the
psychiatrist. He placed due emphasis on the distress she was causing her parents,
but little else was offered in the form of treatment. The pattern continued. Three
more years followed of short-term jobs and time off work because of 'depression'.

In 1972 Frances was encouraged by friends to leave her parents. Starting to
study again, she endeavoured to stay away from home, spending her time in
sexual relationships, some violent, others just a 'one-night job'. In 1976 (her B.Ed
year) Frances started teaching again, but her father became ill and she was told by
her mother that he was dying. Frances, in terror, jettisoned the teaching place-
ment. Her father recovered and Mrs Ashe appealed to her to come back and live at
home. Frances was able to resist the pressure, and returned to teaching.

Frances now took up with Bob, a Buddhist, and became very involved visiting
his Temple, six days a week. She was in love, but Bob was homosexual. This time
there could be no sexual relationship and Buddhism became less attractive; indeed
everything became less attractive. Again she broke her teaching contract and with
it the possibility of a qualification. Depressed, unemployed and disgusted with
Bob, she took a second overdose. This was a far more serious attempt and Frances
was kept in intensive care for several days.

At 31 years of age, Frances still phoned her mother every night, cursing and
contacting her parents with equal regularity. More jobs, more diverse sexual
encounters, moving flats, and a sexual relationship with Jon, a man she had met at
college who was already involved with other women. It was sex on demand, with
Frances trying hard to convince herself that he had some feeling for her. Jon's
demands were perverse and Frances was able only to comply. If she did not hear
from Jon she would seek sexual solace elsewhere – advertisements in *Time Out*,
Computer Dating, anything, anyone for sexual comfort – however dangerous.

In 1980 Frances received Christian baptism in a local church, otherwise all
continued as before: mother's illnesses, father's ill health, one-night stands, dead-
end jobs, depressive, self-destructive behaviour, long days spent masturbating in

bed. In 1983 she was urged to see a psychotherapist. Her parents agreed to pay for her treatment.

To reflect on the features in Frances's life-story, the overt ones concerned the constant ill-health of her mother and father and Frances's desire for self-destruction. The covert ones were later revealed in therapy: Mrs Ashe's use of Frances for sexual titillation of her husband, when taunting her own daughter with intimate details of the 'normal' sex which took place between her and her husband, was a constant sexual abuse of the mind and spirit of her child. Frances experienced strong feelings of guilt about the violent and murderous dreams which were released into consciousness by her therapy, dreams which contained explicit sexual overtures from her father and violent phantasies of knife attacks on her parents.

The therapy

Mr and Mrs Ashe, now 78 years old, continue to complain about their ill-health. Frances has spent most of her life surrounded by their symbols of death and dis-integration. These symbols were introjected by Frances, who also assumed a model of ill-health as she struggled to find a meaning for her life. She assumed that she herself was doomed to an existence dominated by depression, despair and suicide.

In therapy Frances was encouraged to look carefully at this process, to identify the introjection and set it aside, separating the sickness of her mother from her own health, both mental and physical. Neither of her parents was terminally ill and their death threats became meaningless. In the conscious, everyday world faced with the repetitive complaints of arthritis, angina, cataracts and back trouble from her mother, Frances began to understand that these were attempts to hold her in thrall, and began to deal with them in a positive way by resisting the process.

She realized that the clever little girl had become adult as quickly as she could in order to share with her father the burden of a sickly and hypochondriacal mother: a reversal of roles. She was the wifely daughter and her mother the demanding infant. In 'layering down' to the depths of early infantile behaviour, she became aware of her collusion in the events. The price of love was extortionate, and for Frances it was a two-edged sword. Her mother's dependency gave her power, but at a price. At times she *became* her mother, competing with her for the attention of her father and providing both of them with sexual titillation in the bathing rituals which were instigated in early childhood.

Periodically Mrs Ashe would choose to discuss the details of her husband's sexual needs, confiding in Frances at a time when Frances herself felt totally inadequate and despairing of ever achieving a marital relationship.

The therapeutic process did not concentrate on mere translation of symbols or on interpretations which dealt with the symbolic representation of the material presented, but rather with Frances's primary concern, the anxiety and sense of guilt with which she associated her childhood memories. These depths of understanding of her early infantile behaviour became activated by the material which Frances presented over the months of therapy and which touched upon the violent and painful places in her psyche where the strongest latent resistance to adult growth and change had been established. She was willing to resort to murder, if not of her parents then of her herself.

She was ashamed of the seduction scenes (in phantasy) which were played out with her father. These adult sexual attitudes (encouraged at home) were frowned on at school. Frances was labelled 'different'. Sensuality was confined to the 'safe' relationship between her and her parents. Frances had to stay within the walls of her suburban cage, hence the sickness, vomiting and not eating. Illness would ironically defend her against the outside world and encroaching old age, keeping her small and child-like in stature. Her adolescent fancies and dreams, strongly repressed, had veered from phantasies of powerful murder to pseudo-intercourse with her parents.

In therapy Frances was well able to express her feelings. She spoke about the times when she wished she could be like other children, comforting herself with self-imposed ostracism. She had to tell herself that she was more grown-up, sophisticated, intelligent, and had no time for childish games. In the trap of these paranoid-schizoid feelings she was in a time warp which could lead only towards death.

Contrarily, Frances was full of sexual longings, which games with father were unable to fulfil.

> I asked daddy to look behind me today to make sure my bottom wasn't too big! Daddy would sit on the edge of the bath to talk to me but Daddy gives me the creeps sometimes: I just don't want him to kiss me or look at me at all.

Masturbation helped at night but sexually violent and promiscuous phantasies encroached upon her sleep with visions of multiple sex and beatings. When Frances lost her virginity, her mother had waited avidly to share with her a recounting of the event. Vicariousness and voyeurism were salient features of their relationship. Daddy had also to be kept amused and Frances knew *now* how to please her mother. Frances was always kept aware of the avidly waiting but still prostrate figure of Mrs Ashe. Visits or phone calls home on a daily basis were a mixture of dependency and sacrificial appeasement. Every visit was followed by dreams of murder and death, the violent death of her parents which alone would leave her free and independent to enjoy their considerable financial resources.

Throughout her therapy Frances has been unable to lay on the couch: lying down held connotations of her mother's behaviour and of her own previous responses. Beds were also, by association, used for sexual attention and reassurance.

Frances was and still is a hard-working patient. She is eager to help herself. She has good recollection and keeps a diary to chronicle daily events and her dreams. The psychotherapeutic alliance has provided her with the previously unknown qualities inherent in a loving, validating relationship. This was in turn contrasted with the sexual encounters where she had exposed herself to brutalization and subsequent pain and disgust. Over the years the penis had become her substitute for the nutritious nipple to which she had never had access. Oral sex was her preferred method of intercourse; it confirmed subjugation of the self, a woman with no expectation of any return for her lovemaking.

Several significant events took place in the third year of therapy which highlighted Frances's increasing ability to resist parental pressures. Home visits and phone calls decreased. Frances returned to supply teaching, and was able to specialize in infant teaching. She is a good teacher, in demand, the recipient of much affection and respect from the children, but still obviously immersed in an area of childhood from which she was excluded. Frances now lives in a cottage which she has decorated and furnished. She has become an enthusiastic gardener and cook. She dresses well and entertains friends. She has few days off work and periods of depression are short lived.

Her mother asks 'Have you thanked your therapist for what she has been able to do for you?', 'Do you realize how aggressive you have become?' Frances later reported that 'Mummy was very put off by your refusal to see her. I told her I pay for my therapy myself. Blackmail doesn't work now.' Changes in her daughter's self-esteem have obviously disconcerted Mrs Ashe. In babyhood Frances was unable to develop normally. 'Feel sorry for Mummy, be good for Mummy, be quiet for Mummy.' Frances soon learned how to behave. If she felt 'bad' she could only assume that the fault lay not at the door of her ailing mother but within herself. Unacceptable, unlovable Frances, who forced her way into life, became totally responsible for her mother's sorry state.

In retrospect the ingredients for the early development of anorexia were there for all to see. It was wiser for Frances not to take in nourishment. It was safer to stay immured forever in her childlike state, sparse as the pickings at home could be. Her parents colluded with a non-diagnosis. Having a 'bad' daughter enabled them to escape the mutual frustration and anger their own relationship engendered. A 'crazy' daughter could become a diversion. Mrs Ashe, remaining in bed, could throw her hands up in horror at what her daughter made her endure. She would hint that Frances had inherited her illness from Mr Ashe's mother. This in turn would frighten her husband and keep him compliant.

During therapy the schizoid trap became identifiable and unattractive to Frances. She would grow. People liked her and thought she was attractive. She could work, have a home and feel independent. She could survive and she no longer felt MAD or BAD all the time.

In 1990 Frances is firmly anchored in the real world. From time to time she visits her parents but she is selective in the help she offers them and very careful no longer to offer reports on her sexual feelings. Frances has retrieved her friends, many of whom date back to school days, college and teaching. Frances now considers marriage.

She experiences sadness about having no children and there are still black days which have to be endured, but minor setbacks remain as just that and can be tolerated. Frances is beginning to trust her own judgement and gradually to believe in herself with hope for the future.

References

Bowlby, J. (1979) *The Making and Breaking of Affectional Bonds*, London: Tavistock.

Colby, K.M. (1951) *A Primer for Psychotherapists*, New York: Ronald Press.

Cooper, C. (1988) The Jewish mother, in H. Cooper (ed.) *Soul Searching*, London: SCM Press.

Farrell, B.J. (1981) *The Standing of Psycho-analysis*, London: Oxford University Press.

Hinshelwood, R.D. (1989) *A Dictionary of Kleinian Thought*, London: Free Association Books.

Hughes, A. (1974) Contributions of Melanie Klein to psycho-analytic technique, in V.J. Varma (ed.) *Psychotherapy Today*, London: Constable.

Klein, M. (1932) *The Psycho-Analysis of Children*, London: Hogarth.

—— (1950) On the criteria for the termination of a psycho-analysis, *International Journal of Psycho-analysis* 31: 78–80, 204.

—— (1952a) Notes on some schizoid mechanisms, in J. Riviere (ed.) *Developments in Psycho-analysis*, London: Hogarth.

—— (1952b) On the theory of anxiety and guilt, in J. Riviere (ed.) *Developments in Psycho-analysis*, London: Hogarth.

—— (1957) *Envy and Gratitude*, New York: Basic Books.

—— (1960) *Our Adult World and its Roots in Infancy*, London: Tavistock Pamphlets no. 2.

Meltzer, D. (1979) *The Kleinian Development*, London: Clunie Press.

Miller, A. (1983) *For your Own Good*, London: Virago.

Mollon, P.J. (1979) Transforming anxiety: a rationale for verbal psychotherapy, *New Forum Magazine* 5, 4: 18–19.

Riviere, J. (1936) On the genesis of psychical conflict in earliest infancy, *International Journal of Psycho-analysis* 17: 395–422.

Spillius, E.B. (1983) Some developments from the work of Melanie Klein, *International Journal of Psycho-analysis* 64: 321–2.

Tarachow, S. (1970) *Introduction to Psychotherapy*, New York: International University Press.

Waelder, R. (1937) The problem of the genesis of psychical conflict in earliest infancy, *International Journal of Psycho-analysis*, 18: 406–73.

Winnicott, D.W. (1958) *Through Pediatrics to Psychoanalysis*, London: Hogarth.

Suggested further reading

Klein, M. (1961) *Narrative of a Child Analysis*, London: Hogarth.

Grosskurth, P. (1986) *Melanie Klein: Her World and her Work*, London: Hodder & Stoughton.

Meltzer, D. (1967) *The Psychoanalytic Process*, London: Heinemann.

Segal, H. (1974) *Introduction to the Work of Melanie Klein*, London: Heinemann.

Spillius, E.B. (1988) *Melanie Klein Today: Developments in Theory and Practice Vol. 2. Mainly Practice*, London: Karnac.

4

Psychodynamic therapy:
the Jungian approach

RICHARD CARVALHO

Historical context and development in Britain

C.G. Jung lived from 1875 to 1961. He was averse to the idea of schools and, indeed, to the idea of theories of any kind on which schools might be based. He was, none the less, persuaded to sanction the foundation of a school in Zurich. There is now an extensive International Association for Analytical Psychology with affiliates from many countries. In Britain there are three bodies, the largest being the Society of Analytical Psychology which organizes trainings in both adult and child analysis and which runs the C.G. Jung Clinic for both adult and child patients.

Historical context

The theories that go to make up Jung's psychology inevitably reflect his family and cultural background. He had a difficult childhood (Jung 1963a) which was marked by considerable deprivation and illness. His father was a pastor so that he grew up in an explicitly Christian tradition. He was also steeped in the German idealist and romantic tradition: his student essays show an astonishing grasp of a very broad range of philosophical literature which included Goethe, Kant, Schopenhauer, Hegel, Von Carus and Von Hartmann (Jung 1983). Medicine, to which these interests did not primarily incline him, suggested itself as a means of earning a living. But psychiatry, in which he soon became interested, provided a field in which his interests could flourish. He became interested in this subject as a student, and wrote his dissertation on a medium and on her dissociated states of consciousness (Jung 1957: ch. 1).

By the time he met Freud in 1907 he was an established and distinguished psychiatrist. He already had a theory of mind which was distinct from the one developed by Freud. This had been developed through his student essays (Jung 1983), his association experiments (Jung 1973) and his work on dementia praecox (schizophrenia) (Jung 1960). In this model there are autonomous structures in the mind which he later called archetypes: these generate stereotyped imagery and may form the core for the accretion of associated experience into *complexes* (a word which found its way into the psychoanalytic literature). The model included the idea of the unconscious: this included not only material derived from experience but also that derived from the organismic structure of the central nervous system that was the basis of innate predispositions or archetypes.

The relationship between Jung and Freud was evidently one of mutual enrichment though also one of some incompatibility. This had more to do with their personalities than with their theories though the explicit reason for their breach was Freud's adherence to the exclusively sexual nature of the libido, or psychic energy. The difficulties between them had more to do with the difficulty which Freud had in understanding Jung's own developmental problems. These lay at a more primitive level than Freud's theories had hitherto understood. The result was a failure of Jung's 'analysis' and a breakdown in their relationship. This was extremely painful and bitter on both sides and nearly catastrophic for Jung, who underwent a severe emotional crisis which he was, however, able to use creatively (Jung 1953; Satinover 1985). As has been observed (Winnicott 1964), Freud's writings largely assume that the patient has achieved a secure sense of self. There is evidence that Jung's own sense of self was fragile because of his early experiences and that his own self-analytic efforts were aimed at achieving this self. Patients whose sense of self was damaged ('narcissistic', 'borderline' and psychotic patients) were not considered to be amenable to treatment by psychoanalysts until much later. Jung, on the other hand, apart from having to face his own damage, had worked extensively with psychotic patients as a psychiatrist.

As the break with Freud became increasingly inevitable he resumed the work of elaborating his own theories (Jung 1956; 1971). It is important to point out that the polarization between Jungians and psychoanalysts has more to do with the bitterness already described than to the incompatibility of theories, which, as I am suggesting, are about different stages of development. A careful and unprejudiced reading of both Freud and Jung reveal much in common between their ideas and very little that is, in fact, mutually precluded. As psychoanalysis has extended its explorations into the areas of the development of the self and of psychosis it has increasingly developed ideas reminiscent of Jung's and, in some cases, barely distinguishable apart from an insistence on mental structures and contents deriving from experience as opposed to deriving from innate structural predispositions, schemata or 'archetypes'.

Development in Britain

Three major developmental lines have been followed within the International Association (Samuels 1985): there is a 'classical' school which has remained close to what it considers to have been Jung's original methods and which is to be found particularly in Switzerland, New York, Los Angeles, Italy and Israel. It is also represented in London by the Association of Jungian Analysts and its offshoot styled the Independent Group. Another movement has arisen in the USA under the stimulus of Hillman, which concentrates on the cultural and mythological phenomena of the mind, explicitly eschewing any understanding of archetypal processes in terms that might suggest that the 'idea' or *noumenon* can be known as such or related to in what it would see as spurious developmental correlates (Hillman 1983).

This directly conflicts with the mainstream London view as represented by the Society of Analytical Psychology. The work of this society has been largely to remedy the defect it sees in the lack of a developmental scheme in Jung's theories, the absence of any consistent consideration of the child and the lack of consideration of the impact of objects (mother and significant others) or the environment upon him. This development owes a great deal to the work of Michael Fordham with whom it is largely, though not exclusively, identified (see Fordham 1985; Lambert 1981). The present chapter owes much to this development.

Theoretical assumptions

In outlining the theoretical assumptions of analytical psychology, I shall start with Jung's position, before describing developments associated with the London school. It is important to say that Jung insisted that there were 'no Jungians but myself' so that in what follows (as in what has already been described) the views expressed here have to be said to be my own, derived from my own experience and from developments associated with the Society of Analytical Psychology.

Jung's position

Jung's position may be briefly summarized as follows. The matrix for a capacity for psyche and those parts of the psyche which may become available for conscious thought (mind) is called *self*. The self is an organismic concept clearly and explicitly linked to the structures and function of the central nervous system. Because the central nervous system is proactive (as opposed to merely reactive) according to a relatively limited and stereotyped repertoire of perceptive, cognitive and conative behaviours, the resulting psyche with its conscious and unconscious potential is similarly stereotyped. The extent to which these stereotypes can be related to by the individual will determine the extent to which he or she is able to *individuate*, that is have some degree of choice in relation to both internal necessity and to external necessity, without having rigidly to identify with or deny either.

Jung's own experience of let down in relation to his parents and later to Freud meant that he conceived the process of relating to these stereotyped processes (archetypes) in terms of imagery rather than through interpersonal (or 'object') relations. It has, therefore, been justifiably observed that his theories lack this dimension (Satinover 1985).

The term 'archetype' relates not only to processes which are primitive and instinctual but also to ways in which experiences of the evolution of a sense of self and its consciousness are represented. Material that a patient might bring is not, therefore, seen as exclusively defensive, the best compromise between the repression of a forbidden wish and its expressive fulfilment. It may also be seen as the best available expression of the present state of self and of its aspirations. In archetypal terms, the Oedipus complex, for instance, will be seen not only to express the forbidden wish to have intercourse with one's actual mother together with the attendant paranoid anxieties, but also to express the wish (and fear) to penetrate the 'matrix' of unconsciousness (personified by the mother) in order to achieve an identity but at the risk of madness (mutilation) and elimination of consciousness represented by elimination of father. Oedipus as *hero* represents the capacity for emerging and beleaguered consciousness. The 'good mother' represents the capacity for renewal, the 'bad mother' the risk of the loss of differentiation. These represent examples of various archetypal motifs: that of the *great mother* in her positive and negative aspects and of the *hero*. When Oedipus (at Colonnus) can exercise the choice of where and when he is to die and for what purpose, he represents the individual's capacity to exercise some choice in relation to both inner and outer reality, to be individuated, and may, therefore, be described as a *mana personality*. This is a figure who is used to personify the capacity for free access to powerful and frightening experiences of the unconscious conceived of as 'other worlds' and therefore invested with other worldly authority. It will again be noted that the Jungian and psychoanalytic interpretations are not mutually exclusive.

Jung's later work was concerned to a great extent with the study of alchemy and the insights it afforded him into other aspects of the 'primal scene' and the Oedipus complex. This is the way in which the parental intercourse can be used to personify the coming together of different and often conflicting aspects of the self in a creative and generative way. Once again, the difficulties in Jung's own parental marriage meant that he chose to express this through imagery rather than through the means of environmental objects. This coming together of disparate elements in the self in order to achieve a sense of self Jung called the *coniuncto oppositorum* (Jung 1963b). The achievement of this sense of self, Jung thought, was often expressed in the emergence of *mandala forms*: harmonious, symmetrical, geometric designs (Jung 1953).

This very brief sketch of Jung's ideas is a description of some of the major themes that came to be subsumed under the title of *Analytical Psychology*. Jung chose to call his body of thought and the practice that arose from it analytical psychology in order to differentiate it from Freud's psychoanalysis. He assumed that his erstwhile colleague would wish him not to use the latter term and also wished to differentiate his own from Freud's views.

Development in London

Much of the development in London is associated with the name of Michael Fordham. As a child psychiatrist he worked closely with psychoanalytic colleagues, notably Winnicott, and was forced to confront the developmental issues with which Jung had not been so concerned. He was quick to recognize the resemblance between the Kleinian view of innate unconscious ideas and Jung's concept of archetypes. Fordham is largely responsible for a development that bridges the gap that had previously seemed unbridgeable between psychoanalysis and analytical psychology, but more importantly between what had hitherto seemed irreconcilable ideas: that of innate factors (archetypes) and environmental influences.

This development identifies the original and integrated state (the *primary integrate*) as being the *primary self* which contains the innate schemata or archetypal structures with which the environment and self will be explored and out of which the demands of both internal and external experience will be met. These schemata or archetypes begin to unfold in infancy and to manifest themselves in a process which Fordham has called *de-integration*. De-integration can be seen as a process whereby a schema or archetype in infancy, say the behavioural appeal for holding or comforting or the behavioural appeal for feeding, 'searches' for and evokes the appropriate environmental response. If this is forthcoming, the individual has 'sense made' of an internal state which through successive such experiences can then allow the archetypal expectation to be modified in order to permit not only the establishment of the individual's own identity in relation to experience but also the progressive recognition and acceptance of experience which does not fit into archetypal expectation: the individual can now learn from dissonant experience and the raw archetypal response to this (for instance rage) can be modified (for instance to appropriate assertion). Where the appropriate environmental response is not forthcoming, individuals are robbed of an experience that makes sense of them and are left with what may be powerful and fragmenting emotions as a result of the frustration. An example would be of the empathic response of the mother to an infant's stirring when she correctly intuits his need to be fed: the 'de-integrate' would be the not-yet-conscious hunger in relation to its complement, which is the empathically proffered breast or bottle. The gradual, appropriate and tolerable emergence of a sense of discrepancy between the ideal and the reality allows the emergence of feelings associated with disillusion and frustration so that loving feelings may be integrated with hateful and destructive impulses. In this scheme, significant environmental objects are not only the objects of drives and impulses but also their representatives, objects which can be used to personify the self which would otherwise be unavailable for reflection. In this way it differs from many psychoanalytic theories. It also differs from similar theories in psychoanalysis which postulate the containment of aspects of personality by significant objects (for instance, those of Bion and Winnicott) in that the latter do not postulate a primary self. Winnicott, for instance, specifies a primary state of unintegration (Winnicott 1945).

This developmental scheme has important technical considerations especially for the importance granted to the reconstruction of childhood phantasies and environmental influences, which are given less prominence in classical Jungian therapy. It implies a much greater significance for the role of the transference in analysis than Jung always accorded it. The transference becomes the instrument by which analysts can be informed of the processes they are required to complement. This, in turn, implies considerable importance for the counter-transference, emotional experiences, sometimes extreme, whereby the analyst has an experience which corresponds to the phantasy which the patient is using the analyst to embody.

In this way the objects of the parents (and in analysis, the analyst) come to reconcile the opposition between idea and reality in a way that then permits the individual to be 'individuated', that is, neither the involuntary function of his or her internal world nor of the external world. This view suggests that the capacity for symbol formation is contingent on the successful negotiation of object relating as outlined above and gives less importance to mythological and cultural artefacts than does the 'classical' Jungian position. On the contrary, such phenomena may be used defensively in order to avoid the interpersonal conflicts implicit in individuation. There is some evidence that this was a compensatory mechanism used by Jung himself whose parents and later Freud failed to mediate between ideas and reality in certain respects.

Image of the person

The person is seen as a psychosomatic entity with potential for consciousness and personal identity. This potential, its organization and coherence inhere in the *self*. These are realized through the interaction already described between innate potential and the environmental provision that meets it: the *ego* is conceived as being the centre of consciousness derived from the coalescence of multiple experiences of such interaction. Over-identification with either the innate potential (idea or archetype) or with the environment is pathological. In the former case it results in extremes of *introversion* and in the latter extreme *extraversion* (Jung 1971), corresponding to schizoid withdrawal or hysterical personality traits respectively. Extraversion tends to identify excessively with that structure which interfaces between the self and the environment, namely the *persona*. The individual deploys a number of mechanisms to relate himself to the object (Jung 1971: ch. VII) and in health, achieves a position which transcends an exclusive identity with either the innate archetypal disposition or with its environmental complement.

Conceptualization of psychological disturbance and health

Psychological health is conceived as a situation in which individuals are free to interact with themselves and their environment without the experience being so persecuting that it has to be repudiated. By implication healthy individuals will be able to adapt creatively to the tasks set by the environment at the same time as being nourished by a sense of emotional relatedness to their inner world that allows them to have a sense of meaning. Unconscious processes not only are conceived of as arising exclusively from impulses incompatible with conscious intention and, therefore, repressed (the *personal unconscious*) but also are conceived of as arising from innate potential which has not yet been evoked by internal or external exigency (the *collective unconscious*). It is therefore not only forbidden memories or wishes that disturb the individual but also unlived aspects of the self. Where these are denied or split off they will insist in the form of symptoms. Defensive structures mobilized against the experience may be rigidly clung to and lead to maladaptive behaviours.

Acquisition and perpetuation of psychological disturbance

The disordered personality can logically be seen to arise from a situation in which the interaction between innate expectation and the environment is distorted. This may be a result of inborn factors in the personality, the result of inevitable environmental disasters such as the death of a mother or of neonatal illness. There may be a congenital defect which interferes with feeding and which necessitates multiple hospital admissions. There may be difficulties in the maternal personality which mean that the child is unable to experiment with certain emotional experiences. There is evidence, for instance, that Jung's own mother was depressed and that the parental marriage was in difficulties in such a way as apparently to corroborate his phantasy that his destructive feelings were indeed damaging, so that he was deprived of the opportunity for experimenting with aggression in a context where his objects proved their durability. In such a situation the innate potential (in this case, for aggression with its creative as well as its destructive potential) cannot be linked up to reality so that phantasized damage is not differentiated from real damage. This can lead to a compensatory idealization of creativity which has to be divorced from aggression and so is vitiated in turn.

There are many opportunities in day-to-day living and development which allow for a reworking of such distortions. The danger is, however, of the development of rigid defensive structures which perpetuate the phantasy and make it increasingly inaccessible to reality testing. An example of this would be the situation in which dangerous parts of the self are repudiated and attributed to important others, originally perhaps a mother, and then generalized to subsequent relationships. Everything that is manifest by others subsequently is then in danger of being perceived as a product of the repudiated and projected aspects of the self and therefore viewed with suspicion. Evidence of kindness, love, consideration and generosity may in this case be seen as tricks, traps and seductions for the unwary so that individuals are deprived of the emotional reality which might modify their paranoid view of the world and their deprivation is perpetuated in a vicious circle in which the paranoia is apparently repeatedly justified.

It should be added that every individual has a predilection for certain defensive structures and that normality or health is to some extent a reflection of the flexibility and adaptiveness with which these mechanisms can be deployed. It is clearly adaptive to be able to dissociate in certain situations, for instance from pain in war; it would be advantageous to be capable of suspicion and sensitive to attack in dangerous or threatening situations in a way that might be termed paranoid in times of safety. Even 'normal' people will have their breaking point under abnormal degrees of stress or in situations where there is some inhibition against the deployment of their adaptive defensive capacity.

Change

Change involves the recognition of maladaptive patterns; the recognition of the circumstances and environmental failures in relation to which they arose (reconstruction) together with a delineation of the phantasies involved. It will involve repair of the distorted object relations so that the healthy aspect of the available objects are made available. In this way those aspects of the self which have received distorted representation and which have distorted the environment may be repaired so that aspects of the self which have had to be kept in abeyance are now more likely to become available to be tolerated, rather than be split off from ego and each other.

Practice

Goals of therapy

The goals of therapy are broadly to make it possible for individuals to relate adaptively to both their internal and external worlds in a way that not only enables them to cope with these more effectively but also enhances their sense of growth and creativity. The individual will be emancipated from rigid or over-identification with either archetypal processes or external objects: in this way both the internal world and the external world become available for use and mutual enrichment. This is what is meant by Jung when he talks about establishing the possibility for a *compensatory* relationship between unconscious and conscious processes (Jung 1971: para 695).

Selection criteria

Selection criteria for Jungian therapy do not differ from those of other exploratory dynamic therapies, that is patients must show a capacity to engage with the therapist/analyst and their own unconscious processes. This is indicated by a readiness to respond to and elaborate interpretation with conscious or unconscious material. It is necessary for the way in which the patient uses the therapist to be open for discussion (transference readiness) and there needs to be some indication that there is motivation for change and development rather than merely for dependence or for the exercise of destructive impulses.

Where there is a capacity to use interpretation, to examine the transference and where there is motivation for change, it still has to be considered whether patients have the capacity in their social circumstances to move. Patients who are very isolated may find the constraints of therapeutic intimacy unbearable. Married patients may have to face the dilemma of choosing between their health and their spouse. In addition, very careful consideration should be given before risking therapy with anybody who has been actively psychotic, who has a serious psychosomatic illness or who has a tendency to impulsive behaviour which might be provoked by the emergence of unconscious material and conflicts. This is especially the case if these have seemed the inevitable consequences of conflict and stress such as may be provoked by interpretation. Jungian analysts have, however, a long tradition of treating relatively severe psychopathology which has become accessible to their psychoanalytic colleagues only with the exploration of Klein, Bion, Winnicott and Kohut, for instance of areas already considered by Jung.

The issue as to whether the patients are selected for analysis or psychotherapy and, indeed, as to what differentiates analysis from psychotherapy is a vexed one. Some see the two activities as sharply differentiated: therapy implying something relatively supportive with infrequent sessions as opposed to analysis which is thorough-going, aims at profound change in the structure of the personality and requires frequent sessions. It has to be said that patients selected for 'therapy' and seen relatively infrequently often achieve profound psychological change, while patients seen frequently, say five times a week, having been selected for 'analysis' achieve little profound change. It is probably more useful to consider for each individual what 'depth' of interpretation they can tolerate, how much disturbance at any time they can sustain and how much support they need both in the environment and in terms of the therapist's/analyst's behaviour. There are no hard and fast rules for frequency: some patients may require five weekly sessions (of fifty minutes) in order to maintain continuity and in order to feel sufficiently supported to risk an encounter with themselves, some patients, perhaps with equivalent disturbance and damage, may find anything more than once or twice a week more provocative of turbulence than they can cope with.

There may be circumstances where modifications of the analytic method derived from individual work may seem preferable. Isolated individuals, for instance, with problems in social relating may be more effectively helped in groups; individuals whose problems clearly reflect significant difficulties within a marriage may be more greatly helped by a marital focus where both members of the couple are seen. It may become clear that someone who presents as an individual is, in fact, presenting the problem of a deeply enmeshed family in which no change is going to be possible for any individual in the system unless they are all disentangled together and allowed to relate differently. In these circumstances family therapy is the only option.

Qualities of effective therapists

It has to be assumed that therapists have themselves undergone a thorough-going analysis and have made use of it. The vocation for psychotherapeutic work is likely to come from at least some degree of disturbance and pathology, and from the need for repair in the analysts themselves. They need to be capable of resonating with their patients' disturbance where necessary (the counter-transference) in a way that is in the service of the patient, neither responding with inappropriate retaliation, with acting out, with inappropriate identification nor with illness. This may require a very considerable capacity for containing any disturbance elicited by the patient and will make great demands on the analyst's continuing capacity for self-analysis based on the original analysis. Analysts need to have an awareness of their limitations not only in relation to the kinds of patients they can tolerate and work with but also in relation to the amount of disturbed and regressed patients they can manage in their case-load at one time.

Therapeutic style

The interaction of the therapy/analysis is perforce a function of the two personalities involved. The analyst needs to be available as a real person but needs to be so in a way that does not obtrude his or her personality or views on the patient. Analysts need to be contained, consistent and retiring enough to be attentive to the detail of what their patients are bringing. Analysts need to be aware that any invitation to be more interactive may be an invitation by the patient to enact something in the counter-transference. Self-disclosure, for instance, may be the response to an invitation to enact a seduction at a primitive level; humour may be the response to an invitation into a manic collusion. These may not necessarily be the case, however, and therapists need the capacity for spontaneity. On the other hand, acting as a 'screen' may sometimes be technically proper or it may be used as defensive behaviour on the part of the analyst; again, it may be an enactment in the counter-transference, perhaps of the patient's phantasy of a dead object. These considerations apply throughout analysis, though it is likely to be the case that the reality of the analyst becomes more available to the analysand as the reality of his environment in general becomes more accessible to him along with the reality of his self.

Major therapeutic strategies and techniques

Jung's own experience of let-down by his parents and later, of the failure of his relationship with Freud, led him to be wary of a dependence on others and of a regression that would leave him or his patients vulnerable to abandonment. He tended, therefore, to avoid techniques that might 'induce' such regression or that might 'reduce' behaviour to explanation in terms of impulses towards the analyst. He favoured, therefore, a process called *active imagination* over the free-association advocated by Freud. Active imagination was the process whereby patients were encouraged to follow through an imaginative train of thought in a directed manner rather than to allow their thoughts to occur to them in the more spontaneous manner associated with free-association. This latter, Jung felt, merely led patients back into the complexes which already imprisoned them. Patients were encouraged to bring dreams written down in a book with columns prepared with their own associations and one ready for the *amplifications* of the analyst. These amplifications were references to parallel motifs that might be found in cultural material, religious, mythological, and so on. He preferred sessions to be relatively infrequent (three times a week, for instance) and for the analyst and patient to be facing one another in chairs rather than have the patient use the couch.

The London School of Jungians have, on the whole, moved away from these practices. The logic of the developmental scheme outlined above and an understanding of the origin of Jung's suspicion of the object in his own sense of let-down have led Jungians (in the Society of Analytical Psychology at least) to adopt techniques which permit an optimal level of regression within which to facilitate the repair of distorted object relations and the embodiment of de-integrative processes at the putative stage of their distortion and inhibition. There is meticulous attention to the setting, its predictability and safeness within which to allow patients to determine their use of the analyst in such a way that, within reason, let-down can be guaranteed not to happen. The couch is often used and the frequency of the sessions (which may be five times a week in analysis) is that which will optimally facilitate the particular individual's needs. Active imagination tends to be avoided because of its potential use in evading interactive issues with the analyst. Dreams are reported but not demanded any more than is any other sort of material because of the risk of inducing compliance and the perpetuation of a false *persona*. Amplification tends to be avoided because of the opportunities it offers for a collusive or competitive grandiosity in the counter-transference.

It is the analyst's job to create a reflective space in which the patient may begin to have experiences of him or herself. To this end the analyst must find ways of making it clear to the patient that events in the consulting room are not to be controlled or pre-empted by any set format, but, on the contrary, that both must endure the discomfort of not knowing what is going to happen from one moment to the next and perhaps of not understanding it when it does. The patient may invite the analyst to foreclose on this experience and close the analytic space with premature explanation or reassurance and indeed the analyst may be tempted to provide these. Analysts must, however, make it clear by their behaviour and by their interventions that uncertainty and the thoughts, phantasies and emotions that fill it can be endured and examined. Analysts will, therefore, tend to leave the space for their patients' reflections, keeping themselves unobtrusively as a holding presence who represents the reflective space in a way that a mother may hold her child's reverie. The analyst will need to be alert to processes that interfere with this reflection: these may take the form of unbearable affect, perhaps overwhelming anxiety which may need to be acknowledged and identified in order for the patient to continue; it may be in the form of some defensive manoeuvre such as obstinate silence or inconsequential chatter. The analyst will be attentive to the form of the session (silences, the quality of silence, the quality of speech, etc.) as well as the content. Sometimes the content will be quite straightforward, at others it will require great skill in order to make the logical inferences about underlying phantasies which may be heavily disguised, and about transference issues. The analyst may wish from time to time to make an enquiry as to what patients think they mean or to clarify some issue but, on the whole, these interventions will be kept to a minimum and the analyst's attitude will be one of alert restraint while he or she allows the impressions of the session to form and re-form in their mind together with the counter-transference feelings. This process may allow analysts to feel that they have understood something about the session (even if this is about the way in which they are being prevented from understanding something) in such a form as to share this impression with their patient. The process of understanding (which can be only provisional and never final) may take two minutes of the session (very rarely) or it may take several sessions, perhaps even several months. It is quite possible for a patient to be silent for several sessions without anything being said while some realization crystallizes in both patient and analyst.

It is customary to call the form in which understanding is shared an *interpretation*. It is important to understand this not as a final 'truth' so much as interpretation in the sense of translation, of making sense. Such an interpretation is likely to include reference to the symbolic nature of content (verbal, behavioural, etc.); to the phantasies implied by the symbolism; to the archetypal structures which are attempting to find expression; to the original objects which met or failed these expectations; to current relationships, whether vitiated or enhanced by these processes; to the current relationship with the analyst with whom new redemptive solutions are being attempted at the same time as old problems are being relived. The language into which the 'translation' is made will, to a large extent, be determined by the patient's own language and the language negotiated over the process of the analysis between analyst and patient.

The change process in therapy

Most patients who are motivated to change lose interest fairly quickly in any symptoms with which they may have presented and turn towards the significance of the emotional processes which prompted the symptom formation in the first place. If the symptoms return patients tend to be curious as to their internal dynamic meaning rather than merely accepting them as the external visitation of random illness. They tend to develop the capacity for reflection which gives them an element of choice in the way in which they react to situations so that their behaviours may become less compulsive. The result is that the environment becomes more available for real interaction rather than the rehearsal of prejudice and they can, in turn, become more nourished not only by an increasingly rewarding environment but also by a greater sense of richness in their experience of themselves, even when this is painful. Difficulties often arise where patients feel threatened by success. This may be because their sense of guilt makes them feel undeserving of relief and of reward; it may be because of the reluctance to surrender the allure of a psychopathological process which, however painful, none the less offers the illusion of omnipotence; it may be a fear that without this omnipotent phantasy they will have nothing, and on occasion all three processes may combine together to vitiate the analysis. There may be several such cycles in a process whose time scale may be anything from several months to several years.

Limitations of the approach

Much of what has been described comprises more a way of thinking and reflecting than one of doing or technique. Technique is extremely difficult to describe, particularly briefly, and there is an important way in which what happens in the consulting room is a function more of the personalities involved than of any explicit 'approach' or 'technique'. It would, however, be reasonable to suppose that someone who had undergone a personal analysis and a training along the lines suggested would be prepared to treat a broad spectrum of personal difficulties ranging from personalities with complex disorders, occasionally presenting with psychotic features (so-called 'borderline' patients) to patients whose basic personality structure is much more secure and who present with mild neurotic symptoms or with life crises. Certain conditions are notoriously resistant to any therapeutic approach, whether psychodynamic (of any school), behavioural or cognitive: these include diffuse and disabling phobias and severe obsessional compulsive phenomena. It can be dangerous and even life-threatening (to patients, members of the community and therapists) to undertake the treatment of patients whose proven response to the sort of stress that an interpretation constitutes is to act out violently and destructively. Likewise, if the habitual response to stress is the production of life-threatening psychosomatic crises then psychotherapy may again be life-threatening. It is rare that frank psychosis, particularly where it is chronic and severe, is accessible to psychotherapy or analysis and when it is it requires particular personal qualities and skills of the practitioner. Appropriate drug therapies are more likely to hold the patient in psychosis. The management of all of these conditions, however, can be shown to be greatly enhanced if it is informed by psychodynamic sensitivity and, indeed, the lack of such sensitivity can be extremely alienating for the patient. Finally, mono-symptomatic phobias (such as spiders, for instance) in an otherwise untroubled personality tend to do much better with behavioural techniques.

The absolute limitation, however, of the approach lies in the patient's motivation for change, however healthy or however disturbed. Even then a successful result in analysis is often sobering. The restoration of a self may be the restoration of a self which is in reality very ordinary and this ordinary self will suffer ordinary pains and griefs. It is important to realize that analysis of any school may be idealized in terms of the persecuting ideal which the analysand expects him or herself to attain through analysis: it may also imply that the external world is also going to be magically transformed. The fact is that analysis is limited by the motivation and potential of both the analysand and of the analyst and by the realities within which they both exist.

Case example

The client

Miss A was 36 when she came into analysis. Her analysis is now in its final phases and illustrates many of the theoretical points outlined above.

Miss A had been catastrophically failed as a child. Her parents were apart for the first three years of her life; her mother was depressed, ineffectual and, as it turned out later, subtly and sadistically undermining although she was initially idealized in the analysis. Her father was irascible and also drank so there were frequent rows. When my patient was 3 her father returned from his peripatetic existence and a sister was subsequently born.

Miss A had somehow hoisted herself out of and beyond her very humble and deprived beginnings in another country to achieve what, in the light of her circumstances, seemed to have been an almost unbelievable success in a world of intellectuals and the media in this country. She had a reputation for being extremely intimidating and was characterized by a ferocious self-righteousness. Her world was, however, populated with caricatures, particularly of men who were seen either as brutes or as 'wimps' and of women who were all victims.

She broke down at the point at which she could no longer sustain the illusion of golden youth. This was brought in on her not only by her age but also by the realization that she would now have to join the grown-ups and progress to managerial responsibilities in her career. Matters were further complicated by an abortion, which raised the issue of her destructiveness.

Her presenting symptom was of catastrophic states of anxiety and an accompanying feeling of disintegration whenever she felt that her super-confident exterior might be showing any cracks or with any fancied slight from a colleague: this was registered in effect if someone failed to praise her effusively.

The therapy

Miss A's presentation to me was of an almost inert, brittle and stiff person whose movements, gait and demeanour were without any spontaneity. Her phantasy of herself was of a 'stick'. She told me that she thought of herself as 'flat between the legs like a doll'; it was as if she had no orifices that would let anything in or out. She very quickly engaged in the analysis with an initial phase which was to last for around eighteen months; for four times a week she would come and vilify me with considerable violence which I was not always sure that I could go on tolerating and which she would justify in terms of violence which she experienced my doing her. This took the form of implied insults or patronage which she would imagine I had perpetrated. She gradually settled down in this phase and became increasingly aware of her own very primitive violent phantasies which had hitherto located exclusively in her father and more latterly in myself. She was able to see that I had survived these phantasies and had not, in fact, been damaged by them as she assumed I would be, a phantasy which had apparently been corroborated by the actual damage in her own parents. She began to allow herself the experience of feeling refreshed by the sessions and of experiencing some relief. She was reluctantly able to realize that she sometimes enjoyed them and got what she needed.

What we see here is a provision of a safe and predictable setting which allowed Miss A to experiment for the first time with her innate aggressive predisposition which hitherto had been too catastrophic to risk but which could now be contained by a mother/father analyst who was neither damaged nor retaliatory. The aggression, of course, not only was innate but also had been amplified by actual environmental deprivation and by objects which could not mediate her innate predispositions satisfactorily. With the repair of these internal object representations, she was now able to take some nourishment and feel that her expectations (her needs) could be met and embodied in order to afford her a satisfactory personification of herself.

This required and allowed her to assimilate what she had repudiated in herself (Jung called this 'shadow') and had located elsewhere in phantasy, attributing it to men in general and to her father in particular.

With the increasing identification with myself as a benign figure, she was able progressively to allow herself the idea of (maternal) containment on the one hand and of a penetration (paternal) by experience on the other. She became not only increasingly preoccupied but also resistant to representations of herself in dream and phantasy in terms of sadistic and denigratory intercourses between men and women. She was deeply contemptuous of herself as a woman, as somebody who might be penetrated, and terrified of all the evidence of destructiveness that would be discovered in her interior. At the same time she was troubled by her contemptuous and ruthless intrusiveness so that any 'coming together' of herself seemed to threaten an internal catastrophe. She, therefore, fought against it and against any idea of being 'penetrated' by my interpretations, still less any demonstration that she might have retained anything. She worked very hard to destroy the phantasized intercourse between us which represented the phantasized coming together of herself: she maintained that she had no mind, that she was becoming senile and had no memory, that she was becoming deaf and couldn't take in my words, that she was becoming blind and so couldn't 'see the point'; she managed to become quite severely ill.

After about two years of this phase she began to allow herself some glimpses of coming together, of having a mind of her own and of occasionally remembering some insights, though against great resistance. An important event for her, however, was the death of her father with whom her relationship had considerably modified in the previous year. When she was able to return to her country for the funeral she discovered that the coffin was already screwed down and for the first time since she started her analysis she was aware of wondering of how I would approach the problem. This enabled her to ask the undertakers to unscrew the coffin lid so that she could see her father for the last time. This, of course, required the admission that she had both taken me in to the extent of being able to conjure me in need and that there was a receptive part of her with which to contain me.

I have already described that any coming together of herself, in this case symbolized by the idea of myself in her mind, was associated with the catastrophe of sadistic penetration. This development therefore occasioned a rearguard action in that she now produced a contemptuous figure conceived of as a rather pretentious aristocrat who let her know that the ordinary self that might come together in this way would not be as glamorous as her previous omnipotent self and who attacked the ordinary elements of herself that might come together in its creation. The contempt of this figure indicated, however, that her resistance was prompted not only by fear of sadistic catastrophe and fear of ordinariness, but also by envy of anything that might happen outside her control (the parental intercourse, any creativity in myself or ideas that might 'occur to her').

At the end of this phase, however, she had a dream in very abstract and geometrical terms about the coming together of extreme opposites: very hot with very cold, masculine with feminine, and very hard with very soft; in part object terms, penis with breast. The imagery in the dream was of triangular motifs contained in circular surrounds and she chose several parallel images to express this.

This is a culmination of the process that she had deferred until the beginning of her analysis and which she had tried to exclude from the interior of her body by being sterile, rigid and without orifices. She was terrified that 'coming together' would be experienced as the most terrifying and sadistically penetrating cataclysm inside an extraordinarily vulnerable self. This coming together of herself had been rehearsed in successively modified images of her parents' intercourse and her phantasy of the intercourse between herself and me. It was not only important to reconstruct the reality of her actual parental relationship but also important to be aware of her need to embody the innate processes of integration within herself. What was being rehearsed and repaired was not only the actual primal scene between her real parents but also the phantasies which could be represented only by them, her own *coniunctio*, the coming together and the creative, transformative 'matings' of her own creative capacities. This *coniunctio* was the product of what may be characterized as, the archetypal mother, her own capacity for containment, on the one hand, and her *animus* on the other. The creative aspect of this containment could be attained only by thorough analysis of the sadistic and destructive phantasies that in projection constitute the terrible or devouring, negative mother archetype. The animus could be contained only when her own biting, penetrating intrusiveness could be modified by containment in the transference.

In this way her self, her creative matrix, was made available to her, initially identified with me but later on, in a dream, abstracted from me and represented in geometrical form, a *mandala*. It is important to mention that she described someone else, a disembodied voice, in an earlier part of this dream as engaged in 'saving a child with a speech' and that later on an important redemptive act took place in relation to something spoken in her own voice. She has achieved a self by means of identification through the transference but the identification with me and my voice is now 'as if' and no longer rigid: she is to some extent 'individuated'; she has her own voice.

The material that she subsequently progressed to was much more straightforwardly Oedipal in a classical psychoanalytic sense. Once she had a self with unit status, memories became available to her again, both of much more positive aspects of her parents and of her own sense of responsibility in relation to her destructive phantasies and acts, particularly in relation to her sister. Having a sense of self meant that she was no longer prey to the catastrophic sense of fragmentation and annihilation with which she had presented nor with the anxiety attacks. Her sense of self-esteem was much more assured, though tinged with the disappointment that the self she had achieved was not as dramatic as the omnipotent processes she had relinquished. She began to contemplate creative relationships in a way that had not hitherto been possible, though to date she has not achieved one. Meanwhile, however, she has 'joined the grown-ups' by assuming her deferred managerial and administrative responsibilities. To these and to her other activities she brings a creative spontaneity which was unavailable to her before she could trust processes to come together and mate within her, outside her omnipotent and rigid control.

References

CW refers to the collected works of C.G. Jung published in London by Routledge & Kegan Paul.

Fordham, M. (1985) *Explorations into the Self*, Library of Analytical Psychology, Vol. 7, London: Academic Press

Hillman, J. (1983) *Archetypal Psychology: A Brief Account*, Dallas, Tex: Spring.

Jung, C.G. (1953) *Psychology and Alchemy*, CW 2.

—— (1956) *Symbols of Transformation*, CW 5.

—— (1957) *Psychiatric Studies*, CW 1.

—— (1960) *The Psychogenesis of Mental Disease*, CW 3.

—— (1963a) *Memories, Dreams, Reflections*, London: Routledge & Kegan Paul.

—— (1963b) *Mysterium Coniunctionis*, CW 14.

—— (1971) *Psychological Types*, CW 6.

—— (1973) *Experimental Researches*, CW 2.

—— (1983) *The Zofingia Lectures*, CW Suppl. Vol. A.

Lambert, K. (1981) *Analysis, Repair and Individuation*, Library of Analytical Psychology, Vol. 5 London: Academic Press.

Samuels, A. (1985) *Jung and the Post-Jungians*, London: Routledge & Kegan Paul.

Satinover, J. (1985) *At the Mercy of Another: Abandonment and Restitution in Psychosis and the Psychotic Character*, Chiron, 47–86.

Winnicott, D.W. (1945) Primitive emotional development, in D.W. Winnicott (1975) *Through Paediatrics to Psycho-Analysis*, London: Hogarth.

—— (1964) Book review: *Memories, Dreams, Reflections* by C.G. Jung, *International Journal of Psychoanalysis* 45: 450–3.

Suggested further reading

Readers new to Jung will find it helpful to read his autobiography, *Memories, Dreams, Reflections* (referred to above). A useful adjunct to this is the Satinover article also referred to above. Those who wish to continue with Jung might proceed to Volume Seven of the collected works, *Two Essays on Analytical Psychology*. Samuels (1985) (see above) provides a helpful over-view of Jung and of subsequent developments on a wider canvas than attempted in this chapter. A technical over-view along the lines of the London school may be found in Michael Fordham (1986) *Jungian Psychotherapy*, London: Karnac.

5

Adlerian therapy

JENNY CLIFFORD

Historical context and development in Britain

Historical context

Alfred Adler (1870–1937) was a doctor in Vienna who became interested in functional disorders (*neuroses*) in which physically healthy patients complained of and genuinely suffered from physical symptoms which disrupted their lives. In 1911 he founded a new society which later became the Society for Individual Psychology. From 1902 to 1911 Adler attended the Wednesday evening meetings of the Viennese Psychoanalytical Society at Freud's invitation. Adler was the most active member of this group and Freud held him in high esteem. Adler's book, *Study of Organ Inferiority and its Psychical Compensation: A Contribution to Clinical Medicine* (1917), first published in 1907, was well received by Freud and considered by him to complement psychoanalytical theory. In this book Adler described the relative weakness of an organ or a system in the body and the reaction of compensation either by the weak organ, another organ or the nervous system. In 1910 Adler became President and Stekel became Vice President of the Vienna Psychoanalytical Society; both men were joint editors, under Freud, of their new journal, *Centralblatt*. By 1911, however, it became obvious that Adler's views differed greatly from Freud's and Adler and Stekel resigned their positions and with a few others left to form a new Society.

In 1912 Adler published *The Neurotic Constitution*, outlining his theory of neurosis, and laying down many of the basic tenets of Individual Psychology. Adler was now specializing in treating psychiatric patients, neurotic rather than psychotic. In 1914 the *Journal for Individual Psychology* was founded and Adler's ideas spread to Europe and the USA.

Adler was mobilized into the Austrian-Hungarian Army in 1916 and worked as an army physician in a military hospital in Cracow. On returning from the war to a destitute Vienna, Adler directed his energies towards educating people about Individual Psychology. His concept of *social interest* fitted well into the new atmosphere of rebuilding a nation. As well as a welfare programme and a housing and health programme, educational reforms were taking place in Vienna. With respect to the latter, Adler held open sessions with teachers and their problem children so that as many people as possible could learn about his ideas to enable children to grow up mentally healthy. Adler lectured to teachers and at the teachers' request he was appointed professor at the Pedagogical Institute of Vienna in 1924.

In 1923 Adler gave a lecture in Britain for the first time at the International Congress of Psychology in Oxford, although he spoke very little English. In 1926 he was invited back to Britain by a few interested medical and psychological societies and by 1927 an Individual Psychology Club was founded in Gower Street, London; this club later became political and Adler dissociated himself from it. In 1927 Adler's book, *Understanding Human Nature*, was published; this book was based on a year's lectures given at the People's Institute in Vienna. It gives a complete description of Individual Psychology and its aim is to enable people to understand themselves and one another better. From 1926 to 1934 Adler spent the academic year in the USA and June to September in Vienna with his family. He went on lecture tours all over the USA; he was appointed lecturer at Colombia University from 1929 to 1931 and in 1932 a chair of medical psychology was established for him at Long Island Medical College. In 1933 he published *Social Interest: A Challenge to Mankind* describing the concept of *Gemeinschaftsgefuhl* (social interest) and placing it at the centre of his psychological theory. By 1934 Adler had settled permanently in the USA and was eventually joined by his family. A year later he founded the *International Journal of Individual Psychology* in 1935 in Chicago. The theory of Individual Psychology and its application in medicine and education was spreading throughout Europe and the USA. In 1937 Adler had a lecture tour planned in Holland, England and Scotland. In Holland he gave over forty lectures in three weeks and he suffered severe angina before he left for Britain. He and his daughter, Dr Alexandra Adler, herself a psychiatrist, had public and private lectures as well as university vacation courses booked at Aberdeen, York, Hull, Manchester, London, Edinburgh, Liverpool and Exeter. Sadly Adler died of a heart attack on the fourth day in Aberdeen while taking an early morning walk; he was 67 years old. Alexandra Adler arrived in Britain and fulfilled most of her father's and her own lecture commitments. She and her brother Kurt, also a psychiatrist, formed an Adlerian group in New York, which is still functioning today.

During the 1920s Rudolph Dreikurs, a young doctor, had worked with Adler's followers in their child guidance clinics in Vienna. In 1937 he went to the USA and had soon established an open centre for family counselling in Chicago. From 1942 to 1948 he was professor of psychiatry at the Chicago Medical School where he exposed medical students to Adler's theories of personality, behaviour and psychopathology. By 1950 he was teaching a postgraduate course in child guidance at Northwestern University. Manford Sonstegard attended this course and afterwards went on to develop child guidance centres and parent education in Iowa and West Virginia and on his retirement as Professor in Counselling he went to Britain.

Development in Britain

A new Adlerian Society had been formed in London just before Adler's death with Adler as its President. This did not meet during the Second World War but afterwards was reconstituted with Dr Alexandra Adler as its President. It was and still is called the *Adlerian Society of Great Britain*. It was affiliated to the Individual Psychological Medical Society which had been founded in the 1930s.

Dr Joshua Bierer, who was personally trained by Adler, emigrated to Britain and founded the first self-governed social therapeutic group for acute and chronic inpatients at Runwell Hospital, Wickford, Essex. He also set up a social psychotherapy centre – now a Day Hospital – and clubs for outpatients and discharged patients. Group therapy and community psychiatry are legitimate offspring of Alfred Adler's thought and work according to Ellenberger (1970).

In 1958 Rudolph Dreikurs visited England and Scotland and lectured at Edinburgh, Aberdeen, Liverpool and London Universities at Dr Joshua Bierer's invitation. Dreikurs found that Adlerian psychologists in England were engaged in private practice but were not training parents, teachers, other psychologists or psychiatrists. Adler, during the last twenty years of his life, had emphasized the need to educate teachers, who have influence over large numbers of children so that the ideas of Individual Psychology could benefit future generations and prevent mental illness. Dreikurs too concentrated his efforts on teaching parents and teachers so that children could be enabled to grow up mentally healthy and psychologically able to participate in a democratic society. In 1976 Sonstegard came to Britain and trained a group of health professionals in Buckinghamshire. These people joined the Adlerian Society of Great Britain, some of whose members had worked with Adler in Vienna. Sonstegard visited Britain annually and started to train people to do family counselling, life-style assessment, group counselling, self-awareness and psychotherapy. He was particularly interested in training lay counsellors and encouraging parents to form study groups and family education centres.

There are no formal Adlerian psychotherapy training courses in Britain recognized by the Institute for Individual Psychology, which is the training division of the Adlerian Society of Great Britain. British Adlerian therapists have travelled to the USA, Israel and Europe to continue their training as well as attending the International Committee for Adlerian Summer Schools and Institutes (ICASSI) which takes place annually in different countries.

Theoretical assumptions

Image of the person

The *holistic socio-teleological* approach of Adlerian therapy, based on Adler's Individual Psychology, maintains that people should be viewed in their social contexts in order that their goals can be identified. People choose their own goals based on their subjective perceptions of themselves and their world, their bodies, minds and feelings in harmony with their consistent movement towards these goals. Adlerians consider that people are creative, responsible, self-determined and unique. The holistic socio-teleological approach can be defined in three parts.

1 *Holistic* The term, *individual*, of Individual Psychology was used by Adler to describe the indivisibility of a person: as such it is a holistic approach to psychotherapy. Adler wanted to stress the self-consistent unity of a person as opposed to other theories which described conflicting divisions of the personality.
2 *Social* Human beings are socially embedded and their actions can be understood only when observed within a group.
3 *Teleological* All behaviour has a purpose and consequently it is possible to identify people's short- and long-term goals, which are of a social nature and reveal the total personality. Individual Psychology emphasizes that people are unaware of their goals and the private logic which underpins their movement towards the goals.

People can always choose how to respond to their inherited qualities and to the environment in which they grow up. People's basic concept of themselves and life provides a guiding line, a fixed pattern; this is called the life-style. The ideas and beliefs upon which a person operates are called *private logic*. They are not common sense but *biased apperception*. While common sense is shared and understood by all people, private logic is owned and understood by one individual and characterizes his or her own biased perceptions of his or her experiences. A person's private logic is created in childhood and contains generalizations and oversimplifications. Individuals create their own unique life-style and are therefore responsible for their own personality and behaviour; they are creative actors rather than passive reactors.

People will have developed their own characteristic life-style by the time they are 5 years old, based on their own creative and unique perceptions of their situation in their family. Parents and their values and the atmosphere they create in the family will set the scene for children to begin to make some assumptions about themselves, their world and their chosen direction of movement. Siblings and their choices of direction will have a major effect on the individual child.

The Adlerian view is that everyone is born with a desire to belong – to the family, to larger groups, to society and the whole human race. Everyone is born in an inferior position and strives to overcome this position. If this striving for superiority takes place in the context of social interest, the whole group, all society and the future human race benefit. The feeling of belonging (or *gemeinschaftsgefuhl*) is an innate potentiality in every human being. If this potentiality develops in a person he or she feels an equal member of the human race, with a useful part to play, willing to contribute and co-operate; this potentiality can become severely limited or be non-existent when individuals feel inferior to their fellows, unsure of their place and unable to make a useful contribution.

The meaning we attribute to life will determine our behaviour so that we will behave as if our perceptions were true. Life will turn out as we expected and people will respond as we expected; this is a self-fulfilling prophecy.

Conceptualization of psychological disturbance and health

Mental health can be measured by the amount of *social interest* a person has. Mentally healthy people are assured of their place and contribute to the tasks of the groups to which they belong; they co-operate with their fellow human beings and are part of a community. The human race, when looked at from an evolutionary point of view, is always moving towards an improved position from a minus to a plus.

The word *courage* is used by Adlerians to describe activity plus social interest and a person who is said to be acting with social interest is *encouraged*. The encouraged individual has a positive attitude towards him or herself and has self-confidence and self-respect. The goal of mentally healthy people is to belong as *social equals* in the family, in larger groups and in humanity, making their unique and useful contribution to these groups. Social equality was a concept that Rudolph Dreikurs developed and wrote about.

> [Social equality] implies that each individual is entitled to respect and dignity, to full and equal status, regardless of any personal quality or deficiency.
>
> (Dreikurs 1967: 39)

A person who has social interest will feel equal to other people and will treat others as social equals. The mentally healthy person is moving on a *horizontal plane* towards others and is *task-orientated*. Their behaviour is useful and is determined solely by the demands of the situation and by *common sense*. Their feeling of belonging enables them to identify with all human beings and to empathize with them.

Adler considered there were three major *life tasks* required of each member of the human race – work (or occupation), friendship and love. Dreikurs added two more – getting on with oneself and relating to the cosmos. In Adler's time the way that people could fulfil the life tasks was seen as getting a job, having a social life and friendships, getting married and having children. Successful completion of these life tasks was seen as being essential for the healthy perpetuation of the human race. More recently Adlerians give a broader definition of the three life tasks to the account of unemployment and homosexual relationships. Of the three life tasks, forming and maintaining an intimate relationship with one partner is considered to be the most testing of a person's social interest and willingness to co-operate.

Psychological disturbance occurs when individuals *feel inferior* and unworthy of an equal place amongst their fellows. Social interest, which is an innate potentiality in every human being, does not grow in the presence of strong feelings of inferiority. The inferiority feelings are substituted by a *compensatory striving for personal superiority*. People who feel inferior and act superior cannot adequately fulfil the life tasks of occupation, friendship and marriage because they are concerned with preserving their own prestige rather than responding to the needs of the situation and making their contribution to these tasks. Their movement is on a vertical plane away from the group, withdrawing from some or all of the life tasks. An unrealistic, unattainable goal of personal superiority is set by the individual and in the *neurotic individual* alibis then have to be found to explain why the goal is never reached. Neurotic symptoms or behaviours serve as excuses and the mistaken ideas and attitudes that justify the useless behaviour are called *private logic*. An example of private logic might be *I am the best at everything I do – unfortunately I get bad headaches when I am under stress so I am never able to perform at my best*. The goal of being best at everything is unrealistic and unattainable, and the headaches are a neurotic symptom which safeguards an individual from having to admit that he is not as superior as he thinks he is. He likes to think he is superior because he feels inferior; the reality of the situation is that he is socially equal to all human beings. If his feelings of equality and social interest could be developed he could divert his attention away from his own self-esteem, personal security and prestige and concentrate on making his contribution to the tasks of living. His private logic could then be replaced by common sense – Adler's *ironclad logic of social living* (Terner and Pew 1978).

Psychotic individuals in the presence of certain predisposing conditions escape totally from the logic of social living and assume a reality of delusions and hallucinations which conform with their own private logic. *Psychopaths* openly reject common sense and like neurotics and psychotics are motivated only by self-interest but, unlike the other two, have no conscience; they do not need the neurotic's alibis and symptoms nor the psychotic's distorted reality.

Acquisition and perpetuation of psychological disturbance

All human problems are essentially social in nature.

(Dreikurs 1967: 104)

We do not develop neurotic symptoms or behaviour as long as we feel we can function adequately. Neurosis will develop as soon as we feel unable to fulfil our obligations in one of the life tasks – at work, in friendships, in an intimate relationship. The symptoms and behaviour will be the excuse for not fulfilling the tasks adequately, not engaging in them at all, or retreating from them. Rather than facing failure and being found to be inadequate the symptom enables the discouraged individual to hesitate or evade and yet not lose face. Neurotics may not appear to have any difficulties until they meet a crisis situation where they feel unprepared. For example, a crisis situation for one individual might be having to find a job when she feels incapable of fulfilling the demands of employment. Facing the demanding task of marriage might become a crisis situation for another individual so forcing her to break off an engagement. Rather than developing a symptom, individuals may choose safeguarding behaviour such as being totally absorbed in one life task so leaving no time or energy to engage in the other two life tasks in which they feel inadequate.

Individuals feel unable to find their place due to varying degrees of inferiority feelings. As children they learned to feel inferior. Their parents may have spoiled them and given in to their demands, in which case they would have developed the mistaken idea that they were very special people who should be served by others. They may have learned to use displays of emotion to get this service – temper tantrums, tears or sulks. Adler uses spoiling and pampering synonymously in his writings. Sonstegard makes a distinction between the two: spoiling is giving in to children's demands whereas pampering is doing for children those things that children can do for themselves. Pampering is regarded by Sonstegard as the most disabling form of parenting. Pampered children will feel unable to accomplish many tasks and will constantly seek help from others. They will lack self-confidence when they grow into adulthood because they have such limited experience of learning and doing for themselves. Their parents' over-protection stunts their growth so they doubt their ability to be independent or to make choices or to take risks and face hardships. Spoilt children in adult life will still be expecting others to serve them and let them have their own way. Pampered and spoilt people feel that the world is their enemy because it does not respond in the same way as did their parents. Adler pointed out that the children play an active part in enlisting help in the case of pampering or in demanding service in the case of spoiling. Criticized children grow up afraid of taking risks and making mistakes. Neglect is far less common than pampering and spoiling but was acknowledged by Adler to produce discouraged children. Dreikurs was convinced that the parenting methods and education of our competitive society did not encourage mental health. Mistake-centred education and '*You could do better*' *parenting* discourages children.

People's perception of their position in their family constellation will form the basis of their life-style. The parents set family values and create a family atmosphere and the children decide their place in the family. A competitive family will produce discouragement, the children competing against each other and eventually channelling themselves into separate spheres of success. They each choose something they can be best at, even if that is being naughty. As each child strives for superiority this necessitates putting the other siblings down. An eldest child is an only child for a while, possibly the centre of attention until the second child arrives and dethrones the first child. The first child has several options, one of which is to strive to retain her superiority. The second child may want to catch up with the first child and may succeed, in which case the first child will feel discouraged. The second child may give up as the first child is too capable and too far ahead. The youngest child may remain a baby for a long time, the other children acting as pampering parents; they have a vested interest in keeping the youngest a baby as it enhances their superiority. However, some youngest children can become the most accomplished members of their families; they are never dethroned and strive to overcome all the other children. Individual children will make their choice and choose their goals supported by mistaken ideas or private logic, interpreting their position in the family constellation. Neither the child nor the adult is aware of these goals or their private logic.

Even though people may not be co-operating and may not be fulfilling all of the life tasks, as long as their life-style is in harmony with their environment, there will be no disturbing behaviour nor distressing symptoms. An adult, spoiled as a child, may find partners, relatives, children or friends who are willing to give in to her demands. An adult, pampered as a child, may find sufficient rescuers, helpers and advisers who will take over responsibility for his life. If these individuals should lose their slaves or supports, a crisis situation would ensue and disturbing behaviour might emerge in order to attract more applicants for the vacant posts.

People may consciously regret their symptom and seek treatment for it. They may convince themselves and others of their good intentions to get rid of their symptoms or their disturbing behaviour. Their efforts to fight the symptom merely aggravate and perpetuate it. People's private logic maintains their mistaken and unrealistic life goals. Adler referred to this as a *yes-but* personality where individuals are aware of their social obligations (yes) – (but) due to their private logic they have to continue with their useless behaviour. The feared situation is still avoided, the task or duty is evaded and the obligations of a relationship are side-stepped. Sometimes the symptom might be *cured* but it recurs or is replaced by another symptom if its safeguarding tendency is still needed.

Change

Any occurrence in people's lives may become an encouraging experience so causing them to change their perceptions. New behaviours which challenge the old premises of the life-styles may cause a revision in social interest with a consequent decrease in inferiority feelings. The new behaviour may be embarked upon due to encouragement from another person, or less often due to an independent decision on the part of the individual. Changed circumstances e.g. leaving home, partners or parents, or being left by partners or parents, leaving school, passing exams or failing exams, getting a job or losing a job can start the changed behaviour. If the new behaviour has encouraging results then the private logic which underpinned the old behaviour is challenged and possibly revised.

As mentioned in the previous section, people may change their overt behaviour without any change in their motivation. Adlerians would consider that a behavioural change is superficial if not accompanied by an alteration of perception and an increase in social interest. People would need to gain some insight into their mistaken ideas after changing their behaviour. Substituting acceptable behaviour for unacceptable behaviour is not a change in life-style if people still do not feel equal to their fellows. People who feel they must always be the centre of attention, and who change from unacceptable behaviour to acceptable behaviour, are still focused on their own superiority and sense of being special; they are not concentrating on what they can contribute to the task and the needs of the situation.

Practice

Goals of therapy

Adlerian psychotherapy is a learning process where there is re-education of clients' faulty perceptions and social values, and modification of their motivation. It is intended that clients should gain insight into their mistaken ideas and unrealistic goals, both of which are a source of their discouragement. After insight there is a stage of reorientation of short- and long-term goals and readjustment of personal concepts and attitudes. The clients' original feelings of inferiority will be superseded by a growing social interest. They will feel encouraged as they recognize their equality with their fellow human beings. They will concentrate on making their contribution and on co-operating instead of looking at their personal status within groups.

There are four phases, each with its own goal, in the Adlerian psychotherapy process:

1 establishing and maintaining a relationship with the client
2 uncovering dynamics of the client
3 giving insight
4 encouraging reorientation.

Selection criteria

There are no rigid guidelines for selecting individual therapy rather than couples therapy or group therapy. Individual choice on the part of both the therapist and the client is respected, although clients' rights to choose their kind of therapy are limited by what is available. Some therapists prefer to work with people in a group acknowledging that each individual's problems are of a social nature, the group acting as an important agent in the psychotherapeutic process. Some therapists are reluctant to work with married individuals unless their partner is aware of the implications of psychotherapy and the changes it may encourage. When working with children, Adlerian therapists work with the whole family, parents and siblings, as they realize that if one child makes changes then the whole family will need to change too. Dreikurs *et al.* (1952; 1982) introduced multiple psychotherapy, several therapists working with one client. This provides an ideal training opportunity. The client enjoys the attention of more than one therapist; since the atmosphere is educational, discussion of interpretation of the client's life-style, including disagreements between therapists, is enlightening and encouraging to the client. The client participates as an equal in explaining and understanding his or her private logic. It does happen that clients move from individual to group therapy or from a group to individual therapy and this move is mutually agreed between clients and therapists. If a couple have a relationship problem the therapist may want to work with the couple; however, it may emerge that one or both partners need to do some individual work, in which case they would have some individual therapy. Clients who feel ridiculous if they share feelings and personal ideas tend to prefer individual therapy, one therapist being less threatening than a group of people.

Qualities of effective therapists

The effective Adlerian therapist feels truly equal to all human beings and this includes clients and children. The therapist shows respect to the client; this does not necessarily mean that the therapist is always nice and kind and accepting of all the client's behaviours. The relationship with the client is one of mutual respect so the therapist shows herself respect by not tolerating unacceptable behaviour from the client and by giving honest feedback to the client. The therapist shows respect towards the client by genuinely acting as if the client has full responsibility for his decisions and actions. The therapist is warm and accepting of the person *as he is* and sincerely interested in understanding without judgement his life-style, his own unique perception of life and life goals. The Adlerian therapist models social interest and shows herself to be a fallible human being who is making her own contribution, unafraid of making mistakes. The Adlerian approach is based on a clear philosophy of life and the effective therapist will espouse social values that enable all human beings to live together in harmony as equals now and in the future. The relationship with the therapist may be the first one where the client experiences a democratic, co-operative partnership between equals. The therapist will need to have the skills to win people over as well as the personal maturity to model social interest. Many clients will resist entering a partnership between equals because this gives them too much responsibility. The therapist must resist the temptation to dominate, rescue, manipulate or fight with the client: all these therapist behaviours are disrespectful and belong to an authoritarian relationship rather than a democratic one.

There are many varied creative and adaptable Adlerian therapists who use different modes of gaining insight and encouraging reorientation. Art therapy, psychodrama, non-verbal exercises, group exercises and dream analysis are some of the major approaches that Adlerian therapists use in these respects.

Therapeutic style

There is no prescribed style for Adlerian therapists. Initially the therapist will sensitively respond to the client in order to establish quickly an atmosphere of trust and acceptance. The setting is usually relaxed and comfortable, with the therapist and client facing each other in chairs of equal heights. After the presenting problem has been briefly described by the client the Adlerian therapist will want to move on to gathering information in order to be able to understand the client's life-style. The client may be surprised to be moved away from *the problem* and although the therapist's style is directive at this point it is respectful, so that an explanation is given as to why the therapist wishes to move on and the client's agreement is sought. Both client and therapist will embark upon this educational voyage of discovery actively as partners, the client providing the information and the therapist giving interpretations. The therapist's style will vary according to each client's needs so that *empathy* is established. For instance, the therapist might use the client's vocabulary, seeking clarification if she is not sure what the client is saying or the therapist might give time and space for clients to express their feelings. Gradually the private logic will be uncovered and understood by the therapist. Interpretations need to be put tentatively to the client as they are merely hypothesized guessing on the part of the therapist. The therapist will wish to see whether the client will acknowledge that the therapist has made a true interpretation. The whole educational process will not take place unless therapist and client co-operate and share mutually agreed goals. It is in the last phase – reorientation – when it becomes clear whether or not both therapist and client share the same therapy goals. Clients have the right to gain insight and then decide not to make any changes. If clients do wish to make some changes the therapist is there to guide them. Task setting and completing the assignments also require a co-operative relationship. There will be difficult times, there may be strong emotions to work through, disagreements between therapist and client but their resilient relationship endures these tests. The time-scale for the last phase of reorientation will vary with each client. Some clients will spend useful time with their therapist when they want to make some changes; others may need to be away from their therapist, having decided to stick to old familiar patterns. The door is always open for them to return when they feel ready to work on themselves again. The therapist demonstrates complete faith in the client by giving him total responsibility for his own reorientation.

Major therapeutic strategies and techniques

Adlerian psychotherapy can be described as a co-operative educational enterprise between equals – the therapist and client. The first stage of therapy is to *establish a co-operative relationship*; one between equals that is recognized by the presence of mutual respect. A co-operative relationship requires mutually agreed goals. An open approach towards stating goals will prevent ineffectual therapy between a therapist and a client who have different goals. If it is not possible to find mutually agreed goals psychotherapy will be ineffectual and may as well be terminated. Mutual respect is established by the therapist's showing herself respect by refusing to play any *games* with the client, by working only towards agreed therapy goals and by openly commenting about behaviour towards herself that she finds unacceptable. Moreover, the therapist shows respect for clients by listening, accepting and acknowledging clients' rights to make their own decisions and take responsibility for their lives. The client needs to feel that the therapist cares but will not manipulate, dominate nor rescue. Dictatorial prescription and rescuing are equally disrespectful behaviours on the part of the therapist. This democratic relationship becomes part of the client's retraining: it is an action experience.

The second stage of the therapy is to *gather information* and *understand* clients' *life-styles* and then to show clients how the presenting problem fits into their overall characteristic pattern of movement. From the first minutes of meeting clients, information will be available to the therapist from non-verbal clues, how clients enter the room, where they choose to sit, their posture, how they speak, etc. Adler was reportedly very clever at picking up information from this non-verbal behaviour. Verbal information is also available in the client's short subjective description of the presenting problem. The Adlerian therapist will not want to spend too long initially on the presenting problem as she will need to discover the client's life-style before the significance of the problem can be understood. The objective situation of the client is also explored as the therapist finds out how the client is functioning in the three life tasks: work, friendships and intimate relationships. Some therapists may also enquire about relationships to God and moral-ethical beliefs. Clients are then asked *the Question*, i.e. what would be different if you were well/if you didn't have this symptom? Clients' answers will reveal the particular area of difficulty for them and their unrealistic goals.

The therapist will then move on to *life-style assessment*, which consists of understanding the client's *family constellation* and interpreting his *early memories*. A child creates his own unique life-style in the context of his family and in relation to his siblings. The therapists, therefore, asks the client to describe himself and his siblings as children. Family constellation is not just a reflection of birth order. Adlerians might describe typical eldest, second, youngest, middle and only children but as Adler said, '*Everything can also be different*' and children may interpret their positions in the family constellation quite differently. An eldest child chooses how to respond to family values and to the experience of being dethroned by a younger child; all elder children experience being only children for a time. A second child chooses whether to compete with the eldest by overtaking them or by doing something or being something entirely different. A youngest child may decide to remain the baby of the family or surpass all the siblings in achievement. Family values will determine whether the competition takes place in academic achievements or in being an acceptable person or some other realm of behaviour important to that family. Many children will decide to rebel against family values either silently or openly. Most families are competitive; very few are democratic.

The therapist will want additional information in order to verify the hypothesis that she is beginning to form about the client's life-style. Dreikurs said that you needed two points on a line before you could make a hypothesis about a person's life-style. The therapist asks the client for some of his early memories. Adler found that people remembered incidents, often innocuous and ordinary, that fitted in with their life-style. The clients are asked to think back as far as they can and tell the therapist the first thing they think of, if possible something that happened to them before they were 5 years old. People select out of all their life experiences those memories that depict some aspect of their life-style. It may be their view of themselves, their view of their world and the people in it, their view of how life should be or how they have to behave. The therapist has to interpret the early memories and align this information with that already gleaned from the description of the family constellation. The therapist wants to find out clients' life goals and their underlying mistaken assumptions, i.e. their private logic. The overall movement of the client needs to be recognized. The presenting problem and future problems will fit into this basic pattern of living.

The third phase of *interpretation* and *giving insight* is now entered. The therapist's approach is to find enough points on a line to begin to make a hypothesis. This informed guess is then put to the client so that it can be verified. Previously clients were unaware of their goals and private logic, thus this phase of therapy is where the therapist particularly needs to demonstrate her empathy; she needs to be able to describe the client's goals and mistaken ideas in words that the client understands, recognizes and owns. This hypothesis does not have to be perfect at the first attempt. The therapist shows her fallibility and encourages the client to help her shape the life-style summary so that it feels right for the client. The summary usually takes the form of *life is . . . ; others are . . . ; and I am . . . themes*. The therapist explains how clients chose their particular goals so that there is no mystique in the interpretation of the life-style. Private logic once it is verbalized begins to lose its strength. The overgeneralizations, oversimplifications and unrealistic ideas can be challenged. *Is it reasonable to expect . . .?, Is this really how people are? Is it realistic for you to expect always to be . . .?*

Dreams may also be analysed. Adler said dreams were the *factory of the emotions*;

they set the mood that fuels people's actions. Remembered dreams that clients produce always fit within a person's life-style and never contradict it.

The therapist places the client's concerns and problems in the context of the life-style and shows how certain situations, relationships or demands can cause a crisis for them because they challenge the client's life-style. Neurotic symptoms can be understood as alibis which have been necessary because the client was pursuing unattainable goals. Making clients aware of the purpose of their neurotic symptoms was described by Adler as *spitting in the patient's soup*. He can persist with the symptoms but they will not give the same satisfaction as before.

The *reorientation phase* follows on from gaining insight. The Adlerian therapist will use a mirror technique to show clients familiar patterns of movement towards consistent goals in all their behaviour. Attainable assignments will be set for clients that challenge their private logic. If the assignments are completed successfully then there is a weakening of clients' private logic. Clients will begin to catch themselves pursuing the same goals and making the same justifications for their behaviour. Clients will catch themselves after, during and then before they engage in the useless behaviour. Each '*aha*' experience increases clients' new learning and growing understanding of their own personality. Each individual, once they have some insight, will decide whether or not to change and if to change, over how long a period. The old patterns are well tried and tested, automatic and to some extent feel comfortable. New patterns are scary. One method that Adler used when a client was fighting against a symptom or behaviour and actually increasing both was to encourage the client to increase the symptom or behaviour; this is known as paradoxical intention.

The change process in therapy

Once people's mistaken goals are revealed to them they can no longer pursue them with such conviction. Once their mistaken ideas are revealed to them they can choose to change. Gaining insight and choosing to change is one choice; gaining insight and choosing not to change is another choice. Insight will develop as individuals begin to recognize their patterns of behaviour. New behaviours which challenge the old assumptions are then tested out. New behaviours or assignments may be successful: the old private logic is then challenged and weakened and replaced by common sense. New behaviours may have disastrous outcomes, in which case clients may be tempted to retreat back to old ways and to feel comfortable with familiar private logic. As their private logic decreases and common sense grows they will display increased social interest in all spheres of their lives and they will take on responsibility for their own life goals, perceptions and behaviours. As soon as they accept full responsibility for their own behaviour they enable themselves to make changes. Their increased sense of belonging and feeling of equal worth will be a source of encouragement to them. Inferiority feeling will diminish; their focus of interest will be on their personal contribution to the task at hand. They will feel content with themselves. Their unattainable goals will be replaced by the courage to be imperfect, an acknowledgement that all active, co-operating human beings make mistakes. The new behaviours and new goals will be followed by new assumptions. This process can be instant in a child as when one of the Four Mistaken Goals of Misbehaviour (Dreikurs and Soltz 1964) is revealed to them, very quick in a teenager and increasingly slower in a mature adult. It is harder for adults in established relationships to make changes as these changes will inevitably have an effect on partners in intimate relationships, and on close friends. The therapist, who has always treated the client as an equal, encourages the client to contribute as an equal. Clients may make a partial or complete change of personality, their private logic replaced by common sense, their inferiority feelings replaced by social interest and a feelings of belonging. The correction of one mistaken concept will enable growth and release further courage to tackle new behaviours and additional mistakes. The therapist will respect the client's right to choose when and how much to change. Behaviour change can occur years after initially gaining insight. It is best for the therapist not to fight with the client during times of inactivity; the therapist can be available when the client wants to make some changes but does not know how to. Each person, if they choose to change, will do so in their own unique and creative way.

Limitations of the approach

Adler's theory of personality provides Adlerian therapists with a complete under-standing of all human behaviour. The practice of Adlerian therapists is very varied but always based on the foundation of a holistic socio-teleological view of people. Much of Adler's Individual Psychology has permeated other approaches to psychotherapy and counselling; many of his ideas are incorporated into other people's theories without acknowledgement to Adler. Adlerian theory appears to have widespread acceptance and relevance to students of human behaviour.

The psychotherapeutic procedures practised by Adler himself and Rudolf Dreikurs are used today by therapists and any technique which a therapist finds helpful is added to the basic approach. The insight and the skills are only part of Adlerian psychotherapy. Psychotherapists need to have social interests and need to use their skills *for the purpose of establishing an ideal community* (Dreikurs). The Adlerian approach can give therapists a great deal of insight; to use that insight and understanding of people with social interest is an exacting demand on every therapist. Many people, including therapists, have grown up in families where power was used either openly in the form of control by anger or disguisedly in the form of manipulation. Therapists have to work on their own skills in the arena of power before they can work with clients in a truly equal co-operative relationship. Many clients will find the idea of being responsible for their own behaviour distasteful and unacceptable. The client may leave therapy with insight but be unwilling to change. If therapy outcomes are looked at over too short a time the long-term effects of the insight may not be recorded. Changes have been seen everal years after a life-style assessment was done. It is always worth while enabling people to gain insight. It is never worthwhile fighting with them after-wards in order to force, persuade or shame them into change.

There are limitations to using Adlerian psychotherapy only in a one-to-one situation. So much information can be gained by observing clients in groups. So much can be gained by clients when trying out new behaviours in a safe group. So much can be gained by clients experiencing equal membership of a group with a shared goal of mutual growth.

Case example

The client

Keith was in a self-help group for people who stammer. They met in each other's homes and invited the speech therapists they had previously worked with to join them. Two years previously Keith and his group had received a two-week intensive speech therapy course learning a technique to speak fluently. Keith always managed to appear to be the least able in the group and with the most noticeable stammer; he received a lot of concern and help from the other group members and the therapists. He was always late.

Keith was 40 years old, divorced five years previously, with three children that he saw once or twice a week. He owned his own house and worked at an international airport. He was lonely, without friends and without an intimate partner. He said his children kept him going and he felt depressed at times. He felt that if he did not stammer he would have a better chance of making friends.

The therapy

During one of the self-help group sessions Keith had his life-style assessed. He was the youngest of three children – with two sisters, one nine years and one five years older. His description of his elder sister when they were children showed her to be a *typical eldest* – bossy, achieving, popular and selfish, she was father's favourite. The second sister was described as more placid, gentle, helpful and considerate towards the family. The elder sister had taken up the position in the family of the achiever and was successful academically and socially with her peers. The second sister had taken up the pleasing role, particularly directing her behaviour towards adults. Then Keith arrived three years later, the first boy. Keith described himself, as a child, as a bit of a loner, who made friends with a bully at school; he was mother's favourite. Keith described his mother as always trying to help. She could not understand Keith in his teens; he joined a gang and became rebellious. She also found it hard to believe he was living on his own, looking after himself. Keith described his father as wanting a quiet life, avoiding arguments, usually giving in to his wife, taking jobs with little responsibility, harming no one. He had a big future ahead of him at work but he used to worry and eventually, after serious illness with a duodenal ulcer, gave up his responsible job; his wife was disappointed about this. Keith's place in the family was that of the pampered baby who had to behave very rebelliously in his teens, within the safety of a peer group, in order to assert his independence.

Keith gave three early memories. In the first one he described how as an infant he used to cry and drop his bottom lip which his sisters found amusing. They found it so amusing that they used to find ways of making him cry. He gave a feeling of fear for this memory. In the second memory he was in infant school and the teacher was calling the register. He couldn't say *here* so a little girl in front of him said it for him. He has always remembered her; she always used to do that for him. He felt pleased that she helped him. In the third memory he was having a fight in the playground with a boy bigger than himself. This boy was always teasing Keith, who lost his temper, knocked the boy to the ground and started kicking him. A couple of prefects had to part them. He felt that he had got something out of his system as he did not like being humiliated. He could laugh off so much and then his tolerance reached its limit.

Keith's life-style was interpreted in the group thus:

1 Keith feels victimized – he is always the victim.
2 He is afraid of doing many things as he is afraid of becoming a victim.

This was revealed to Keith who acknowledged that this is how he feels and thinks; he actually used the word *crucified*. There was no ongoing therapy after the initial life-style assessment and the group stopped meeting after a few months.

Five years later Keith referred himself for individual therapy. During that time he had married and acquired a teenage step daughter. A great deal of growth had obviously taken place since I had first met Keith. He was participating in the relationship with his wife as an equal valued adult. His capacity for loving was being given an opportunity to be expressed. He was in the same job as when I first met him. He described his concerns as 'blockages' and mentioned certain situations where his stammer was a hindrance, such as using the telephone at home and at a court appearance in a social services tribunal. He was able to use the phone at work and when speaking to his wife and daughter and on the two-way radio at work. I asked him if he would be prepared to have his life-style assessed so that I could have a more complete picture of him as he was now. He agreed to do this next session.

We started off with Keith's family constellation. I asked him to describe his sisters and himself as children. As Keith talked about his sisters five years after his initial life-style assessment it was noticeable how his perceptions of them had changed. His elder sister he said was *Daddy's girl* and broad-minded; she could talk to anyone about anything. She was in charge of the situation and very kind. The second sister was obstinate, determined and sympathetic. Keith said he was happy as a child – a loner. He found girls easier to talk to. He could not communicate so he was always having fights at school. He was *special*. His father worked away from home a lot and was in charge of the situation, had a very kind nature and was peace-loving. His mother was very understanding and caring. These descriptions showed Keith's present preoccupation with communication and control as well as his continuing interest in peoples being kind. He saw both his sisters as being assertive and kind. Keith saw his family as being able to communicate and therefore control their lives whereas he could not communicate and so required very special understanding from others. I asked Keith for an early memory, requesting that he think back as far as he could to something that happened to him, if possible something that happened before he was 5 years old. He gave one early memory this time: he was 6 years old in class at school, and could not say *here*. A girl always said it for him and he felt relief. This memory was the same as the first one he produced five years before. I suggested to Keith that this memory could be interpreted that Keith was still thinking that he needs help and feels relief when he gets it. He acknowledged that this was how he felt.

Keith's description of his sisters and himself had been focused on communication and control so I asked Keith to complete a grid, rating himself and his sisters as children on various characteristics, e.g. who was the best student? And the least? Who was the naughtiest? And the least naughty? His elder sister was the hard worker, the striver and popular with her peers; the second sister was naughty, helpful to mother and popular with her peers. Keith was the most intelligent and the most lazy. Here Keith gave new information of his awareness of his ability that he hid by being lazy. I asked why he was lazy and he said he did not want to put himself above others; he acknowledged my comment, *so you put yourself at the bottom of the pile*. Here I converted Keith's negative statement into a positive description of his behaviour and highlighted it with visual imagery. Once this particular image was acknowledged as meaningful by Keith I continued to use it. I explained to Keith that being at the bottom of the pile was his chosen position; he could not compete with either sister, although he considered he could achieve more than both of them. He needed to have an alibi for hiding at the bottom of the pile; the stammer was his alibi. Keith's perception of his elder sister was unrealistic and showed the unattainable goals he had set himself when communicating or controlling situations. Keith's view of himself as a victim had changed. Five years ago he was a superior good person who was being crucified by bad people in a frightening world; he was lying low, avoiding people and escaping further victimization. Now he had made many moves towards people. He still had unattainable goals and unrealistic ideas. We needed to look together at detailed areas of his life so we could set some realistic goals for him.

He said he did not express his viewpoint as he thought people would not understand him. More discussion about this revealed Keith's high standards and high expectations. He needed to give perfect explanations to people which were immediately understood. He then used his blocking stammer for thinking time so he could get this performance perfect. This perfection was never attained and the stammer was always blamed. I gave Keith the assignment to talk to a colleague at work and use something else for thinking time, not the stammer. He was given the broader task of making conversation when he had something to say. After a month he was talking more to his wife, friends and people at work.

Part of Keith's wish not to express his viewpoint to people was his unrealistic goal of wanting to please people all the time. He started to be less pleasing to his mother and openly disagreed with her; he felt he was being too hard on her. This is a common reaction when a person changes his habitual behaviour. The new behaviour will feel uncomfortable and frightening and may be perceived as very extreme. Keith perceived his disagreement with his mother as being *hard*. People who have pleased others all their lives may interpret their first attempt at assertion as aggression. Their private logic will still be operating and telling them they must please everyone at all times or else they will be rejected by everyone. We discussed this and I explained to Keith that new behaviours always feel uncomfortable.

Keith's other concern was whether to take on more responsibility at work. He had spent his life avoiding pressure and stress and he was not sure he wanted to change. This was a realistic and honest approach with the stammer no longer being used as an alibi. I said to Keith that he had a right to choose whether or not he wanted to take on more stress and pointed out that he was making the decision honestly instead of deceiving himself and others by saying that he would take on more responsibility at work if only his stammer went away.

We ended our therapy sessions at this point as Keith had no more concerns to work on. Keith's social interest had grown considerably and he was participating in all three life tasks, making a contribution and comparing himself less with others.

References

Adler, A. (1912) *The Neurotic Constitution*, London: Kegan Paul, Trench, Trubner & Co.
—— (1917) *Study of Organ Inferiority and its Psychical Compensation: A Contribution to Clinical Medicine*, New York: Nervous and Mental Diseases Publishing.
—— (1927) *Understanding Human Nature*, London: Allen & Unwin.
—— (1933) *Social Interest: A Challenge to Mankind*, London: Faber & Faber.
Dreikurs, R. (1967) *Psychodynamics, Psychotherapy and Counselling: Collected Papers*, Chicago, Ill: Alfred Adler Institute.
Dreikurs, R. and Soltz, V. (1964) *Happy Children*, Glasgow: Fontana/Collins.
Dreikurs, R., Mosak, H.H. and Shulman, B.H. (1952) Patient–therapist relationship in multiple psychotherapy. 11: Its advantage for the patient, *Psychiatric Quarterly* 26: 590–6.
—— (1982) *Multiple Psychotherapy*, Chicago, Ill: Alfred Adler Institute.
Ellenberger, H.F. (1970) *The Discovery of the Unconscious*, Ch. 8, 'Alfred Adler and individual psychology', New York: Basic Books.
Terner, J. and Pew, W.L. (1978) *The Courage to be Imperfect: The Life and Work of Rudolf Dreikurs*, New York: Hawthorn Books Inc.

Suggested further reading

Adler, A. (1962) *What Life Should Mean to You*, London: Allen & Unwin.
—— (1964) *Superiority and Social Interest: A Collection of Later Writings*, H.L. Ansbacher and R.R. Ansbacher (eds), New York: Norton.
Ansbacher, H.L. and Ansbacher, R.R. (eds) (1956) *The Individual Psychology of Alfred Adler*, New York: Basic Books.
Corsini, R.J. (1984) *Current Psychotherapies*, Ch. 3, 'Adlerian psychotherapy', Itasca, Ill: Peacock.
Dreikurs, R. (1971) *Social Equality: The Challenge of Today*, Chicago, Ill: Henry Regnery.

6

Person-centred therapy

BRIAN THORNE

Historical context and development in Britain

Historical context

Dr Carl Rogers (1902–87), the American psychologist and founder of what has now become known as person-centred counselling or psychotherapy, always claimed to be grateful that he never had one particular mentor. He was influenced by many significant figures, often holding widely differing viewpoints, but above all he claimed to be the student of his own experience and of that of his clients and colleagues.

While accepting Rogers's undoubtedly honest claim about his primary sources of learning there is much about his thought and practice which places him within a recognizable tradition. Oatley has described this as

> the distinguished American tradition exemplified by John Dewey: the tradition of no nonsense, of vigorous self-reliance, of exposing oneself thoughtfully to experience, practical innovation, and of careful concern for others.
>
> (Oatley 1981: 192)

In fact in 1925, while still a student at Teachers College, Columbia, New York, Rogers was directly exposed to Dewey's thought and to progressive education through his attendance at a course led by the famous William Heard Kilpatrick, a student of Dewey and himself a teacher of extraordinary magnetism. Not that Dewey and Kilpatrick formed the mainstream of the ideas to which Rogers was introduced during his professional training and early clinical experience. Indeed, when he took up his first appointment in 1928 as a member of the Child Study Department of the Society for the Prevention of Cruelty to Children in Rochester, New York, he joined an institution where the three fields of psychology, psychiatry and social work were combining forces in diagnosing and treating problems. This context appealed to Rogers's essentially pragmatic temperament.

Rogers's biographer, Kirschenbaum (1979), while acknowledging the variety of influences to which Rogers was subjected at the outset of his professional career, suggests nevertheless that when Rogers went to Rochester he saw himself essentially as a diagnostician and as an interpretative therapist whose goal, very much in the analytical tradition, was to help a child or a parent gain insight into their own behaviour and motivation. Diagnosis and interpretation are far removed from the primary concerns of a contemporary person-centred therapist and in an important sense Rogers's progressive disillusionment with both these activities during his time at Rochester mark the beginning of his own unique approach. He tells the story of how, near the end of his time at Rochester, he had been working with a highly intelligent mother whose son was presenting serious behavioural problems. Rogers was convinced that the root of the trouble lay in the mother's early rejection of the boy but no amount of gentle strategy on his part could bring her to this insight. In the end he gave up and they were about to part when she asked if adults were taken for counselling on their own account. When Rogers assured her that they were she immediately requested help for herself and launched into an impassioned outpouring of her own despair, her marital difficulties and her confusion and sense of failure. Real therapy, it seems, began at that moment and was ultimately successful. Rogers commented:

> This incident was one of a number which helped me to experience the fact – only fully realized later – that it is the client who knows what hurts, what direction to go, what problems are crucial, what experiences have been deeply buried. It began to occur to me that unless I had a need to demon-strate my own cleverness and learning, I would do better to rely upon the client for the direction of movement in the process.
>
> (cited in Kirschenbaum 1979: 89)

The essential step from diagnosis and interpretation to listening had been taken and from that point onwards Rogers was launched on his own path.

By 1940 Rogers was a professor of psychology at Ohio State University and his first book, *Counseling and Psychotherapy*, appeared two years later. From 1945 to 1957 he was professor of psychology at Chicago and director of the university counselling centre. This was a period of intense activity, not least in the research field. Rogers's pragmatic nature had led to much research being carried out on person-centred therapy. With the publication of *Client-Centered Therapy* in 1951 Rogers became a major force in the world of psychotherapy and established his position as a practitioner, theorist and researcher who warranted respect. In an address to the American Psychological Association in 1973 Rogers maintained that during this Chicago period he was for the first time giving clear expression to an idea whose time had come. The idea was

> the gradually formed and tested hypothesis that the individual has within himself vast resources for self-understanding, for altering his self concept, his attitudes and his self-directed behavior – and that these resources can be tapped if only a definable climate of facilitative psychological attitudes can be provided.
>
> (Rogers 1974: 116)

From this 'gradually formed and tested hypothesis' non-directive therapy was born as a protest against the diagnostic, prescriptive point of view prevalent at the time. Emphasis was placed on a relationship between counsellor and client based upon acceptance and clarification. This was a period, too, of excitement generated by the use of recorded interviews for research and training purposes and there was a focus on 'non-directive techniques'. Those coming for help were no longer referred to as patients but as clients with the inference that they were self-responsible human beings, not objects for treatment. As experience increased and both theory building and research developed, the term 'client-centred therapy' was adopted which put the emphasis on the internal world of the client and focused attention on the attitudes of therapists towards their clients rather than on particular techniques. The term 'person-centred' won Rogers's approval in the decade before his death, because it can be applied to the many fields outside therapy where his ideas are becoming increasingly accepted and valued and because in the therapy context itself it underlines the person-to-person nature of the interaction where not only the phenomenological world of the client but also the therapist's state of being are of crucial significance. This 'I–Thou' quality of the therapeutic relationship indicates a certain kinship with the existential philosophy of Kierkegaard and Buber and the stress on personal experience recalls the work of the British philosopher/scientist Michael Polanyi (whom Rogers knew and admired). In recent times, too, Rogers himself reported his own deepening respect for certain aspects of Zen teaching and became fond of quoting sayings of Lao-Tse, especially those that stress the undesirability of imposing on people instead of allowing them the space in which to find themselves.

Development in Britain

Although the influence of Rogers percolated spasmodically into Britain in the post-war years – mainly through the work of the Marriage Guidance Council (now known as 'Relate') and then often in an unacknowledged form – it was not until the mid-1960s that he came to be studied in depth in British universities. Interestingly enough the reason for this development was the establishment of the first training courses in Britain for school counsellors. These programmes (initially at the Universities of Keele and Reading) were largely dependent in their first years on American Fulbright professors of psychology or counselling, many of whom were steeped in the client-centred tradition and introduced their British students to both the theory and practice of client-centred therapy. It is therefore with the growth of counselling in Britain that the work of Rogers has become more widely known; it is probably true to say that the largest recognizable group of person-centred practitioners currently working in Britain are counsellors operating within the educational sector. It is also significant that when Rogers started working in the 1920s psychologists in the USA were not permitted to practise psychotherapy so he called his activity 'counselling'. British practitioners of person-centred therapy have tended to use the word 'counsellor' and to eschew the word 'psychotherapist' for perhaps different reasons. They have seen the word 'psychotherapist' as somehow conducive to an aura of mystification and expertise which runs counter to the egalitarian relationship which the person-centred approach seeks to establish between therapist and client. In the last fifteen years or so, partly thanks to the growth of the Association for Humanistic Psychology in Britain, there are many signs that the person-centred approach is moving out of the educational arena and making its impact felt more widely. The work of the British Centre of the Facilitator Development Institute (founded in 1974 on the initiative of Rogers's close associate, Dr Charles Devonshire) has introduced person-centred ideas to a wide variety of psychologists, social workers, psychiatrists and others, while the establishment in 1980 of the Norwich Centre for personal and professional development gave Britain its first independent therapy and training agency committed to the person-centred approach. The last five years have also seen the emergence of two substantial in-depth training courses for those seeking to become person-centred therapists. One is run by the Facilitator Development Institute (Mearns and Thorne 1988) and the other is the British programme of the Person-Centered Approach Institute International, which is gradually extending its training opportunities throughout Europe.

Theoretical assumptions

Image of the person

Person-centred therapists start from the assumption that both they and their clients are trustworthy. This trust resides in the belief that every organism – the human being included – has an underlying and instinctive movement towards the constructive accomplishment of its inherent potential. Rogers (1979) often recalled a boyhood memory of his parents' potato bin in which they stored the winter supply of potatoes. This bin was placed in the basement several feet below a small window and yet despite the highly unfavourable conditions the potatoes would nevertheless begin to send out spindly shoots groping towards the distant light of the window. Rogers compared these pathetic potatoes in their desperate struggle to develop with clients whose lives have been warped by circumstances and experience but who continue against all the odds to strive towards growth, towards becoming. This directional, or actualizing, tendency in the human being can be trusted and the therapist's task is to help create the best possible conditions for its fulfilment.

The elevated view of human nature which person-centred therapists hold is paralleled by their insistence on individual uniqueness. They believe that no two persons are ever alike and that the human personality is so complex that no diagnostic labelling of persons can ever be fully justified. Indeed, person-centred therapists know that they cannot hope to uncover fully the subjective perceptual world of the client and that clients themselves can do this only with great effort. Furthermore clients' perceptual worlds will be determined by the experiences they have rejected or assimilated into the self-concept.

Conceptualization of psychological disturbance and health

The self-concept is of crucial importance in person-centred therapy and needs to be distinguished from the self. Nelson-Jones (1982) has made the helpful distinction of regarding the self as the real, underlying organismic self – that is the essentially trustworthy human organism which is discernible in the physiological processes of the entire body and through the growth process by which potentialities and capacities are brought to realization – and contrasting this with the self-concept which is a person's conceptual construction of him or herself (however poorly articulated) and which does not by any means always correspond with the direct and untrammelled experiencing of the organismic self.

The self-concept develops over time and is heavily dependent on the attitudes of those who constitute the individual's significant others. It follows therefore that where a person is surrounded by those who are quick to condemn or punish (however subtly) the behaviour which emanates from the experiencing of the organismic self he or she will become rapidly confused. The need for positive regard or approval from others is overwhelming and is present from earliest infancy. If therefore behaviour arising from what is actually experienced by the individual fails to win approval an immediate conflict is established. A baby, for example, may gain considerable satisfaction or relief from howling full-throatedly but may then quickly learn that such behaviour is condemned or punished by the mother. At this point the need to win the mother's approval is in immediate conflict with the promptings of the organismic self which wishes to howl. In the person-centred tradition disturbance is conceptualized in terms of the degree of success or failure experienced by the individual in resolving such conflicts. The badly disturbed person on this criterion will have lost almost complete contact with the experiencing of the organismic self, for the basic need for self-regard can in the most adverse circumstances lead to behaviour which is totally geared to the desperate search for acceptance and approval. The voice of the organismic self in such cases is silenced and a self-concept is developed which bears little relationship to people's deepest promptings from which they are essentially cut off. Not surprisingly, perhaps, such attempts to create a self-concept which denies the nature of the self cannot in the long run be successful. In most cases individuals, whatever face they may present to the world, hold themselves in low esteem and a negative self-concept is usually a further sign of disturbance at some level. In those rarer instances where the self-deception is more extreme the self-concept may at a conscious level appear largely positive but it will be quickly evident to others that such self-affirmation has been won at the cost of a deliberate and sustained refusal to allow adverse judgements into awareness whether these threaten from within or from outside sources. Disturbed people can seldom trust their own judgement and for the person-centred therapist another sure mark of disturbance is the absence of an internalized locus of evaluation. This somewhat cumbersome term describes the faculty which determines individuals' capacity to trust their own thoughts and feelings when making decisions or choosing courses of action. Disturbed people show little sign of possessing such a faculty: instead they constantly turn to external authorities or find themselves caught in a paralysis of indecision. In summary, then, disturbance may be conceptualized as a greater or lesser degree of alienation from the organismic self prompted by the fundamental need for self-regard. The resulting self-concept, usually negative and always falsely based, is linked to a defective capacity to make decisions which in turn indicates the absence of an internalized locus of evaluation.

If individuals are unfortunate enough to be brought up amongst a number of significant others who are highly censorious or judgemental, a self-concept can develop which may serve to estrange them almost totally from their organismic experiencing. In such cases the self-concept, often developed after years of oppression of the organismic self, becomes the fiercest enemy of the self and must undergo radical transformation if the actualizing tendency is to reassert itself.

The person-centred therapist is constantly working with clients who have all but lost touch with the actualizing tendency within themselves and who have been surrounded by others who have no confidence in the innate capacity of human beings to move towards the fulfilment of their potential. Psychologically healthy persons on the other hand are men and women who have been lucky enough to live in contexts which have been conducive to the development of self-concepts which allow them to be in touch for at least some of the time with their deepest experiences and feelings without having to censure them or distort them. Such people are well placed to achieve a level of psychological freedom which will enable them to move in the direction of becoming more *fully functioning* persons. 'Fully functioning' is a term used by Rogers to denote individuals who are using their talents and abilities, realizing their potential and moving towards a more complete knowledge of themselves. They are demonstrating what it means to have attained a high level of psychological health and Rogers has outlined some of the major personality characteristics which they seem to share in common. The first and most striking characteristic is *openness to experience*. Individuals who are open to experience are able to listen to themselves and to others and to experience what is happening without feeling threatened. They demonstrate a high level of awareness especially in the world of the feelings. Second, allied to this characteristic, is the *ability to live fully* in each moment of one's existence. Experience is trusted rather than feared and is therefore the moulding force for the emerging personality rather than being twisted or manipulated to fit some preconceived structure of reality or some rigidly safeguarded self-concept. The third characteristic is the *organismic trusting* which is so clearly lacking in those who have constantly fallen victim to the adverse judgements of others. Such trusting is best displayed in the process of decision-making. Whereas many people defer continually to outside sources of influence when making decisions, fully functioning persons regard their organismic experiences as the most valid sources of information for deciding what to do in any given situation. Rogers put it succinctly when he said 'doing what "feels right" proves to be a . . . trustworthy guide to behaviour' (1961: 190). Further characteristics of the fully functioning person are concerned with the issues of personal freedom and creativity. For Rogers a mark of psychological health is the sense of responsibility for determining one's own actions and their consequences based on a feeling of freedom and power to choose from the many options that life presents. There is no feeling within the individual of being imprisoned by circumstances, or fate or genetic inheritance although this is not to suggest that Rogers denies the powerful influences of biological make-up, social forces or past experience. Subjectively, however, people experience themselves as free agents. Finally, the fully functioning person is typically creative in the sense that he or she can adjust to changing conditions and is likely to produce creative ideas or initiate creative projects and actions. Such people are unlikely to be conformists, although they will relate to society in a way which permits them to be fully involved without being imprisoned by convention or tradition.

Acquisition of psychological disturbance

In person-centred terminology the mother's requirement that the baby cease to howl constitutes a *condition of worth*: 'I shall love you if you do not howl'. The concept of conditions of worth bears a striking similarity to the British therapist George Lyward's notion of contractual living. Lyward believed that most of his disturbed adolescent clients had had no chance to contact their real selves because they were too busy attempting – usually in vain – to fulfil contracts, in order to win approval (Burn 1956). Lyward used to speak of usurped lives and Rogers in similar vein sees many individuals as the victims of countless internalized conditions of worth which have almost totally estranged them from their organismic experiencing. Such people will be preoccupied with a sense of strain at having to come up to the mark or with feelings of worthlessness at having failed to do so. They will be the victims of countless introjected conditions of worth so that they no longer have any sense of their inherent value as unique persons. The proliferation of introjections is an inevitable outcome of the desperate need for positive regard. Introjection is the process whereby the beliefs, judgements, attitudes or values of another person (most often the parent) are taken into the individual and become part of his or her armamentarium for coping with experience, however alien they may have been initially. The child, it seems, will do almost anything to satisfy the need for positive regard even if this means taking on board (introjecting) attitudes and beliefs which run quite counter to its own organismic reaction to experience. Once such attitudes and beliefs have become thoroughly absorbed into the personality they are said to have become internalized. Thus it is that introjection and internalization of conditions of worth imposed by significant others whose approval is desperately desired often constitute the gloomy road to a deeply negative self-concept as individuals discover that they can never come up to the high demands and expectations which such conditions inevitably imply.

Once this negative self-concept has taken root in an individual the likelihood is that the separation from the essential organismic self will become increasingly complete. It is as if individuals become cut off from their own inner resources and their own sense of value and are governed by a secondary and treacherous valuing process which is based on the internalization of other people's judgements and evaluations. Once caught in this trap the person is likely to become increasingly disturbed, for the negative self-concept induces behaviour which reinforces the image of inadequacy and worthlessness. It is a fundamental thesis of the person-centred point of view that behaviour is not only the result of what happens to us from the external world but also a function of how we feel about ourselves on the inside. In other words, we are likely to behave in accordance with our perception of ourselves. What we do is often an accurate reflection of how we evalute ourselves and if this evaluation is low our behaviour will be correspondingly unacceptable to ourselves and in all probability to others as well. It is likely, too, that we shall be highly conscious of a sense of inadequacy and although we may conceal this from others the awareness that all is not well will usually be with us.

The person-centred therapist recognizes, however, that psychological distur-bance is not always available to awareness. It is possible for a person to establish a self-concept which, because of the overriding need to win the approval of others, cannot permit highly significant sensory or visceral (a favourite word with Rogers) experience into consciousness. Such people cannot be open to the full range of their organismic experiencing because to be so would threaten the self-concept which must be maintained in order to win continuing favour. An example of such a person might be the man who has established a picture of himself as honourable, virtuous, responsible and loving. Such a man may be progressively divorced from those feelings which would threaten to undermine such a self-concept. He may arrive at a point where he no longer knows, for example, that he is angry or hostile or sexually hungry, for to admit to such feelings would be to throw his whole pic-ture of himself into question. Disturbed people therefore are by no means always aware of their disturbance nor will they necessarily be perceived as disturbed by others who may have a vested interest in maintaining what is in effect a tragic but often rigorous act of self-deception.

Perpetuation of psychological disturbance

It follows from the person-centred view of psychological disturbance that it will be perpetuated if an individual continues to be dependent to a high degree on the judgement of others for a sense of self-worth. Such persons will be at pains to preserve and defend at all costs the self-concept which wins approval and esteem and will be thrown into anxiety and confusion whenever incongruity arises between the self-concept and actual experience. In the example above the 'virtuous' man would be subject to feelings of threat and confusion if he directly experienced his hostility or sexual hunger, although to do so would, of course, be a first step towards the recovery of contact with the organismic self. He will be likely, however, to avoid the threat and confusion by resorting to one or other of two basic mechanisms of defence – perceptual distortion or denial. In this way he avoids confusion and anxiety and thereby perpetuates his disturbance while mistakenly believing that he is maintaining his integrity. Perceptual distortion takes place whenever an incongruent experience is allowed into awareness but only in a form that is in harmony with the person's current self-concept. The virtuous man, for instance, might permit himself to experience hostility but would distort this as a justifiable reaction to wickedness in others: for him his hostility would be rationalized into righteous indignation. Denial is a less common defence but is in some ways the more impregnable. In this case individuals preserve their self-concept by completely avoiding any conscious recognition of experiences or feelings which threaten them. The virtuous man would therefore be totally unaware of his constantly angry attitudes in a committee meeting and might perceive himself as simply speaking with truth and sincerity. Distortion and denial can have formidable psychological consequences and can sometimes protect a person for a lifetime from the confusion and anxiety which could herald the recovery of contact with the alienated self.

Change

For people who are trapped by a negative self-concept and by behaviour which tends to demonstrate and even reinforce the validity of such a self-assessment, there is little hope of positive change unless there is movement in the psychological environment which surrounds them. Most commonly this will be the advent of a new person on the scene or a marked change in attitude of someone who is already closely involved. A child, for example, may be abused and ignored at home but may discover, to her initial bewilderment, that her teachers respect and like her. If she gradually acquires the courage to trust this unexpected acceptance she may be fortunate enough to gain further reassurance through the discovery that her teachers' respect for her is not dependent on her 'being a good girl'. For the young adult a love relationship can often revolutionize the self-concept. A girl who has come to think of herself as both stupid and ugly will find such a self-concept severely challenged by a young man who both enjoys her conversation and finds her physically desirable. There are, of course, dangers in this situation, for if the man's ardour rapidly cools and he abandons her the young woman's negative self-concept may be mightily reinforced by this painful episode. Where love runs deep, however, the beloved may be enabled to rediscover contact with the organismic core of her being and to experience her own essential worth. For clients beginning therapy the most important fact initially is the entry of a new person (the therapist) into their psychological environment. As we shall see it is the quality of this new person and the nature of the relationship which the therapist offers that will ultimately determine whether or not change will ensue.

Practice

Goals of therapy

The person-centred therapist seeks to establish a relationship with a client in which the latter can gradually dare to face the anxiety and confusion which inevitably arise once the self-concept is challenged by the movement into awareness of experiences which do not fit its current configuration. If such a relationship can be achieved the client can then hope to move beyond the confusion and gradually to experience the freedom to choose a way of being which approximates more closely to his or her deepest feelings and values. The therapist will therefore focus not on problems and solutions but on communion or on what has been described as a person-in-person relationship (Boy and Pine 1982: 129). Person-centred therapists do not hesitate therefore to invest themselves freely and fully in the relationship with their clients. They believe that they will gain entrance into the world of the client through an emotional commitment in which they are willing to involve themselves as people and to reveal themselves, if appropriate, with their own strengths and weaknesses. For the person-centred therapist a primary goal is to see, feel and experience the world as the client sees, feels and experiences it and this is not possible if the therapist stands aloof and maintains a psychological distance in the interests of a quasi-scientific objectivity.

The theoretical end-point of person-centred therapy must be the fully functioning person who is' the embodiment of psychological health and whose primary characteristics were outlined above. It would be fairly safe to assert that no client has achieved such an end-point and that no therapist has been in a position to model such perfection. On the other hand there is now abundant evidence, not only from the USA but also, for example, from the extensive research activities of Reinhard Tausch and his colleagues at Hamburg University (Tausch 1975) that clients undergoing person-centred therapy frequently demonstrate similar changes. From my own experience I can also readily confirm the perception of client movement that Rogers and other person-centred practitioners have repeatedly noted. A listing of these perceptions will show that for many clients the achievement of any one of the developments recorded could well constitute a 'goal' of therapy and might for the time being at least constitute a valid and satisfactory reason for terminating therapy. Clients in person-centred therapy are often perceived to move, then, in the following directions:

1 away from facades and the constant preoccupation with keeping up appearances
2 away from 'oughts' and an internalized sense of duty springing from externally imposed obligations
3 away from living up to the expectations of others
4 towards valuing honesty and 'realness' in oneself and others
5 towards valuing the capacity to direct one's own life
6 towards accepting and valuing one's self and one's feelings whether they are positive or negative
7 towards valuing the experience of the moment and the process of growth rather than continually striving for objectives
8 towards a greater respect for and understanding of others
9 towards a cherishing of close relationships and a longing for more intimacy
10 towards a valuing of all forms of experience and a willingness to risk being open to all inner and outer experiences however uncongenial or unexpected.
(Frick 1971: 179)

Selection criteria

Person-centred therapy has proved its effectiveness with clients of many kinds presenting a wide range of difficulties and concerns. Its usefulness even with psychotics was established many years ago when Rogers and his associates participated in an elaborate investigation of the effect of psychotherapy on schizophrenics. Rogers himself, however, offered the opinion that psychotherapy of any kind, including person-centred therapy, is probably of the greatest help to the people who are closest to a reasonable adjustment to life. It is my own belief that the limitations of person-centred therapy reside not in the approach itself but in the limitations of particular therapists and in their ability or lack of it to offer their clients the necessary conditions for change and development. Having said this I freely admit that in my own experience there are certain kinds of clients who are unlikely to be much helped by the approach. Such people are usually somewhat rigid and authoritarian in their attitude to life. They look for certainties, for secure structures and often for experts to direct them in how they should be and what they should do. Their craving for such direction often makes it difficult for them to relate to the person-centred therapist in such a way that they can begin to get in touch with their own inner resources. Overly intellectual or logically rational people may also find it difficult to engage in the kind of relationship encouraged by person-centred therapy, where often the greatest changes result from a preparedness to face painful and confusing feelings which cannot initially be clearly articulated. Clients falling into these categories often turn out to be poorly motivated in any case and not infrequently they have been referred in desperation by an overworked medical practitioner, priest or social worker. Inarticulacy is in itself no barrier to effective therapeutic work, for inarticulate people are often brimming over with unexpressed feeling which begins to pour out once a relationship of trust has been established.

Clients who perhaps have most to gain from person-centred therapy are those who are strongly motivated to face painful feelings and who are deeply committed to change. They are prepared to take emotional risks and they want to trust even if they are fearful of intimacy. In my own work I often ask myself three questions as I consider working with a prospective client:

1 Is the client really desirous of change?
2 Is the client prepared to share responsibility for our work together?
3 Is the client willing to get in touch with his or her feelings, however difficult that may be?

Reassuring answers to these three questions are usually reliable indicators that person-centred therapy is likely to be beneficial.

The person-centred approach has made significant contributions to small group and large group work and the person-centred therapy group (with two therapists or 'facilitators') is a common modality. Clients who give evidence of at least some degree of self-acceptance and whose self-concept is not entirely negative may well be encouraged (but never obliged) to join a group from the outset. More commonly, however, membership of a counselling group will occur at the point when a client in individual therapy is beginning to experience a measure of self-affirmation and is keen to take further risks in relating. At such a stage membership of a group may replace individual therapy or may be undertaken concurrently. In all cases it is the client who will decide whether to seek group membership and whether or not this should replace or complement individual therapy.

The person-centred therapist will be at pains to ensure that a client whose self-concept it very low is not plunged into a group setting prematurely. Such an experience could have the disastrous outcome of reinforcing the client's sense of worthlessness. In such cases individual therapy is almost invariably indicated.

Person-centred therapists can work successfully with couples and with family groups but in these contexts much will depend on the therapist's ability to create the environment in which the couple or the family members can interact with each other without fear. In order for this to be possible it is likely that the therapist will undertake extensive preparatory work with each individual in a one-to-one relationship. Ultimately the principal criterion for embarking on couple or family therapy (apart, of course, from the willingness of all members to participate) is the therapist's confidence in his or her own ability to relate authentically to each member. Such confidence is unlikely to be achieved in the absence of in-depth preliminary meetings with each person involved. Indeed, in couple therapy it is common for the therapist to agree to work for a negotiated period with each partner separately before all three come together in order to tackle the relationship directly. With a family the process is clearly more complex and the preparatory work even more time-consuming. Perhaps this is the main reason why person-centred family therapy remains comparatively rare. In a sense it is therapists who select themselves for such work and not the clients who are selected.

Qualities of effective therapists

It has often been suggested that of all the various 'schools' of psychotherapy the person-centred approach makes the heaviest demands upon the therapist. Whether this is so or not I have no way of knowing. What I do know is that unless person-centred therapists can relate in such a way that their clients perceive them as trustworthy and dependable *as people*, therapy cannot take place. Person-centred therapists can have no recourse to diagnostic labelling nor can they find security in a complex and detailed theory of personality which will allow them to foster 'insight' in their clients through interpretation however gently offered. In brief, they cannot win their clients' confidence by demonstrating their psychological expertise for to do so would be to place yet another obstacle in the way of clients' movement towards trusting their own innate resources. To be a trustworthy person is not something which can be simulated for very long and in a very real sense person-centred therapists can only be as trustworthy for another as they are for themselves. Therapists' attitudes to themselves thus become of cardinal importance. If I am to be acceptant of another's feelings and experiences and to be open to the possible expression of material long since blocked off from awareness I must feel a deep level of acceptance for myself. If I cannot trust myself to acknowledge and accept my own feelings without adverse judgement or self-recrimination it is unlikely that I shall appear sufficiently trustworthy to a client who may have much deeper cause to feel ashamed or worthless. If, too, I am in constant fear that I shall be overwhelmed by an upsurging of unacceptable data into my own awareness then I am unlikely to convey to my client that I am genuinely open to the full exploration of his own doubts and fears.

The ability of the therapist to be genuine, accepting and empathic (fundamental attitudes in person-centred therapy which will be explored more fully later) is not developed overnight. It is unlikely, too, that such an ability will be present in people who are not continually seeking to broaden their own life experience. No therapist can confidently invite his client to travel further than he has journeyed himself but for the person-centred therapist the quality, depth and continuity of his own experiencing becomes the very cornerstone of the competence which he brings to his professional activity. Unless I have a sense of my own continuing development as a person I shall lose faith in the process of becoming and shall be tempted to relate to my clients in a way which may well reinforce them in a past self-concept. What is more I shall myself become stuck in a past image of myself and will no longer be in contact with that part of my organism which challenges me to go on growing as a person even if my body is beginning to show every sign of wearing out. It follows, too, that an excessive reliance on particular skills for relating or communicating can present a subtle trap because such skills may lead to a professional behavioural pattern which is itself resistant to change because it becomes set or stylized.

Therapeutic style

Person-centred therapists differ widely in therapeutic style. They share in common, however, a desire to create a climate of facilitative psychological attitudes in which clients can begin to get in touch with their own wisdom and their capacity for self-understanding and for altering their self-concept and self-defeating behaviours. For person-centred therapists their ability to establish this climate is crucial to the whole therapeutic enterprise, since if they fail to do so there is no hope of forming the kind of relationship with their clients which will bring about the desired therapeutic movement. It will become apparent, however, that the way in which they attempt to create and convey the necessary climate will depend very much on the nature of their own personality.

The first element in the creation of the climate has to do with what has variously been called the therapist's *genuineness*, realness, authenticity or congruence. In essence this realness depends on therapists' capacities for being properly in touch with the complexity of feelings, thoughts and attitudes which will be flowing through them as they seek to track their clients' thoughts and feelings. The more they can do this the more they will be perceived by their clients as people of real flesh and blood who are willing to be seen and known and not as clinical professionals intent on concealing themselves behind a metaphorical white coat. The issue of the therapist's genuineness is more complex, however, than might initially appear. Although clients need to experience their therapists' essential humanity and to feel their emotional involvement they certainly do not need to have all the therapist's feelings and thoughts thrust down their throats. Therapists therefore must not only attempt to remain firmly in touch with the flow of their own experience but must also have the discrimination to know how and when to communicate what they are experiencing. It is here that to the objective observer person-centred therapists might well appear to differ widely in style. In my own attempts to be congruent, for example, I find that verbally I often communicate little. I am aware, however, that my bodily posture does convey a deep willingness to be involved with my client and that my eyes are highly expressive of a wide range of feeling – often to the point of tears. It would seem therefore that in my own case there is frequently little need for me to communicate my feelings verbally: I am transparent enough already and I know from experience that my clients are sensitive to this transparency. Another therapist might well behave in a manner far removed from mine but with the same concern to be genuine. Therapists are just as much unique human beings as their clients and the way in which they make their humanity available by following the flow of their own experiencing and communicating it when appropriate will be an expression of their own uniqueness. Whatever the precise form of their behaviour, however, person-centred therapists will be exercising their skill in order to communicate to their clients an attitude expressive of their desire to be deeply and fully involved in the relationship without pretence and without the protection of professional impersonality.

For many clients entering therapy, the second attitude of importance in creating a facilitative climate for change – *total acceptance* – may seem to be the most critical. The conditions of worth which have in so many cases warped and undermined the self-concept of the client so that it bears little relation to the actualizing organism are the outcome of the judgemental and conditional attitudes of those close to the client which have often been reinforced by societal or cultural norms. In contrast, the therapist seeks to offer the client an unconditional acceptance, a positive regard or caring, a non-possessive love. This acceptance is not of the person as she might become, a respect for her as yet unfulfilled potential, but a total and unconditional acceptance of the client as she seems to herself *in the present*. Such an attitude on the part of the therapist cannot be simulated and cannot be offered by someone who remains largely frightened or threatened by feelings in himself. Nor again can such acceptance be offered by someone who is disturbed when confronted by a person who possesses values, attitudes and feelings different from his own. Genuine acceptance is totally unaffected by differences of background or belief system between client and therapist, for it is in no way dependent on moral, ethical or social criteria. As with genuineness, however, the attitude of acceptance requires great skill on the part of the therapist if it is to be communicated at the depth which will enable clients to feel safe to be whatever they are currently experiencing. After what may well be a lifetime of highly conditional acceptance clients will not recognize unconditionality easily. When they do they will tend to regard it as a miracle which will demand continual checking out before it can be fully trusted. The way in which a therapist conveys unconditional acceptance will again be dependent to a large extent on the nature of his or her personality. For my own part I have found increasingly that the non-verbal aspects of my responsiveness are powerfully effective. A smile can often convey more acceptance than a statement which, however sensitive, may still run the risk of seeming patronizing. I have discovered, too, that the gentle pressing of the hand or the light touch on the knee will enable clients to realize that all is well and that there will be no judgement however confused or negative they are or however silent and hostile.

The third facilitative attitude is that of *empathic understanding*. Rogers (1975) himself wrote extensively about empathy and suggested that of the three 'core conditions' (as genuineness, acceptance and empathy are often known), empathy is the most trainable. The crucial importance of empathic understanding springs from the person-centred therapist's overriding concern with the client's subjective perceptual world. Only through as full an understanding as possible of the way in which clients view themselves and the world can the therapist hope to encourage the subtle changes in self-concept which make for growth. Such understanding involves on the therapist's part a willingness to enter the private perceptual world of the client and to become thoroughly conversant with it. This demands a high degree of sensitivity to the moment-to-moment experiencing of the client so that the therapist is recognized as a reliable companion even when contradictory feelings follow on each other in rapid succession. In a certain sense therapists must lay themselves aside for the time being with all their prejudices and values if they are to enter into the perceptual world of the other. Such an undertaking would be foolhardy if the therapist feels insecure in the presence of a particular client for there would be the danger of getting lost in a perhaps frightening or confusing world. The task of empathic understanding can be accomplished only by people who are secure enough in their own identity to move into another's world without the fear of being overwhelmed by it. Once there therapists have to move around with extreme delicacy and with an utter absence of judgement. They will probably sense meanings of which the client is scarcely aware and might even become dimly aware of feelings of which there is no consciousness on the part of the client at all. Such moments call for extreme caution for there is the danger that the therapist could express understanding at too deep a level and frighten the client away from therapy altogether. Rogers, on a recording made for *Psychology Today* in the 1970s, described such a blunder as 'blitz therapy' and contrasted this with an empathic response which is constructive because it conveys an understanding of what is currently going on in the client and of meanings that are just below the level of awareness but does not slip over into unconscious motivations which frighten the client.

If the communication of genuineness and acceptance presents difficulties the communication of empathic understanding is even more challenging. In this domain there can, I believe, be less reliance on non-verbal signals. Often a client's inner world is complex and confusing as well as a source of pain and guilt. Sometimes clients have little understanding of their own feelings. Therapists need therefore to marshal the full range of their emotional and cognitive abilities if they are to convey their understanding thoroughly. On the other hand if they do not succeed there is ample evidence to suggest that their very attempt to do so, however bumbling and incomplete, will be experienced by the client as supportive and validating. What is always essential is the therapist's willingness to check out the accuracy of his understanding. I find my own struggles at communicating empathic understanding are littered with such questions as 'Am I getting it right? Is that what you mean?' When I do get a complex feeling right the effect is often electrifying and the sense of wonder and thankfulness in the client can be one of the most moving experiences in therapy. There can be little doubt that the rarity of empathic understanding of this kind is what endows it with such power and makes it the most reliable force for creative change in the whole of the therapeutic process.

It was Rogers's contention – and he held firm to it for over forty years – that if the therapist proves able to offer a facilitative climate where genuineness, acceptance and empathy are all present then therapeutic movement will almost invariably occur. In such a climate clients will gradually get in touch with their own resources for self-understanding and will prove capable of changing their self-concept and taking over the direction of their life. Therapists need only to be faithful companions, following the lead which their clients provide and staying with them for as long as is necessary. Nothing in my own experience leads me to dispute Rogers's contention that the core conditions are both necessary and sufficient for therapeutic movement, although I have argued that when a fourth quality is present, which I have defined as tenderness, then something qualitatively different may occur (Thorne 1985). This fourth quality is characterized chiefly by an ability on the part of the therapist to move between the worlds of the physical, the emotional, the cognitive and the mystical without strain and by a willingness to accept and celebrate the desire to love and to be loved if and when it appears in the therapeutic relationship. I cite my own thinking as evidence for the fact that person-centred theory and practice is in no sense a closed system and is constantly being refined and developed by person-centred practitioners.

Major therapeutic strategies and techniques

There are no strategies or techniques which are integral to the person-centred approach. Person-centred therapy is essentially based on the experiencing and communication of attitudes and these attitudes cannot be packaged up in techniques. At an earlier point in the history of the approach there was an understandable emphasis on the ebb and flow of the therapeutic interview and much was gained from the microscopic study of client-therapist exchanges. To Rogers's horror, however, the tendency to focus on the therapist's responses had the effect of so debasing the approach that it became known as a technique. Even nowadays it is possible to meet people who believe that person-centred therapy is simply the technique of reflecting the client's feelings or, worse still, that it is primarily a matter of repeating the last words spoken by the client. I hope I have shown that nothing could be further from the truth. The attitudes required of the therapist demand the highest level of self-knowledge and self-acceptance and the translation of them into communicable form requires of each therapist the most delicate skill which for the most part must spring from his or her unique personality and cannot be learned through pale imitations of Carl Rogers or anyone else.

In a recent work (Mearns and Thorne 1988) a colleague and I have drawn attention to the fact that the most productive outcomes seem to result from therapeutic relationships which move through three distinct phases. The first stage is characterized by the establishing of *trust* on the part of the client. This may happen very rapidly or it can take months. The second stage sees the development of *intimacy* during which the client is enabled to reveal some of the deepest levels of his experiencing. The third stage is characterized by an increasing *mutuality* between therapist and client. When such a stage is reached it is likely that therapists will be increasingly self-disclosing and will be challenged to risk more of themselves in the relationship. When it occurs this three-stage process is so deeply rewarding for the therapist that a cynical critic might view it as the outcome of an unconscious strategizing on the therapist's part. So insidious is this accusation that I am now deeply concerned to monitor my own behaviour with the utmost vigilance in order to ensure that I am *not* embarked on a manipulative plot which is aimed at achieving a mutuality which may be deeply satisfying for me but quite irrelevant to the client's needs.

The change process in therapy

When person-centred therapy goes well clients will move from a position where their self-concept, typically poor at the entry into therapy and finding expression in behaviour which is reinforcing of the negative evaluation of self, will shift to a position where it more closely approaches the essential worth of the organismic self. As the self-concept moves towards a more positive view so, too, clients' behaviour begins to reflect the improvement and to enhance further their perception of themselves. The therapist's ability to create a relationship in which the three facilitative attitudes are consistently present will to a large extent determine the extent to which clients are able to move towards a more positive perception of themselves and to the point where they are able to be in greater contact with the promptings of the organismic self.

If therapy has been successful clients will also have learned how to be their own therapist. It seems that when people experience the genuineness of another and a real attentive caring and valuing by that other person they begin to adopt the same attitude towards themselves. In short, a person who is cared for begins to feel at a deep level that perhaps she is after all *worth* caring for. In a similar way, the experience of being on the receiving end of the concentrated listening and the empathic understanding which characterize the therapist's response tends to develop a listening attitude in the client towards herself. It is as if she gradually becomes less afraid to get in touch with what is going on inside her and dares to listen attentively to her own feelings. With this growing attentiveness there comes increased self-understanding and a tentative grasp of some of her most central personal meanings. Many clients have told me that after person-centred therapy they never lose this ability to treat themselves with respect and to take the risk of listening to what they are experiencing. If they do lose it temporarily or find themselves becoming hopelessly confused they will not hesitate to return to therapy to engage once more in the process which is in many ways an education for living.

In Rogers and Dymond (1954) one of Rogers's chapters explores in detail a client's successful process through therapy. The case of Mrs Oak has become a rich source of learning for person-centred therapists ever since and towards the end of the chapter Rogers attempts a summary of the therapeutic process which Mrs Oak has experienced with such obvious benefits to herself. What is described there seems to me to be so characteristic of the person-centred experience of therapy that I make no apology for providing a further summary of some of Rogers's findings.

The process begins with the therapist's providing an atmosphere of warm caring and acceptance which over the first few sessions is gradually experienced by the client, Mrs Oak, as genuinely *safe*. With this realization the client finds that she changes the emphasis of her sessions from dealing with reality problems to experiencing herself. The effect of this change of emphasis is that she begins to experience her feelings in the immediate present without inhibition. She can be angry, hurt, childish, joyful, self-deprecating, self-appreciative and as she allows this to occur she discovers many feelings bubbling through into awareness of which she was not previously conscious. With new feelings there come new thoughts and the admission of all this fresh material to awareness leads to a *breakdown of the previously held self-concept*. There then follows a period of disorganization and confusion although there remains a feeling that the path is the right one and that reorganization will ultimately take place. What is being learned during this process is that it pays to recognize an experience for what it is rather than denying it or distorting it. In this way the client becomes more open to experience and begins to realize that it is healthy to accept feelings whether they be positive or negative, for this permits a movement towards greater completeness. At this stage the client increasingly comes to realize that *she can begin to define herself and does not have to accept the definition and judgements of others*. There is, too, a more conscious appreciation of the nature of the relationship with the therapist and the value of a love which is not possessive and makes no demands. At about this stage the client finds that she can make relationships outside of therapy which enable others to be self-experiencing and self-directing and she becomes progressively aware that at the core of her being she is not destructive but genuinely desires the well-being of others. Self-responsibility continues to increase to the point where the client feels able to make her own choices – although this is not always pleasant – and to trust herself in a world which, although it may often seem to be disintegrating, yet offers many opportunities for creative activity and relating (Rogers 1954).

Limitations of the approach

After twenty years as a person-centred therapist I am drawn to the conclusion, as I stated earlier, that the limitations of the approach are a reflection of the personal limitations of the therapist. As these will clearly vary from individual to individual and are unlikely to be constant over time I am sceptical about the usefulness of exploring the limitations of the approach in any generalized fashion. None the less I am intrigued by the question with respect to two particular issues. I believe that person-centred therapy may be in danger of selling itself short because of its traditional emphasis on the 'here and now' and because of what is seen as its heavy reliance on verbal interaction. Both these tendencies are likely to be reinforced when the therapist's congruence remains at a relatively superficial level.

In my own practice I have discovered that the more I am able to be fully present to myself in the therapeutic relationship the more likely it is that I shall come to trust the promptings of a deeper and more intuitive level within myself. Cautiously and with constant safeguards against self-deception I have come to value this intuitive part of my being and to discover its efficacy in the therapeutic relationship. (For a further discussion of this issue see my chapter in *Key Cases in Psychotherapy*: Thorne 1987.) What is more, when I have risked articulating a thought or feeling which emanates from this deeper level I have done so in the full knowledge that it may appear unconnected to what is currently happening in the relationship or even bizarre to my client. More often than not, however, the client's response has been immediate and sometimes dramatic. It is as if the quality of the relationship which has been established, thanks to the powerful offering of the core conditions, goes a long way towards ensuring that my own intuitive promptings are deeply and immediately significant for the client. Often, too, the significance lies in the triggering of past experience for the client – not in the sense simply of looking at memories of past events but in releasing a veritable flow of feeling whose origin lies in past experience which is then vividly re-lived. Commonly, too, the therapist's intuitive response seems to touch a part of the client's being which cannot find immediate expression in words. I am astonished, too, how often at such moments the client reaches out for physical reassurance or plunges into deep but overflowing silence or even requests materials for writing or sketching.

The person-centred approach is frequently applauded for its usefulness in promoting beneficial changes in self-concept and criticized at the same time for its failure to change behaviour. There may well be some truth in this judgement but I do not believe that this limitation is inherent to the approach. I am increasingly convinced that it is in the area of therapist congruence that the greatest advances can and should be made. In my own case this has meant a developing trust in my intuitive responses and the discovery that for my client this has often resulted in a profound re-living of past experience and an engagement with me on a non-verbal level which has proved remarkably productive. These outcomes, not commonly associated with the person-centred approach as it has been traditionally practised, are, of course, powerfully conducive to behavioural change both within and beyond the therapeutic relationship. This having been said I suspect that clients who are in the grips of behavioural disorders such as phobias or obsessive compulsive neuroses are unlikely to be much helped by person-centred therapy unless, that is, they conceptualize their difficulties as being an outcome of their way of being in the world. If, as is often the case, they view their disorder as a disability to be cured then they are more likely to be rewarded by a visit to the nearest behavioural therapist.

Case example

The client

Louise, a married postgraduate student in her mid-20s, presented herself for the first time at the university counselling service in the early autumn. She had been persuaded to come by her GP. She seemed taut and uncertain and began smoking within minutes of the start of the interview. She announced in a somewhat staccato fashion that she had a long history of tension and anxiety and was determined to tackle this directly. Recent asthma attacks had further strengthened her motivation to do something about her 'screwed-up' state. As if to reassure me that not everything was negative she added the astonishing information that she had cured herself of a stammer and was an absolute expert at evolving strategies for coping. In fact, she was constantly preoccupied with the detailed working out of such schemes and strategies.

All this came out in an enormous rush with Louise scarcely seeming to draw breath; nor did she look at me much during her monologue. When she stopped it was to convey to me that she was sceptical about the likely value of counselling and to ask me what I thought about continuing with her.

The therapy

I was astonished by the strength of feeling within myself during these opening minutes. I was aware of a deep compassion for Louise and of sheer admiration at the way in which she was apparently holding her life together despite the great cost she was paying in tension and anxiety. I was also conscious of the difficulty of making contact with her. She seemed almost incarcerated in her anxiety and therefore insulated from me. I responded to her scepticism about the value of therapy by describing my own approach with particular reference to the core conditions and by suggesting that she might like to consider an 'experimental' period of, say, four sessions at the end of which she could decide whether she would like to continue. The proposal seemed to reassure her and for the first time she relaxed a little. She then began to talk about her earlier years and especially about the difficult relationship with her parents.

When she left I felt puzzled. I had no idea how she had experienced the session nor did I feel that I had made much contact. I was sure, however, that I liked her and only hoped that she had sensed something of my respect for and acceptance of her. When she came a fortnight later for the first of three weekly sessions, I made what could have been a costly mistake. For some reason I needed to prove to this highly intelligent woman that I, too, was intellectually alert. I made prodigious efforts to empathize with her thought processes and constantly interjected 'understanding' responses. Almost every time I miscued disastrously. It seemed as if her frame of reference was so removed from my own that the more I tried to come alongside her the more elusive she became. Somewhat crestfallen I gave up, stopped trying to be empathic and contented myself with listening and simply being present to her. As in the first session, she began to relax at this and talked at length about her annual depressive bouts, sometimes lasting weeks and involving almost total withdrawal, which invariably began in the month of February. She spoke of the effect of these bouts on her marriage and of her concern for her husband, even though she was not at all sure that she actually loved him.

In the third session Louise began to look me in the eye for the first time. There was a new liveliness about her which did not seem fuelled by her anxiety. She told me that she was rather proud of the way in which she had coped with much of her adult life, especially with motherhood and its demands. She smiled at this and actually exuded the confidence which she was expressing. A few minutes later, however, she took me quite by surprise by plunging into the most painful recollections of her childhood and adolescence. There was no way, it seemed, in which she could win her parents' approval. Two stories exemplified her predicament. Her parents apparently admired those who had the courage to own up to their misdemeanours. Louise therefore concluded that she should deliberately commit an offence so that she could own up to it and thus win her parents' love. She stole biscuits and then openly admitted the theft. The plan, of course, backfired and she was punished for her criminal behaviour. On another occasion she achieved outstanding results in her O level examinations only to be told by her father that it was typical of her to excel in the wrong subjects.

After this third session I found myself profoundly moved at the process. I was aware of the fact that not only was Louise already prepared to experience deep feelings, both positive and negative, in my presence but also that she was doing so on only the flimsiest evidence of my capacity to receive and understand her. She seemed to be letting me or allowing me to experience directly that she was both strong and weak, coping and confused, self-affirming and yet craving for approval. What is more I began dimly to perceive that it was these apparent contradictions which made life intolerable for her. It was as if she experienced herself as many conflicting elements and could consequently find no firm identity on which to build.

During the weeks which followed (she was in no doubt after the fourth session that she wished to continue) Louise experienced breathless attacks in my presence and short periods of agitation when she would shake or chain-smoke. She even ran out on one occasion because the fear of suffocation was so overwhelming. Gradually, however, it became clear that her life outside the counselling room was becoming increasingly satisfactory to her. She was making friendships at a deeper level than ever before. She had overcome her awe of her academic supervisor and as Christmas approached she coped effectively with a visit from her parents. It was only in the seventh session that she referred directly to me and our relationship. In the most delicate way possible she indicated how much she had felt able to have confidence in me almost from the outset ('something about how you listen and how you sit') and that this permitted her to feel free to be whatever she happened to be and to 'leave things behind' with me in a way which was not possible even with her friends. Because I was clearly not out to pass judgement she felt able to experiment freely with the situation and to take risks which would not have been possible in the 'real' world.

By the time February arrived (the month of the cyclical depression) Louise seemed in fine fettle. She declared that she seldom now engineered particular responses from others and that she no longer saw herself as a permanently anxious person. On the other hand she was still aware of tension within herself and wondered if this might be to do with blocked energy. This was the prelude to a period of intense self-exploration during which she discovered new resources in herself and became deeply involved in student politics and radical activism. Perhaps more importantly, she began to face her feelings about her marriage and to acknowledge her dissatisfaction with many aspects of it. One day she appeared in different clothes and announced that she now felt happy about the person she was discovering herself to be and that other people seemed to like her, too.

By the beginning of May it seemed that Louise was approaching the end of therapy. She admitted that she came now to her weekly sessions mainly because she enjoyed them rather than because she needed them. Completely taken in by this apparent breakthrough into psychological health, I asked Louise if she would be interested in working with me on a new video project in which I had been asked to participate with a long-term client. She readily agreed and the fact that the project would require us to spend many hours together as we travelled to another university some distance away seemed to make the proposal all the more attractive to her. Five days later (and a week before the video was due to be made) I was telephoned in alarm by one of Louise's close friends, who reported that Louise had cut her wrist and was hopelessly drunk. The following day Louise herself arrived unexpectedly and asked to be seen as an emergency. She was totally incoherent, unable to focus and clearly very frightened. Although her behaviour was bizarre in the extreme I found myself able to contain my own anxiety, to hold her silently for some minutes and to let her go at the end of the session although she literally staggered from the building and remained slumped against the wall outside for a further half-hour before moving off. The agitation of others in a neighbouring building was such that I went out to her during this period and asked if she could manage. 'I shall be all right', she said although she was crying. An hour or so later she sent a message from the university's Health Centre to assure me that she was not in danger.

It is clear in retrospect that for Louise this was her final test of my acceptance of her and of my trust in her own inner resources. I am not suggesting that she consciously planned the whole episode and it is evident that she experienced great fear as she allowed herself to move into chaos. Suffice it to say that four days later we travelled together to make the video film and actually spent almost eight hours in each other's company, during which we established a depth of mutuality which had not been possible previously. (Readers who are interested in seeing the video can purchase it or hire it from the Audio Visual Services Department, University of Leicester.)

Therapy continued for another ten months during which time Louise fell deeply in love, faced the complexities of her marriage and found a new direction for her life. To all intents and purposes hers is a success story. For me, however, the experience of working with her reinforced in a moving and dramatic way the truth that the client knows best even if this means, as in Louise's case, the rejection of coping behaviours and the descent into chaos. What is more my relationship with her showed me that as a therapist I can be taken completely by surprise and make apparently profound errors of judgement without losing the privilege of being a faithful companion who goes on trying to be accepting, empathic and open to the flow of my own experiencing within a relationship.

References

Boy, A.V. and Pine, G.J. (1982) *Client-Centered Counseling: A Renewal*, Boston, Mass: Allyn & Bacon.

Burn, M. (1956) *Mr Lyward's Answer*, London: Hamish Hamilton.

Frick, W.B. (1971) *Humanistic Psychology: Interviews with Maslow, Murphy and Rogers*, Columbus, Ohio: Charles E. Merrill.

Kirschenbaum, H. (1979) *On Becoming Carl Rogers*, New York: Delacorte Press.

Mearns, D. and Thorne, B.J. (1988) *Person-Centred Counselling in Action*, London and Beverly Hills, Calif: Sage.

Nelson-Jones, R. (1982) *The Theory and Practice of Counselling Psychology*, London: Holt, Rinehart & Winston.

Oatley, K. (1981) The self with others: the person and the interpersonal context in the approaches of C.R. Rogers and R.D. Laing, in F. Fransella (ed.) *Personality*, London: Methuen.

Rogers, C.R. (1954) The case of Mrs Oak: a research analysis, in C.R. Rogers and R.F. Dymond (eds) *Psychology and Personality Change*, Chicago, Ill: University of Chicago Press.

—— (1961) *On Becoming a Person*, Boston: Houghton Mifflin.

—— (1964) 'Towards a modern approach to values: the valuing process in the mature person', *Journal of Abnormal and Social Psychology*, 68, 4: 160–7.

—— (1974) In retrospect: forty-six years, *American Psychologist* 2: 115–23.

—— (1975) Empathic: an unappreciated way of being, *The Counseling Psychologist* 2: 2–10.

—— (1979) The foundations of the person-centered approach, unpublished manuscript.

Rogers, C.R. and Dymond, R.F. (eds) (1954) *Psychology and Personality Change*, Chicago, Ill: University of Chicago Press.

Tausch, R. (1975) Ergebnisse und Prozesse der klienten-zentrierten
   Gesprächspsychotherapie bei 550 Klienten und 115 Psychotherapeuten. Eine
   Zusammenfassung des Hamburger Forschungsprojektes, *Zeitschrift für Praktische
   Psychologie* 13: 293–307.
Thorne, B.J. (1985) *The Quality of Tenderness*, Norwich: Norwich Centre Occasional
   Publications.
—— (1987) Beyond the core conditions, in W. Dryden (ed.) *Key Cases in Psychotherapy*,
   Beckenham: Croom Helm.

Suggested further reading

Boy, A.V. and Pine, C.J. (1982) *Client-Centered Counseling: A Renewal*, Boston, Mass: Allyn
   & Bacon.
Mearns, D. and Thorne, B.J. (1988) *Person-Centred Counselling in Action*. London and
   Beverly Hills, Calif: Sage.
Rogers, C.R. (1951) *Client-Centered Therapy*, Boston, Mass: Houghton Mifflin.
—— (1961) *On Becoming a Person*, Boston, Mass: Houghton Mifflin.
—— (1980) *A Way of Being*, Boston, Mass: Houghton Mifflin.

7

Personal construct therapy

FAY FRANSELLA

Historical context and development in Britain

Historical context

Philosophers have argued about the nature of science and of human beings throughout the centuries, but never more vehemently than in the seventeenth and eighteenth. During this period two streams of thought were developing about the nature of human beings. First, Isaac Newton was expanding Galileo's methods of inquiry into the form we recognize today as scientific method. The entire cosmos was regarded as functioning like a perfect machine with precise laws governing its movements, so science was defined as the discovery of these laws by experiment. These thoughts pointed us in the direction of twentieth-century behaviourism and B.F. Skinner.

Then Immanuel Kant (1724–1804) rebelled against the prevailing ideas of these seventeenth-century philosophers, including Hobbes and Locke. In particular, he was against their emphasis on the essential passivity of the individual and the view of science that truth could be found 'out there' by applying the experimental methods of physics. Kant argued that individuals are active upon the world and have at least some control over their actions; also, that they are never able to perceive reality directly (the noumena) but only to see things filtered through *mental categories* (the phenomena). Thus Kant offers us the model of a person who is active rather than passive, and incapable of making direct contact with reality. The person cannot therefore be studied by the use of the scientific method as in physics but can be understood only through an examination of consciousness. This line of thinking led towards the whole humanistic movement and the theoretical formulations of George Kelly (1955).

Many of Kelly's ideas can be seen as springing directly from those of Kant, but there is an additional and very important source of influence: Vaihinger's (1924) 'as if'. Vaihinger suggested that since we have no way of gaining direct access to truth we should look at God and reality in a hypothetical way, 'as if' they were true. This appears as a fundamental idea in Kelly's own philosophy of *constructive alternativism* and his *psychology of personal constructs*.

Behaviourism dominated psychological thinking for the first sixty years of the twentieth century, and it is in this context that the development of Kelly's ideas should be considered. Immanuel Kant was a philosophical revolutionary; George Kelly was a psychological one. Just as Kant rebelled against the prevailing view that human beings are passive and powerless over their own destinies, so Kelly came to psychology at the time when the establishment view was behaviourism, with its doctrine of the essential passivity and powerlessness of humanity. Kelly (1969a) describes how he sat through endless lectures in his psychology course watching innumerable 'Stimulus→Response' pairs being written on the blackboard. He waited patiently for someone to discuss the nature of the arrow in between. They never did – at least, not to Kelly's satisfaction.

Kelly received his PhD in psychology – with particular emphasis on physiology – in the early 1930s. He became Professor and Director of Clinical Psychology at Ohio State University in 1946. However, in order to gain a fuller insight into the context in which his ideas developed it is important to know something of his earlier studies: in 1926 he obtained a BA degree in physics and mathematics, later a master's degree in educational sociology, and in 1930 a Bachelor of Education degree in Edinburgh.

Knowing now of his training in physics and mathematics, it comes as no surprise to find that Kelly's model of the person is couched in the language of science, as is his whole theory (see Fransella 1984 for a more detailed discussion of how training in physics may have influenced Kelly's theorizing). But it is important to bear in mind that his is a science based on the philosophy of *constructive alternativism*: a science in which there are no 'facts', only support for current hypotheses. These hypotheses may lead to others, which encompass new events, and so on. At some infinite moment in time we may learn all there is to know about the universe, for there *is* a reality 'out there'; but this is unlikely since the universe, like the person, is in a constant state of motion.

The person is a form of motion. Kelly's whole approach is about action, prediction and change. The client, for instance, may 'test out' alternative ways of making sense of the world in the relative safety of the consulting 'laboratory', using role-play or enactment. Here we find the influence of Moreno, who was developing his ideas on psychodrama when Kelly was formulating his theory.

Although certain threads running through Kelly's work bear a close resemblance to existentialist thinking, there is no evidence that translations of the works of Sartre and others were available in the USA in the late 1930s and early 1940s; in fact, it is very difficult to find out what precisely did influence Kelly, the man, in his formulation of one of the most comprehensive theories known to psychology.

Development in Britain

Kelly, an American, found receptive readers first and foremost in Britain, and there are many reasons why this might be so. Only in the 1980s has there been a quickening of interest in his work in its country of origin. Neimeyer (1983) has described its development in the context of the sociology of science. He uses

Mullins's (1973) model of the socio-historical development of new theory groups, which focuses on the changing patterns of communication.

The development of personal construct theory goes, according to Neimeyer, something like this. Before and for some time after the publication of Kelly's *magnum opus* in 1955, he and others worked largely in isolation. However, by 1966 workers in Britain had attained a *cluster* status; that is local groups with a minimum of seven people had developed plus a publication explosion. The major force behind the development of interest in the theory in Britain was the lecturing and publications of Don Bannister.

Neimeyer finds that by 1972 the major clusters in Britain were beginning to dissolve and that personal construct theory was steadily establishing itself as a mature speciality; by contrast, the USA and the rest of Europe started to enter the *cluster* stage of development only in the 1980s.

Up to 1978 there was surprisingly little work published on the application of personal construct psychology (PCP) to psychotherapy – surprising since this is its 'focus of convenience'. But things have now changed, and the quantity of publications in the therapy field is now considerable.

Interest is now world-wide. Conferences take place in Australia, the USA and Britain independently of the biennial international congresses which were started in 1975. The first centre devoted solely to teaching, therapy and the general application of personal construct theory was set up in London in 1982 founded by Fay Fransella.

Theoretical assumptions

Image of the person

Kelly suggests we might look at the person 'as if' you and I were scientists. By this he meant that we could all be seen as doing the same sorts of things that scientists traditionally do. We have theories about why things happen; erect hypotheses derived from these theories; and put these hypotheses to the test to see whether the predictions arising from them are validated or invalidated. We test our predictions by behaving. Viewing all behaviour 'as if' it were an experiment is one of Kelly's unique contributions to our understanding of the person.

Kelly's formulation of the psychology of personal constructs relates to this image of the person. He suggests that we might come to understand ourselves and others *in psychological terms* by studying the personal constructs we have each evolved in order to help us predict events in our personal worlds.

We approach the world not as it *is* but as it appears to us to be; we gaze at it through our construing *goggles*. We make predictions about events constantly and continually; there is no let-up. We are active beings, 'forms of motion'.

Construing is not all going on in the head though; we construe just as much with our bodies as with our minds. Kelly gives as an example our digestive system. Our stomach anticipates food, secretes gastric juices, behaves towards what it receives in an accepting manner if the food is in line with expectation, or rejects the food if it is not up to expectation and so forth. Kelly considered dualistic thinking a hindrance to our understanding of the person. At any given moment it is just as appropriate to ask what a person is feeling as what he is thinking, for many constructs (discriminations between events) have either been formed before we have formulated the words to express them or else the discriminations have never acquired verbal labels. Personal construct theory is thus a theory of human experiencing.

For example, a child may discriminate between types of voices; a harsh, grating voice and a soft, smooth one. The harsh, grating voice is related to feelings of reassurance, a large body to snuggle up to, and is there before the child goes to bed. The soft, smooth one gives conflicting messages; sometimes it is comforting like the harsh, grating one, but at other times – often when it is *particularly* soft and smooth – there are feelings of unease, of all not being well. Later, as an adult, that person may never be able to put into words exactly why he cannot abide women who have soft, smooth voices and why he himself has developed a harsh, grating one. His pre-verbal construing is thus being applied in adult life.

Conceptualization of psychological disturbance and health

Kelly argued fiercely against the use of the medical model in the field of psychological disorder. Like many others, he felt that those with psychological problems were not 'ill' and did not need to be 'treated' by medical doctors. He believed that the use of the medical model hampers our attempts to understand people and to help them deal with whatever it is that is troubling them. If there is no 'illness' there can be no 'health'.

Instead, he suggests that we might use the concept of *functioning*. A person who is functioning fully is one who is able to construe the world in such a way that predictions are, for the most part, validated. When invalidation *does* occur, the person deals with it by reconstruing. For example, you are at a party and go up to a stranger whom you construe as likely to be friendly. You start a general conversation and, before a few moments have passed, that 'friendly' person is arguing fiercely with you and being quite unpleasant. He is certainly not being 'friendly'. You have been invalidated in your prediction that this was a friendly person. If you are a well-functioning person, you will accept this invalidation and reconstrue the person, perhaps as someone who has a very deceptive facade and that you were stupid not to have seen through the veneer. You leave the incident behind you and put it down to *experience*.

But someone else, who is incapable of dealing with invalidation like that, may not come out so unscathed. She may become more and more embarrassed, flustered and bereft of words. She would then become increasingly anxious since she has been confronted by an event which she now has difficulty in construing at all. Not only is she unable to predict the outcome of this event, but also she finds she is increasingly unable to predict herself. The situation is a traumatic one. Hopefully, either someone will soon come to her rescue, or the stranger will move off. The person who experiences a considerable number of such predictive failures will often consider herself to 'have a problem'.

Another way of dealing with invalidation is to 'make' things work out the way we have predicted. When we do this we are being 'hostile' (extorting validational evidence for a social prediction that we have already seen to be a failure). For example, having construed the stranger as friendly, you might behave in such a way that he thought you were going to faint. He then puts his arm under your elbow to support you and guides you towards a chair. Now you can say to yourself: 'There you are! I knew he was really a friendly person!' Such hostility as this is well known in counselling and therapy, and will be discussed further later. Yet there is nothing essentially 'bad' about hostility; it is a way of dealing with events when our construing lets us down.

Nevertheless, the person who functions reasonably well is one who does not use too much hostility to deal with invalidation, does not find himself too often confronted by events he cannot construe (and thus be overwhelmed with anxiety), and whose system for construing the world has had potentially troublesome pre-verbal constructs 'up-dated'. This means that he has been able to explore, at some level of awareness, those early childhood discriminations. For instance, is it valid, in adult life, to take an instant dislike to people who have soft, smooth voices? Perhaps the construction does not now lead to useful predictions.

Acquisition of psychological disturbance

Kelly argued theoretically that the person is an integrated, indivisible whole; but that does *not* mean that individuals necessarily see themselves that way. Many of us are dualists in the way we understand ourselves. Likewise, it makes no theoretical sense to ask how a disturbance in construing is acquired; since personal construct theory takes the position that we act upon the world and construe (predict) events in the world, we cannot 'acquire' something as if we were buying it in a shop or having it imposed upon us, like measles.

Yet a client may construe his vomiting, for instance, as a 'bodily symptom' which he 'acquired' as a result of some stressful psychological event. It is the client's construing that the therapist has to understand. To the therapist, however, the vomiting is as much construing as is the way the client describes it. There is no body/mind dichotomy in Kelly's system. As the therapist examines the client's construing system (in verbal and non-verbal terms), she will be examining the context within which the vomiting arose. She will be asking herself such questions as: 'What experiment is the client conducting when he vomits?' 'What answers is he seeking from himself or others around him by behaving in that way?'

It is important to remember here that *behaviour is the experiment*. So we look at the event as if the child's first vomit was his way of asking a question of his world. It might have gone something like this: 'As far as I can see, if I go on as I am doing, I will grow up and be successful like my father. But I don't want to be successful like my father. He is aggressive and weak, like all men. Perhaps if I'm sick I won't grow up and can remain a child'. He vomits. He is treated differently. Has he 'acquired a disturbance'? I think not. He has tried an experiment which, according to the way in which he construes the world, works. He is successful, but not in the way his father is.

I must add that, although I have spelt out a possible process in words, this does not mean that the thought goes consciously through the child's head in this way. We do a lot of our experimenting at a non-verbal level.

Perpetuation of psychological disturbance

The vomiting is perpetuated because 'it works'. The child's predictions are validated; he has succeeded in stopping the process of maturation. It now takes on a meaning of its own: 'I am someone who is sick. I can't lead the sort of life which, were I able to, would make me a highly successful person'. When as an adult this person came for help we find that he has hedged his bets. The opposite of being successful is not, as one might expect, being unsuccessful but is being 'not yet successful'; this means he may still be a potential genius. He sought help because he was getting some invalidation of this construing. He had begun to see 'not yet being successful' as rather ludicrous at the age of 40 when he also saw himself as a potential genius. Something had to yield.

Invalidation of our important notions of our selves comes, most often of course, from other people in our lives. Our experiments in life succeed or fail in relation to our understanding of others' understandings of us. But it can also come from within. Like the potential genius who could be successful any time he chose except that he had suddenly become aware that he was approaching 40 years of age.

Problems persist until the person is able to find acceptable alternative ways of dealing with the world. Many long-standing problems, such as stuttering, become enmeshed in the person's core-role construing. The person comes to see himself as 'a stutterer', 'a vomiter', 'a useless person'. The longer a problem exists for a person, the more likely it is to become part of the construing of the self and the more likely it is to persist: to change construing of one's self is no easy undertaking.

It is not only core-role construing that takes place at a very important (superordinate) level. The *organization corollary* of personal construct theory states that constructs are organized into a system and that a superordinate construct is one that includes others as elements in its context. Hinkle (1965) demonstrated that the more abstract (superordinate) constructs are the more implications (other constructs) they imply and, incidentally, the more resistant they are to change.

Hinkle also described 'implicative dilemmas' in construing. These may occur because the person has not worked out the meaning of (or lines of implication for) a particular superordinate construct. The subtle changes in meaning in different contexts are unclear; and with such a lack of clarity, few useful predictions can be made or, if they are made, can lead to invalidation. Alternatively, the lines of implication are there, but in conflict. This aspect of 'implicative dilemmas' has been elaborated by Tschudi (1977) as described on p. 140. An example of such a dilemma can be seen in the case study at the end of this chapter.

The reasons for problems persisting must be sought within a person's construing of himself and his world. He behaves in a particular way because that is most meaningful to him; it is in that way he is able to achieve maximal control over events – and over himself. The problem becomes enmeshed in his core-role superordinate construing system. The longer the problem persists, the more difficulty the person is likely to have in changing. He is not able to complete the cycle of experience.

Change

Since part of the model of the person in personal construct psychology is that we are a form of motion, the process of change is built into the theory. Kelly wrote his theory at two levels. There is the structure in the form of postulate, corollaries and other theoretical constructs. There is also the theory of human experiencing in the form of cycles of movement and transition.

The *fundamental postulate* states that 'a person's processes are psychologically channelized by the ways in which he anticipates events'. Three of the elaborative corollaries are specifically concerned with change.

The *experience corollary* states that 'a person's construction system varies as he successively construes the replication of events'. Merely being in a situation does not, of itself, mean that one has had experience; it is only experience if one has cause to construe some aspect of it in a way that differs from the way one construed before. An agoraphobic woman placed in a situation at some point in her behaviour therapy hierarchy will have experience of that situation only if her construing of the world is in some way different from what it was before. Kelly (1955) equates experience with learning:

> The burden of our assumption is that learning is not a special class of psychological process; it is synonymous with any and all psychological processes. It is not something that happens to a person on occasion; it is what makes him a person in the first place.

The *choice corollary* states that 'a person chooses for himself that alternative in a dichotomized construct through which he anticipates the greater possibility for extension and definition of his system'. This is a basic motivation construct. As living beings we strive to make our world a more predictable and personally meaningful place. We may not like the world in which we are living, but it is preferable to live in it than to launch ourselves into a vast sea of uncertainty.

In a certain sense, the client is 'choosing' to remain as he is rather than change. The person who has stuttered since early childhood sees no alternative but to continue stuttering in adulthood; that is the way he can make sense of the interaction – it is personally meaningful to him. If he were to suddenly become a fluent speaker, he would be launched into chaos (Fransella 1972). In much the same way, smoking is meaningful for the smoker, obesity for the obese and depression for the depressed.

A personal construct approach involves helping the client construe what he or she is going to become and not simply eliminating the undesired behaviour directly.

The *modulation corollary* discusses a third aspect of change. It states that any variation within a construing system 'is limited by the permeability of the constructs within whose range of convenience the variants lie'. Construing new events is difficult if many of a person's constructs are not open to receive them;

they are pumice rather than sponge. Someone who stutters and knows too precisely how people respond to his attempts at communication will find it difficult to employ new constructions of those interactions. He will not 'see' different responses.

While the corollaries describe the theoretical structure underpinning change, the cycles of movement describe the change process. These are the cycles of experience, creativity and circumspection, pre-emption and control (CPC) (or decision-making).

The cycle of experience is about the process of reconstruing itself. The whole of psychotherapy therefore is seen in terms of human experiencing rather than as treatment. Kelly puts it like this:

> Psychotherapy needs to be understood as an experience, and experience, in turn, understood as a process that reflects human vitality. Thus to define psychotherapy as a form of treatment – something that one person does to another – is misleading.
>
> (Kelly 1980: 21)

In the first place we have to have *anticipation*. Behaving is our experimentation to test out our anticipations about what confronts us. But we also have to be committed to these anticipations. We have to care what happens. We have to invest something in our experiments. But it is not experience as Kelly uses the term if we do not reconstrue as a consequence of the consequences of our experiment to which we have committed ourselves. The problem with problems is that we continue to conduct the same old experiments again and again without adding the final, essential component – reconstruing.

Creativity starts with loosening up our construing of events and then tightening them again, hopefully in a different pattern. We have a problem. We go for a long walk and 'mull it over'. We allow the ideas to come and go as they please (we are construing loosely). Then we suddenly have a flash of light. Quickly, before it can slip away, we tighten things up again so we can look to see whether or not we have indeed found a solution. This cycle of loosening and tightening repeats itself again and again. Kelly puts it like this:

> The loosening releases facts, long taken as self-evident, from their rigid conceptual moorings. Once so freed, they may be seen in new aspects hitherto unsuspected, and the creativity cycle may get under way.
>
> (Kelly 1955: 1,031)

The ability to loosen the construing of events is often one of the first lessons the client has to be taught. Problems very often result in our tightening our construing so as to make it more manageable, more predictable. It can therefore be quite threatening to a client to be asked to let go the anchors that hold the construing together – even for a short time.

The decision-making or CPC cycle is independent of tightening or loosening construing. We have a decision to make. First of all we look at the alternatives available to us (we circumspect). Eventually we come up with the way that makes the most sense (we pre-empt the issue). Now we are in a position to be in control of the situation and are precipitated into action.

Practice

Goals of therapy

The person with a psychological problem is 'stuck': he or she keeps repeating the same old behavioural experiments over and over again. Since personal construct psychology views the person (amongst other things) as a form of motion, enabling the person to 'get on the move again' becomes the goal of therapy. As Kelly puts it:

> The task of psychotherapy is to get the human process going again so that life may go on and on from where psychotherapy left off. There is no particular kind of psychotherapeutic relationship – no particular kind of feelings – no particular kind of interaction that is in itself a psychotherapeutic panacea.
>
> (Kelly 1969b: 223)

Selection criteria

Since all are seen as a construing process, then no one construing person would be deemed unsuitable for personal construct psychotherapy. What usually provides the limiting factor is the context in which the therapy will take place. Not all places can deal with the over-active, the catatonic, the violent. There is also another limiting factor, but less easy to define – the psychotherapist him or herself. There are very few therapists who would wish to say that they are equally successful with any client with any form of problem. The limitations are thus in the physical therapy context and the therapist and not in the client.

There are a few criteria which help the therapist decide whether or not the client is likely to benefit from personal construct psychotherapy. But none would automatically lead to a rejection of the client. One is that the client is willing to go along with the idea that the therapist does not have the answers – the client does. All the therapist has is a theory about how people may go about the business of making sense of themselves and the world around them. If the client is basically looking for psychological 'pills' or hypnosis, then they are not likely to take to the idea that psychotherapy means work.

Clients do best if they have some existing construct to do with psychological change. Not only that it is possible to change, but also that they, themselves, may find it possible to change.

In choosing whether the client is most likely to be able to contemplate change in the one-to-one situation or in the presence of others, a number of factors have to be considered. For instance, a very withdrawn adult would rarely be seen without any contact being made with those caring for that person. The choice is then between seeing the client only in the company of one or two relatives; seeing client and relatives on different occasions; or seeing the client alone for part of the session with the relative(s) joining later.

The choice will depend on the problem as seen by all parties. If the problem seems to be very definitely one that focuses on interactions and the withdrawn client not seeming to want to communicate more, then the emphasis would probably be on seeing client and relative(s) together. If the client is clearly withdrawn because of the experience of some internal turmoil, most work would be done with the client alone.

However, the die is not cast forever. As the withdrawn client becomes less so, the relatives may increasingly be brought into the sessions; as they come to understand what their interactions with their client are all about *from the client's point of view* and vice versa, the client may well increasingly be seen alone.

Clients are referred for group therapy if their problem is clearly related to interpersonal issues. For instance, if they feel poorly understood by others or that others do not understand them.

It is not uncommon for a client to be seen both individually and in a group. Here it is important that the same therapist is not involved in both. The client needs to be able to separate out the two experiences. There are experiments which the client may wish to conduct with or upon the therapist individually which would not be appropriate in a group. However, such a combination of therapies requires very close collaboration between the therapists, for it is they who must ensure that the client moves along a single path toward reconstruing and does not get mixed messages. For instance, it is counter-therapeutic for one therapist to be working with the client on the basis that the client needs to be helped to 'tighten' aspects of their construing while the other therapist is focusing on 'loosening'.

Qualities of effective therapists

Although no one has yet tried to relate the qualities of personal construct therapists either to success or failure with clients or to the qualities of other types of therapist, Kelly specifies a number of skills that they need to acquire: these are outlined below.

A subsuming system of constructs

Above all, therapists must have a 'subsuming construct system' and be skilled in its use. Every therapist needs a set of professional constructs within which to subsume a client's own personal system of constructs. For the analyst, it is spelt out in psychoanalytic terms; for the cognitive therapist, in cognitive terms; for the personal construct therapist it is spelt out in terms of the theoretical constructs stated in the psychology of personal constructs. Kelly describes it thus:

> Since all clients have their own personal systems my system should be *a system of approach* by means of which I can quickly come to understand and subsume the widely varying systems which my clients can be expected to present.

> (Kelly 1955: 595)

Therapists should be able to specify precisely what constructs are being used whenever a therapeutic decision is made: for example, if therapists systematically use the writing of a self-characterization (see 'fixed role therapy', p. 141) with clients, they should be able to state precisely what this procedure is designed to do.

In personal construct therapy, the subsuming system is that which defines the theory itself. Those constructs most commonly used in psychotherapy are referred to as 'professional constructs'. One such is *loose* versus *tight*: is the client using constructs in a way that leads to varying prediction (loosened construing) or to predictions which state that events will definitely be one way or another (unvarying or tight construing)? Bannister (1962) based his theory of the origins and maintenance of schizophrenic thought disorder on this construct.

To be effective, personal construct therapists must be able to 'work within' a client's construing system whether it be overly tight or overly loose. They have to understand these process differences both experientially and theoretically.

Therapists who lack an adequate subsuming system of constructs, or who lack the skill of using such a system in an experental way, may fail to help a client change. Once therapists allow their *own* construing to intervene between themselves and their clients, they may find themselves being used by their clients and have difficulty extricating themselves.

Creativity and aggression
Given the focus on the client and therapist as personal scientists, the therapist needs to be creative, versatile and aggressive. Kelly (1955) comments that 'Every case a psychotherapist handles requires him to devise techniques and formulate constructs he has never used before.' Such creativity means the readiness to try out unverbalized hunches, and a willingness to look at things in new ways:

> Creation is therefore an act of daring, an act of daring through which the creator abandons those literal defenses behind which he might hide if his act is questioned or its results proven invalid. The psychotherapist who dares not try anything he cannot verbally defend is likely to be sterile in a psychotherapeutic relationship.
>
> (Kelly 1955: 601)

To be creative the therapist must be able to adopt a variety of roles and be aggressive in testing out hypotheses (aggression being the active elaboration of one's construing). In psychotherapy, both client and therapist must be prepared to be aggressive and to take risks.

It must be borne in mind that an unwritten basic tenet of personal construct psychology is that we have created ourselves and can therefore re-create ourselves if we so wish.

Verbal ability
The therapist must be skilled both verbally and in observation. A therapist must be able to speak the client's language in addition to having a wide-ranging vocabulary. By understanding the meanings that word-symbols have for the client the therapist can minimize the risk of misunderstandings.

Therapeutic style

The personal construct therapist's style can best be understood by looking once again at the model of the 'person as scientist': both struggle to understand the same problem and to find a solution to it. The therapist, like a research supervisor, knows something about designing experiments, has experience of some of the pitfalls involved in any type of research and knows that, ultimately, only the research student can carry out the research. This supervisor-research student model may sound cold and calculating, but it is not: anyone who has ever been in one or both of those positions knows only too well how totally involving and challenging is the task.

One of the most important aspects of such a relationship is that both client and therapist must have a personal commitment to solving the problem and to the necessary work and experimentation that this involves. Within this research framework, the therapist initially adopts the *credulous approach*: all personal evaluation is suspended; there are no judgements. Everything the client says is accepted as 'true'.

As the therapist gains access to the client's world and begins to formulate hypotheses about the nature of the problem, the therapist begins to put these to the test. However, being active in therapy does not mean that the therapist necessarily adopts a directive role; she may, in fact, be very quiet and give the client absolute freedom to do, say or think whatever he wishes. Nevertheless, the role is decided on by the therapist. The therapist's construing of the client's constructions leads the therapist to consider that this 'quiet' role is something the client can use *at this stage of the therapy*. The personal construct therapist therefore *acts as validator or invalidator of the client's construing*.

One implication of construing the therapist as validator of the client's construing, is that the therapist uses the relationship as another valuable 'tool' for helping the client's reconstructions. For instance, 'transference' or 'dependency' is not a general problem to be 'dealt with'. At a particular stage in therapy it may be useful, such as when attempts are being made to verbalize pre-verbal constructs; at another time or with other clients, dependence on the therapist may prevent the client from conducting useful experiments outside the therapy consulting room.

The therapeutic style is thus dictated by the ways in which the therapist construes the needs of the client, always remembering that client and therapist are *both* in the experimenting and reconstruing business.

Major therapeutic strategies and techniques

The therapist hopes that all interactions with the client will aid the client in reconstruing. The therapist's principal goal is to help the client find alternative ways of looking at himself, life, the problem. But before the therapist can be reasonably sure about these possible alternative ways, she has to have a moderately clear idea of what it is that is holding the client back from doing this on his own.

Most of the techniques stemming directly from personal construct psychology are concerned with providing the therapist as well as the client with a picture of how the client views the world at the present time. In that sense they can be called 'diagnostic'. Only fixed role therapy is a therapeutic tool in its own right – designed specifically to bring about reconstruing (alternative constructions). However, the diagnostic techniques do themselves bring about reconstruing in many instances, although this is not their prime aim.

Kelly talks about techniques thus:

Personal construct psychotherapy is a way of getting on with the human enterprise and it may embody and mobilize all of the techniques for doing this that man has yet devised. Certainly there is no one psychotherapeutic technique and certainly no one kind of inter-personal compatibility between psychotherapist and client. The techniques employed are the techniques for living and the task of the skillful psychotherapist is the proper orchestration of all of these varieties of techniques. Hence one may find a personal construct psychotherapist employing a huge variety of procedures – not helter-skelter, but always as part of a plan for helping himself and his client get on with the job of human exploration and checking out the appropriateness of the constructions they have devised for placing upon the world around them.

(Kelly 1969b: 221–2)

Repertory grid technique
This technique has been modified a number of times since Kelly first described it in 1955 (see Fransella and Bannister 1977). Its uses are many and its analyses often complex. It is basically a technique which enables the therapist to obtain some degree of quantification of the relationships between the constructs of clients and those of the individuals who people their worlds. Though it has a place in the psychotherapy setting, it is not essential to it. It is only useful if the therapist sees it as such. It can be used to validate therapists' hunches, in monitoring change over time, or in helping clients explore their construing of events more fully. In the last-named context, it becomes part of therapy if the results are fed back to the client.

Laddering, pyramiding and the ABC model
These are all methods for exploring construct relationships without getting into the complexities of statistical analyses that are often necessary with repertory grids.

Laddering   helps the client explore the relationships between constructs at more and more abstract levels (Hinkle 1965). For instance, if the client uses the construct *dominant* versus *submissive*, the client would be asked which he would prefer to be. If the answer were *submissive*, the therapist would ask 'Why? What are the advantages of being a submissive rather than a dominant person?' The client might answer that submissive people do not get attacked, whereas dominant people do. The client is again asked why he prefers not to be attacked. The reply might be that he would not know how to respond if he were attacked; he would not know what to do. And so the questioning goes on, until the construing has reached such a superordinate level that it has nowhere else to go to (in this example, it might be something to do with self-preservation).

Laddering is an art and one that is not easy to learn; but having learned it, most people find it an invaluable tool for getting insight very quickly into the most important values the client holds about himself and others. Not only does it enable the therapist to learn about the client, but also it frequently enables the client to gain considerable insight into his own construing.

Pyramiding   aims at identifying the more concrete levels of the construing system of the client (Landfield 1971). Instead of asking 'Why?', the client is asked: 'What?' or 'How?'; 'What sort of person is a submissive person?'; 'How would you know that a person is being submissive?' This method can be useful when planning behavioural experiments.

The ABC model   involves finding out the advantages and disadvantages to the client of each pole of a construct (Tschudi 1977). This can be used to advantage with constructs connected with 'the problem'. In the case of a woman whose 'problem' was being overweight, the client would be asked first to state an advantage of being the desired weight (perhaps she would be able to wear nice clothes); then for a disadvantage of being overweight (perhaps she gets out of breath when going upstairs). Next, she is asked for a disadvantage of being the normal weight (perhaps she would find there was too much choice around and so get confused), and finally for an advantage of being overweight (perhaps men not bothering her). These answers are regarded not as 'truths' but as guidelines for understanding and further exploration.

Techniques from other therapies
The choice of technique is always determined by the current formulation of the problem, which is couched in the language of the professional theoretical constructs. Personal construct therapists find the use of dream material, guided fantasy, systematic desensitization and many other techniques of great value for specific purposes, but it must be emphasized that the choice of technique is guided by theory.

The self-characterization
Kelly is reported as saying that if he were to be remembered for one thing only, he would like it to be his first principle: 'If you do not know what is wrong with a person, ask him, he may tell you.' A working model for this is the self-characterization he described. The instructions are carefully worded as follows:

> I want you to write a character sketch of (e.g. Mary) just as if she were the principal character in a play. Write it as it might be written by a friend who knew her very *intimately* and very *sympathetically*, perhaps better than anyone ever really could know her. Be sure to write it in the third person. For example, start out by saying 'Mary is . . .'.

There is no formal method of analysis. However, one might look at the first sentence as if it were a statement of where the person is now and at the last as a statement of where the person is going. One might look for themes running through the whole piece. What one tries to do is to go beyond the words and glimpse inside where the person lives. These character sketches can be written from a variety of standpoints: 'Mary as she will be in ten years' time', '. . . as she will be when her problem has disappeared', or any other form which seems to offer the person a way of exploring and communicating her constructions of the world. An example of the use of the self-characterization as a therapeutic instrument can be found in Fransella (1981).

Fixed role therapy

This is the only method that is offered by Kelly as a therapeutic tool in its own right. He gave it as an example of the theory in action and based it on the self-characterization. In his description of fixed role therapy, he also gives an implicit account of the way we invent and create ourselves.

The therapist writes a second version of the client's original self-characterization. This is not a replica of the first, since that would only lead back to where the client is now; nor should it be a complete opposite, since no one will readily turn his life on its head – instead, the client's *fixed role sketch* is written so as to be 'orthogonal' to the first. For instance, if the client is using the construct *aggressive* versus *submissive* in relation to his boss, the sketch might talk of being *respectful*.

When the sketch has been written, client and therapist pore over it together. They modify it until it describes a person who the client feels it would be possible for him to be. The client now lives the life of that person for a few weeks; he eats what this new person eats, dresses as he would dress and relates to others as this person would relate. During this period of fixed role enactment the therapist has to see the client fairly frequently. The sessions focus on what the client sees as going on, which ventures were successful and which were not, what messages he is getting from others and so forth.

The purpose of this fixed role enactment is to get over the idea that we can, indeed, change ourselves; that even the client can change, though he seems so stuck at the moment. He learns about self-inventiveness; he learns what happens when he alters a particular item of behaviour, and whether it is useful to explore this line of inquiry further or whether he should try something else. He discovers how the way we construe others and behave towards them influences how they behave towards us. He learns to read new messages from others. This is particularly important since the person we have invented is, in large part, the result of the way we have construed the reactions of others to us.

Fixed role therapy is certainly not suitable for everyone; it can, however, be very useful in modified form. For instance, the client and the therapist may choose to work out just one experiment for the former to carry out during the period before the next appointment: this might be to experiment with being respectful to his boss on just one occasion and see what difference it makes to how the boss reacts, to how the client feels about himself. These 'mini' fixed roles need to be worked out carefully with the client, but can give useful insights into the direction in which both client and therapist think he might profitably travel.

The change process in therapy

There are no clear stages in the change process that are applicable to all clients. We have to refer back to the theory. How permeable is the client's construing in the problem area? What is at stake for him if he were to contemplate changing in some radical way? How loosely or tightly knit is his construing in areas relating to anticipated change? And so on. In other words, the change process will be determined by the 'diagnosis' the therapist makes of why the client is unable to move forward.

Diagnosis is the planning stage of treatment for the therapist. This does NOT imply that the therapist is placing the client in some medical pigeon-hole such as 'depression', 'schizophrenia', or 'psychopathic'. Personal construct diagnosis does not imply any illness or disturbance on the part of the client. It is couched in the language of the theory to provide guidance for the therapist as to a possible way forward for the client. There is no one way forward for all-comers.

There are some specific factors that may impede the reconstruction process by the client. These factors are to be found in the constructs to do with transition. The change process can involve anxiety, threat, or hostility. All can impede movement if not dealt with sensitively by the therapist.

Any change is accompanied by anxiety as we move into areas we find it difficult or impossible to construe for a while. But this is rarely a problem if the client moves forward in moderate steps. Threat can bring the client up short as she perceives that, if things go on as they are at the moment, she will have to change how she construes some essential aspect of her 'self'. As one client put it after writing a self-characterization:

> Writing the self-characterization focused on something which I suppose has been associated with panic – although not consciously associated with panic – the feeling that I was going to have to change more drastically – in a sense either remain more or less the same or the change would have to be more drastic than I had thought. Writing the self-characterization focused my attention on *not wanting to change*. Not wanting to change because I felt that if I was going to have to change as dramatically as I was feeling was necessary, I'd lose 'me'.
>
> (Fransella 1981: 228)

If a client is able to put the threat into words like that, it is usually possible to move on forward from there. He has to elaborate precisely what this 'me' is that is in danger of being lost and whether, on close examination, this is necessarily true. But some clients are not able to put the threat into words. Often the client realizes, at some level of awareness, that these radical changes are just too much to be contemplated. He relapses. He has made a positive choice – in his terms – and has signalled that an alternative therapeutic strategy is required. Relapse is not a negative event, but the client's safety-net.

The problem becomes more difficult if the client defends his position by being hostile; that is, by extorting evidence to prove that he really should be the sort of person he always knew himself to be. He can 'make' the therapy fail. It is really the therapist's fault not the client's. He can produce evidence that there has really been no great change at all by pointing out that the experience indicating psychological movement to the therapist was really 'a chance event – those combination of circumstances will never happen again!'

Hostility is dealt with by discovering, on the one hand, what it is that is so important for the client to retain and, on the other hand, areas of construing that will help elaborate the sort of self the client wants to become. Exploration with the client just mentioned revealed that the 'me' he was afraid of losing was 'the child me'. This was to do with a rich fantasy life and a world of deep experiencing. He evolved for himself a way in which he could change to becoming 'an adult' while retaining areas of living in which he could still experience the valued child-like qualities.

Limitations of the approach

A major undeveloped area for personal construct therapy is group work. Although Kelly did provide a chapter devoted to working with groups of people, little use has been made of it. Its focus has always been on the one-to-one situation.

Apart from this, limitations lie with the therapist rather than with personal construct therapy. The therapist finds it easier if she has the full co-operation of the client – at least implicitly. She finds it easier to work with those who are verbally fluent, but that is not essential. She finds it easier to work with those from a culture similar to that of the therapist but, again, this is by no means essential. If all human beings are seen as experiencing, construing beings, then personal construct therapy should be able to be used by all.

Case example

The client

Rowena is 35 years old, smartly dressed as befits a career woman who has some success in the banking business. Her hair is brushed softly so as to frame her face. She is tall – about 5 feet 10 inches – and normally talks in a lively, bright, high-pitched way.

Rowena described her problem as failing to make long and lasting relationships with men. At one time she was so desperate that she took an overdose but was found in time and taken to hospital. She gives her suitors her genuine love and does her utmost to ensure the man of her choice responds likewise, but the relationship always founders. She cannot understand why.

She also talked at length about her mother who 'is a pain in the neck', a 'martyr who is engulfed by self-pity' and who 'does not know the meaning of love'. She did not make any connection between her own inability to sustain love in others and her experience of lack of love from her mother.

She also complained of having migraine headaches.

The personal construct approach was explained to her and she was given the opportunity to go away and think it over. But she made up her mind then and there, agreeing to come on a course of ten one-hour weekly sessions. This was on the clear understanding that improvement was not guaranteed in that time, but that it was a long enough period for us both to see whether or not we were on the right tack and whether or not more sessions were likely to lead to substantial movement in the direction she wanted to take.

The therapy

The philosophical position of constructive alternativism means assuming that there are several ways in which the client's dilemmas may be construed. There can thus be no one and only one path along which therapy may proceed. However, without some formulation of the client's problem nothing can happen at all. Kelly therefore coined the term 'transitive diagnosis'. This is construed as the planning stage of the client's reconstructions. Kelly explains his use of this term thus:

> The term suggests that we are concerned with transitions in the client's life, that we are looking for bridges between the client's past and his future. Moreover, we expect to take an active part in helping the client select or build the bridges to be used and in helping him cross them safely. The client does not ordinarily sit cooped up in a nosological pigeonhole; he proceeds along his way.
>
> (Kelly 1955: 773)

To come to any depth of understanding of what is the most likely reason why a client cannot continue moving forward in life one has to have data. Reaching an initial diagnosis can take several sessions. In Rowena's case these data were gleaned by my adopting the 'credulous approach' to listening in that first session and my asking her to bring a self-characterization with her to the second session.

Rowena's self-characterization was hand-written in rather spidery writing and said that

> Rowena is a warm, loving and very thoughtful person. She loves her best friend and her best friend's son without reservation and is loyal, affectionate and caring toward her friends and most of her family. She enjoys developing and maintaining friendships with people of considerable character. She is intolerant when she has little respect or liking for someone. She dislikes her mother. . . . She has two or three close platonic men friends, but seems unable to maintain an intimate stable relationship with a man. She is very excited and happy when both mentally and physically powerfully attracted but possibly her anxiety to have a relationship makes her too demonstrative, willing and available. . . . She has a great fear of being alone through her life. She would love to have a family and feels a total failure in this respect because of her inability to achieve it.
>
> She is very direct in communication and is stimulated by ideas and change. She likes serious discussion tempered by humour, has great integrity and a reasonable degree of compassion. She is romantic, emotional, rather unrealistic and fairly independent. She can be impatient and irritated. She dreads boredom.

The theme is one that was to be expected. Kelly suggests that the first sentence may usefully be looked at as if it were a statement of where the person is now: 'Rowena has a lot to give in terms of warmth and affection'.

The last sentence may give an indication of where the person sees themselves as going: 'She dreads boredom'. Perhaps this is how she sees the future with no marriage and family – just living alone and being bored: 'She has a great fear of being alone through life'. Anxiety about an empty future appears to be fuelling the impatience at no man staying with her for long.

There are no special ways of analysing such characterizations, but they are often valuable in indicating important personal themes and in giving a 'feel' for how people see themselves and their life. The question raised by Rowena's script is why it is she cannot combine her obvious warm nature with a physical relationship without the latter overwhelming her and her partner. What is she seeking by being 'too demonstrative'?

One thing that is missing from Rowena's writing is any construct centred on movement. She talks of being stimulated by change, but the impression is that it is change from without rather than within herself. This, of course, may prove to be wrong. Kelly suggests that a construct of *movement* is for the personal construct psychologist, one of the indications that the person may be amenable to psychotherapy.

My initial transitive diagnosis was not a very hopeful one. For one thing there was this lack of any construing to do with the possibility of change. But, more importantly, Rowena's main problem was likely to be at a pre-verbal level. In spite of her verbal sophistication, she gave evidence of feelings about herself and her need for love which she was quite unable to put into words.

At the first session I had been concerned to get behind the rapid flow of words. As she finished telling me about a married woman friend with whom she has a really good relationship, I asked, 'What's going on *now* inside you?' There was a long pause before she said, 'I am thinking about my friend as I tell you about her and about how lucky she is to be happily married and have two lovely children'. That was not what I meant. She had given me thoughts and I was after feelings. I gently pressed the point, 'Yes, and can you tell me what you are *feeling* – now – this instant?' There was an even longer pause. Her face fell, her eyes misted over and tears welled up and flowed slowly down her cheeks: 'I am feeling how deeply I love David – my friend's son – I have so much love to give and no one seems to want it'.

Additional support for a major involvement of pre-verbal construing was that Rowena also had problems with migraine headaches. In personal construct theory 'psychosomatic symptoms' are often expressions of dependency and core, pre-verbal construing.

If pre-verbal construing is hypothesized as being involved in the client's complaint, the therapist knows she may have an uphill struggle. In particular, she has to consider the nature of the therapeutic relationship. As a female, middle-aged therapist I had to work out very carefully what my role in relation to Rowena should be. What did I have to do so as not to be cast as 'like my rejecting mother'?

Diagnosing the involvement of pre-verbal construing is, in itself, not enough. You have to hypothesize the nature of this construing. One way of gaining some insight into another's construing is to look for possible submerged poles of constructs (all constructs being bi-polar).

A most useful question can be 'What is my client NOT doing by behaving as she currently is?' Seeking meaning in the opposites of what a client is saying, seeking those submerged poles of constructs, seeking those poles of constructs that have yet to be elaborated, there lies a great wealth of information about the private world of the client.

Rowena knows about rejection. What she may not know about is how to construe herself as someone being loved in return.

One final hypothesis completes the picture. If you do *not* have a clear idea of what sort of person you are likely to be when you become as you want to be – you can never let it happen (or not easily in any case). In Rowena's case she had developed as a person who is rejected by all those from whom she wants (demands?) love. She has to learn what it is like to be someone who is loved in return. Until that time she has to make sure that she gets evidence that she is, indeed, someone who is rejected. That is her validation of her 'self'. She is therefore more than likely to 'cook the books'. She makes sure that she so overpowers her men that they cannot bear with her any longer. They reject her. That is hostility.

The transitive diagnosis was thus that Rowena construed rejection by her mother at a very early age as rejection of herself and this core dependency construing had remained at a pre-verbal level into adulthood. She is someone who is rejected whenever she tries to give all the love she possesses. The opposite pole of that construing has never been elaborated. To maintain her sense of self-hood she has to retain herself as a rejected person by being hostile whenever in a situation in which she might be invalidated (forced to see herself as someone loved).

Having made one's transitive diagnosis one acts 'as if' it were true. In essence, one tests it out.

My relationship with Rowena was that of a caring, helpful but not emotionally involved person helping an intelligent but over-emotional person. The strategy, guided by the diagnosis, was to help Rowena put some verbal anchors on those elusive pre-verbal constructs.

Our starting place was at the submerged pole of her 'loving' constructs. We explored the differences between her enduring relationship with her woman friend (who, it transpired, also did not love her in return) and her men friends. We looked at her relationships with men in detail. Exactly what did she do that caused them to leave her?

She quickly saw that she actually smothered them with her love as early on as their second meeting. We examined what might happen if she played a waiting game. This had never occurred to her. At no time did we touch upon her relationship with her mother and she never tried to bring it up. Personal construct therapy works very much in the here and now, especially when the contract is for a relatively short period of time.

By the fifth session Rowena was elaborating her feelings about these relationships at considerable speed. Possibly too fast for sustained reconstruing to be taking place. However, a natural experiment presented itself. Personal construct therapy involves regular 'homework' and Rowena had been observing how other people managed their relationships. She now reported meeting a man who attracted her very much. We now designed specific experiments for her to conduct. In the main, they were concerned with biding her time; getting an understanding of what he was feeling about her; he being the one to decide when they had intercourse, not her and so forth.

After two weeks she had managed to hold on to the relationship and had still not had intercourse. She was delighted with this new form of experimentation and its results. We now worked hard at trying to elaborate what sort of person she now was. What did she think, feel, do as this person who was accepted?

By the time the tenth session came, all was still going well. She felt there was no reason to go on coming to see me. She was delighted with her progress. I did nothing to try to dissuade her.

My prognosis was not too good. Rowena had moved very fast – as always. I do believe that there had been some elaboration in the direction we were moving toward but I doubted if she could maintain the new caution. With this client it had been a mistake to make a short time contract before I had assessed the full implications of her problem. I had underestimated the massive changes she would have to embark on. Ten sessions was just too short for me to have any confidence that the changes would be maintained. The making of time contracts is always something of a gamble because the client wants to have some idea of their commitment before agreeing to go ahead with therapy. In Rowena's case I believe I should have re-negotiated the contract before the end. But, who knows? She has not come back nor answered follow-up letters.

References

Bannister, D. (1962) The nature and measurement of schizophrenic thought disorder, *Journal of Mental Science* 108: 825–42.

Fransella, F. (1972) *Personal Change and Reconstruction: Research on a Treatment of Stuttering,* London: Academic Press.

—— (1981) Nature babbling to herself: the self characterisation as a therapeutic tool, in H. Bonarius, R. Holland and S. Rosenberg (eds) *Personal Construct Psychology: Recent Advances in Theory and Practice,* London: Macmillan.

—— (1984) What sort of scientist is the person-as-scientist?, in J.R. Adams-Webber and J.C. Mancuso (eds) *Applications of Personal Construct Theory,* Ontario: Academic Press.

Fransella, F. and Bannister, D. (1977) *A Manual for Repertory Grid Technique,* London: Academic Press.

Hinkle, D. (1965) The change of personal constructs from the viewpoint of a theory of construct implication, unpublished PhD thesis, Ohio State University.

Kelly, G.A. (1955) *The Psychology of Personal Constructs,* Vols 1 and 2, New York: Norton.

—— (1969a) The autobiography of a theory, in B. Maher (ed.) *Clinical Psychology and Personality: The Selected Papers of George Kelly,* New York: Krieger.

—— (1969b) The psychotherapeutic relationship, in B. Maher (ed.) *Clinical Psychology and Personality: The Selected Papers of George Kelly,* New York: Krieger.

—— (1980) A psychology of optimal man, in A.W. Landfield and L.M. Leitner (eds) *Personal Construct Psychology: Psychotherapy and Personality,* New York: Wiley.

Landfield, A.W. (1971) *Personal Construct Systems in Psychotherapy,* New York: Rand McNally.

Mullins, N. (1973) *Theories and Theory Groups in Contemporary American Sociology,* New York: Harper & Row.

Neimeyer, R.A. (1983) Uneven growth of personal construct theory, *Constructs* 2: 5, London: Centre for Personal Construct Psychology.

Tschudi, F. (1977) Loaded and honest questions, in D. Bannister (ed.) *New Perspectives in Personal Construct Theory,* London: Academic Press.

Vaihinger, H. (1924) *The Philosophy of 'as if': A System of the Theoretical, Practical and Religious Fictions of Mankind,* trans. C.K. Ogden, London: Routledge & Kegan Paul.

Suggested further reading

Bannister, D. and Fransella, F. (1985) *Inquiring Man*, 3rd ed, London: Routledge.
Button, E. (ed.) (1985) *Personal Construct Theory and Mental Health*, London: Croom Helm.
Dunnett, G. (ed.) (1988) *Working with People: Clinical Uses of Personal Construct Psychology*, London: Routledge.
Landfield, A.W. and Leitner, L.M. (eds) (1980) *Personal Construct Psychology: Psychotherapy and Personality*, New York: Wiley.
Neimeyer, R.A. and Neimeyer, G.J. (eds) (1987) *Personal Construct Therapy Casebook*, New York: Springer.

8

Existential therapy

EMMY VAN DEURZEN-SMITH

Historical context and development in Britain

Historical context

The existential approach is first and foremost philosophical. It is concerned with the understanding of people's position in the world and with the clarification of what it means to be alive. It is also committed to exploring these questions with a receptive attitude, rather than with a dogmatic one: the search for truth with an open mind and an attitude of wonder is the aim, not the fitting of the client into pre-established categories and interpretations.

In this sense the historical background to this approach is that of 3,000 years of philosophy. Throughout the history of humankind people have tried to make sense of human existence in general and of their personal predicament in particular. The whole philosophical tradition is relevant and can help us to understand an individual's position with regard to existential issues. The philosophers who are particularly pertinent are those whose work is directly aimed at making sense of human existence. But the philosophical movement that is of special importance and that has been directly responsible for the generation of existential therapy is that of phenomenology and existential philosophy.

This movement (see Warnock 1970; Macquarrie 1972) can be traced back to the last century, and the work of Kierkegaard and Nietzsche, two unorthodox and original thinkers. Both were in conflict with the predominant ideologies of their time and were committed to the exploration of reality as experienced in a passionate and personal manner.

Kierkegaard (1813–55) protested violently against Christian dogma and the so-called objectivity of science (Kierkegaard 1941; 1944). He thought that both were ways of avoiding the anxiety inherent in human existence. He had great contempt for the way life was being lived all around him. Truth, he said, could ultimately come forth only from being, not from thinking. What was most lacking was people's courage to live with passion and commitment from the inward depth of existence. As Kierkegaard lived by his own word he was lonely and much ridiculed during his lifetime.

Nietzsche (1844–1900) took this philosophy of life a step further. He took as his starting-point the notion that God was dead (Nietzsche 1961; 1974; 1986) and that we are at our own mercy in the project of achieving a new and more intense reality. It was in this way that he came to formulate a philosophy of freedom that invited people to shake off the shackles of moral constraint and to discover their own will and with it a new power to live. He encouraged people not to remain part of the herd, but to stand out and reach for a greater destiny. The important existential themes of freedom, choice, responsibility and courage are thus introduced.

While Kierkegaard and Nietzsche were undoubtedly the forerunners of the existential movement, the intellectual impetus for it came from Husserl's phenomenology (Husserl 1960; 1962). Husserl contended that natural sciences are based on the assumption that subject and object are separate and that this kind of dualism can lead only to error and must be replaced with a whole new mode of investigation and understanding of the world.

Prejudice and assumptions have to be put aside, in order to meet the world afresh and discover what is absolutely fundamental and directly available to us only through intuition. Instead of explaining and analysing things we have to describe and understand them.

Heidegger (1889–1976) applied this method to understanding the meaning of being (Heidegger 1962; 1968). He highlighted how poetry and deep philosophical thinking can bring greater insight into what it means to be in the world than scientific knowledge. He also favoured hermeneutics, an old philosophical method of investigation which is the art of interpretation. Unlike interpretation as practised in psychoanalysis (which consists of referring a person's experience to a pre-established theoretical framework) this kind of interpretation seeks to understand how something is experienced by the person herself.

Most recent contributions to existential exploration are based on Heidegger's work. There is a vast literature on the subject by many well-known authors such as Jaspers (1951; 1963) Tillich and Gadamer within the Germanic tradition and Sartre, Camus, Marcel, Ricoeur, Merleau Ponty and Levinas within the French tradition (see for instance Spiegelberg 1972; Kearney 1986). Few psychotherapists are aware of this literature, or interested in exploring it. Psychotherapy has traditionally grown within a medical rather than a philosophical milieu and it has to a large extent yet to discover the possibility of a more radical philosophical approach and method.

From the beginning of this century some therapists were however inspired by phenomenology and its possibilities for working with people. Binswanger, in Switzerland, was the first to attempt to bring existential insights to his work with patients in the Kreuzlingen sanatorium where he was a psychiatrist. Much of his work was translated into English during the 1940s and 1950s and, together with the immigration to the USA of Tillich and others, this had a considerable impact on the popularization of existential ideas as a basis for therapy (Valle and King 1978). Rollo May played an important role in this and his writing (May 1969; 1983; May *et al.* 1958) kept the existential influence alive in the USA leading eventually to a specific formulation of therapy (May and Yalom 1985; Yalom 1980).

Much of humanistic psychology was influenced by these ideas, but it invariably diluted and sometimes distorted the original meanings.

In Europe the original existential ideas were combined with some psychoanalytic insights and a method of existential analysis was developed by Boss (1957a; 1957b; 1979). Frankl developed an existential therapy called logotherapy (Frankl 1964; 1967), which focused particularly on finding meaning. In France the ideas of Sartre (1956; 1962) and Merleau Ponty (1962) and of a number of practitioners (Minkowski 1970) were important and influential but no specific therapeutic method was developed from them.

Development in Britain

Britain became a fertile ground for the further development of the existential approach when Laing and Cooper took Sartre's existential ideas as the basis for some of their writing (Laing 1960; 1961; Laing and Cooper 1964; Cooper 1967). Without developing a concrete method of therapy they critically reconsidered the notion of mental illness and its treatment. In the late 1960s they established an experimental therapeutic community at Kingsley Hall in the East End of London, where people could come to explore their madness without the usual medical treatment. They also founded the Philadelphia Association, an organization providing alternative living, therapy and therapeutic training from this perspective. The Philadelphia Association is still in existence today and is now particularly committed to the exploration of the works of philosophers such as Wittgenstein, Derrida, Levinas and Foucault as well as the work of the French psychoanalyst Lacan. It also runs a number of small therapeutic households along these lines. The Arbours Association is another group that grew out of the Kingsley Hall experiment. Founded by Berke and Schatzman in the 1970s, it now runs a training programme in psychotherapy, a crisis centre and several therapeutic communities. The existential input in the Arbours has gradually diminished and has been replaced with a predominantly Kleinian approach. Regent's College, London, runs an MA in Psychotherapy and Counselling that features a large existential input as well as a post-qualifying diploma in Existential Therapy will be on offer through Regent's College from September 1990.

Major British publications dealing with existential therapy include contributions by Jenner (de Koning and Jenner 1982), Heaton (1968; in preparation), Ledermann (1972; 1984), Spinelli (1989), Cooper (1989) and van Deurzen–Smith (1988). Other writers such as Lomas (1981) and Smail (1978; 1987) have published work relevant to the approach although not explicitly 'existential' in orientation. The *Journal of the British Society for Phenomenology* regularly publishes work on existential/phenomenological psychotherapy.

An important recent development is that of the founding of the Society for Existential Analysis in July 1988. This is a professional society which brings together therapists, psychologists, psychiatrists, counsellors and philosophers working from an existential perspective and which aims to strengthen and further develop this approach. The first conference of the society took place in December 1988 and was immensely successful, attracting well over a hundred therapists from different training organizations from all over Britain. The society now edits a Newsletter and Journal and contacts have been made with representatives of the approach both in the USA and in Europe.

Theoretical assumptions

Image of the person

The existential approach considers human nature to be open-ended, flexible and capable of an enormous range of experience. The person is a constant process of becoming. I create myself as I exist. There is no essential, solid self, no given definition of one's personality and abilities. This impermanence and uncertainty give rise to a deep sense of anxiety (*Angst*), in response to the realization of one's insignificance, and simultaneous responsibility to have to create something in place of that emptiness. Everything passes and nothing lasts. One finds oneself somewhere in the middle of this passing of time, grappling with the givens of the past and the possibilities of the future, without any sure knowledge of what it all means.

Existential thinkers avoid restrictive models that categorize or label people. Instead they look for the universals that can be observed transculturally. There is no existential personality theory which divides humanity up into types or reduces people to part components. Instead there is a description of the different levels of experience and existence that people are inevitably confronted with.

The way in which a person is in the world at a particular stage can be charted on to this general territory map of human existence (Binswanger 1963; Yalom 1980; van Deurzen–Smith 1984). There are four basic dimensions of human existence: the physical, the social, the psychological and the spiritual. On each of these dimensions people encounter the world and shape their attitude out of their experience.

Physical dimension

On the physical dimension (*Umwelt*) we relate to our environment and to the givens of the *natural world* around us. This includes our attitude to the body we have, to the concrete surroundings we find ourselves in, to the climate and the weather, to objects and material possessions, to health and illness and to our own mortality. The struggle on this dimension is, in general terms, between the search for domination over the elements and natural law (as in technology, or in sports) and the need to accept the limitations of natural boundaries (as in ecology or old age). While people generally aim for security on this dimension (through health and wealth), much of life brings a gradual disillusionment and realization that such security can only be temporary.

Social dimension

On the social dimension (*Mitwelt*) we relate to others, as we interact with the *public world* around us. This dimension includes our response to the particular culture we live in, as well as to the class and race we belong to (and also those we do not belong to). Attitudes here range from love to hate and from co-operation to competition. The contradictions can be understood in terms of acceptance versus rejection or belonging versus isolation. Many people blindly chase public acceptance by going along with the rules and fashions of the moment. Otherwise they try to rise above these by becoming trendsetters themselves. By acquiring fame or other forms of power, dominance over others can be attained temporarily. Sooner or later we are, however, all confronted with both failure and aloneness.

Psychological dimension

On the psychological dimension (*Eigenwelt*) we relate to ourselves and in this way create a *personal world*. This dimension includes views about our character, our past experience and our future possibilities. Contradictions here are often seen in terms of personal strengths and weaknesses. People often search for a sense of identity, a feeling of being substantial and having a self. But inevitably many events will confront us with evidence to the contrary and plunge us into a state of confusion or disintegration. Activity and passivity are an important polarity here. Self-affirmation and resolution go with the former and surrender and yielding come with the latter. Facing the final dissolution of self with death brings anxiety and confusion to many who haven't yet given up their sense of self-importance.

Spiritual dimension

On the spiritual dimension (*Uberwelt*) we relate to the unknown and thus create a sense of an *ideal world*, an ideology and a philosophical outlook. For some people this is about religion and one's relationship to God or gods, for others it is about finding meaning during life on earth without reference to the transcendental. Contradictions here are often between finding purpose and meaning or suffering a sense of absurdity and despair. In between these extremes people create their values in search of something that matters enough to live or die for, something that may even be ultimate and universally valid. Faith and doubt are central in this domain. Usually the aim is that of the conquest of a soul, or something that will substantially surpass human mortality (as for instance in having contributed something valuable to humankind). Facing the void and the possibility of nothingness are the indispensable counterparts of this quest for the eternal.

Conceptualization of psychological disturbance and health

Disturbance and health are two sides of the same coin. Living creatively means welcoming both. Well-being coincides with the ability to be transparent and open to what life can bring: both good and bad. In trying to evade the negative side of existence we get stuck as surely as we do when we cannot see the positive side. It is only in facing both positive and negative poles of existence that we generate the necessary power to move ahead. Thus well-being is not the naive enjoyment of a state of total balance given to one by mother nature and perfect parents. It can only be negotiated gradually by coming to terms with life, the world and oneself. It doesn't require a clean record of childhood experience, nor a total devotion to the cult of body and mind. It simply requires an openness to being and to an increasing understanding of what the business of living is all about. Psychological well-being is closest to wisdom and psychological disturbance is closest to self-deception in a blind following of popular opinions, habits, beliefs, rules and reasons on the one hand, or a drowning in the paradox of life on the other hand.

Finding one's inner authority and learning to create an increasingly comfortable space inside and around oneself, no matter what the circumstances, no matter what the past experience is to become authentically alive. To be authentic is to be true to oneself. This is not about setting one's own rules and living without regard for others. It is about recognizing necessities and givens as much as about affirming freedom and taking personal rights.

Many people avoid authentic living, because it is terrifying to face the reality of constant failing and of the possibility of ultimate disappearance into nothingness. It is superficially far more rewarding to play at being important or role-defined. Even the solidity of a self-image of sickness or madness can seem more attractive than having to struggle with yourself and face your unsubstantiality.

But ultimately it is an essential aspect of being human to long for truth. One is reminded of truth by the pangs of one's conscience, which expose one's evasion of reality. An immediate sense of courage and possibility can be found by stopping the dialogue with the internalized voices of other people's laws and expectations. In the quietude of being with myself I can sense where truth lies and where lies have obscured the truth. The call of conscience reaches me through a feeling of guilt, that is existential guilt, which tells me that something is lacking, something is being owed to life by me: I am in debt to myself.

The call of conscience comes through an attitude of openness to possibilities and limitations. This openness leads to *Angst* as it exposes me to my responsibilities and possible failure. But when I accept this anxiety it becomes the source of energy that allows me to be ready for whatever the future holds in store. And so, in facing up to the worst, I prepare myself for the best. I can live resolutely only when I can also surrender. I can be free only when I know what is necessary. I can be fully alive only when I face up to the possibility of my death.

Acquisition of psychological disturbance

With this definition of well-being disturbance can obviously be generated at any time in life, not necessarily only through childhood trauma. Problems are first of all problems in living and will occur at any stage in human development. In fact the only thing you can be sure of is that life will inevitably confront you with new situations that are a challenge to your established ways and evasions of the human paradox. When people are shocked out of their ordinary routine into a sudden awareness of their inability to face up to the realities of living, the clouds start to gather. Even though we may think of ourselves as well-adjusted people who have had a moderately acceptable upbringing, unexpected events – such as the death of a loved one, the loss of a job or another significant situation – may still trigger a new sense of failure, despair or extreme anxiety. Everything around us suddenly seems absurd or impossible and our own and other people's motives are questioned. The value of what used to be taken for granted becomes uncertain and life loses its appeal. The basic vulnerability of being human has emerged from behind the well-guarded self-deception of social adaptation. Sometimes a similar disenchantment and profound disturbance arise not out of an external catastrophe but out of a sense of the futility of everyday routine. Boredom can be just as important a factor in generating disturbance as losses or other forms of crisis.

No matter how securely a person is established in the world some events will shake the foundations of that security and transform the appearance of existence. For some people however such false self-security is not at first available. They never achieve 'ontological security' (Laing 1960), which consists of having a firm sense of one's own and other people's reality and identity. Genetic predisposition obviously makes some of us capable of greater sensory awareness and psychological susceptibility than others. People who have such extraordinary sensitivity may easily get caught up in the conflicts that others are trying to avoid. If they are exposed to particularly intense contradictions (as in certain family conflicts) they may fall into a state of extreme confusion and despair and withdraw into the relative security of a world of their own creation.

Both the ontologically secure person who is disturbed by a crisis (or boredom) and the ontologically insecure person who is overwhelmed by the less pleasant sides of ordinary human existence is struggling with an absence of the usual protective armour of self-deception. Life is suddenly seen in all its negativity, harshness and reality. Without the redeeming factor of some of the more positive aspects of life such realism can be utterly distressing.

This does not mean that this kind of crisis or generation of anxiety should be avoided. It can be faced and overcome by making sense of it. The existential view of disturbance is therefore that it is an inevitable and even welcome event that everyone will sooner or later encounter. The question is not how to avoid it, but on the contrary how to approach it with determination and curiosity.

Perpetuation of psychological disturbance

Problems start to become more serious when the challenge of disturbance is not faced but evaded. Then a self-perpetuating negative spiralling downwards can happen which leads to destruction of self and other. This type of vicious circle is most likely to occur if we are not part of a vital support system. As long as our family situation or other close relationship is strong and open enough to face and tackle the contradictions that we get caught up in, distress can be eased and overcome: the balance can be redressed. But if we find ourselves in isolation, without the understanding and challenge of a relative or a partner it is easy to get lost in our problems. Society's rituals and beliefs for safeguarding the individual are these days less and less powerful and secure. Few people get a sense of ultimate meaning or direction from their relationship to a God or from other essential beliefs. Many feel at the mercy of temporary, ever-changing, but incessant demands, needs and desires.

In time of distress all too often there seems to be nowhere to turn. Relatives and friends, who themselves are only just holding their heads above water, may be unavailable. If they are available, they may have a tendency to want to soothe the distress instead of facing and tackling it at the root. Spiritual authority and support has gradually been eroded and has been replaced with scientific or medical authority and support. The latter does not provide understanding and strengthening of personal resources, but a mechanistic cure-oriented salvage operation which leaves people uninspired and often victimized. It is hardly surprising that more and more people are turning to psychotherapists or counsellors in an attempt to break out of these vicious circles. Unfortunately there is little evidence that therapy and counselling significantly achieve this goal. To some extent a reliance on therapeutic cure may present another perpetuation of disturbance, as long as the basic existential issues are not dealt with and the client is kept in a passive role.

This illustrates the paradoxical nature of the institutions in our society that often seem to encourage the very opposite of what they are supposed to be about. When the family becomes a place of loneliness and alienation instead of togetherness and intimacy, when schools become places of boredom and reluctance instead of curiosity and learning and surgeries places of dependence and addiction instead of healing and renewal of strength, it is time that basics and essentials get reconsidered. Much disturbance is not only generated but also maintained by a society that is out of touch with the essential principles of life.

Often it is in the distress of those who face a crisis that the disturbance of society is expressed. It is therefore hardly surprising that we are inclined to want to smother such distress which reminds us of the basic fallacies and failings at the heart of our own existence. If we are willing to hear the message of such distress we however give ourselves a chance to be reminded of the ways in which we usually perpetuate our own misunderstanding and avoidance of life.

Change

Life is one long process of change and transformation. Although people often think they want to change, more often than not their lives reflect their attempts at maintaining a status quo. As soon as a person becomes convinced of the inevitability of change she can usually become aware also of the many ways in which she has resisted such change. Almost every minute of the day people make small choices that together determine the direction of their life. Often that direction is embarked upon in a passive way: people just follow their own negative or mediocre predictions of the future. But once insight is gained into the possibility of reinterpreting a situation and opting for more constructive predictions a change for the better comes about.

It is not easy to break the force of habit, but there are always times when habits are broken by force. Crises are times when old patterns have to be revised and when changes for the better can be initiated. This is why existential therapists often talk about a breakdown as a possible breakthrough and why people often note with astonishment that the disaster they tried so hard to avoid became a blessing in disguise. In times of crisis the attention gets refocused on where priorities lie so that choices can be made with more understanding than previously.

Whether such an event is self-imposed (as in emigration or marriage) or not (as in natural disasters or death) it has the effect of removing the previously taken-for-granted securities. When this happens it becomes harder for us to obscure the aspects of existence that we would rather not think about and we have to reassess our own attitudes and values. In the ensuing chaos we then have to make choices about how to proceed and how to bring a new order into our lives. If we can stand the uncertainty of the situation instead of fleeing towards a new routine, such times can be an opportunity for getting life's direction right.

Once a crisis has been faced in such a constructive manner it becomes increasingly easier to be open to change at other times as well. People can learn to re-evaluate their values and reassess their priorities on an almost permanent basis, thus achieving a flexibility and vitality that allows them to make the most of life's natural transformative character. Many other people dread change and hide from it even if they have to face it at a time of crisis. Existential therapy can be particularly helpful in those circumstances.

Practice

Goals of therapy

The goals of existential therapy are

1 to enable people to become truthful with themselves again
2 to widen their perspective on themselves and the world around them
3 to find clarity on how to proceed into the future whilst taking lessons from the past and creating something valuable to live for in the present.

The word authenticity is often used to indicate this goal of becoming true to oneself and therefore more real. But it is a much abused word, which misleadingly suggests that there is a true and solid self, when the existential view is that self is a process – not an entity or substance. The notion of authenticity can also become an excuse for people who want to have their cake and eat it. Under the aegis of authenticity anything can be licensed: crude egoism may very well be the consequence.

In fact authenticity can never be fully achieved. It is a gradual ongoing process of self-understanding. It means getting to know the self as it is created in one's relationships to the world on all its different levels. Helping people to become authentic means assisting them in gaining an increasing understanding of the human condition, so that they can respond to it with a sense of mastery, instead of being at its mercy.

The task of the therapist is therefore to have reached sufficient depth of clarity and openness to be able to venture along with any client into murky waters and explore (without getting lost) how this person's experience fits into the wider map of existence. Clients are safely guided through the disturbances they had become caught up in and they are helped to look at their assumptions, values and aspirations, so that a new direction can be taken. The therapist is fully available to this exploration and will therefore often be changed in the process. The poignancy of each particular new adventure over the dangerous grounds of life will involve the therapist to become aware of always new aspects and dimensions of life. Therapy is not about putting yet another client through a number of pre-established paces and interpretations; it is an adventure that client and therapist embark on together. In the process both will be transformed, as they will let themselves be touched by life.

Selection criteria

Clients who come specifically for existential therapy usually already have the idea that their problems are about living, not a form of pathology. This basic assumption must be acceptable to clients if they are to benefit from the approach. A genuine commitment to an intense and very personal philosophical investigation is therefore a requirement. A critical mind and a desire to think for oneself are a decided advantage. People who want another's opinion on what ails them and who would rather find quick symptom relief than a search for meaning should be referred on to other forms of therapy.

The approach is particularly suitable for people who feel alienated from the current expectations of society or for those who are in search of meaning in the sense of looking to clarify their personal ideology (rather than belonging to a church or a political group). The approach is relevant to people living in a foreign culture, class or race, as it does not dictate a particular way of looking at reality. It also works well with people who are confronting particular upheavals in their lives or who are trying to cope with changes of personal circumstances (or want to bring those about). Bereavement, job-loss or biological changes (in adolescence or middle age) are a prime time for the reconsideration of the rules and values one has lived by so far.

Generally speaking the existential approach works better with those who question the state of affairs in the world, than with those who would like to see the status quo confirmed and consolidated. This approach seems to be most right for those at the edge of existence: people who are dying or contemplating suicide, people who are just starting on a new phase of life (like teenagers), people in crisis, or people who feel they no longer belong in their surroundings. It is less relevant for people who do not want to examine their assumptions and who would rather not explore the foundation of human existence. People who specifically just want to relieve a particular symptom should be referred on.

But even though existential work consists in gaining understanding through talking, the client's level of verbal ability is not important. Very young children or people who are speaking a foreign language, for instance, will often find that the simpler the way of expressing things, the easier it becomes to grasp the essence of their world-view and experience. The approach is not about intellectualizing, but about verbalizing the basic impressions, ideas, intuitions and feelings a person has about life.

The existential approach favours individual therapy over group, family or marital therapy, though the individual work may sometimes take place within such a setting. The focus is always on the individual's experience, rather than on the actual interactions or dynamics at work. Some more directive and manipulative forms of therapy would not fit very well alongside existential work, as the objects and aims would be contradictory and confusing to the client. But it is possible to combine existential work with an analytic approach, a person-centred approach or other specific compatible methods, such as Gestalt.

Qualities of effective therapists

Good existential therapists combine personal qualities with accomplishment in method, but on balance it is more important that they are the right sort of people than that they have a high level of skill and technology. Qualities can be described as falling into four categories: life experience, attitude and personality, theoretical knowledge and professional training.

Life experience
The existential therapist will characteristically be mature as a human being. This maturity will manifest itself in an ability to make room in oneself for all sorts of, even contradictory, opinions, attitudes, feelings, thoughts and experiences. Rather than clinging to one point of view, existential therapists will be capable of overseeing reality from a wide range of perspectives. There are a number of life experiences that appear to be particularly helpful in preparing people for such maturation. First, it is cross-cultural experience that stretches the mind and one's views on what it means to be human. People who have had to permanently adjust their whole way of perceiving and dealing with the world (especially when this includes a change of language) have had the all-important experience of questioning previous assumptions and opening up to a new culture and perspective. Going through this experience several times can allow one to reach a place where it is more clear what the essential human experiences are.

Second, raising a family or caring for dependants in a close relationship is another invaluable source of life experience relevant to creating an open attitude. There are many women who have little academic schooling but great practical experience in this area. Their life experience can become one of the building blocks of the kind of maturity needed to become a therapist.

Third, the experience of having been immersed in society from several angles, in different jobs, different academic studies, different social classes and so on, is a definite advantage. The existential therapist must be someone who has lived life seriously and intensely in a different field than that of the caring professions only. People opting for psychotherapy as a second career are often particularly suitable.

The final *sine qua non* of the required maturity is that the therapist has personally negotiated a sufficient number of significant crossroads in his or her life.

Existential therapists will have had their share of existential crises. Of course they will also have had to develop their ability to deal with these situations satisfactorily, so that their own lives were enriched rather than impoverished through the experience. Although all this maturity conjures up the image of someone advanced in age, it must be noted that maturity is not always commensurate with years. Some fairly young people may have weathered greater storms than their elders and what is more may have lived their relatively shorter lives with greater intensity maturing into fuller human beings.

Attitude and personality
Existential therapists are capable of critical, yet not cynical consideration of situations, people and ideas. They are serious, but not heavy-handed or downtrodden by life. They can be lighthearted, hopeful and humorous about the

human condition, while intensely aware of the true tragic poignancy of much of existence.

They are eminently capable of self-reflection, recognizing the particular manner in which they themselves represent the paradoxes, ups and downs, strengths and weaknesses that people are capable of. They have a genuine sense of curiosity about the universe and a strong urge to find out what it means to be human. Rather than reaching for doctrines to explain experience they are capable of an attitude of wonder. Existential therapists will now and then abandon psychological theory altogether and reach for poetry, art or religion instead.

Theoretical knowledge

A good working knowledge of philosophy, that is of the essential controversies and different perspectives that the human race has produced over the centuries, is more useful to this approach than any other kind of knowledge. Included in this would be a familarity with the history of psychology and psychoanalysis and a wide study of the many different approaches to psychotherapy that have been developed over the years. This will provide a map of different views on human nature, health and illness, happiness and unhappiness, which again will train and broaden the mind and personal outlook of the therapist.

Professional training

The existential therapist needs the kind of training that an eclectic therapist needs: an all-round one. But instead of borrowing bits and pieces of technique from each to produce a complex amalgam, the essentials are distilled and applied within a consistent and firmly philosophical framework.

The training will consist of a significant amount of clinical work under supervision and of work of self-reflection and analysis. Here again it is the quality that will be judged instead of the quantity. Numbers of hours of individual and group therapy are irrelevant. Some people will not reach the necessary perspective and depth with any amount of therapy. Others will be well ahead by having engaged in a discipline of self-reflection for years. The degree of readiness usually becomes obvious in supervision sessions, for one's response to other people's troubles is an excellent test of one's own attitude to life and level of self-knowledge.

Therapeutic style

It is important for the existential therapist to have a flexible attitude towards therapeutic style. Not only do different therapists interpret the approach in diverse ways, but also clients have their own individual requirements which may vary over time. The existential therapist is therefore ready and willing to shift her stance when the situation requires this. In a sense, then, this variability is characteristic of the existential therapeutic style.

There are, of course, common features running through all of this. All existential therapists, for example, strive to abandon their preconceptions and prejudices as much as possible in their work. There is also a consistent appreciation of the unique and particular situation of the client. The existential therapist takes the dilemmas of the client seriously – eschewing glib diagnoses and solutions. The seriousness includes openness and wonder as essential attributes of the existential attitude and certainly does not preclude humour when appropriate.

The existential therapist is fundamentally concerned with what matters most to the client. He or she therefore avoids normative theories, and renounces any ambition to, even implicitly, push the client in any particular direction. The attitude is non-directive, but is not directionless. The client is assisted in finding his or her own perspective and position in the world.

At times the therapist might facilitate this through an attitude of relative passivity. At other times activity and confrontation are required. On such occasions the therapist intervenes to point out contradictions in or implications of the client's avowed point of view. The use of 'confrontation' to offer opinions or moral evaluations of the client is not consistent with the existential attitude.

The existential therapist resists the temptation to change the client. The therapy is an opportunity for the client to take stock of her life and ways of being in the world. Nothing is gained from interfering with these. The client is simply given the space, time and understanding to help her come to terms with what is true for her. What she wants to do with this afterwards is up to her. The therapist does not teach or preach about how life should be lived, but lets the client's personal taste in the art of living evolve naturally.

The only times when the therapist does follow a didactic line is when she reminds the client of aspects of a problem that have been overlooked. She gently encourages the client to notice a lack of perspective and puts forward missing links and underlying principles. The therapist never does the work for the client but makes sure that the work gets done. The client's inevitable attempts to shirk and flee from the task in hand are reflected on and used as concrete evidence of the client's attitude to life. The same can be said of the actual encounter between the client and the therapist, which is also reflected on and seen as evidence of the client's usual ways of relating.

Generally speaking the therapeutic style follows a conversational pattern. Issues are considered and explored in dialogue. The rhythm of the sessions will follow that of the client's preoccupations – faster when emotions are expressed and slower when complex ideas are disentangled.

Existential sessions are usually quite intense, as deep and significant issues will tend to emerge. Moreover, the therapist is personally engaged with the work and is willing to be touched and moved by the client's conflicts and questions. The human dilemmas expressed in the therapeutic encounter have just as much relevance to the therapist as to the client. This commonality of experience makes it possible for client and therapist to work together as a team, in a co-operative effort to throw light on human existence. Every new challenge in the client's experience is grist for the mill. The therapeutic relationship itself brings many opportunities to grasp something of the nature of human interaction. The therapist, in principle, is ready to consider any past, present or future matter that is relevant to the client.

Major therapeutic strategies and techniques

The existential approach is well known for its anti-technique orientation. It prefers description, understanding and interpretation of reality to diagnosis, treatment and prognosis. Existential therapists will not generally use specified techniques, strategies or skills, but they will follow a specific philosophical method of enquiry which requires a consistent professional attitude. This method and attitude may be interpreted in various ways, but it usually includes some or all of the following ingredients.

Cultivating a naive attitude
By meeting the client with an open mind and in the spirit of exploration and discovery a fresh perspective on the world will emerge.

Themes   Clear themes will run through the apparently confused discourse of the client. The therapist listens for the unspoken links that are implicit in what is said. When the theme is obvious and has been confirmed several times the client's attention can be drawn to it.

Assumptions   Much of what the client says will be based on a number of basic assumptions about the world. Generally people take their assumptions for granted and they are consequently unaware of them. Clarifying the implicit assumptions can be very revealing and may throw a new light on a dilemma.

Vicious circles   Many people are caught up in self-fulfilling prophecies of doom and destruction without realizing that they set their own low standards and goals. Making such vicious circles explicit can be a crucial step forward.

Meanings   Most often people naturally assume that they know what they mean when they talk about something. But the words they use can hide, even from themselves, the significance of what they really mean. By questioning the super-ficial meaning of the client's words and asking her to think again of what she really wants to express, a new awareness may be brought about.

Facing limitations
As the existential approach is essentially concerned with the need to face the limitations of the human condition, the therapist will be alert for opportunities to help the client identify these.

Self-deception   Much of the time we pretend that life has determined our situation and character so much that we have no choices left. Crises provide us with proof to the contrary. The safe crisis of the therapeutic interaction is a good place for rediscovering opportunities and challenges that had been forgotten.

Existential anxiety   The anxiety that indicates one's awareness of inevitable limita-tions and death is also a dizziness in the face of freedom. Existential anxiety is the *sine qua non* of individual awareness and full aliveness. Some people have dulled their sensitivity so as to avoid the basic challenges of life, others are overwhelmed by them and yet others have found ways of disguising them. The therapist will recognize existential anxiety and guide the client in finding ways of dealing with it constructively.

Existential guilt   The sense of being in debt to life and owing it to oneself to do or not do something is another source of insight into limitations and priorities that have to be dealt with. Therapists will watch for existential guilt hidden underneath various disguises (such as anxiety, boredom, depression or even apparent self-confidence).

Consequences   Clients are sometimes challenged to think through the consequences of choices, both past and future. In facing the implications of one's actions it becomes necessary to recognize limitations as well as possibilities. Some choices become easier to make, others become less attractive.

Paradoxes   In helping the client to become more authentic the concept of paradox can be of great help. If clients are inclined to evade the basic human dilemma of life and death and other contradictions that flow from it their self-affirmation is almost invariably misinformed ego-centricity. Checking that a person is aware of her capacity for both life and death, success and failure, freedom and necessity, certainty and doubt, allows one to remain in touch with a fundamental search for truth.

Exploring personal worldview

The existential approach aims at covering all of life's dimensions, tasks and problems and the therapist will in principle explore together with the client all information that the latter brings along.

The fourfold world   Using the model of four dimensions of existence discussed earlier (see pp. 152–3), it becomes possible to listen to the client's account of herself as revealing her preoccupations with particular levels of her existence. A systematic analysis of how the client expresses her relationship to the natural, public, private and ideal dimensions of her world can provide much insight into imbalance, priorities and impasse. An impression can be formed this way of where on the whole territory of human existence the client is struggling for clarity.

Dreams   Listening to dreams with this model of human experience in mind can be particularly enlightening. The dream is seen as a message of the dreamer to herself. The dream experience reflects the dreamer's attitudes on the different dimensions of existence. Of course the same thing applies to the fantasies or stories the client reports. Each of these is a miniature picture of the way in which she relates to the world.

Questions   Exploring the client's worldview is an ongoing enterprise and it is best done with an observation-oriented attitude. Questions are asked as little as possible, but deductions are arrived at whenever there is enough evidence to suggest a particular orientation. The therapist draws the client's attention to what seems to be the case. Sometimes in order to clarify a perception an enquiry might be made, along the lines of an exploration: 'What makes this so important to you?', or 'What is this like for you?' or 'What does it mean to you?' The question in this case never suggests a solution nor judges right or wrong, but investigates the client's personal opinion and inclination.

Enquiring into meaning
All investigations eventually lead to gaining a greater understanding of what makes the world meaningful to the client. The idea is to assist the client in finding purpose and motivation. In the process a number of irrelevant and misleading motivations may be encountered and eliminated.

Emotions   Feelings are of great help in this process. Understanding the meaning of one's emotions and the message they contain in terms of what one aspires to or is afraid to lose is of crucial help in finding the pattern of purpose currently at work. Each emotion has its own significance (van Deurzen–Smith 1988) and the whole emotional spectrum can be used as a compass in indicating one's direction in life. For example, emotions like shame, envy and hope are indicators of values that are still missing but implicitly longed for. Love, joy and pride are within the range of emotions that indicate a sense of ownership of what is valued. Whereas jealousy and anger express an active response to the threat of what is valued, fear and sorrow come with the giving up and eventual loss of what really mattered.

Beliefs   All observations on what it is that makes the client tick lead to a picture of her opinions, beliefs and values. It is important to extract these with an attitude of absolute respect. Nothing can be gained from opposing the client's values with an alternative set of values. It is the client's conscience that has to be uncovered. If deeply held values are contested or criticized conformity will be encouraged rather than reliance on an inner source of truth.

Talents   Many small talents and abilities will have been hidden by the client's preoccupation with what is wrong with her. The therapist will be sensitive to these and draw attention to the wisdom that lies fallow inside of them. Often it will be useful for the therapist to use particular practical talents of the client as metaphors or similes for further understanding.

Recollection   Past memories will be seen as flexible and open to interpretation. While clients often set out with fixed views of their past they discover the possibility of reinterpreting the same events and experiences in different ways. It is essential to encourage clients to discover how they influence their future with their particular version of the past and how it is within their power to recollect themselves in new ways, thereby opening new vistas for the future. In addition to this the absolutely determining factors from the past will be moderated by a knowledge of the possibility for positive or negative transformation. When the client realizes that she is the ultimate source of the meaning of her life, past, present and future, living is experienced as an art rather than as a duty.

The change process in therapy

The aim of existential therapy is not to change people but to help them to come to terms with life in all its contradictions. The assumption is that when people do face up to reality they will eventually find a satisfactory way forward. People are often hurried and under the impression that they can speed life up and force great rewards out of it with relatively little effort. One of the aims of existential therapy is to enable people to stop deceiving themselves about both their lack of responsibility for what is happening to them and their excessive demands on life and themselves. Learning to measure one's distress by the standards of the human condition brings great relief to pressure and at the same time provides a clearer ideological basis for making sense of personal preoccupations and aspirations. Clients change through existential therapy by gradually taking more and more of life's ups and downs in their stride. They become more steadfast in facing death, crises, personal shortcomings, losses and failures. They accept the reality of constant transformation that we are all part of. They find ways of tuning into these changes, instead of fighting them or trying to speed them up.

In other words they acquire a measure of wisdom in learning to distinguish between the things they can change and those they cannot change. They come to terms with the givens and find the courage to tackle the uncertainties. They find out what matters enough to them to be committed to it, live for it and ultimately perhaps even die for it.

As they are constantly reminded to do their own thinking on these issues, they learn to monitor their own actions, attitudes and moods. The therapy gives an opportunity to rediscover the importance of relating to themselves and take time for contemplation and recreation.

The process of change, in other words, is initiated in the sessions, but not accomplished in them. The process of change takes place in between the sessions and after the therapy is terminated. The therapeutic hour itself can never be more than a small contribution to the person's renewed engagement with life. The change process is a never-ending one. As long as there is life there will be change. There is never any place for complacency or self-congratulatory belief in complete cure.

As existential therapy has no criterion for cure, it could in theory be an endless process. To make sure this doesn't happen the criterion for finishing a series of sessions is simply to stop when the client feels ready to manage alone again. To encourage such self-reliance, relatively short-term therapy is encouraged (six months to two years).

Limitations of the approach

The emphasis that the existential approach places on self-reflection and understanding can lead to certain limitations. The approach often attracts clients who feel disinclined to trust other human beings as they perceive the existential approach as leaving them in total control. This limitation can be overcome only by a therapist who neither fights the need, nor leaves it unchallenged, but who assists the client in turning such self-reliance to a positive end.

The approach is also often misconstrued as intellectual. Some existential therapists tend to emphasize the cognitive aspect of their client's preoccupations and some clients are attracted to the approach with the hope of avoiding senses, feeling and intuition. A good existential therapist would heed all these different levels of experience, as full self-understanding can be achieved only through openness to all different aspects of being.

The practical limitations of the approach have already been referred to in the section on selection criteria (p. 158). As the approach doesn't stress the illness–health dimension people who want to relieve specific symptoms will generally find the existential approach unhelpful.

The existential therapist neither encourages the client to regress to a deep level of dependency nor seeks to become a significant other in the client's life and nurture the client back to health. Rather, the therapist is a consultant who can provide the client with a method and systematic support in facing up to the truth and in this sense is there to allow the client to relate to herself more than to the therapist. This might be considered a limitation of the approach by clients who wish to regress and rely on the therapist as a substitute parental figure. Good existential therapists would obviously enable the client to confront that issue just as bravely as any other issue and come through with greater self-understanding.

The final limitation is that of the level of maturity, life-experience and intensive training that is required of practitioners in this field. It should be clear from the above that existential therapists are required to be wise and capable of profound and wide-ranging understanding of what it means to be human. The criteria of what makes for a good existential therapist are so high that the chances of finding bad existential therapists must be considerable.

One can imagine the danger of therapists' pretending to be capable of this kind of wisdom without actual substance or inner authority. Little would be gained in replacing technological or medical models of therapy, which can be concretely learnt and applied by practitioners, with a range of would-be existential advisers who are incapable of facing life's problems with dignity and creativity themselves. The only way around this is to create training organizations that select candidates extremely carefully on personal qualities and experience before it puts them through a thorough training in both philosophy and psychology and a long period of intensively supervised work.

Case example

The client

Vicky is a determined professional lady in her late 30s. She is referred by a colleague and makes contact in writing, presenting herself as 'stuck at a number of crossroads in my life, carrying too much baggage to proceed and therefore in imperative need of personal therapy'. At the initial interview she turns out to be of average height with short-cropped ash-blond hair and small, expressive metallic blue eyes. The overall effect of her appearance is the more striking as she is considerably overweight and dressed in colourful kingsize dungarees. Although she gives the impression of being solidly self-confident there are all over her face thick layers of masking cream barely hiding severe acne, betraying her inner turmoil and her vain efforts to cover it up. There is similarly an air of tiredness and defeat in the manner in which she sinks down to sit on the couch.

She says that she is a residential social worker, in charge of a large unit for severely emotionally disturbed children and that she generally enjoys her work. It is her sexuality and her marriage that are problematic. Although she and her husband Jim have a son (Mark), who is now 7 years old, they have been unable to have another child, because she has had innumerable miscarriages. She is convinced that this has made her into a burden for her husband and she has given up hope that he is genuinely interested in her. She fears that she is nothing but an impediment to his freedom and therapy is meant to help her make up her mind about whether to remain with him or let him go. She is only fleetingly aware of the possibility that she is actually encouraging Jim to turn away from her. She knows that she has pushed him to go on a forthcoming trip to Canada by himself. He is half-Canadian and has not been back there for fifteen years, but is to leave in a few weeks to go and stay with his Canadian family for two months. Vicky presents this as the inevitable crisis that will take him away from her forever. It is not clear whether she longs for him to leave and stay away, to leave and come back, or not to leave at all. It is as if she has no confidence in her ability to love him, and be loved back. She almost hopes that he will stay away so that he won't have left because he wanted to but because she sent him away. Her suffering is evident only when she speaks about their son, Mark, who is trying hard to keep them together. She fears that Jim might persuade Mark to come and live with him in Canada if he really decides to settle there without her.

Most of the initial interview is spent on her descriptions of what she imagines Jim, Mark, her parents and her colleagues think of her. She is particularly preoccupied with her belief that she has deceived and disappointed Jim. She reckons that he was attracted to her because she seemed to be strong and nurturing, capable of taking care of him, whereas in fact she has turned out to be someone who forced him into marrying her because she got pregnant and who then slumped into illness and dependency following the miscarriages. She thinks that Jim must feel trapped and fed up and she feels she owes it to him to help him free himself from this unfair situation. In all these situations she displays an extraordinary ability to remain in control of what she describes as a desperate situation. For someone who describes herself as dependent she appears to be remarkably in charge of the destiny of the person she thinks she depends on. It is not surprising that she requests a short-term once-weekly therapy. We agree on a six months' working period, as this fits in with mutual schedules and commitments.

The therapy

At the first session after this initial interview Vicky is much more concerned with her parents, and in particular with her father, than with Jim. Because her father is suddenly seriously ill in hospital after what should have been a routine operation, she is now very concerned with her own mortality and that of those whom she loves. The role of the therapist at this stage is simply to point out that there is a theme of the unfairness of life. This is expressed, for instance, in her thinking it unfair that her father should be in worse health than her mother. He has always done the right things, like not drinking and smoking, while her mother has always pretty much done as she pleased and seems to fare much better than him physically. Also, later on in the session while she is talking about her father's affection for her she remarks that 'she just can't win'. When I ask her what she means, Vicky explains that she thought she was pleasing her father by moving up the social ladder and by having been promoted to become 'Head of Unit'. Then she discovered to her dismay that life once more was not fair as her father would have preferred her to be at home with her son and husband instead. She is prepared to dismiss the whole idea of not being able to win with stoicism, but when pressed to examine her view on what 'winning' would consist of, she discovers that her whole attitude to life hinges on this; winning would mean living life on her own terms and doing everything she likes while still being liked and respected by everybody.

At first Vicky is rather casually dismissive about this and calls it her perfectionism. When asked equally casually 'and why not be a perfectionist?' she begins to investigate the contradictions inherent in her own attitude. Now the emphasis shifts from all this talk about other people and the outside world to her sadness about her mixed-up relationship with herself. Of course she is nothing as simplistic as a perfectionist: her house is a mess that she wants to escape from, her body seems out of control, even her work-life takes up too much of her time. It is as if she is greedy for work, things, people, food, love, and wants ever more just to get a sense of fullness and worth. But once she has it all, the fulfilment doesn't follow. So all her efforts seem in vain. No wonder she feels that life isn't fair.

The next week she speaks of wanting to be in the real world instead of in a fantasy world. When asked, she defines the real world as where she is in touch with other people rather than where she constructs images that do not connect. When asked what is wrong with a fantasy world she launches on to a long list of bad experiences in her childhood and adolescence. Each of these involved her expectations of other people being disappointed, sometimes violently so. Yet another theme also emerges – that of the discovery of her own power over others. She speaks of her memories of sexual play with her stepfather at the age of 9 and 10. First she sees this only in the light of his abuse of her and her guilt feelings when he turned alcoholic some time after she had refused to carry on with the games. When I point out how she is implying having had quite a lot of influence she remembers the sense of victory: the victory in the knowledge that he picked her and not her sister, victory also in that he gave her a valuable piece of jewellery one day and victory in the sense of having had such an impact on him that he would need to turn to drink after she refused him. All this leaves her very thoughtful.

We are able to discover how this theme is repeated many times over in other relationships where she turns a sense of being abused into one of being in control and having mastery over others. The bitter after-taste in all this is that she can never believe that it is she who matters to people. She may have some power and influence, but always indirectly, for people do not choose her for what she is, but for what she can provide. Her only consolation is that of having discovered in herself the strength to say 'no' when she can't bear this any longer. In distilling the essence of this we conclude that her relationships to other people seem to take place in a dimension of competition, where her only chance of winning is to take the upper hand, impressing people with her superior abilities (taking on lots of work, going out with lots of boyfriends in her teenage years, having lots of friends over to play with her son, eating lots of food to become huge and powerful). Of course the only thing she really 'wins' in this way is exhaustion and disappointment when people are not fooled by this behaviour. She also alienates herself from any possible appreciation of others as they are cast as the inevitable enemy.

At the third session this new understanding has translated into an image. She sees herself as stuck on a ridge on a mountainside overlooking the sea: she is comfortable and can see the whole world from up there, but is cold and isolated and looking for a path down. She is aware of many ways in which she remains aloof from other people, including from Jim and Mark. Then she says: 'I am often told that I should trust people more and believe they will like me'. As this is said with scepticism I respond by saying: 'Why should you be so rash? What certainty do you have that they will like you? Why should they come to you on your ridge on the mountainside when you are the one who is not coming down?'

This changes her rather flippant attitude into one of self-reflection as she realizes that she has not *wanted* to trust others. She takes a long time to respond and finally says with tears in her eyes and with the surprise of having made a new discovery: 'Yes. I am really alone – I am the only one who can do it. I'm on my own'. As it is near the end of the session, I merely reply: 'Yes, and that's where I will have to leave you; it is time for us to stop'. That moment carries a seriousness and understanding of being touched by the inevitability of human limitations. It carries her forward into a more certain direction, for she now realizes what she is up against.

During the fourth session for the first time she is capable of exploring some of her strengths: she reports that she is a keen gardener and has her own allotment. Putting order into nature's growing process is a source of unlimited enjoyment for her, especially as she is good at it. The metaphor of this talent becomes a source of inspiration during future sessions. With some assistance, she learns to translate her difficulties at work, for instance, into terms of sowing and reaping, planting and weeding and pruning. This makes her see new possibilities in her work and gives her much courage for facing problems as if they were just part of the enjoyable activity of her gardening life. This gives her the concrete model she craved: life seems within her grasp. She knows she is good at gardening and she feels confident that she would know what to trim and cut and where to encourage flowering and blossoming. She glows with pride as she realizes that this turns everything that seemed like a bore, a duty and a danger into something that can only be a source of challenge and enjoyment. For the first time she sees her problems in perspective.

The next few weeks a number of concrete events in her life provide plenty of challenges for her. Among other things Jim has now gone to Canada and her mother has moved in with her. She easily loses sight of her gardening metaphor as the clouds gather and she feels threatened in many ways. During this time she explores other issues for which other understandings and metaphors are needed. One of the themes that now emerges is that of her fantasy of being self-sufficient. It is of course related both to her negative view of other people and to her joy in gardening. She has a longing to live in a small cottage on her allotment, surviving entirely within her own resources. As self-sufficiency is her ideal, one of the things she most despises is 'middle-class women living off their husbands' salaries and prancing around to art classes'. In exploring this statement it becomes clear that what she does not understand at all is why these women, while being totally dependent and in her opinion virtually useless, still expect to be loved and desired by their husbands. Vicky does not in the least expect to be loved even though she thinks of herself as fairly deserving. So how can those women who don't do anything to deserve it expect to be loved and what's more: how do they actually manage to *be* loved? I point out to her that she has forgotten that by climbing away, on to her mountain ridge in her aloof self-sufficiency she is the one not available to others. She is the one not open for love. Be denying her own need for others she is pushing them away. These contradictions in her own attitude are gradually becoming explicit in our dialogue together. She can grasp this in theory but it is harder to recognize her implicit rejection of others in practice. She often needs me to make her implicit attitude explicit to her, so that she can recognize it.

This issue is particularly poignant in her relationship with her mother. Both try to outdo each other in independence and self-sufficiency, while reproaching the other for not being more loving or needy. It seems extremely difficult for Vicky to let it sink in that to love means, among other things, to make oneself available and therefore vulnerable to needing the other. She has protected herself carefully from being hurt by others by pretending never to need anything from anyone. She does not, for instance, expect Jim to be faithful to her in Canada and has told him so in as many words before he left. She makes it generally clear to him that she wants nothing from him at all, but is amazed that this pushes him away rather than bringing him closer. Each time I draw her attention to such contradictions in her attitude, she is surprised and somewhat relieved at rediscovering the logic of the situation, which previously seemed strange and confusing.

There are many complex past and present relationships that we examine in this light, but it is as if Vicky remains blind to the contradictions of her own attitude. She still prefers to believe that she really is open to others and does not like to think that this might be an illusion.

This paradox finally comes to a head in a real sense through an apparently unrelated event in her working life which becomes a powerful vehicle for a new understanding. One day she arrives for therapy in a shocked and somewhat distraught state about something that has taken place at the weekend. Some of the adolescents in her unit have been to a holiday camp with some of the staff and Vicky decided to surprise them by paying them a visit. Far from being rewarded for this generous extra bit of work, she was fiercely disappointed upon finding the staff drunk, drugged and so much out of control of the children in their charge that they are thrown out of the resort the following day in spite of Vicky's intervention. Although she does not want to take official action against the staff, because it would have severe repercussions for them and for the establishment (and perhaps for her), she knows that her relationship with them will never be the same again. Her professional self-confidence is shocked to its very foundation.

When we look, together, and calmly at the implications of this experience, we find that up to this point she has always been the popular, friendly colleague and superior: it is her pride to be 'one of the boys' with the mostly male staff. This time she has had to resort to authoritarian behaviour and has been mocked by them for being a spoil-sport. She is outraged and wonders if she has always been too gullible, not strict enough, too eager to please. Yet she is also profoundly hurt, especially for having been let down by a staff that she thought she could trust and whom she has done so much for. But in the end the most painful aspect of the experience is that they have called her uptight and considered her to be on the other side of the divide: no longer 'one of the boys'. More than their reproaches, it is the realization that she herself is no longer able to condone such behaviour that shocks her. She is discovering with astonishment that the values that she thought she stood for have been replaced by a new set of values that she has not so far dared to make explicit to herself.

Our discussion brings out that she was always the sort of person who fought for freedom and against the establishment: she used to smoke dope and drink quite a lot herself and believed that experience to be part of the rights of the individual. She used to think of herself as something of a revolutionary and as an outright liberated and democratic sort of person. This was precisely why she used to hate her name: Victoria. It always seemed so out of keeping with what she believed in and wanted to be. And now suddenly, through this one event she notices that for a long time she has lied to herself. She is really proud of her name and the values that it conjures up do not seem so terrible at all. When she sees that I do not condemn her for her hesitant reclaiming of old values, it is with some glee, as if in a long last homecoming, that she admits to identifying secretly with Queen Victoria and all she stands for, even though that is hard to acknowledge and goes against what she long thought ought to be the case. While these things are clearly difficult to express there is an obvious release of pent-up longing to be more true to herself and with much sighing and wide-eyed tearfulness she finds relief in facing her new position in life.

It is now possible for us to see the past in a new light too. It has been such a struggle for her all those years to try and take everything in her stride and everyone under her wing. She has been so caught up in this one-sided attempt at being broad-minded and understanding that she is surprised at her own relief when her forced composure and unrealistic accepting attitude are broken. Floods of resentment and sadness come streaming out now that she lets down the barrier. Suddenly she can see all the contradictions in her attitude. Accepting everything that comes her way and bending over backwards to accommodate everybody's demands on her, but never daring to reject anything or anyone for fear of rejection, she has got herself into an untenable position. She can only keep on expanding and expanding without ever having the possibility of decompressing or eliminating. It is obvious that such one-sided behaviour can lead only to explosion.

The next few sessions are so many variations on this theme. Each elaboration of this small revelation of inner truth makes her understand herself a little better. Every week a little piece of the puzzle falls into place. Often she describes a situation that apparently has no relation to the puzzle until her attention is drawn to its relevance in terms of her basic choices and challenges. Then sometimes it clicks into place and the world makes a bit more sense. At other times she just needs to explore her experience, finding it too painful to consider the ways in which she limits herself by overexpanding herself. She goes through a phase where she loses her self-esteem when I challenge her rather too forcefully on the way in which she controls Jim by pretending to be all accepting of him, while actually punishing him with further withdrawal and independence whenever he does something she inwardly disapproves of.

This clearly still is the blind spot in her understanding. It is almost impossible for her to notice the impact of her own withholding of demands. Although she recognizes the effect of her withdrawal from Jim when he becomes alienated from her, she finds it much harder to catch herself doing it, let alone stop doing it. She would love to be able to tell him that she needs his love so that he would not be pushed away, but she is not ready even to allow herself to experience that fully. There are still too many deeply ingrained reasons for her wanting to maintain the independent, aloof and outwardly tolerant, but inwardly suffering and judgemental attitude that keeps him away from her.

Vicky still deeply believes that she cannot have any impact on others unless she puts up with everything they dish out to her. The fundamental purpose for her is to have an effect and be in control of others. But this purpose is dressed up as an attitude of great acceptance and capacity to include anything and anyone. The straightforward making of demands and setting of boundaries that could lead to a positive control of her relationships to others is lacking: she does not dare to announce and affirm her exclusive rights and needs. When she is asked to muse over what it means to her to be exclusive one session she discovers the entire concept to have long been taboo – exciting – but strictly taboo. Being selective and choosy is dangerous, for how can she know that what she will pick is right? Also how can she continue to be acceptable to all if she is not accepting? When I point out to her that she is just as non-accepting and selective in excluding selectivity as an option she is shocked.

The idea that she may have been only fooling herself makes it easier to abandon her old ways. She begins to wonder about what it is she really wants out of life and other people rather than to continue assuming that she already knows what she wants. This brings up many new aspects, new questions and issues that need exploring. Around this time Vicky begins to take an active interest in undertaking various projects for her own enjoyment instead of for her professional ambition. She finds that she can use some of this ambition for personal purposes and use her energy to achieve joy for herself instead of success at work which impresses nobody. Her priorities are gradually shifting. She is loosening her own expectations of herself and opening up to the terror and longing underneath.

When the sessions finish, after six months as planned, she evaluates her progress with great optimism. A follow-up session two months later shows that although she is managing well she is perhaps a little too keen on proving to herself and me that the therapy has been a success. It is clear that she is not always allowing her experience to touch her deeply and that she is looking still to outside achievements to fill up the inner longing. Perhaps the therapy should have continued longer to stabilize a new attitude of self-reflection and monitoring of experience. But as Vicky herself puts it: there is enough for her to go on. Her attitude is constructive and confident. She will know where to find further assistance if and when she needs it.

References

Binswanger, L. (1963) *Being-in-the-World*, trans. J. Needleman, New York: Basic Books.
Boss, M. (1957a) *Psychoanalysis and Daseinsanalysis*, trans. J.B. Lefebre, New York: Basic Books.
—— (1957b) *The Analysis of Dreams*, London: Rider.
—— (1979) *Existential Foundations of Medicine and Psychology*, New York: Jason Aronson.
Cooper, D. (1967) *Psychiatry and Anti-psychiatry*, New York: Barnes & Noble.
Cooper, R. (ed.) (1989) *Thresholds between Philosophy and Psychoanalysis*, London: Free Association Books.
Deurzen–Smith, E. van (1984) Existential therapy, in W. Dryden (ed.) *Individual Therapy in Britain*, Milton Keynes: Open University Press.
—— (1988) *Existential Counselling in Practice*, London: Sage.
Frankl, V.E. (1964) *Man's Search for Meaning*, London: Hodder & Stoughton.
—— (1967) *Psychotherapy and Existentialism*, Harmondsworth: Penguin.
Heaton, J. (1968) *The Eye: Phenomenology and Psychology of Functions and Disorders*, London: Tavistock.
—— (in preparation) *Differences: Wittgenstein and Psychotherapy*.
Heidegger, M. (1962) *Being and Time*, trans. J. Macquarrie and E.S. Robinson, New York: Harper & Row.
—— (1968) *What is Called Thinking?*, New York: Harper & Row.
Husserl, E. (1960) *Cartesian Meditations*, The Hague: Nijhoff.
—— (1962) *Ideas*, New York: Collier.
Jaspers, K. (1951) *The Way to Wisdom*, trans. R. Manheim, New Haven, Conn. and London: Yale University Press.
—— (1963) *General Psychopathology*, Chicago, Ill: University of Chicago Press.
Kearney, R. (1986) *Modern Movements in European Philosophy*, Manchester: Manchester University Press.
Kierkegaard S. (1941) *Concluding Unscientific Postscript*, trans. D.F. Swenson and W. Lowrie, Princeton, NJ: Princeton University Press.
—— (1944) *The Concept of Dread*, trans. W. Lowrie, Princeton, NJ: Princeton University Press.
Koning, A.J.J. de and Jenner, F.A. (1982) *Phenomenology and Psychiatry*, New York: Academic Press.
Laing, R.D. (1960) *The Divided Self*, Harmondsworth: Penguin.
—— (1961) *Self and Others*, Harmondsworth: Penguin.
Laing, R.D. and Cooper, D. (1964) *Reason and Violence*, London: Tavistock.
Ledermann, E.K. (1972) *Existential Neurosis*, London: Butterworth.
—— (1984) *Mental Health and Human Conscience*, Amersham: Avebury.
Lomas, P. (1981) *The Case for a Personal Psychotherapy*, Oxford: Oxford University Press.
Macquarrie, J. (1972) *Existentialism: An Introduction, Guide and Assessment*, Harmondsworth: Penguin.
May, R. (1969) *Love and Will*, New York: Norton.
—— (1983) *The Discovery of Being*, New York: Norton.
May, R. and Yalom, I. (1985) 'Existential psychotherapy', in R.J. Corsini (ed.) *Current Psychotherapies*, Itasca, Ill: Peacock.
May, R., Angel, E. and Ellenberger, H.F. (1958) *Existence*, New York: Basic Books.
Merleau Ponty, M. (1962) *Phenomenology of Perception*, trans. C. Smith, London: Routledge & Kegan Paul.
Minkowski E. (1970) *Lived Time*, Evanston, Ill: Northwestern University Press.
Nietzsche, F. (1961) *Thus Spoke Zarathustra*, trans. R.J. Hollingdale, Harmondsworth: Penguin.
—— (1974) *The Gay Science*, trans. W. Kaufmann, New York: Random House.

—— (1986) *Human, All Too Human, A Book for Free Spirits*, trans. R.J. Hollingdale, Cambridge: Cambridge University Press.

Sartre, J.P. (1956) *Being and Nothingness: An Essay on Phenomenological Ontology*, trans. H. Barnes, New York: New York Philosophical Library.

—— (1962) *Sketch for a Theory of the Emotions*, London: Methuen.

Smail, D.J. (1978) *Psychotherapy: A Personal Approach*, London: Dent.

—— (1987) *Taking Care*, London: Dent.

Spiegelberg, H. (1972) *Phenomenology in Psychology and Psychiatry*, Evanston, Ill: Northwestern University Press.

Spinelli, E. (1989) *The Interpreted World: An Introduction to Phenomenological Psychology*, London: Sage.

Valle, R.S. and King, M. (1978) *Existential Phenomenological Alternatives for Psychology*, New York: Oxford University Press.

Warnock, M. (1970) *Existentialism*, Oxford: Oxford University Press.

Yalom, I. (1980) *Existential Psychotherapy*, New York: Basic Books.

Suggestions for further reading

Deurzen-Smith, E. van (1988) *Existential Counselling in Practice*, London: Sage.

Macquarrie, J. (1972) *Existentialism: An Introduction, Guide and Assessment*, Harmondsworth: Penguin.

May, R., Angel, E. and Ellenberger, H.F. (1958) *Existence*, New York: Basic Books.

Sartre, J.P. (1962) *Existential Psychoanalysis*, Chicago: Gateway, Henri Regnery Co.

Yalom, I. (1980) *Existential Psychotherapy*, New York: Basic Books.

9

Gestalt therapy

MALCOLM PARLETT AND FAYE PAGE

Historical context and development in Britain

Historical context

Gestalt therapy emerged as a distinctive approach in the early 1950s in New York, shortly after Frederick (Fritz) Perls and his wife and collaborator, Laura Perls, had moved there from South Africa. To trace the historical development of Gestalt therapy we must begin in Germany in the years following the First World War, a time of great intellectual upheaval, and a formative period in the lives of the Perls.

Fritz Perls, after active service in the German army, trained and practised as a psychiatrist and psychoanalyst in the 1920s and 1930s. He began analysis with several orthodox Freudians but was dissatisfied with their passivity and rigidity. On Karen Horney's advice, Perls entered analysis with Wilhelm Reich, and the Reichian view – that the body is as important as the mind in the development and maintenance of resistances – became a major influence in the Perls' later approach.

While working at the Institute for Brain-Damaged Soldiers in Frankfurt in 1926, Perls met Laura, working as a Gestalt psychologist. She was an accomplished scholar and concert-level musician, who also worked with Paul Tillich and Martin Buber. The latter had a long-term influence on Gestalt therapy with his emphasis on 'I–Thou' communication and other existentialist ideals. The Institute in Frankfurt was directed by the physician and neurologist Kurt Goldstein, and it was in Goldstein's work – he invented the terms 'holism' and 'self-actualization' – along with the writings of Gestalt psychologists (e.g. Wertheimer, Koffka, Kohler, and Kurt Lewin), that the Perls found valuable ideas in their first departures from psychoanalysis. They were also influenced by the ferment of ideas and cultural climate of Frankfurt, Berlin, and Vienna in the 1920s – the era of the Bauhaus movement and a time of great hope. Fritz had also been involved in theatre with the director Max Reinhardt and his love of dramatization was later to be reflected in his training workshops.

By 1933, Fritz and Laura Perls were on the Nazi black list. Unlike many Jewish intellectuals they realized what was to come and moved to South Africa, where they founded its first psychoanalytic institute. They continued to absorb other ideas and influences – e.g. from semantics – and were moving away from Freudian orthodoxy. Their first major statement, *Ego, Hunger, and Aggression* (Perls 1969a) was written while Fritz was a psychiatrist in the South African Medical Corps during the Second World War. When the National Party came to power in South Africa after the war, promising more apartheid, they emigrated to the USA.

In New York they became the focus for a small group of writers, political activists, and therapists, including the poet and social critic Paul Goodman, who was to write the important theoretical statement contained in *Gestalt Therapy* (Perls *et al.* 1974), first published in 1951. As the new approach took shape, the group debated possible names: integrative, existential, and concentration therapy were all mooted. 'Gestalt' was taken from the earlier Gestalt school of psychology, which pointed out that humans did not perceive the world as individual shapes or sounds but in coherent, meaningful configurations, or 'gestalts'. This holistic perspective was carried over into Gestalt therapy along with the respect it implies for people's actual or 'phenomenological' experience.

The first Institute of Gestalt Therapy was set up in New York in 1952 and Laura Perls has remained its focus and inspiration ever since. Fritz Perls meanwhile moved restlessly between different locations, never able to set down roots or build a practice. It was only when he arrived at the Esalen Institute in California that he became widely known and that Gestalt therapy became linked to the human potential movement.

Many popular assumptions, stereotypes and misconceptions about Gestalt stem from this time. Many would-be Gestalt practitioners imitated Perls and his personal style of work, taking the techniques he happened to be experimenting with at the time to be the essence of Gestalt. Fritz Perls was a brilliant, dramatic, controversial and charismatic teacher. He often appeared confrontational and dismissive of intellectual explanation, partly because he was demonstrating Gestalt therapy often with groups of psychiatrists and therapists who used intellectualizing as a strategy of avoidance.

The legacy from this era has been that Gestalt therapy has sometimes been abused, practised in an overly confrontative way, and regarded as anti-intellectual. In the last ten years there has been a re-evaluation of these attitudes and a wholesale change back towards the original fundamental ideas, and a recognition that the therapy needs to be grounded in a deep appreciation of its underlying theory. At the same time there has been belated recognition of the central influence of Laura Perls. The practice of Gestalt therapy has matured, with less emphasis on flamboyant group activities, more on steady work to heighten awareness and enhance the quality of interaction. There is more acknowledgement, in groups, of group processes. Practitioners have also extended Gestalt thinking and methodology into other fields, including organizational development and management training (Herman and Korenich 1977) and education (Brown 1971). There is a new emphasis on the importance of adequate training, and a scepticism towards those who claim to have grasped Gestalt ideas in the course of a few weekend workshops.

Development in Britain

In Britain in the late 1960s and early 1970s there was an upsurge of interest in the human potential movement. 'Growth centres' sprang up in various places, especially in London. These centres invited visiting leaders from North America to facilitate seminars and workshops, which were usually experientially based. A number of Gestalt trainers, including Laura Perls, worked in Britain.

From these early beginnings there has been a growing interest in Gestalt in this country and the opportunities for training have increased during the past few years. The longest established programmes which offer extensive training are the Gestalt Centre in London and the Scottish Association for Gestalt Education. There are other organizations which offer Gestalt training – they include the Pellin Institute, metanoia Psychotherapy Training Institute, and Gestalt Southwest. There are also smaller training programmes available in Brighton, Leeds, Dublin, Manchester, Nottingham, Cambridge, Leamington Spa and Exeter.

Although Gestalt therapy has no national body nor professional association as such, discussions are proceeding to establish one. Meanwhile there are signs of increasing collaboration between groups. For instance, trainees from Gestalt Southwest and metanoia Psychotherapy Training Institute now work towards a common diploma organized by the recently established Gestalt Psychotherapy Training Institute set up in 1985 as a federation of trainers in various parts of the country. Three bi-annual national conferences have taken place and a fourth is to be held in July 1990. The Gestalt Centre has a programme of advanced training for experienced Gestalt trainers and supervisors.

The Gestalt Psychotherapy Training Institute and the Gestalt Centre, London are member organizations of the recently established UK Standing Conference for Psychotherapy. Altogether the present-day British experience is characterized by a rapidly growing interest in Gestalt therapy which has overwhelmed training facilities and by an increased concern for greater professionalism and high ethical standards.

Theoretical assumptions

Image of the person

Gestalt therapy is based on a holistic view of the individual relating to his or her environment. As with all organisms, human beings are not self-sufficient; they engage with their surroundings in order to live and grow (Perls 1969a; 1973). We make demands on the outside world and it, too, makes demands on us. Central to the Gestalt approach is the view that personality is comprised of a number of functions – bodily, perceptual, verbal/cognitive – that interrelate closely and exist in relation to the environment.

Perls stated that 'every individual, every plant, every animal has only one inborn goal – to actualize itself as it is' (1969b: 19). Involved in their striving for self-actualization, individuals have many needs: biological, physical, psychological, social and spiritual. Fulfilling these requires full phenomenological awareness, that is recognizing and attending to the sensations, feelings and thoughts which come together as an experience of need; open-ended creativity in adjusting to situations in order to meet needs; and sufficient self-support to make choices about what needs can be met, when and how.

Conceptualization of psychological disturbance and health

In Gestalt therapy, psychological health and disturbance are not mental but are 'organismic': they relate to the functioning of the whole mind-body-spirit system of the organism (Latner 1974). In healthy functioning there is continuous creative adjustment at the interface of the organism with the environment. This involves both responding to, and also acting upon, the environment in order to maintain balance and equilibrium with it. In disturbed functioning this process is interrupted and the person's ability to maintain herself in relation to life situations is impaired.

When an imbalance occurs within the person, or in her relation to her environment, this is experienced as a need. If awareness is not suppressed, this need stands out and she recognizes it as such within her 'life space' at that moment. At any given time there will be several imbalances or needs. In healthy functioning, the one which is most important for the person's survival or self-actualization will stand out as the most distinct; the person clearly differentiates this dominant need from the rest of what she is experiencing. This temporary configuration of her experience is called a gestalt. A gestalt comprises something being attended to which is interesting, called the figure, which stands out from the rest of her conscious life temporarily held in abeyance, called the ground.

As the need increases, excitement or tension is generated, activating the person to satisfy the need. In healthy functioning, the person will then mobilize herself and actively engage with the environment in order to meet that need, for example by encountering another person in a certain way or by manipulating and destroying a part of the environment, as in taking in food. When the need is met and the results integrated or digested, the gestalt dissolves. The temporary configuration breaks up; interest is lost in whatever it was that stood out as figure in the first place, for example food in the case of hunger – and the balance is restored. The next most important need now emerges, and a new gestalt is formed.

This process can be depicted diagrammatically (Figure 9.1). Recognition of the dominant need or imbalance rests on the person's being able to sense and feel (Stage One) and then to allow these feelings and sensations into awareness (Stage Two), for instance she may experience tension in her legs and realizes that she needs to move around. Stage Three occurs when the person mobilizes herself, using physical energy in this case to stand up. At this point she is in a state of readiness to take action (Stage Four); in the example, the action is to start moving and to get into the experience of doing so. The next stage (Five) is when the person is in full flight, so to speak, engaging in whatever she needs to do – in this case to move; she will be sensorily, emotionally and physically in contact with herself, her movements, the floor and her experience; she will be concentrating on what she is doing and be involved in it. At some point (Stage Six) engagement reaches its high point or 'final contact' after which the action stops – the need has dissipated. Then

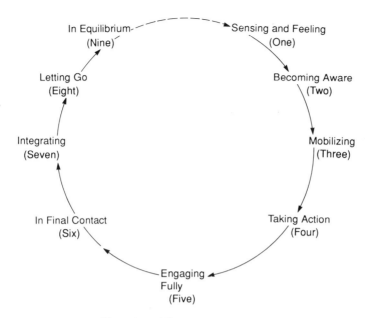

Figure 9.1   The cycle of awareness

follows a crucial stage (Seven) of integrating, or taking in fully, what has happened: the person may realize how much she needs 'to put her foot down' in other ways or she may simply be noticing the loss of felt tension in her legs. Stage Eight involves letting go; it is marked by loss of interest and concentration and a return to equilibrium (Stage Nine) in which temporarily no need or imbalance is registered. The person is clearly satisfied and her attention is no longer on her legs or on wishing to move – her experience has moved on.

This cycle is portrayed in many different forms (e.g. Zinker 1977; Hall 1976) and represents a healthy functioning process in which a gestalt forms, evolves and self-destructs. The emerging and receding of different gestalts is a continuous, unending process which, when operating freely, represents successful creative adjustment.

The cycle can be interrupted at every stage. Thus a block may occur near the beginning, so that the individual fails to recognize she has a particular need. Alternatively, she may be aware of her need but not mobilize herself to do anything about it. A third example, later in the cycle, might involve an interruption, say, between Stages Seven and Eight; after successfully engaging with something in her environment, she is unable to let go, and 'hangs on' to the experience at the expense of relaxing and being still. Obviously a block at any stage of the cycle prevents its being completed and the person remains dissatisfied. Uncompleted cycles or incomplete gestalts, Perls called 'unfinished business', a term that has wide currency.

In focusing on the process of self-regulation and transaction with the environ-

ment, and the impairment of this process, we pay particular attention to 'awareness' and 'contact', which have specialized meanings in Gestalt theory.

Awareness and contact

Perls described awareness as covering three zones: 'awareness of self, awareness of
the world, and awareness of what's between' (1969b: 49). Awareness of self
includes the person's direct experience of his feelings, emotions and physical
sensations at the time he is having them; awareness of the world occurs through a
person's five senses; 'what's between' (the intermediate zone) refers to the
person's representation of his internal and external reality and includes thinking,
planning, worrying, day-dreaming, anticipating, remembering, and so on. In
healthy functioning, by accurately representing his internal and external reality, a
person is able to integrate the two in creative adjustment.

'Awareness develops "with" and is integrally "part of" the organismic
environmental transaction' (Enwright 1972: 136). Awareness occurs spontaneously as transactions take place between self and environment and relates to
ongoing need and/or demands. Awareness, therefore, can be only in the here-and-
now and is not the same as intellectual understanding.

'Contact' occurs when the organism is fully in touch with the environment and
engaging with it. There is full sensory awareness and activation of the motoric
system as well as an accompanying internal feeling state. In everyday language we
refer to people being 'in touch', meaning they are in contact with what is going on
and with themselves: they are 'all there'. In dysfunctioning, this ability to be
present and in touch is lost: the differentiation of the individual's experience of
himself from his experience of the environment – in Gestalt theory this is termed
the 'contact boundary' – is distorted, leading to an interruption of contact.

Interruptions and confusions at the contact boundary

Four patterns of disturbance at the contact boundary have become central to
Gestalt theory and practice (e.g. Polster and Polster 1973). These can result in a
person's self-regulation being severely distorted. In each case there is confusion
about what part of the person's total field of experience at a particular time is truly
'self' and what is 'not-self' or is in the environment.

Introjection – taking in from the environment without evaluation   When a person is
overloaded by forces in the environment or is punished for rejecting such forces,
he may introject or 'take in whole bits' of his environment rather than biting off a
manageable portion, chewing it and assimilating it or spitting it out if it is not good
for him. These 'whole bits' can take the form of injunctions, beliefs and values.
Thus he may have introjected the message 'I should be helpless' or 'I should not
get angry'. He then behaves 'as if' he were helpless or not angry (Ward and
Rouzer 1974). The contact boundary is moved inside the province of 'self' so that
little remains of self (Perls 1973). The person makes himself responsible for what is
effectively part of his environment, albeit carried over into his belief system.

Projection – displacing from self into the environment   Here the contact boundary is
moved outside the normal province of self and the person locates his own feelings,
needs and preferences beyond his own self in the realm of the environment. He
thus may avoid taking responsibility for his own feelings (e.g. 'my anger takes me

over'), parts of his body (e.g. 'my neck is stiff and is killing me'), and aspects of his own experience which, being 'unacceptable' to him, he has attributed elsewhere instead (e.g. 'I know she is fed up with me' may substitute for 'I am fed up with her', an awareness which is being avoided).

Retroflection – self-manipulation rather than engagement with the environment This occurs when doing something to oneself substitutes for creatively engaging with the environment, because doing the latter is experienced as too 'dangerous'. Thus, if a person is harbouring aggressive impulses which, accurately or not, are perceived as impossible to express, he may direct it back on himself unawares, usually in a physical way – for example he may hit his knee with a clenched fist. Retroflection also involves giving to oneself what one wants or needs from others but cannot get. If this is affection, the person may hug himself. He treats a part of his being as if it was part of the environment.

Confluence – merging with the environment and avoiding separateness This is when the contact boundary weakens with the person feeling unsure where he and his environment begin and end. He cannot make good contact with others nor can he withdraw from them. He may automatically acquiesce with others or want their experience to be the same as his. He may merge in with a crowd, avoid conflict, and fail to differentiate his needs.

Everyone uses these mechanisms and they are often necessary. For instance, projection is essential for creative art and in therapy where it takes the form of empathy; retroflection of aggression may be necessary for survival. However, with continued and inappropriate use, healthy functioning becomes impossible.

Acquisition of psychological disturbance

Returning to the cycle of awareness (see Figure 9.1), as we said, the sequence of stages does not and cannot always be completed. There are interruptions of all kinds. Sometimes particular needs cannot be met due to a genuine lack of availability in the environment – for instance, in cases of war, famine, imprisonment and poverty. In the case of young children, they learn progressively what their environments offer and what they forbid. They may learn that particular needs are dangerous to express, since they invite ridicule or censure; or that the stages in the cycle represented by mobilizing energy, taking action and engaging fully do not achieve satisfaction or integration – indeed, some children are punished for their vigour and assertiveness rather than rewarded.

In developmental terms, the younger the child the more he or she depends on a supportive environment for survival. It is inevitable that children are frustrated at times in satisfying their needs, and some frustration is necessary for developing their potential to grow. However, if they are continually prevented from expressing and meeting their needs, they learn to suppress the excitement which accompanies emerging needs, using effort instead to suppress their feelings and spontaneous movements. If this occurs persistently – i.e the cycle is repeatedly interrupted – the developing person is likely to find it increasingly difficult, first, to register and express her needs at all; second, to distinguish what her own needs are from what she is expected to do or feel in the eyes of other people; and, third, to obtain for herself what she actually requires for her well-being.

When there is persistent interruption of the cycle, there is an accumulation of uncompleted gestalts (unfinished business), leaving the organism in a constantly unfulfilled state. Experience is fragmented and a sense of integration and wholeness is lost. As a result, the person is likely to become bored, confused, anxious, rigid, self-conscious, or otherwise alienated (Perls *et al.* 1974). The individual continues to have needs – e.g for affection, to express resentment, to explore freely, or whatever it is – but instead of operating in the natural, unselfconscious ways of organismic self-regulation to meet these needs, she tries to satisfy them in unhealthy, roundabout ways, or to change herself or her environment to fit a preconceived image of how she or it 'should be'.

With early life traumas, the capacities to be aware and in contact with herself and others are themselves affected, and through desensitization and physical withholding, through developing internal controls of self, the child learns to blot out parts of her experience, to substitute intentional behaviour for an organismic response, or to suppress his or her vitality and assertiveness. Disturbed patterns of adaptation and engagement with the environment and loss of natural impulses and spontaneous behaviour are the long-term results. There is a loss of growth and of potency.

Perpetuation of psychological disturbance

Even though a person's disturbed functioning may have been acquired in the past, the perpetuation of the disturbance occurs in the present. Individuals develop fixed patterns of adapting, getting by, or manipulating, which are so habitual and taken for granted that they are not easily accessible to the person's present awareness. They can be thought of as fixed gestalts, with the person's cycles of experience being interrupted in a similar way over and over again, leading to stereotyped reactions and behaviour. The person does not realize that she has a choice, that she does not have to be stuck with an obsolete response – and it usually is obsolete in that the original adverse conditions are no longer present. The unaware person effectively is making choices about how to live and to be, many of them not life-enhancing or creative choices, without realizing that she is choosing at all.

Suppose that a need from the past – for example, a need to be left alone – was frequently ignored in childhood; it may have been suppressed, perhaps by introjecting the admonition 'it is good to be with other people'. Though the person will attempt to conform to the introjected belief, even perhaps to the extent of deliberately seeking out gregarious situations, the unmet need continues to assert itself; for instance, her attention might be caught by advertisements for retreats or holidays in remote places, although she will never allow herself to go on one. She is ignoring, as she has done for so long, her attraction to solitude. Real organismic satisfaction will continue to elude her as she seeks to conform with her introject rather than with her organismically based need. Confusions such as these arise in a person's middle zone of awareness, characterized by 'fantasy activity' such as internal debates, imaginings, giving oneself a talking to, or day-dreaming. In the terms mentioned, this is a form of retroflection. It often substitutes for contactful engagement with the real situation, a prerequisite for organismic (or natural) self-regulation. Instead of dealing with actual, present situations a person may become preoccupied with the future, what might happen or how she will perform; she will render the future threatening by imagining scenarios – her catastrophic expectations might be fulfilled or her overly optimistic ones might not be (Perls 1969b). Such mental activity in the intermediate zone will often provoke anxiety.

Automatic patterns of thinking, moving, feeling or holding herself posturally – many of them self-damaging or self-limiting – remain in existence because the person keeps trying to actualize her self-image rather than her actual self, and to grasp that the two are not identical means unsettling the status quo; she would rather act as if nothing has changed or could do so. At the same time she may want herself or other people or her circumstances to be different, and she may report feeling dissatisfied. She may be playing games, asserting that she 'should be nicer' or that she 'ought to be happy', which Perls (1969b) locates in the 'phoney' or role-layer of neurosis or growth disorder. If an individual becomes aware of these in-authentic roles and attempts to be more honest, she is likely to encounter her fears at the deeper level of the 'impasse' – fears, perhaps, of being rejected, of possible embarrassment, or of pain. She is afraid of going through the suffering and frus-tration, often charged with emotion, and she withdraws into known, if unsatisfy-ing, patterns of avoidance. The archaic responses are thus maintained, as though they were necessary for the present, and the person fails to take a step towards greater maturity. She is not prepared to risk change.

Change

Gestalt therapy provides a means for speeding up the evolution of a person, although evolution occurs anyway. Individuals change and grow as a result of life experiences of all kinds. People 'grow up', 'take on a new lease of life', 'come to their senses', or 'are forced to come to terms with things', as a result of changes in the environment which have to be assimilated – changes like promotion at work, meeting a new partner, coping with accidents, becoming a grandparent. A person with a disturbed pattern of relating to the environment has a reduced capacity for creative adjustment to novel or stressful situations; his or her capacity for assimila-tion may be impaired but human creativity and resourcefulness are not easily extinguished. Just because a person has a pattern, say, of retreating from social contacts does not mean that he will retain this as a fixed personal characteristic throughout his whole life; he may well find himself in a new work group where he is stimulated and encouraged to break his habit of withdrawal, and then finds that he 'is taken out of himself'. The next time he is less reluctant to take part. Such growth experiences occur for all of us, throughout life, and many people change, mature and mellow as a result of un-learning patterns of avoidance and stereo-typed reactions they acquired earlier in life. The requirements are, first, an environmental challenge or opportunity; second, some re-experiencing of past patterns of reaction; and, third, a willingness now to take the risk to do something differently.

Incremental change through assimilating new life experiences is quite different from intentional self-reform or 'improvement' according to rules (like diets or some religious teachings). This difference is reflected in Gestalt therapy in what is called the Paradoxical Theory of Change (Beisser 1972), that is, change occurs when a person 'becomes what he is, not when he tries to become what he is not'. In other words, deliberate attempts to change by conscious control, either by a part of the self acting upon another part – what Perls (1969b: 19) calls the 'topdog' and the 'underdog' – or by the efforts of an external (often well-meaning) change agent, are ultimately counter-productive: they reinforce tendencies within the individual which are anti-organismic. Instead, change occurs through recovering the potential to engage creatively with the environment through reinstatement of healthy functioning, whether through the challenges of ordinary life or as a result of therapy.

Gestalt therapy seeks to promote assimilation of new, maturing life experiences not through any programme of intentional change, but through simply providing a context and stimulus for a person to experiment with 'being who he is'. He will change as a result of increased awareness of the choices he is in fact making all the time. The expansion of consciousness and sense of inner freedom, as a result of training and practice in awareness, leads in turn to his allowing into full awareness unfinished situations from the past. These incomplete gestalts press for completion; to do so requires letting go of self-protective strategies of avoidance, allowing some entirely new experience to develop, and actually doing or feeling what was formerly inhibited or diverted. For the individual to complete whatever he needs to complete (e.g. mourning a loss, expressing a resentment, liberating his physical energy), he must risk a new adaptation or response. Ordinary life situations call for these and so does Gestalt therapy. In each case there is an environmental challenge, an openness on the part of the individual to 'suffer' some of the old feelings and reactions, and a willingness to take risks with doing something new. In other words, Gestalt therapy seeks to promote a change strategy which builds on the normal ways in which people develop and mature, and extends them.

Practice

Goals of therapy

Much psychotherapy, deliberately or unwittingly, subscribes to 'the medical model' – emphasizing the expertise of the doctor or specialist helper and the dependency of the patient. Gestalt therapy does not fit this model at all. The emphasis from the outset is on encouraging the person to recognize his own expert status – i.e. that he is the author of his own life (his own 'author-ity'). At the beginning of therapy this may be impossible for the person to assimilate, in which case this issue itself becomes a focus of therapy. The aim is to promote self-support sufficient for the person to live a life of freedom and responsibility (or to increase his 'response-ability').

Personal development of this kind requires, first, that we become more continuously aware of our own actual experience of sensing, feeling and thinking on a moment-by-moment basis; second, that we have adequate self-support (i.e. inner strength so that we are not automatically dependent on favourable aspects of the environment in order to function); third, that we operate in a more integrated way – recognizing when we are at odds with ourselves and experimenting with utilizing more of our potential; and, fourth, that we realize more consciously our status as social beings and discover how we relate satisfyingly (or less so) to others, individually and in community.

The work of therapy is to foster conditions in which the self-researching individual, at whatever level of awareness he starts from, becomes an active participant in his own personal growth: he 'grows himself' in the areas above – awareness, self-support, integration and ability to interact with others. These interrelate closely. As aspects of our personal evolution they are never attained once and for all: Perls noted that 'there is always the possibility of richer maturation – of taking more and more responsibility for yourself' (1969b: 65); 'integration is never completed' (1969b: 64). The therapeutic journey, as conceived in Gestalt therapy, is therefore life-long and for many people can lead into being something akin to a meditative discipline or path. Of course, not everyone engaged in Gestalt therapy as a patient, client or customer goes this far; many will stop when they have restored, or learnt, more satisfying ways of functioning in the world.

Concerned as it is with speeding up the process of personal evolution, Gestalt therapy is not a normative approach designed to elicit 'well-adjusted' behaviour as conventionally defined. Rather it values individuals finding unique solutions to unique situations – recognizing the special nature of each person's history, circumstances, values, needs and preferences. The emphasis is on the person finding his own goals within his own life and discovering his potential to meet those goals, even if these go against commonly held values (like making money) or lead the individual into radical questioning of society, its institutions and its norms.

Selection criteria

The Gestalt therapy system orientates the work of its practitioners, but each one applies the principles of the system in individual ways and uses different methods according to her training, professional background and personal style.

It follows from this that each 'therapist–client dyad' is also individual and that to argue that certain individuals are 'suitable' for Gestalt therapy as such, while others are unsuitable, does not make sense. A clinical psychologist working, say, in a hospital setting and from a Gestalt therapy base, may work therapeutically with severely fragmented and disoriented individuals, applying Gestalt principles appropriately and effectively. A school counsellor, on the other hand, though trained in Gestalt, would almost certainly not work with such individuals, although she might be well qualified to apply Gestalt thinking and practice to working with the children referred to her.

Issues of selection, therefore, turn on the suitability of the therapist and the match between therapist and patient. The match has to do not only with professional background and length of time working in the field but also with the therapist's own life experience. A therapist who suffered extreme physical abuse in childhood may choose, despite having resolved all that can be resolved about this in her own therapy, not to work with someone similarly abused; alternatively, she may choose to specialize in this area. These are personal decisions of a kind that probably all psychotherapists are likely to want to make. Such decisions are particularly sensitive ones in Gestalt therapy in that therapists need to be open to sharing some of their own feelings and reactions, as part of sustaining the dialogic relationship (see below).

The most likely course of action for a practitioner, faced with an enquirer interested in pursuing Gestalt therapy, will be to have an introductory meeting in order to assess what the individual might benefit from most – perhaps once or twice weekly individual sessions, joining an ongoing therapy group, or participating in a weekend workshop.

Practitioners of Gestalt therapy, following the axiom that each person/situation 'field' is unique, give emphasis to the singular nature of each person's therapeutic needs. Suppose, for instance, that the extent of disturbance is such that the client has little contact with reality, such that he has been labelled 'psychotic' or 'borderline'. In this case a high degree of environmental support and time, commitment, and attention on the part of the therapist may be called for. This might entail residential care and the necessity for the therapist to see the client every day for a period of time. Such conditions, even in hospital settings, are often not available, and it would be highly irresponsible to engage the client in intensive exploration without the necessary environmental support. Stratford and Brallier (1979) argue that when working with profoundly disturbed persons, 'glue' rather than 'solvent' is required: instead of 'loosening structure, allowing new experiences, and expanding possibilities', which can heighten anxiety, the Gestalt therapist needs to focus on 'the familiar and/or comfortable', on 'decreasing stimuli', and 'organizing energy', all of which can begin to 'stabilize and "re-glue" ' a person's disintegrated experience.

Obviously, then, the initial meeting and contacts are very significant. The person's presenting problem may indicate one form of intervention rather than another – e.g. a relationship problem might best be explored with the partner in couples therapy and someone cut off and lonely might benefit most from a group. But the emphasis is on the special nature of each enquiry, not on any rule.

In weighing up what the person might benefit from most, the Gestalt therapist does not ignore usual psychiatric diagnostic categories. However, she will want most to observe how aware the person is of his own process – i.e. of the current direction of his interest, his bodily state, his feeling sense, and how capable he is of externalizing his inner experience. She will also note how he communicates with her, and how he interrupts his ongoing self-regulation (e.g by being insensitive to his physical feelings, by continuously changing the subject, or by restricting his breathing) and what type of contact boundary confusions (introjection, confluence, etc.) are most evident. The therapist may also be influenced by what strikes her as 'missing' with this person: e.g. he may manifest no assertiveness or, though married, fail to mention his wife or children. All of this may suggest to the therapist the appropriateness of a particular course of action. At this stage, someone who was very unaware or unable to externalize his inner experience might be considered a candidate for one-to-one therapy: joining a group might be thought desirable at a later stage, when the person has become more familiar with the Gestalt method – i.e. has acquired facility with its self-investigative procedures (which constitute both a demand for, as well as a means to, greater awareness).

Often, in the choice of modality, practical considerations weigh heavily – for instance, the availability of Gestalt courses and therapy (now increasing in Britain), the financial commitment the individual is able (or prepared) to make, and in the case of groups, whether others in the group will be at a similar level of development and whether there are vacancies.

Qualities of effective therapists

Basic to all training of Gestalt psychotherapists is that all trainees have prolonged individual and group therapy themselves. Gestalt therapy is not an approach which can be applied – at least responsibly or effectively applied – by people who are themselves not capable of being aware of their own processes; it is not an approach based on acquiring techniques or on theoretical understanding from books. Rather it has to be known from the inside, experienced as a powerful means of self-enquiry and progressively incorporated in one's personal life and work.

Effective Gestalt therapists vary greatly in their personal and professional qualities. Along with their diversity, and their having achieved a satisfying level of integration themselves, effective Gestalt therapists are distinguished by their authenticity and openness about their feelings and reactions, as well as by their competence in handling a broad spectrum of interpersonal transactions (including intimacy, conflict, physical contact, emotional expression, separation, and maintaining clear boundaries). In addition, they need to have acquired the ability to 'bracket off' (set aside for the time being, not forget or suppress) their own preoccupations and problems in order to be fully present (or 'all there') for the client and, even more, to recognize occasions when they are unable to do this and are therefore not competent to practise for the time being. Finally, they need to have a strong ethical base, to be non-exploitative, and to have a fundamental respect for the integrity of the therapy process.

Therapeutic style

Although there are wide differences in style between Gestalt therapists, most would conceptualize what they do along the following (or similar) lines.

They aim to provide a relationship and setting which supports and provokes the person's exploration of her 'here and now' experience, that is, what she is aware of in the actual, present context of being in the therapy room, relating to another person, the therapist (or, in a group, with the other members).

Such open-ended enquiry can flourish only within a 'dialogic' relationship (Yontef 1984) based on the 'I–Thou' kind of person-to-person meeting and dialogue described by Martin Buber (1970). This involves each party meeting the other as a person, not as a role. Gestalt therapists let themselves be themselves and encourage those they work with to do the same. Thus, they may communicate some of their own life experience and express their own feelings, albeit with respect and a sense of timing, honouring the validity of the other's reality and not imposing their own views and values. Relating dialogically also calls for the therapist to 'show his caring by his honesty more than by his constant softness' (Yontef 1984: 47).

Along with the emphases on reporting present awareness and on establishing a person-to-person equality, Gestalt therapists tend also to foster an attitude of experimentation ('try it rather than talk about it') and playful creativity. Specifically, they encourage metaphorical and intuitive thinking, which in the majority of people is less developed than the capacity to be verbal and explanatory. (The two types of thinking have been found to be localized in the right and left hemispheres of the brain respectively and to have separate qualities and uses; much research has been done in this field, both in the laboratory and also with artists and writers: Zdenek 1983). Although there is much variation, most Gestalt therapists incline towards using a variety of active methods – e.g. dramatizations, dance or other physical movement, dialogues between parts of the self – which can heighten awareness of the whole mind/body system and of inner feeling states.

When it comes to the style of the Gestalt therapist, it is difficult to generalize. The competent therapist employs different styles according to the person, situation and stage of therapy. His choices are based on skills and experience and his response in a particular instance depends on his creativeness in finding a way to heighten the person's awareness at that time. The therapist may at one time be confrontational and challenging, pointing out that a pattern of behaviour is manipulative or self-destructive; at another time he may extend a hand, literally, to establish a channel of support when the person he is working with requires it in order to take a risk. He may listen intently and sympathetically to an emotionally laden account of an early trauma now being recounted for the first time. In contrast, with another person at another time, he may yawn openly at the repeated recital of some well-known facts, perhaps provoking a shift or a new realization thereby. He is, after all, attending to individuals' unfolding reality, to their unique experience, and this demands spontaneous and creative responses – not stereotyped reactions, fixed techniques, and stale routines.

In his response at a particular moment, the experienced therapist is likely to be affected by many different factors: the person's severity of disturbance, her prior experience in therapy and the stage of the therapeutic relationship, her confusions at the contact boundary, the degree of essential support available to her, and 'procedural' concerns such as the time available.

It is appropriate that each practitioner has a range of styles; it is also appropriate that Gestalt therapists as a group diverge considerably in their overall style and disposition to therapy. Each is enjoined to find his own way of integrating and applying the philosophy and methodology of Gestalt therapy in a creative, intelligent, sensitive and ethical fashion.

Major therapeutic strategies and techniques

Awareness training
The Gestalt therapist is an awareness expert. She actively stimulates the person to attend to his own ongoing present experience (sensations, feelings, images, etc.) and is herself aware of her own: the dialogue is a shared exploration of their immediate experience together. The therapist will be attending to and following the person's changing sense of reality, moment by moment. Characteristically she will be asking him such questions as 'What are you aware of?'; 'What is happening? Can you say?', 'What are you doing now?', 'How did you feel when

you said that?' (Notice that the questions begin with What and How, which help to focus attention on the specifics of experience, and not with Why, which invites explanation and generality.)

The therapist will also report her own observations of the other – e.g 'I noticed your voice dropped and you gulped as you said that'; or 'Now you are breathing more heavily'; or 'I am conscious that you are changing the subject again'. In addition, she is likely to report selectively what she is aware of in herself: 'I notice that I'm feeling sad as you tell me this', or 'I am left hanging', or 'What is going on for me is that I do not feel moved, despite what you are saying'.

Persistently, the person is encouraged to connect with the actuality of his existence in the 'here and now' of the therapy room and the dialogic relationship. There is nothing ritualistic in this focus on immediate experience: it is central to both Gestalt theory and practice. Nor should the concentration on the present be misunderstood. References to what is happening outside, or to events in the past, or to future plans do of course occur: there is nothing impermissible in this. At the same time, the Gestalt therapist will want to enquire about their present significance. Something from the past may be recalled, yet the remembering is taking place now – so there must be some significance now. What is of interest (the figure) is, at least for the moment, centre stage in the person's life-space. It is present. It may also be important. Memories do not pop up randomly – they relate to incomplete gestalts from the past, to unmet needs which survive into the present as potent activators of current behaviour or internal feeling states.

Recognizing interruptions and avoidances
There are numerous ways in which human beings attempt to avoid painful or unpleasant memories, emotions, or realizations. They interrupt their awareness of these by such means as cutting out (e.g. by looking away) and sliding over the difficulty by joking or talking a lot. Or they restrict their feelings by holding their breath, at the same time as tensing the musculature in certain parts of the body. Inhibition (wholesale avoidance of certain impulses), intellectualizing (often in the form of 'explaining away'), and displacement (instead of dealing with his wife he lets it out on his employee), are among other common patterns of avoidance.

By staying close to what is happening for the person exploring his reality, almost on a moment-by-moment basis, the therapist is able to spot possible points of interruption in this ongoing process: e.g. shifts in vitality, changes in eye contact, movements in body position, a sentence left unfinished, all of which may indicate some avoidance – something withheld, glossed over, or blotted out. She may on occasions draw attention frequently to such interruptions, at other times she may not intervene for long periods, perhaps letting the person tell his story (Polster 1987) or leaving him to struggle to articulate some hitherto indefinable feeling. All depends on the total situation.

The patterns of avoidance and interruption relate to the awareness cycle (see pp.178–9 and Figure 9.1). Avoidance of crying, for instance, may relate to an incomplete gestalt relating to mourning the loss of a friend. Instead of experiencing fully the grief at the time of loss, the person may have interrupted the cycle – perhaps by not recognizing fully his need at the time to grieve (telling himself 'to get over it and stop making a fuss') or by 'fighting back tears' at the point of engaging with the felt emotion of sadness. Such interruptions to a person's system of self-regulation lead to incomplete gestalts or unfinished cycles – in this case, the full grief reaction was stopped mid-way. The need to grieve fully, though kept out of awareness, still survives. As the individual attends to his present experience, he may – if necessary prompted by the therapist – become aware of (i.e. actually notice) his eye-tension or restricted breathing; that the feeling inside him is one of sadness; and that he has grieving still to do.

The skilled Gestalt therapist focuses with precision on two aspects of interruption or avoidance. First, she notices at what point in the awareness cycle (see pp. 178–9 and Figure 9.1) the interruption occurs: is he not recognizing his need? Is he stopping from mobilizing his energy? Is he accomplishing these but holding back from engaging fully – i.e. is he not making contact with what will meet his need? Is he doing all these but not integrating (or not being permanently affected by) his experience? Or is he unable to let go?

Second, the therapist identifies which major contact boundary disturbance (introjection, projection, retroflection, confluence) is involved at the point of interruption. For instance, suppose a person suppresses his laughter in a therapy group session (i.e. he is not mobilizing his energy fully). He may be doing so through having an introject that 'it is impolite to laugh noisily'. Or he may imagine that others will 'think he is silly' if he laughs uproariously (projection). In addition, he is trying to swallow his laughter (retroflection), and to conform to others around him who are not laughing (confluence). Here, as is often the case, several disturbances occur together.

By noticing, discovering and clarifying together the points and mechanisms of interruption, the therapist and patient are together focusing on the ways, often numerous, that the person's process of creatively adjusting to the environment has been distorted unawares.

Working with 'resistance'

There are, at any point of interruption, two competing forces at work in the individual: one impulse to change in an attempt to complete the unfinished situation, the other to 'resist' or stay with familiar patterns of self-interruption. 'Resistance' is often regarded by psychotherapists as an obstacle to be broken through or overcome. This implies the therapist's taking sides, as it were, with one party to the conflict.

Gestalt therapists – eschewing the role of the change agent with a normative view of how people 'should' be – adopt a position of neutrality, or 'seeming desirelessness' towards a person's changing (Appelbaum 1983). If the person has been punished for crying in the past the therapist does not want to be appearing to support only crying and to disapprove of what appears to be 'resistance' to crying.

Working as they do with 'what is', Gestalt therapists are looking for where the person's interest and vitality is, which may well be evident in the so-called resisting part, not in the person's intending-to-change part. Accordingly, the therapist may encourage the person to exaggerate or amplify her supposedly resistant behaviour, even suggest that she does not change. The therapist will certainly signal her acceptance of its validity – particularly the benefits the person has derived in the past from having 'resisted'.

The goal is achieving integration between the two forces, not the triumph of one. An example might be that the therapist will effectively 'neutralize the patient's stubbornness and negativism by offering him the feeling of independence and control which oppositional people actually crave' (Appelbaum 1983: 762). Paradoxically, by working with rather than against the 'resistance', often there is a shift which involves its dissolution.

This approach to working with resistance is one of the hallmarks of Gestalt therapy. For the therapist to be active in promoting change, seeking 'break-throughs' or having intentions about how her client 'should' develop, is seriously to misunderstand the essence of the approach. The task of the Gestalt therapist is to assist in heightening awareness, not in promoting change. The paradox is that the more the therapist practises 'therapeutic abstinence' in this regard, the more likely it is that her client will herself want and be able to change.

Experimentation and techniques
Gestalt therapy is a form of experiential learning and the experiment is central: 'It transforms talking about into doing, stale reminiscing and theorizing into being fully here with all one's imagination, energy, and excitement' (Zinker 1977: 124). It is the pursuit of increased awareness through active behavioural expression involving the senses, skeletal muscles, and full bodily and emotional involvement.

Experiments grow out of themes emerging during the tracking of ongoing awareness and are ways of 'thinking out loud, [concretizing] one's imagination' (Zinker 1977: 137). There are no set structures or techniques, though necessary preconditions for a successful experiment include ensuring that the person is 'grounded' and has sufficient self-support; that the experiment is pitched at the right level of risk for him at the time; that he understands what he is doing and has agreed to it; and that it incorporates the person's own language and images, not the therapist's.

Some experiments have become classics – for instance, the 'empty chair', in which a person speaks to someone with whom he has unfinished business, or to another part of himself, a polar opposite (the 'weak' him may speak to the 'strong' him). He may then move to the other chair and react from that position – either being the other person or other aspect of self. Another is when someone re-enacts or re-lives some episode from the past but does so with his present resources: what was formerly wanted but not proceeded with, usually out of fear, now becomes possible.

Working with dreams, guided (or unguided) fantasies, or art work may involve identification with and living or acting the parts of the dream, fantasy, or drawing, switching between different elements or characters, all of which may reveal parts of the self.

Although these techniques have been widely copied, their use in isolation from the rest of the Gestalt therapy system is highly questionable. They are not recipes. As Yontef has remarked: 'There is no Gestalt therapy cookbook . . . therapy is an art [requiring] all of the therapist's creativity and love' (1988: 32).

The change process in therapy

As we have seen, work with awareness is at the heart of Gestalt therapy: attending to present experience, noticing what the person is doing, and recognizing her processes of contact and avoidance. Yontef (1988) has suggested a developmental sequence within therapy from naive to more disciplined awareness. Thus the person at the beginning of therapy may talk about her problem but may have little awareness of what she is actually doing – for example how she is talking in a complaining voice and how, by talking about the problem repeatedly, she is actually avoiding facing and dealing with it.

In the course of therapy she recognizes how unaware she was previously; she begins to notice her avoidance; in time, she learns to recognize the ways she has been interrupting the natural process of gestalt formation and completion. She becomes aware of being aware.

The third stage is reached when the person 'becomes aware of [her] overall character structure', her general patterns and the conditions which give rise to her being less aware. The fourth level is when the (by then) high level of awareness reached in therapy 'permeates the person's ordinary life'.

Another way that Gestalt therapists think of change is in terms of the awareness cycle. Later stages of the cycle depend on earlier stages being undergone. Movement in therapy is signalled by the person's being able to complete more unfinished situations both from the past and new ones arising in the present. She learns to avoid her avoidance; she interrupts more of her interruptions as they occur. In the process she is acquiring greater facility in gestalt completion and experiences more fulfilment and less dissatisfaction.

Limitations of the approach

There are many voices today in the international Gestalt therapy community which point to limitations in the approach, an indication in itself that Gestalt therapy has entered a new phase. Having survived its period of being fashionable, it has become an accepted form of psychotherapy that deserves powerful critical scrutiny, most urgently by Gestalt therapists themselves.

Taking a broad view, by far the greatest limitation is that Gestalt therapy 'has been simplified and falsified and distorted and misrepresented', to quote Laura Perls (Rosenfeld 1982). There are numerous therapists of other persuasions who, on the basis of a few weekends' experience of Gestalt therapy, remark that they 'use Gestalt' which, from the perspective of a properly trained Gestalt therapist, is as absurd as it is disquieting.

That the approach has been trivialized, and its theories not understood, is in part due to a paucity of adequate research and writing by Gestalt therapists themselves. This is, in turn, a product of an unfortunate tendency to devalue the use of the intellect – a bias which was present for many years in Gestalt therapy, although there were some notable exceptions – like Laura Perls and the New York Institute. Perhaps, too, there has been a reluctance to abandon the initial phase of excitement, innovation and improvisation – which attends all new ventures – and to settle down to building a more substantial theoretical and organizational base out of fear that it might become a rigidified structure or 'fixed gestalt'.

For whatever reasons, there has been little clinical documentation, too few explications of essential concepts, and an unwillingness to 'professionalize'. There is also acknowledgement that Gestalt therapy has suffered 'from the fact that the growing numbers of those who practise it have not carried the insights of its founders into new territory in a way that remains consistent with its principles' (Miller 1985: 53). All of this has contributed in the past, especially in Britain, to many Gestalt practitioners feeling isolated and without a professional network or base.

In short, there are limitations in the understanding, public perception, avail-ability and organization of Gestalt therapy and – an inevitable consequence – in the variable standards of practitioners. These issues are now being seriously addressed, in Britain as elsewhere. That Gestalt therapy has survived despite its lack of worldly realism, effective education or professional solidarity is remarkable. That it has done so is perhaps because those who engage with it react in a similar way to how Nevis reacted when she encountered the Gestalt approach:

> suddenly I could make sense of the way the world was and that sense has stayed, and deepened, and widened. And, in that way, I think we have a theory that does, indeed, fit the functioning of humans on this earth.
>
> (Nevis 1985: 62)

Case example

The client

Susan was referred to me (F.P.) by one of the doctors in the chest clinic where she works as a nurse. The doctor had several talks with her about the difficulties she seemed to be having with other staff members. In the first meeting with me Susan expressed her gratitude to this doctor for suggesting she seek help, as she had experienced similar difficulties before.

During this session I observed how slow Susan's movements were and how unfit she seemed. Her body appeared angular, with no softness, and she stooped when standing or sitting. Her breathing was shallow and her skin looked pale. When asked about her hands, which were raw and red, she said that she gnawed them continuously. A most striking aspect of Susan's appearance was her facial expression much of the time. It was almost a grimace.

Susan complained of having either no energy or too much, of tiring easily, and of having numerous colds and intermittent stomach problems. She described herself as 'boring' and said that other people did not like her. I asked her what she wanted from therapy: she said she wanted to get on better with people; have a close relationship with a man; feel happy and stop biting her hands.

In the first few sessions Susan told me some of her background. She is the only child of elderly parents and felt she was over-protected. Her father has been retired for some years; her mother has always been at home. They lived in the country and Susan remembered her early life as 'quiet' and 'boring'; she said she often felt 'isolated' and 'lonely'.

Although she went to school in the nearby town, there were no other children around for her to play with where she lived. At school she was often bullied and did not know what to do about it. Her parents told her these children were 'bad' and to 'ignore them', that getting angry 'never did anyone any good'. She remembered being frightened and having fantasies of what she would do to the bullies. In time she became fearful of the fantasies as well and thought this was when she started biting her hands.

Susan could not recall her parents' being angry nor her showing any anger at home herself. She thought they smoothed over any display of emotion by telling her she 'must be coming down with something' or she 'must be over-tired'. Her parents did encourage her to study hard and be better and cleverer than anyone else.

Susan left one job as a community nurse because she said she could not cope with the children. In conflict situations, particularly when her authority was challenged, she said she felt 'intimidated', 'angry', 'bewildered' and 'frightened'. She was then 'authoritarian' or 'ineffective'. She quit her next job in a private hospital after several disputes with a manager whom she said was too 'authoritarian' and co-workers who were 'uncooperative'.

Susan had been working in the chest clinic for eighteen months when she first came to see me, and said she was really trying to 'fit in'. She had requested meetings with her line manager and in these had complained about her co-workers, her feeling dissatisfied and not having enough support in her job. She said the manager did make suggestions, but they were not working.

She said she tried very hard with some people, both colleagues and patients, to be helpful and accommodating but felt this was never appreciated. Susan then felt she was being 'used' and decided to ignore them. Although she liked her work in the chest clinic, Susan reported she was now thinking about looking for another job.

When I asked Susan what she did in her spare time she said she was very busy. She was studying for a higher qualification, and she belonged to a film club. She rang her parents two or three times a week or they rang her. She went to stay with them nearly every weekend and helped with the gardening. Susan said if she did not contact her parents frequently they would worry and ring her at work.

The therapy

As our sessions progressed, Susan appeared to talk easily about how miserable she felt, how difficult things were for her and how lonely she was. During these times, I was aware of her low energy level. Susan would sit still, shoulders hunched, with little movement anywhere in her body. Her breathing was shallow and restricted. Her voice sounded either monotonous or whining. She would often stare at me without looking away and some of the time it was as though she was not seeing me. When I shared this with her, she said she was waiting for me to say something. When I asked 'What do you want me to say?', she looked surprised and said she did not know.

Susan said she often bit her hands at home until they were raw and she would occasionally start to chew her fingers during a session, most noticeably when she was challenged. If I mentioned this, she would stop. When asked what she was experiencing, she replied 'Scared'. However, she rarely looked frightened.

From my observation and what she had told me, my speculation was that as a child, particularly when she was bullied, she had no way of managing situations in which she felt fear and/or anger. Susan was denied the expression of these feelings so she retroflected them, turned them inward on herself and began biting her own hands.

When I encouraged her to pay attention to her breathing, she would do so for a short while and breathe more deeply. As her expression began to change, she would stop breathing fully and, simultaneously, stop attending to her breathing and experiencing. When asked, she would report feeling scared and confused. She seemed unclear about her thoughts and fantasies about her fear at these times. When I suggested she stay with her fear, she then reported she was confused and often said, 'You are scaring me' or 'You must be angry with me'.

I thought by constricting her breathing she was blocking her feelings from her awareness (see Figure 9.1: Stage Two). As I was not angry with her, she was likely to be projecting her feelings on to me. She disowned her own experiences of anger (fear, etc.) and attributed them to her environment, in this instance to me.

Susan appeared to have little access to how she blocked her ongoing awareness. I supposed she was not connecting with her present experience and was not in touch with herself or me. I concluded it was important to work slowly and gently as it seemed any experience of emotion was risky and frightening for her. I encouraged her when she shared anything with me and emphasized my acceptance of her experience, as her self-support seemed minimal.

After some time I realized Susan's pattern was to wait for me to do or say something; rarely would she spontaneously report her own experience. She would either look down at the floor and fidget or stare at me for long periods without moving, her face and mouth looking tense. My experience was one of inadvertently trying to feed Susan with her not taking much in. The 'image' I had was one of my offering Susan spoonful after spoonful of food and her keeping her mouth closed most of the time. Occasionally, however, she did take a 'spoonful' and she made some changes in her life. One such change which she considered beneficial was to make social arrangements with friends and colleagues, thus decreasing her sense of isolation.

At times, I would offer her my observations such as: 'I notice you are picking at your sweater', 'Your voice is quite low', 'You are very still'. Or I would share my feelings with her: 'I felt sad when you said that', 'I felt warm when you looked at me then', 'I was uncomfortable and wanted to move back at that moment'. Susan would sometimes nod her head or other times just look at me and say she thought I was 'criticizing' her and she felt 'bad'. When I assured her my statements were not judgemental, she seemed unable to believe me.

After a few months I began to have some uncomfortable feelings, almost of boredom. I was puzzled about what was going on. I felt I was struggling to engage her excitement in any experiment and she was resisting me: the work we were doing together was not a co-operative venture. I shared this with her. Susan tightened up her face, looked frightened and said she did not know what I meant. She was 'really trying' but she was not 'feeling any better': 'perhaps it was a waste of time and therapy was not helping'. I imagined this statement might mean 'I was not helping her'. This pattern of 'the other' not fulfilling her expectations had similarities with her experiences at work. My notion was Susan expected me (and others) to be responsible for her and I usually failed. She reacted to me (and others) based on her projected interpretations of what I was thinking and feeling, sometimes supported by reality and sometimes not.

By acknowledging and exploring my feelings and thoughts, I recognized I was investing more energy in the therapeutic process than she was. My hunch was that acknowledging her own anger or fear was unbearable for Susan so she would withdraw from her own experiencing (by constricting her breathing, blaming, etc.) and from me (by looking away, staring, etc.). She held back, or retroflected, her energy (kept her body rigid, her voice as monotone, etc.) and then reported feeling 'depressed' or 'bad'. Susan seemed unaware of her emotional reactions.

Most attempts I made to intervene at increasing her awareness would trigger this process. Each time I interrupted Susan's interruptions, she said she felt 'confused and overwhelmed' and seemed unable to mobilize her energy.

To reduce the potency of this triggering process, I suggested we experiment with one situation in detail and focus on each aspect slowly, step by step. I emphasized this to enable Susan to develop more self-support so she could feel confident enough to take a risk. This is similar to a person's making sure of her footing before moving forward, often referred to as 'being grounded'.

The preparation for an experiment is extremely important. If the experiment is too easy, there is no risk and will simply cover old material. If it is too difficult, the client might comply (go through the motions) but end up feeling embarrassed or ashamed, blocking her feelings so no integration could occur.

Susan eventually chose an experiment which re-enacted the time when she worked in the children's clinic. I said I would 'play' her, as the nurse in charge, and she could act out the roles of some of the children. Having Susan take the roles of the children would reduce the degree of risk and, therefore, would be less threatening. I assured her we would stop any time she wanted. Susan agreed.

I adopted her body posture and facial expression as closely as I could and 'played' her in response to her 'playing' several of the more difficult children.

Susan was quite adept in adopting different child roles. She even got angry and stamped her feet. Some of my responses as Susan the nurse resulted in her, as a child, obeying. At these times Susan (as the child) reported feeling 'uncomfortable' and 'dissatisfied' and thought I was 'unreasonable'. Most of my behaviours got me nowhere with her (as the child). And on these occasions Susan, still as a child, reported feeling 'powerful' when she shouted at me, stood her ground, and so on. She stood upright, shoulders straight, looking strong, and she breathed more deeply than I had previously seen her do. At one point she said, 'I was not allowed to be like this when I was little'. From her statement, and the changes in her body posture and voice, she appeared to be more in touch with her own sensations and feelings: she listened, and experienced what she said (as the child) and thereby contacted some aspects of herself which she had disowned.

Further, the experiment enabled Susan to increase her awareness of her everyday functioning. Whereas previously she had denied ever getting angry with people or ignoring them, she now recognized herself in my role-play of her, and she was able to acknowledge that she was indeed at times angry with people, and did ignore them. She accepted that she was doing to others what she accused them of doing to her.

After this session, Susan started being aware of previously being unaware. This was a rich discovery for Susan. She tapped the reservoir of her inner liveliness that she had so long blocked. She acknowledged some of her own experience without feeling overwhelmed. There was no tremendous breakthrough, rather a small turning-point.

At the time of writing, five months on, Susan is still in therapy. Her awareness and self-support continue to grow. Susan smiles more and her face looks softer. She stoops less and her breathing is deeper. Her hands are slowly healing and she bites them only occasionally. As she allowed her nails to grow, she began using nail varnish, saying it helped to 'remind' her that hands could look nice. Where before Susan used to hide her hands, she is now beginning to use them to emphasize points when she is speaking. Her voice is stronger and more animated.

Susan shares some of her 'good' feelings with me and asks me what I am thinking and/or feeling at times. She is more willing to report her experiences spontaneously and to own them as hers. Her therapy is more of a shared venture now.

Susan is still in the same job and has fewer difficulties with her colleagues. She has bought a house and, although her energy varies, is decorating it slowly. Buying her house was an important event for Susan. She said she realized that she had always thought of her parents' house as 'home'. Now that is different. She has her own 'home' and 'felt better' about not visiting them so often. Although she found it 'difficult' and 'uncomfortable' at first, she has negotiated with her parents to write to them once a week and telephone them when she wants to, rather than them contacting her continuously. When she telephones now she has more to tell them and does not feel it is such 'heavy going'. Susan was surprised they did not protest more and later discovered they had decided she was very busy 'fixing up her house'. She laughed when she told me this.

Although Susan is going out more she does not have a close relationship with a man. She says she still wants this, but does not feel 'desperate' about it any more. She is initiating more social activities and says she is 'allowing herself to have fun'. Susan will join a therapy group in the near future.

References

Appelbaum, S.A. (1983) A psychoanalyst looks at Gestalt therapy, in C. Hatcher and P. Himelstein (eds) *The Handbook of Gestalt Therapy*, New York: Jason Aronson.

Beisser, A. (1972) The paradoxical theory of change, in J. Fagan and I. Shepherd (eds) *Gestalt Therapy Now*, Harmondsworth: Penguin.

Brown, G.I. (1971) *Human Teaching for Human Learning: An Introduction to Confluent Education*, New York: Viking Press (An Esalen Book).

Buber, M. (1970) *I and Thou*, New York: Scribners.

Enwright, J. (1972) An introduction to Gestalt techniques, in J. Fagan and I. Shepherd (eds) *Gestalt Therapy Now*, Harmondsworth: Penguin.

Hall, R.A. (1976) A schema of the Gestalt concept of the organismic flow and its disturbance, in E.W.L. Smith (ed.) *The Growing Edge of Gestalt Therapy*, New York: Brunner Mazel.

Herman, S.M. and Korenich, M. (1977) *Authentic Management: A Gestalt Orientation to Organizations and their Development*, Reading, Mass: Addison-Wesley.

Latner, J. (1974) *The Gestalt Therapy Book*, New York: Bantam Books.

Miller, M.V. (1985) Some historical limitations of Gestalt therapy, *The Gestalt Journal* 8, 1: 51–4.

Nevis, S. (1985) Bringing the background into the foreground, *The Gestalt Journal* 8, 1: 61–4.

Perls, F.S. (1969a) *Ego, Hunger, and Aggression: The Beginning of Gestalt Therapy*, New York: Vintage Books.

—— (1969b) *Gestalt Therapy Verbatim*, Lafayette, Calif: Real People Press.

—— (1973) *The Gestalt Approach and Eye Witness to Therapy*, Ben Lomond, Calif: Science and Behavior Books.

Perls, F.S., Hefferline, R.F. and Goodman, P. (1974) *Gestalt Therapy*, Harmondsworth: Penguin.

Polster, E. (1987) *Every Person's Life is Worth a Novel*, New York: Norton.

Polster, E. and Polster, M. (1973) *Gestalt Therapy Integrated*, New York: Brunner Mazel.

Rosenfeld, E. (1982) A conversation between Laura Perls and Edward Rosenfeld, *Voices* 18, 2: 22–8.

Stratford, C.D. and Brallier, L.W. (1979) Gestalt therapy with profoundly disturbed persons, *The Gestalt Journal* 2, 1: 90–104.

Ward, P. and Rouzer, D.L. (1974) The nature of pathological functioning from a Gestalt perspective, *The Counseling Psychologist* 4: 24–7.

Yontef, G. (1984) Modes of thinking in Gestalt therapy, *The Gestalt Journal* 7, 1: 33–74.

—— (1988) Assimilating diagnostic and psychoanalytic perspectives into Gestalt therapy, *The Gestalt Journal* 11, 1: 5–32.

Zdenek, M. (1983) *The Right-Brain Experience*, London: Corgi.

Zinker, J. (1977) *Creative Process in Gestalt Therapy*, New York: Brunner Mazel.

Suggested further reading

Clarkson, P. (1989) *Gestalt Counselling in Action*, London: Sage.

Passons, W.R. (1975) *Gestalt Approaches in Counseling*, New York: Holt, Rinehart & Winston.

Perls, F.S. (1969) *Gestalt Therapy Verbatim*, Lafayette, Calif: Real People Press.

—— (1973) *The Gestalt Approach and Eye Witness to Therapy*, Ben Lomond, Calif: Science and Behavior Books.

Polster, E. and Polster, M. (1973) *Gestalt Therapy Integrated*, New York: Brunner Mazel.

Zinker, J. (1977) *Creative Process in Gestalt Therapy*, New York: Brunner Mazel.

10

Transactional Analysis

PETRŪSKA CLARKSON AND MARIA GILBERT

Historical context and development in Britain

Historical Context

Transactional Analysis as first developed by Eric Berne (1958) is a multifaceted system of psychotherapy. Berne's emphasis on the interactional aspect of communication is reflected in the name *Transactional* Analysis. He saw this as an extension to the in-depth emphasis of psychoanalysis with its focus on intrapsychic dynamics. Transactional Analysis as a theory of psychotherapy integrates intrapsychic dynamics with interpersonal behaviours in an original and creative manner and is based on the ego State Psychology of Federn (1953).

Berne saw Transactional Analysis as a 'systematic phenomenology' which could usefully fill a gap in psychological theory (Berne 1975: 244). Phenomenology as a philosophical approach values the importance of the person's subjective experience above any interpretation, prejudgement or preconceived theories or ideas. Throughout his life, Berne adhered to his belief in the person's inner drive to health and growth, which places him firmly in the humanistic tradition. However, he was far from being optimistic in a simplistic way. As is demonstrated throughout his writings, he had a vivid respect for the power of people's destructive potential, both as individuals and as nations.

Eric Berne, born Eric Leonard Bernstein (1910–70), was a Canadian psychiatrist who originally trained as a psychoanalyst at the New York Psychoanalytic Institute. Although he never officially qualified as a psychoanalyst, the influence of his training analysts is manifest in his theory. The intrapsychic phenomenological interests of Federn combined with the social-developmental emphasis of Erikson is reflected in Berne's integrative approach.

Berne's first interest in research was in the field of intuition. He sharpened his skills personally and professionally during his work at an army induction centre where he recognized the continuing existence of the person's 'inner Child'. He saw such 'ego images' persisting through adult life as reproductions of the person's earlier experiences. These observations led to the development of ego state theory (Structural Analysis).

In 1958 Berne began a series of meetings of mental health professionals interested in Transactional Analysis under the name the San Francisco Social Psychiatry Seminar. On 6 May 1960 the group was granted a charter by the State of California as a non-profit educational corporation offering alternative approaches to earlier types of psychotherapy. This period of time was also notable for the incorporation of a strong behaviourist influence into Transactional Analysis. Later, as theory developed, the group took the name of the San Francisco Transactional Analysis Seminars. The year 1965 saw the establishment of the International Transactional Analysis Association (ITAA), which now has over 5,000 members in 50 countries throughout the world.

Berne wrote prolifically about Transactional Analysis (TA) in a creative and original style with enormous popular appeal. Along with his wit, accessibility, humour and common sense, there is also a depth of wisdom and clinical experience that lends an impressive character to his written work. He made a genuine contribution to twentieth-century psychology which is often unacknowledged. However, his influence is manifested in the ubiquitous references, for example, to 'the Child' in the person, psychological 'games' and other TA concepts which have been absorbed into popular vocabulary and other approaches to psychotherapy.

Eric Berne was an imaginative thinker, widely read and with an insatiable curiosity and intellectual courage. He had a great capacity for self-reflection, experimentation and innovation. He was both an iconoclast and keenly aware of the social responsibilities of psychologists and psychotherapists. He had the courage to cut loose from what did not work and to risk the disapproval of establishment psychiatry by, for example, introducing the radical practice of having patients present at hospital case conferences. Such departures marked him as a radical humanist committed to a basic value system which recognized the worth of every person.

Development in Britain

According to the best information available (Allaway 1983), John Allaway and Joe Richards created the first evening courses in Transactional Analysis for mature students of the University of Leicester in the early 1960s, both in Leicester and in Northampton. Laurence Collinson and David Porter started the first TA discussion group in London in April 1972. In November 1972 Warren Cheney, a psychotherapist from Berkeley, California, and a teaching Member of ITAA, led the first official TA Introductory Course (101) in Sheffield organized by Dr Alan Byron.

From 1975 onwards Dr Margaret Turpin and Dr Michael Reddy were teaching official TA Training Programmes as Provisional Teaching Members under supervision from sponsors in the USA. Michael Reddy subsequently became Britain's first Teaching Member, followed by Margaret Turpin. From this evolved a series of official TA training programmes in Britain and the Institute for Transactional Analysis (ITA) as the country's official link with the ITAA. David Porter, followed by Laurence Collinson, were the first editors of the ITA Bulletin. Michael Reddy played a key role in the establishment of TA in the rest of Europe and in the formation of the European Association for Transactional Analysis (EATA). The ITA's first annual conference was at Heythrop College in London in October 1974. Since then an ITA conference has been held annually, reflecting a corresponding growth in the organization in Britain.

The Institute for Transactional Analysis is the professional body which defines and safeguards standards of competence, professional guidelines and ethical practice for all practitioners, psychotherapists and teachers and supervisors of Transactional Analysis in Britain. The Institute holds a register of members (1) who are in contractual supervised training, (2) who have qualified as Transactional Analysts, (3) who are provisionally endorsed supervisors and trainers, and (4) who have qualified as trainers and supervisors of Transactional Analysis (by virtue of rigorous international examination of their theoretical knowledge and demonstrated competence in teaching and supervision).

The Level 1 TA Clinical Examination is an internationally accredited and standardized qualification which is awarded on completion of stringent written and oral requirements. This externally assessed competency-based examination certifies an individual psychotherapist to practise Transactional Analysis.

Currently TA, with its emphasis on professionalism and international standards of accreditation, is taking its place alongside other psychotherapies in Britain.

Theoretical assumptions

The image of the person

Basic to TA theory and philosophy is Berne's concept of the fundamental worth of the human being, for which his shorthand was 'OK-ness'. This concept embraces valuing and respecting human beings and is not to be confused with blatant approval of all of their behaviour. It is, however, predicated upon an assumption that the infant is born with a basic drive for health and growth and a need for loving recognition (in Berne's terminology 'OK'). In his discussion of child development, Berne (1975) had already adopted an object relations approach which he used within an existential framework. Berne took from Melanie Klein the term 'position' to indicate an internal psychological condition, formed in early childhood and always potentially present in the personality. However, he did not see this as necessarily defensive or negative.

The three not-OK positions that Berne identified are I'm OK – You're not OK (paranoid); I'm not OK – You're OK (depressive) and I'm not OK – You're not OK (schizoid). Berne's unique contribution was the addition of position number one, I'm OK – You're OK, which Klein omitted. He regarded this position as intrinsically constructive and existentially possible. In this way he envisaged the nature of the person as having an inborn potential available from birth, for fulfilment and self-actualization. Transactional Analysts believe that it is possible to maintain an existential position of OK-ness.

Berne postulated the existence of three drives: Mortido (the death instinct), Libido (the sexual instinct) and Physis (a general creative force which eternally strives to make things grow and to make growing things more perfect). The first two correspond to the Freudian ideas of Thanatos and Eros, whereas Physis is Berne's addition which he defines as 'the creative force of Nature which makes all things grow in an orderly and "progressive" way' (Berne 1957: 68). TA recognizes the constraints of heredity, specifically the relationship of temperament or basic limitations of intellect and physique to psychological health (James 1981: 24–7) but considers that the drive towards psychological health in the person can modify, adapt to or overcome many apparent limitations.

Berne's central contribution is his elaboration of ego states and his development of therapeutic techniques to directly influence and change these. An ego state is the subjectively experienced reality of a person's mental and bodily ego with the original contents of the time period it represents. Clarkson and Gilbert (1988: 21) describe ego states as ' "chunks of psychic time" – complete and discrete units of psychological reality' or 'natural psychological epochs'.

Berne integrated the neurosurgical findings of Penfield (1952), which demonstrated that human beings can *relive* earlier experiences in their lives given the appropriate stimulation. To quote Penfield: 'The subject feels again the emotion which the situation originally produced in him and he is aware of the same interpretation, true or false, which he himself gave to the experience in the first place' (Penfield 1952: 178). This experiential difference between· remembering an earlier experience and *reliving* a past event as if it were happening in the present occurs as age regression in hypnosis and also occasionally occurs in more or less complete forms in everyday life. Berne used this as validation for the existence of ego states together with the clinical evidence he was gathering from his patients.

In his contact with patients Berne observed three different *categories* among the multitude of ego states which constitute the personality. One category is concerned with here-and-now reality (the Adult), one with the person's past experience (the Child) and one with the introjects or internalizations of significant authority figures (the Parent).

An 'Adult ego state is characterized by an autonomous set of feelings, attitudes, and behavior patterns which are adapted to current reality' (Berne 1975: 76). The integrated Adult ego state therefore represents the biologically mature person with full emotional responsivity (pathos), a guiding set of considered values (ethos) and the capacity to think clearly and to deal effectively with need-fulfilment in the here-and-now (logos).

A 'Child ego state is a set of feelings, attitudes and behavior patterns which are relics of the individual's own childhood' (Berne 1975: 77). When Berne writes about Child ego state he is often referring to a multitude of such Child ego states which represent the entire earlier developmental history of an individual. These are accessible to being relived as such, in the present, by the adult person. This phenomenon is of particular value in psychotherapy.

A Parent 'ego state is a set of feelings, attitudes, and behavior patterns which resemble those of a parental figure' (Berne 1975: 75). The person whose Parent predominates habitually, or at a given moment is not acting 'like her mother', she is actually reproducing without editing her mother's total behaviour, including her mother's inhibitions, her mother's reasoning and her mother's impulses, as well as her mother's Child ego states. The Parent ego state may be actively reproduced as in when the person is behaving like an historical parent towards another person or may be active internally as in the person's own mental dialogue, for example in self-criticism.

Figure 10.1 is a diagrammatic representation of these three categories of ego states. The diagnosis of ego states is at the heart of Berne's psychotherapeutic approach. He outlines four different methods of ego state diagnosis, all of which are essential for the complete identification of an ego state:

1 *Behavioural* diagnosis of any ego state is based on the observable words, voice tone, gestures, expressions, posture and attitudes of a person.
2 *Social* diagnosis of any ego state is made by observing the kinds of reactions which the person elicits from other people.
3 *Historical* diagnosis of any ego state is based on historical validation – that a past experience actually did occur in a particular ego state.
4 *Phenomenologically*, the diagnosis of any ego state can be confirmed on the basis of subjective self-examination, particularly of intense experiences.

In normal life people may find themselves in different ego states at different times. In everyday life people experience themselves for longer or shorter periods as younger than they are, for example when going for job interviews, or when ill, or when going through customs. This is the everyday appearance of Child ego states. Equally people may find themselves responding to their children exactly as one of their parents reacted to them (for example, by admonishing them not to stare rudely at people, or to be brave at the dentist, or to respect their elders). This is the everyday experience of Parent ego states.

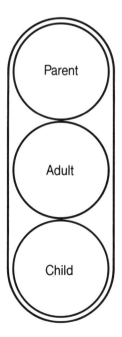

Figure 10.1 Structural diagram of a personality (Berne 1975/1978: 12)

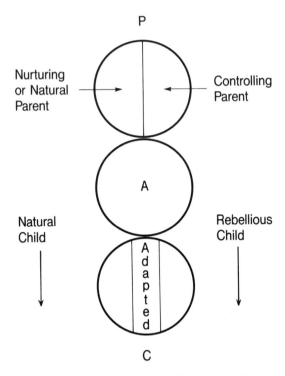

P

Nurturing
or Natural
Parent

Controlling
Parent

A

Natural
Child

Rebellious
Child

A
d
a
p
t
e
d

C

Figure 10.2 Descriptive aspects of the personality (personality functions) (Berne 1975/1978: 13)

Functional Analysis is the subdivision of Transactional Analysis which relates primarily to the behavioural and social components of ego state diagnosis. In this model, which is most useful for communication training and behavioural change, *behaviours* are classified under the following *descriptive* headings: Controlling Parent, Nurturing Parent, Adult, Free Child and Adapted Child. Figure 10.2 is a diagram representing the functional description of these observable behaviours.

Conceptualization of psychological disturbance and health

There are three different ways of conceptualizing psychological disturbance: through affective and cognitive interference in the functioning of the integrated ego (confusion model), through the existence of internal conflict between different parts of the ego (conflict model), and through developmental deficits and inadequate parenting (deficit model).

Confusion model

In the confusion model, psychological health can be structurally defined as the strengthening of integrated Adult functioning. The efficiency of the Adult ego state is dependent on the quality of its information and problem-solving abilities as these are integrated into the personality. The concept of *contamination* describes the

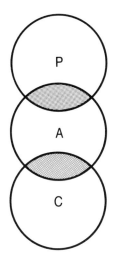

Figure 10.3 Double contamination of the Adult ego state (Berne 1975: 48)

way in which effective Adult functioning is impeded by limiting beliefs, traumatic experiences and learnt emotional and physiological responses.

Contaminations can occur when the Parent ego state intrudes upon the Adult (e.g. prejudices) or when the Child ego state intrudes upon the Adult (e.g. phobias). Figure 10.3 shows a double contamination of the Adult Ego State by both Parent and Child contaminations, which can severely impede reality testing and effective functioning. In terms of Berne's original structural model of ego states, the psychotherapeutic goal would be the achievement of a fully integrated Adult ego state without interference from unresolved experiences from a person's past (Child ego states) or from the influence of internalized significant others (Parent ego states).

Conflict model
In the conflict model, best represented by impasse theory in TA, psychological disturbance is conceptualized in terms of intrapsychic 'stuck points' between different ego states. For example, the Parent may be 'driving' the person to work harder and harder, while the Child may need to play more. If the early decision in the Child ego state has involved shutting down on the expression of feelings, then a conflict or 'impasse' will arise when such a person starts wanting to assert herself, for example, in an abusive marital relationship. Health represents the ability to resolve such impasses within the personality and to function smoothly without blocking needs, values or emotions.

Developmental deficit model
In the developmental deficit model, psychological disturbance results from inadequate, pathological or neglectful parenting at critical development stages in a

child's life. For example, children of alcoholics may need the corrective experience of a relationship where consistency of response is provided in the context of a reparative therapeutic relationship. As an additional example, people with narcissistic personality disorders have often lacked the mirroring or reflecting essential for a healthy sense of self – this can be supplied in the therapeutic relationship. In radical reparenting (such as developed by Schiff *et al.* 1975) schizophrenics have the opportunity to regress and then to move through important child developmental stages while introjecting a new Parent ego state. As a result of this process the healthy person has at his or her disposal a supportive and challenging set of guiding values which he or she has autonomously integrated as the end result of good parenting.

Acquisition of psychological disturbance

Berne introduced the concept of *scripting* to describe the process by which a person, usually in early childhood, makes far-reaching decisions that influence and shape her subsequent life experiences. A *script* is formed out of the child's response to the environment, particularly to her interaction with her parents and/or significant others. The combination of inherited limitations and/or predispositions interact with trauma (e.g. shock) or cumulative conditioning events (e.g. frequent criticism) so that the infant makes survival conclusions (pre-verbal and physiolog-ical) or script decisions (e.g. never to depend on others again). Such conclusions or decisions are fundamentally aimed at survival in the particular set of circum-stances in which the child finds herself. The result may be any one or more of the kinds of psychological disturbances described above. Woollams and Brown (1979) speak about the *vulnerability quotient* of the young child and list five factors that play a determining role in a person's script decisions: lack of power, inability to handle stress, immature thinking capacity, lack of information, and lack of options.

The script matrix is a simplified diagrammatic representation of the origin of the script messages/influences and prohibitions from the parents or significant others in the child's life (see Figure 10.4). S (Script) refers to the negative inhibiting messages (e.g. do not have satisfactory intimate relationships). C (Counterscript) refers to the precepts or positive instructions about how to live (e.g. work hard). R (Release) refers to an outside intervention or condition by which the individual is released from the script (e.g. a heart attack in a young stock broker). A (Aspiration) refers to the individual's autonomous aspirations (e.g. the drive to health and intimacy). P (Pattern) refers to the modelling of significant figures (e.g. a father who never stopped working at the cost of his family life).

Scripting is the process by which the growing person limits her own capacity for spontaneity, awareness and intimacy in the interests of survival. This is usually practically and psychologically equated with acceptance from the care-taking figures. The premature and far-reaching script decisions, based on inadequate information and immature undeveloped mental capacities, hamper the normal developmental processes. Script decisions may also occur in response to trauma or a repeated series of sub-acute injurious events or psychological strain. Psycholog-ical disturbance, often acquired in childhood, can also be acquired in adulthood through similar damaging experiences (e.g. torture of political prisoners).

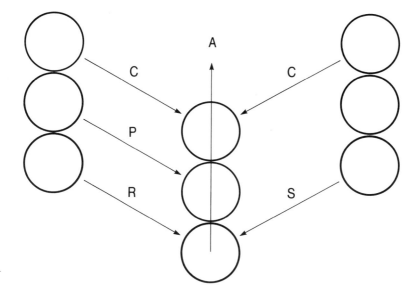

S = Script
C = Counterscript
R = Release
A = Aspiration
P = Pattern

Figure 10.4   Script matrix (Berne 1975/1978: 128)

Berne stressed the importance of the human infant's capacity to love and his need for love and recognition as basic to human psychological development. His concept of *stroking* grew from his appreciation of the enormous power which the provision or withdrawal of recognition can have on human behaviour, particularly on infants and children. He drew on studies (e.g. Spitz 1945) which found that human infants, even though adequately cared for physiologically, fail to thrive, or may even die in the absence of genuine interpersonal recognition. Giving or withholding strokes is, therefore, intimately related to the scripting process, since that which gets stroked will tend to develop (repeat) even to the child's detriment. A child whose parents applaud restraint and stoicism may never feel free to show emotion even in intimate relationships. Both learning theory and the common human response to solitary confinement attest to the power of stroking (negative or positive reinforcement) to modify behaviour.

Perpetuation of psychological disturbance

The major way in which psychological disturbance is perpetuated is in the person's seeking out the same strokes to which he or she became habituated in childhood (motivation) or in the person's construing current situations in a way that fits the preconceived requirements of the script (cognitive mediation). Erskine and Zalcman (1979) in their *Racket System* provide a visual model for viewing the script in action with a particular focus on the self-reinforcing nature of the script process as it is played out in the person's current life. It presents a combination of intrapsychic and interpersonal factors as well as the interface between them. The *Script Beliefs* refer to the self-limiting beliefs about self, others and quality of life related to early decisions. The *Repressed Feelings* are the feelings repressed at the time of such script decisions. The *Rackety Displays* are the behaviours which a person engages in as a result of such script beliefs. The *Reinforcing Memories* refer to all the memories a person collects to reinforce their basic script position. People within the environment will either reinforce the basic script beliefs by repetition of earlier patterns or the individual may construe even positive or ambiguous events in the environment to support the basic script beliefs. In this way, intrapersonal and interpersonal mechanisms interact within the environment to perpetuate the script. An example is shown in Figure 10.5.

Dana's intrapsychic cognitive beliefs about herself, others and the world influence her behaviours, internal experiences and fantasies. Behaving then in the ways described (e.g. charming or tantrumming to get her needs met), she enacts the external manifestations of her intrapersonal process in the interpersonal field. People then react to her manifest behaviours in ways which repeat earlier trauma (e.g. being hurt by her behaviour, or acting in destructive or unhelpful ways towards her). In this way further reinforcing memories are created which fuel her original script beliefs while the underlying feelings related to the original trauma remain suppressed. In this way, a self-reinforcing system is created and maintained until an intervention in the system changes its functioning.

The racket system is useful to show how a person constantly seeks the approval that he or she did not get as a child, but he or she does it in such a way that it guarantees a repetition of the earlier traumatic outcome or deficit. The person may become increasingly desperate and escalate his or her behaviour to the point of the most tragic outcome, for example suicide.

Berne's concept of the *script pay-off* refers to the destructive outcome of self-limiting script decisions in a person's life. Unless the person changes his or her self-chosen destiny, psychological disturbance is maintained by the person's continuing to behave in self-destructive ways. This is the unconscious operation of mortido (the death instinct) in the person's life.

The smallest unit in which human beings recreate the original stimulus–response sequences which maintain the racket system is the *transaction*. This is the central component in TA theory which makes it possible to analyse in a moment-to-moment way the manner in which people repeat their relationships with important figures in their early childhood. For example, if a child is continually victimized by parents, this process may manifest as a tendency to apologize for everything she does (e.g. 'I'm sorry . . .', 'I didn't mean to do that . . .'). In subsequent relationships she may tend to repeat transactions with people in which she overtly or covertly takes the 'victim' position. So any sequence of communication between her and others may be analysed minutely into its covert and overt transactional components so that she may be helped out of these self-defeating patterns.

Dana's Racket System

SCRIPT BELIEFS/FEELINGS
(Intrapsychic System)

┌─ Beliefs about: ─▼─────────────┐

1. Self
  Core: I'm bad and harmful
  Supporting: I'm different/special

2. Others
  Core: Others are all powerful
        able to save or destroy
  Supporting: Others cannot
        handle my feelings

3. Quality of life
  Core: Life is about rejection,
        disappointment and treachery
  Supporting: Wear a mask in
        order to survive

└─ ▶Repressed Feelings ──────────┘

  Sadness and fear

RACKETY DISPLAYS
(Behavioural interface)

1. Observable Behaviour:
  Charmingly manipulative
  Clings and then pushes away
  Temper tantrums
  Seeks special favours

2. Reported Internal Experiences:
  So tired she is hardly able to move
  or agitated and restless

3. Fantasies:
  Grandiose – I can be the greatest
  without effort
  Fantasy of being destroyed or of
  destroying

REINFORCING MEMORIES

I was so large that my mother nearly
died in childbirth

Sexual abuse at 6 years

Short intense relationships ending
badly

Repeated conflicts at work resulting
in frequent changes of job

Two unsuccessful periods of
previous psychotherapy including
one hospitalization for suicide
attempt by overdose of tranquillizers

Figure 10.5 Dana's Racket System

Berne categorized transactions into three types: complementary (predictable), crossed (unpredictable), and ulterior (with hidden or covert agenda). These divisions facilitate the easy analysis of functional and dysfunctional communication between people so enabling people to identify those transactions that further the script and to practise new options.

Transactional Analysis of this type also forms the basis of *Games Analysis*. The psychological game forms the interactional sequence by which a person perpetuates the script in his communication with others and ensures a negative, though familiar, outcome. A game is defined as a series of transactions with an ulterior purpose that proceeds to a well-defined predictable payoff. Such games are played outside of Adult ego state awareness and promote the script through the patterned repetition of negative outcomes. A great deal of Berne's fame arose from his book *Games People Play* (Berne 1968/1975); with its unprecedented popularity it made useful psychological information accessible to vast numbers of ordinary people.

Change

Change from psychological disturbance to psychological health can be conceptualized in Transactional Analysis as a manifestation of Physis – the drive towards psychological health and growth in every human being towards autonomy.

Berne saw autonomy as the aim of the well-functioning person. Autonomy is manifested by three qualities: awareness, spontaneity and intimacy.

1 *Awareness* refers to a freshness of perception freed from archaic conditioning, related to the current reality and an appreciation of the sensory richness of the environment.
2 *Spontaneity* means the option to choose and express one's feelings freely and the liberation from the compulsion to play psychological games.
3 *Intimacy* means spontaneous, game-free, honest quality of relationship which is not an adaptation to parental influences.

> For certain fortunate people there is something which transcends all classifications of behaviour, and that is awareness; something which rises above the programming of the past, and that is spontaneity; and something that is more rewarding than games, and that is intimacy.
>
> (Berne 1968/1975: 162)

Since the force for growth and change is a basic human drive, it can occur in a variety of settings of which the psychotherapeutic relationship is one. In the course of the normal developmental phases of childhood and adulthood, the person continues to develop and grow under the influence of Physis. But when this natural self-actualizing process has been damaged and the person has become locked in a self-reinforcing destructive life pattern, *force majeure* may be required to effect a shift. Clarkson (1989) has identified that religious conversion, crisis, love, and education, along with psychotherapy, are all circumstances which can facilitate sudden and long-lasting fundamental changes in human beings. All of these may involve a profound change in the person's frame of reference (or beliefs), physiology, behaviour, emotions and interpersonal transactions.

Practice

Goals of therapy

The goal of TA is twofold: symptom relief (social control) and/or script release (autonomy). The ultimate aim is for the person to become self-actualizing and take responsibility for his or her own life choices and personal development.

TA sets very specific therapeutic goals (the contract system) which allows for precision in meeting well-defined psychotherapeutic goals (for example to have regular orgasms with a partner). The contract system is one of the chief hallmarks of TA psychotherapy. In this way, a Transactional Analyst can work in brief, focused ways towards verifiable outcomes. Therefore, this approach within TA is well-suited to short-term psychotherapy with circumscribed goals, as well as marking accomplished stage-posts in the course of long-term psychotherapy.

Some Transactional Analysts (who have the required knowledge of theory and experience of personal psychotherapy) are also interested in depth psychotherapy, frequently of a long-term nature, which has 'script cure' as a goal. Script cure is achieved when the person breaks out of his script and becomes autonomous. He puts a new 'show on the road, with new characters, new roles, and a new plot and payoff' (Berne 1975/1978: 362). The metaphor Berne repeatedly used was to change princes and princesses (who had become 'frogs' through social and parental influences) back into princes and princesses so that they could continue their development as autonomous, spontaneous and aware individuals.

Transactional Analysts continue to investigate the concept of cure and its meanings in clinical practice (Clarkson 1988; Erskine 1980; Goulding and Goulding 1979). Berne also gave many warnings against claiming 'cure' without checking out very carefully the nature and stability of the psychotherapeutic change that has apparently taken place.

Selection criteria

Transactional Analysis has been successfully used with a very wide range of clients, for example people who are mentally handicapped, schizophrenic, anti-social, alcoholic, as well as those with the full spectrum of adjustment disorders, personality disorders and clinical syndromes such as anxiety, phobias and compulsions (Harris 1973; Goulding and Goulding 1979; Schiff *et al.* 1975; Woods and Woods 1982; Loomis and Landsman 1980; 1981; Thomson 1986; Steiner 1971; and Groder, cited in Barnes 1977). So the method *per se* is adaptable to almost any client population in the hands of skilled and experienced practitioners. The theoretical scope and the methodological diversity of Transactional Analysis lends itself to applications limited only by the personality, preferences and training of the individual psychotherapist. Because of this diversity, there is practically no category of client that has not been treated by a Transactional Analyst.

Because Transactional Analysis works with the whole system, whether intrapsychically or interpersonally, any component/s of the client system may be the focus of psychotherapeutic intervention at any one time. It is not unusual that a combination of individual and group or family/couples therapy may be considered appropriate.

A detailed discussion of the criteria for such decisions is beyond the scope of an introductory chapter. It would depend on the developmental needs of the client, for example, a client who was very traumatized shortly after birth may need to have a long period of individual psychotherapy in order to build and test a relationship of trust. The nature of the transference relationship would also influence choice of individual psychotherapy as the preferred modality. For example, this may be appropriate with a person who has an intense need to develop a strong transference relationship with the psychotherapist integrating a split between good and bad to the exclusion of others (dyadic transference) as is the case in some people with borderline traits.

Many people prefer individual psychotherapy because it can provide a reparative experience for difficulties experienced in childhood with the earliest caretaker. Some people, who have never had the experience of being in a caring affirmative relationship with a significant other, may deserve the exclusive attention of the psychotherapist in an individual setting. Individual psychotherapy is also the modality of choice when individuals are so damaged or fragmented that they may be unable to benefit from the healing culture of a group or when they behave in anti-social, offensive ways or engage in provocative games likely to lead to scapegoating or undermining of the effectiveness of the group for other members.

Qualities of effective therapists

TA is a psychotherapeutic approach which lends itself to interpretation by a wide variety of personalities. In the study of effectiveness of different group leaders, Lieberman *et al.* (1973) found Transactional Analysts among the most effective as well as among the least effective. However, there are certain common criteria which are evaluated in the clinical training and by written and oral examination in qualifying as Transactional Analysts. These include:

1 a sound theoretical background in Transactional Analysis, an ability to explain and apply different TA approaches
2 clarity of contracts and treatment direction
3 awareness of distortions of reality and of incongruities
4 perceptual and cognitive clarity of client assessment
5 potency or personal power of the therapist, and protection or the ability to create a safe environment for the client
6 intuition and creativity (range of options for therapeutic interventions)
7 effectiveness and professionalism (awareness of privileges and limitations of training by relating clearly to ethical principles).

Ideally the TA therapist will model healthy living and psychological well-being most of the time. This does not mean that therapists have to be perfect, but that they be willing and able to engage in mutually satisfactory intimate relationships, and an emotionally rich and varied psychological life. This transparency can be demanding on the therapist but is also a most powerful tool for change.

The TA therapist assumes that the client can become an equal partner in the therapy process, and in fact expects that clients will assume responsibility for contributing to their own healing process. Integrated Adult functioning on the part of the therapist is facilitated by both personal therapy and regular supervision.

Therapeutic style

Berne's model of self-reflection in the process of therapy with his clients is a valuable tradition within TA and has encouraged therapists to be alert to their own process (counter-transference) and potential for playing games. Berne provided a detailed method for analysing games which enables therapists to identify the points at which they may be invited to participate in a potential game. Games analysis can be helpful to both psychotherapist and client in focusing on both the psychotherapeutic relationship and the client's wider network of interaction. This calls for therapists who are willing to be active and interventionist, as well as clients who are informed, questioning and active on their own behalf.

The adoption of any one attitude, such as neutrality towards a client, is anathema to an approach which values uniqueness and difference, and requires from therapists range and flexibility in approach. Sometimes the therapist may be substantially more active, for example in crisis intervention or in the treatment of serious clinical depression. At other times, the therapist may indeed take a position of objective neutrality, such as in working with some people who have borderline symptomatology. The involvement of the person of the therapist will vary from client to client, and depend on the stage of psychotherapy. This may range from using humour and personal experiences to giving information, confrontation or a determined neutrality.

There are several levels of relationship which therapists may use depending on their training, their own individual psychotherapy, their personal preferences or the appropriateness of a particular level of relationship to a particular client or client group.

The core foundation stone in Transactional Analysis is respect for yourself and the other person. This forms the basis of the *contractual therapeutic relationship* (the I'm OK – You're OK position). This kind of working alliance is exemplified by involving clients in their own goal setting and treatment planning, and encouraging their reading and acquiring psychological knowledge where appropriate.

The *transference relationship* is the externalization of the original intrapsychic relationship on to the therapist. If a therapist has both personal experience and training in working with transference, it can form the fulcrum for most in-depth long-term psychotherapy in Transactional Analysis.

The reparative or *developmentally needed relationship* is the relationship which the therapist may assume to help the client to correct developmental deficiencies overcome trauma and provide what was lacking in the original situation.

For example, for a person who was hospitalized at the exploratory period of child development and over-protected by nervous parents, the psychotherapist may need to provide support and encouragement for risk-taking and experimentation.

The *core relationship* as described by Barr (1987: 137) refers to the integrated Adult to Adult relationship between the psychotherapist and the client. The core relationship, in this sense, is based on the therapist's willingness to be available as a genuine and authentic person in an I–Thou encounter with another human being.

Transactional Analysts range from counsellors with a very specific focus and narrow range of educational/behavioural skills who work with short-term contracts to psychotherapists who engage *inter alia* in long-term in-depth work with their clients involving a radical restructuring of personality within the context of a transferential relationship. It is a tribute to the International Transactional Analysis Association (ITAA) that practitioners from such diverse orientations can find an identity within this approach.

Major therapeutic strategies and techniques

All the strategies and techniques used by the therapist will be determined by his or her assessment (or diagnosis) of the particular client's developmental needs. We shall briefly outline some general strategies and indicate related techniques.

Contracting

The treatment contract is an integral part of TA therapy and defines the responsibility of both parties involved in the therapeutic relationship. A contract worded in specific terms, for which the outcome can be observed and measured, not only avoids disappointment and misunderstanding about goals but also gives clarity to the therapeutic process. A well-defined or 'hard' contract is to be distinguished from a 'soft' contract which is vague and may lead to confusion or deliberate or accidental misunderstandings. The contract is a primary vehicle for emphasizing the client's responsibility for his or her own treatment process. It maximizes co-operation and facilitates positive motivation on the part of the client.

The contract establishes a working alliance between therapist and client, based on the belief that the client has an active drive for health, contrasted with approaches where dealing with the client's resistance to change is a core feature of therapeutic technique. The skill of the therapist resides in finding creative ways to actualize the client's positive forces for growth, while both people take into account the important 'survival' functions of the client's defences which have been built up over many years and under considerable pressure. The contractual nature of TA psychotherapy is one of its distinctive features which Berne saw as a prime vehicle for minimizing the destructive effects of psychological games in the therapeutic relationship.

Decontamination

The strategy of decontamination involves the strengthening of the integrated Adult ego state. The therapist deals with unintegrated material from Parent ego states that may be impeding effective functioning by techniques which highlight the nature of Parental beliefs and assumptions that are out of date and no longer apply in the person's current situation. For example, a man who has an 'ingrained belief' that women cannot be trusted, incorporated from a paranoid father, may engage in a lifetime of repetitive, destructive sexual relationships. Such contaminations from the Parent ego state are by definition outside of the person's conscious awareness. What parents believe often appears to the child to be inviolate truths. The therapist also deals with unresolved childhood fears and traumatic archaic Child ego states as they currently interfere with effective reality testing in the Adult ego state. For example, an unreasonable fear that people in authority will cause damage, may result from a childhood blighted by abusive parenting. By separating the contents of the different ego states (through techniques ranging from transference interpretation to symbolic enactment), the therapist can facilitate the client's awareness of untested automatic assumptions about themselves, others or the nature of reality. In this sense, all transference interpretations can be said to be decontamination interventions since they are designed to separate out current reality from archaic experiences.

Berne describes the eight major categories of therapeutic operations which are particularly effective for decontamination. Southey Swede (1977) summarizes these therapeutic operations as follows:

1 *Interrogation*   Asking questions to document and elicit important information
2 *Specification*   Categorizing and clearly stating certain relevant information
3 *Confrontation*   Using information previously obtained to point out inconsistencies [to a client]
4 *Explanation*   Stating what the therapist's Adult thinks is going on
5 *Illustration*   Using an anecdote, simile or comparison to reinforce a confrontation or explanation
6 *Confirmation*   Using new confrontations to confirm the same issues (previously confronted)
7 *Interpretation*   Stating ways of understanding a situation, thereby correcting distortions and regrouping past experiences
8 *Crystallization*   Making summary statements of a patient's position to facilitate decision-making.

(Swede 1977: 25)

Impasse resolution in the conflict model
TA is based on the concept of script decisions made in early childhood, which determines the person's subsequent behaviour. This original decision was made as a protective measure by the child under parental and/or environmental pressure and persists into adult life. As long as there is no desire to contest such a limitation, the person may be unhappy, disturbed or psychologically ill, and unaware of any possibility of change. As the person mobilizes energy (or the urge to healthy growth asserts itself) different parts of the ego come into conflict with one another. As this conflict intensifies, the person moves into an 'impasse' or 'stuck point'. This is often the time when they seek the help of the therapist and are well-motivated for change although they are experiencing quite intensely the counter-pull of the script.

Redecision therapy (Goulding and Goulding 1979) is a set of therapeutic procedures aimed at resolving impasses between Child ego states and Parent ego states, and different aspects of Child ego states. The purpose of redecision is for the client to reverse the earlier script decisions which maintain a self-defeating and unsatisfactory life so that they can reclaim their intrinsic health, effectiveness and autonomy.

The fact that historical Child ego states can be relived in the present in their full original vividness as if the person were experiencing them now makes it possible to access these intentionally in the course of psychotherapy. Of course, there are also spontaneous regressions to Child ego states (e.g. experiencing the therapist as a 'withholding father'), which the therapist can use to facilitate redecision.

Redecision *techniques* include allowing the client to re-experience past traumatic events with full affective, cognitive and physiological expression. This *reliving*, in the present, of the original experience, allows the client fully to cathect the particular Child ego state of that time when the script decision was made and to express earlier unmet needs or hurts emotionally.

The client is then encouraged to explore and experience the advantages and disadvantages of perpetuating the particular decision in the present time. Then the client can take the opportunity to replace the self-defeating decisions of the past with fresh decisions in that particular Child ego state, witnessed by the Parent and the decontaminated Adult ego state. An important aspect of this technique is to validate the client for constructive decisions (made in the interest of survival) in their childhood. The final steps in this process involve practising the redecisions in and outside of the therapy sessions through rehearsal, experimentation and self-monitoring until the new behaviours and related feelings are firmly grounded in the personality (Pulleybank and McCormick 1985). Such redecisions involve significant restructuring of the Child ego state. Redecisions made at sufficient depth, intensity and at the appropriate stage of treatment for that particular individual, can result in lasting personality changes.

Parenting and reparenting techniques in the deficit model
Generally the paradigm for all parenting and reparenting types of strategies is providing the 'inner child' of the patient with the kind of parenting experiences that were lacking in the individual's childhood. Such corrective emotional experiences are contractually provided by the psychotherapist in the context of the therapeutic relationship.

Time-limited reparenting   involves providing the reparative experiences related to a particular deficit in a past Child ego state which is contributing to the person's current psychopathology. For example, a child may have been unsupported when involved in an accident, so the therapist provides the support that was missing at the time during a symbolic enactment in the consulting room.

Radical reparenting   involves a wide range of techniques for providing adequate Parent ego states often for psychotic patients. This treatment is usually provided in a therapeutic community setting in which the patients are provided with parenting by the new 'therapist' parents. The new parenting experience is provided while fostering a complete regression which allows the patient's Child to move through the developmental cycle once again in a healthier way. This involves the decathexis (withdrawal of energy) of the original pathological Parent ego state and the voluntary contractual incorporation of a complete new Parent ego state, usually that of the psychotherapist. Further psychotherapy is usually still necessary to integrate the replaced Parent ego state structure fully into integrated Adult functioning. The originators of this approach were Schiff and her collaborators (1975).

Self-reparenting is a technique developed by James (1981; 1985) and James and Savary (1977/1983). Individuals provide themselves with new parent messages without necessarily introjecting or incorporating from the therapist. This is possible with non-psychotic clients because of the relative integrity of their personality in contrast with the fragmentation and the destructiveness of the Parent ego states found in psychotics. This technique presupposes a healthy level of Adult ego state functioning.

Clearly these techniques need to be used with extreme care, under intensive supervision, taking into consideration the needs of a particular client, their diagnosis and the nature of the therapeutic contract.

Working with the Parent ego state
One of the most fruitful developments in Transactional Analysis was the discovery that clinicians can contact a client's Parent ego states as vividly real phenomena. In the same way that a Child ego state can be accessed and relived in the present in the psychotherapy, Parent ego states can also be made available for any of the therapeutic strategies and techniques discussed above (Dashiell 1978; Mellor and Andrewartha 1980). Changes can be affected in the Parent ego state through decontamination, redecision or varieties of parenting techniques. Since these incorporated parental figures from a person's past can therefore be interviewed or treated 'as if' they were real people, significant changes in the structure in the Parent ego states can be achieved. Although integrated Adult functioning would still be the major therapeutic goal, more benign internal Parent ego states can support psychotherapeutic changes more effectively. For example, a person can replace hypercritical self-commentary with encouraging interior messages.

The change process in therapy

Berne was interested in the kind of cure which meant that a person could break out of script entirely and put 'his own show on the road, with new characters, new roles, and a new plot and payoff' (Berne 1975/1978: 362). A script cure involves a basic redecision about the course of a person's life which is accompanied by changes in thoughts, feelings and behaviours. 'Such a script cure, which changes his character and his destiny, is also a clinical cure since most of his symptoms will be relieved by his redecision' (Berne 1975/1978: 362).

The process of moving out of script can be achieved by Transactional Analysis treatment. Woollams and Brown (1979) give a description of the phases of treatment in Transactional Analysis psychotherapy. We will give a brief outline of these stages, following Woollams and Brown. Although these are discrete and recognizable phases, there may be movement between stages and a return to earlier stages when new issues are addressed.

Stage 1: motivation
As clients become aware of unhappiness and discomfort, they become motivated to gain information about TA psychotherapy and the nature of the change process. When clients realize that it is possible to change and make a commitment to such change then this stage is complete.

Stage 2: awareness
At this stage clients who desire to change clarify for themselves what they want to change. This process involves the decontamination of the Adult ego state, so that clients become aware of unassimilated Parental ego state material and unresolved archaic issues in the Child ego state.

Stage 3: treatment contract
From their decontaminated Adult ego state, clients are now in a position to make a treatment contract. A TA treatment contract is operationally verifiable and stated in specific terms so that both the client and the therapist can assess the psychotherapeutic goals. Reviewing the treatment contract is done regularly during the course of treatment on the path to autonomy.

Stage 4: de-confusing the Child ego state
At this stage clients are helped to identify and express the unmet needs and feelings in the Child ego state which were suppressed at the time of the script decision in the interests of psychological and/or physical survival. It is important in this phase for clients to develop a sense of internal safety in order to support a redecision in the next stage.

Stage 5: redecision
The redecision stage of therapy involves clients in changing earlier decisions which gave rise to the script. Redecision is usually a process that takes place over time, rather than a one-off statement of change. A redecision is made in the Child ego state with full Adult understanding of the implications of change. It may also be necessary for clients to make redecisions in the Parent ego state.

Stage 6: relearning
For a redecision to be lasting and meaningful it must be integrated into the client's life and functioning. At this stage the client practices the new unfamiliar behaviours with the support of the therapist, who is there to provide information and feedback on the client's progress.

Stage 7: termination
Termination follows the reorientation and reintegration phase of psychotherapy. The psychotherapeutic goals have been met and the client is ready to leave

psychotherapy. Both the client and the psychotherapist take part in the process of assessing the fulfilment of goals.

Lack of therapeutic progress may be due to inadequate diagnosis and chaotic treatment planning. We believe that one of the major reasons for lack of progress is the therapist's inability or unwillingness to enter into the phenomenological world of the client.

Limitations of the approach

In practice, the limitations of the approach are the limitations of the individual practitioner. Clients or referring colleagues need to question the nature and duration of an individual practitioner's own psychotherapy, for example, whether or not they have had experience of long-term individual psychotherapy on a weekly or twice-weekly basis and their previous professional background (e.g. psychiatry or teaching) for suitability for the work to be undertaken.

Although Transactional Analysis benefits from a rich repertoire of diverse techniques, there is considerable scope for the development of more theoretical and applied approaches to dealing with bodily awareness, affective work and transpersonal perspectives. A major strength of Transactional Analysis is its accessibility in that concepts can be translated into simple language that can be understood and used by lay people. The disadvantage of this virtue has been the unwise popularization of misconceived notions which are not based on an adequate study of the primary sources of Transactional Analysis literature on the one hand, and ignorance of the more recent theoretical developments as represented in the *Transactional Analysis Journal*.

Clinical practice in Transactional Analysis far outstrips in complexity, sophistication and subtlety the available written material on the subject. It is hoped that in the future the accumulated experience of veteran clinicians will become more freely available in the professional literature to the benefit of colleagues of other approaches as well as beginning clinicians in Transactional Analysis. The future hope and development of Transactional Analysis as a psychotherapy depends on increasing standards of professionalism in practice; an integration into Transactional Analysis theory of major trends from mainstream psychology and developments in other approaches to psychotherapy; and a return to understanding the historical conceptual framework from which Berne evolved his thought and work.

Case example

The client

Huntley is a successful, dedicated and conscientious professional. He works for 60 hours per week as a GP in a medical practice. He believes that he hardly ever 'delivers' enough and feels responsible for everyone and everything. He displays irritation and impatience with other people who do not take life as seriously as he does. He has no time for fun and recreation. Huntley smokes heavily and his smoking acts as a stimulant when he is tired. His family complain that he is seldom available to them. His immediate motivation for coming to psychotherapy is that his wife has threatened to leave him because he does not spend enough time with her and the children.

Huntley is sincere and earnest about psychotherapy. He has given the matter a great deal of thought, having talked to several people to find out about TA psychotherapy. He spoke to a friend who reported great benefit from TA. However, he says that immediately it may be difficult to find regular times for psychotherapy in the midst of his busy schedule.

Huntley feels that he should be working harder and better than he does. He seldom asks for help. He displays a very high anxiety level, especially over financial matters, and is afraid to work less for fear of financial insecurity. For this reason, psychotherapy may impose an additional strain on his life.

Huntley's presenting problems are as follows: family problems, overwork, tiredness and irritability, tension headaches, reduced libido, worrying especially about his own inadequacies and a lack of drive. As regards the last, he feels he should be able 'to cope better' with his life. His initial contract with the therapist is to explore time-structure and look for alternatives that allow him to be with his family, have fun and relax.

The therapist makes a diagnostic evaluation and formulates a treatment plan. The therapist views Huntley's situation as a serious, possibly life-threatening problem. She hypothesizes that Huntley has a third degree or hamartic script, a type of script which leads to a tragic outcome, for example a heart attack. One clue is the 'Harried Game' – Huntley reports being constantly hurried and having a sense of pushing appointments. In terms of Berne's 'process scripts' the therapist views his script as an 'until' script. The myth associated with this script is the story of Hercules (or Jason) who could not get his reward until he had performed certain tasks. Because of the many responsibilities that Huntley takes on, the rewarding rest after work seldom comes.

The therapist derives a script matrix (see Figure 10.4) from the information Huntley gives about his background and current life. Huntley's script matrix is included here (see Figure 10.6) as part of the TA diagnostic assessment together with a summary of the script decisions Huntley made in response to the messages he received from his parents.

Decisions I will do my duty by my parents if it's the last thing I do. I will be self-sufficient and take care of my own needs. I will not 'need' other people.

According to Paul Ware (1983), one of the TA writers who have systematically addressed diagnosis and treatment planning, Huntley would be described as having an obsessive-compulsive personality adaptation. In the therapist's view Huntley clearly fits the obsessive-compulsive description of being perfectionistic, overly inhibited and over-dutiful, while striving for conformity and respectability.

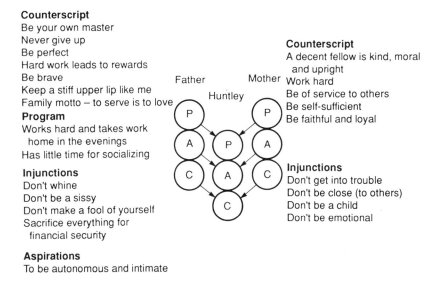

Counterscript
Be your own master
Never give up
Be perfect
Hard work leads to rewards
Be brave
Keep a stiff upper lip like me
Family motto – to serve is to love
Program
Works hard and takes work
   home in the evenings
Has little time for socializing

Injunctions
Don't whine
Don't be a sissy
Don't make a fool of yourself
Sacrifice everything for
   financial security

Aspirations
To be autonomous and intimate

Father   Mother

Huntley

Counterscript
A decent fellow is kind, moral
   and upright
Work hard
Be of service to others
Be self-sufficient
Be faithful and loyal

Injunctions
Don't get into trouble
Don't be close (to others)
Don't be a child
Don't be emotional

Figure 10.6   Huntley's script matrix

The Counterscript messages in this adaptation are 'Be Strong' and 'Be Perfect'. The characteristic injunctions, 'Don't Be a Child', 'Don't Feel', 'Don't be Close' and 'Don't Enjoy' are all present in Huntley's script matrix.

Ware's classification suggests that thinking is the major modality through which therapeutic contact and relationship can easily be formed with Huntley. However, at a depth level, affective (feeling) work is what the client not only is most defending against but also most needs to do. Ware postulated that, with clients like Huntley, attempts to change behaviour in the first instance are not very successful – he consequently describes this superficially attractive but ultimately ineffective available modality as a 'trap door' – but behavioural changes become possible as the affective work takes hold. In Huntley's case, therefore, the therapist's first approach is on the cognitive level, that is through exploration, explanation and interpretation for example.

The therapy

In the description of Huntley's therapy in this section we are following Woollams and Brown's (1979) stages of treatment outlined above. These stages do not always progress in this order. A therapist may go backwards and forwards through these stages with the client, depending on the nature of the problem and the process of psychotherapy.

Stage 1: motivation

Huntley enters therapy owing to other people's pressure rather than out of his own desire to change. He discusses his life history but cannot understand why people are complaining about him. The therapist then intervenes by asking: 'If I were a patient of yours, complaining of tension headaches, reduced sexual drive, tired-ness, excessive worrying and irritability, while working 60 hours per week, would you as a doctor say there was no threat to my health?' This confrontation presents the information to Huntley in a different way, even though one may have expected him to make this connection before. In response to the therapist's confrontation, Huntley realizes the extent of his self-deception. He has enough information about burn-out syndromes in professionals to know that he is engaged in an extremely destructive life pattern. Once he accepts that this applies to him as well he commits himself to the process of change. As a devoted family man he is also motivated, when he realizes there is a very real risk of his children being orphaned at an early age.

Stage 2: awareness
The therapist extends the work, started in the previous stage, by doing structural analysis of ego states with the client to identify the nature of the conflict between the messages in the Parent ego state and the desires of the Child that results in the driven quality of Huntley's behaviour. Structural analysis reveals to both Huntley and the therapist that not only did Huntley as a child decide that the only way to survive was to become a long-suffering, over-committed burn-out risk, but also he had internalized from his father a programme of hard work and no play. In his father's Child ego state, this process originated from a life commitment to escape from a working-class, poverty-stricken mining background. The therapist interviews Huntley's Child ego state at 11 years old, which reveals him as a conscientious boy who stays at home to sit at his books while his mates go out to play. At this stage Huntley is becoming gradually aware of what a restricted and joyless childhood (and adulthood) he has had.

Stage 3: treatment contract
The therapist is now in a position to negotiate a treatment contract with Huntley. Having understood the nature of the influences from his parents and his own archaic childhood experiences, Huntley is ready for this process. Together with the therapist Huntley formulates the following TA treatment contract:

1 To restructure his time so that he will be working a 40-hour week, leaving time for relaxation and fun on his own and with his family.
2 To learn to say 'No' and to delegate to his assistants or to other professionals.
3 To make a new decision about his right to be taken care of and to learn to ask for care, affection and nurturing from others.
4 To contract not to harm himself by accident or on purpose, directly or indirectly by neglect or overwork, realizing the seriousness of his scripting.
5 To give up smoking immediately, recognizing that this is one of the major ways he prevents himself from feeling.

In the process of setting the treatment contract the therapist engages with Huntley largely on a cognitive level. This follows Paul Ware's (1983) recommendations for this personality type, who respond best to initial approaches on an intellectual level.

Stage 4: de-confusing the Child ego state

Having built a therapeutic relationship with Huntley by making contact through thinking, the therapist is now able to do emotional or affective work with his Child ego state. This process continued for a substantial period, so we shall give only a representative sample of a therapeutic vignette related to this stage.

Huntley makes a mistake with the time of an appointment and is mortified on realizing his mistake. In the ensuing session the therapist enables him to intensify his experience of involuntary regression to an early scene in his childhood. He vividly and poignantly relives an occasion when his father beats him severely for not coming first in class (this was the last time he did not come first in class). In the safety provided by the therapeutic relationship, Huntley relives his terror, the pain and humiliation he suffered on this occasion as if it were happening now. He identifies his need for understanding and compassion towards his fallibility, which was lacking in his own family. Huntley weeps bitterly for his lost childhood. He comes out of this experience with a deepened compassion for his own inner Child and an Adult commitment to an improved quality of life in the future. The therapist facilitates this process by using a two-chair technique to enable Huntley to express his newly found compassion towards his inner Child.

Stage 5: redecision

Following this cathartic work, the therapist enables Huntley to claim his right to live joyfully and fully by revoking the script decision made in his Child ego state to shut down on his feelings in order to ensure his parents' love. This limiting decision was not based on the above traumatic incident alone, but on the pervasive quality of his relationship with his parents. Huntley now feels a sense of relief from his previous tension and anxiety. In discussion with the therapist, he realizes that his work schedule and practice management will have to undergo serious changes, resulting perhaps in a lesser income for a period, to allow him to reorganize his life on all levels. Now that Huntley has made this redecision, he is available for such behavioural changes.

Stage 6: relearning

With the therapist's assistance, Huntley reviews all aspects of his life. Huntley's first move is to give up smoking. Then he takes on another partner in his practice. Instead of seeing a patient every five minutes, he now arranges for ten minutes per patient. This both reduces his tension and his concern about making mistakes, and creates a calmer atmosphere at the surgery.

At home Huntley contracts to take regular holidays with his whole family. He joins his wife at her tennis club. He agrees to attend a couples' enrichment work-shop with her. He also takes regular times on his own to walk or read. A natural result of his increased energy is their improved sex life. He also starts a diary to record his own internal feelings and processes 'to build on his new life'.

At this stage the therapist applauds and reinforces Huntley's new behaviours. She shows delight in his growing sense of self and in his newly found autonomy. Suddenly Huntley becomes excessively worried if he does not make an entry in his diary every day. The psychotherapist knows that, towards the end of therapy, there is frequently a recycling of earlier issues. She points out to Huntley that his compassionate acceptance of his human fallibility could extend also to his attempts to be autonomous.

Stage 7: termination
In the last stage of his therapy Huntley reviews his achievements in a process of evaluating his therapy. He sees that he has met all the contracts that he originally made. He allows himself the satisfaction of a task well done, even though it may still fall short of perfection. This is no longer a worry to him, rather a reassurance that he is a fallible, lovable human being.

This case example is a condensed version of a much longer and more complex psychotherapeutic process. We have attempted to give here only some of the major highlights of the TA psychotherapeutic process as it applies to this particular client.

References

Allaway, J. (1983) Transactional Analysis in Britain: the beginnings, *Transactions: Journal of the Institute of Transactional Analysis* 1: 5–10.

Barnes, G. (ed.) (1977) *Transactional Analysis after Eric Berne: Teachings and Practices of Three TA Schools*, New York: Harper & Row.

Barr, J. (1987) The Therapeutic Relationship Model: perspectives on the core of the healing process, *Transactional Analysis Journal* 17, 4: 134–40.

Berne, E. (1957) *A Layman's Guide to Psychiatry and Psychoanalysis*, New York: Grove Press (first published in 1947 as *The Mind in Action*).

—— (1958) Transactional Analysis: a new and effective method of group therapy, *American Journal of Psychotherapy* 12: 735–43.

—— (1968/1975) *Games People Play*, Harmondsworth: Penguin (first published 1964).

—— (1975) *Transactional Analysis in Psychotherapy: A Systematic Individual and Social Psychiatry*, London: Souvenir Press (originally published 1961).

—— (1975/1978) *What Do You Say After You Say Hello: The Psychology of Human Destiny*, London: Corgi (originally published 1972).

Clarkson, P. (1988) Script cure? A diagnostic pentagon of types of therapeutic change, *Transactional Analysis Journal* 18, 3: 211–19.

—— (1989) 'Metanoia', *ITA News* 23: 5–14.

Clarkson, P. and Gilbert, M. (1988) Berne's original model of ego states: some theoretical considerations, *Transactional Analysis Journal* 18, 1: 20–9.

Dashiell, S.R. (1978) The parent resolution process: reprogramming psychic incorporations in the parent, *Transactional Analysis Journal* 8, 4: 289–94.

Erskine, R.G. (1980) Script cure: Behavioral, intrapsychic and physiological, *Transactional Analysis Journal* 10, 2: 102–3.

Erskine, R.G. and Zalcman, M.J. (1979) The racket system: a model for racket analysis, *Transactional Analysis Journal* 9, 1: 51–9.

Fedem, P. (1953) *Ego Psychology and the Psychoses*, London: Maresfield Reprints.

Goulding, M.M. and Goulding, R.L. (1979) *Changing Lives Through Redecision Therapy*, New York: Brunner Mazel.

Harris, T.A. (1973) *I'm OK – You're OK*, London: Pan (first published 1967).

James, M. (1981) *Breaking Free: Self-Reparenting for a New Life*, Reading, Mass: Addison-Wesley.

—— (1985) *It's Never Too Late to Be Happy: The Psychology of Self-Reparenting*, Reading, Mass: Addison-Wesley.

James, M. and Savary, L. (1977/1983) *A New Self: Self-Therapy with Transactional Analysis*, Reading, Mass: Addison-Wesley.

Lieberman, M.A., Yalom, I.D. and Miles, M.B. (1973) *Encounter Groups: First Facts*, New York: Basic Books.

Loomis, M.E. and Landsman, S.G. (1980) Manic-depressive structure: assessment and development, *Transactional Analysis Journal* 10, 4: 284–90.

—— (1981) 'Manic depressive structure: treatment strategies, *Transactional Analysis Journal* 11, 4: 346–51.

Mellor, K. and Andrewartha, G. (1980) New directions: reparenting the parent in support of redecisions, *Transactional Analysis Journal* 10, 3: 197–203.

Penfield, W. (1952) Memory mechanisms, *Archives of Neurology and Psychiatry* 67: 178–98.

Pulleybank, E. and McCormick, P. (1985) The stages of redecision therapy, in L.B. Kadis (ed.) *Redecision Therapy: Expanded Perspectives*, Watsonville, Calif: Western Institute for Group and Family Therapy.

Schiff, J.L., Schiff, A.W., Mellor, K., Schiff, E., Schiff, S., Richman, D., Fishman, J., Wolz, L., Fishman, C., and Momb, D. (1975) *Cathexis Reader: Transactional Analysis Treatment of Psychosis*, New York: Harper & Row.

Spitz, R. (1945) Hospitalism: genesis of psychiatric conditions in early childhood, *Psychoanalytic Study of the Child* 1: 53–74.

Steiner, C. (1971) *Games Alchoholics Play*, New York: Grove Press.

Swede, S. (1977) *How to Cure: How Eric Berne Practiced Transactional Analysis*, Corte Madera, Calif: Boyce Productions.

Thomson, G. (1986) Agoraphobia: the ethiology and treatment of an attachment /separation disorder, *Transactional Analysis Journal* 16, 1: 11–17.

Ware, P. (1983) Personality adaptations (doors to therapy), *Transactional Analysis Journal* 13, 1: 11–19.

Woods, K. and Woods, M. (1982) Treatment of borderline conditions, *Transactional Analysis Journal* 12, 4: 288–300.

Woollams, S. and Brown, M. (1979) *TA: The Total Handbook of Transactional Analysis*, Englewood Cliffs, NJ: Prentice-Hall.

Suggested further reading

Berne, E. (1975) *Transactional Analysis in Psychotherapy: A Systematic Individual and Social Psychiatry*, London: Souvenir Press (originally published 1961).

—— (1975/1978) *What Do You Say After You Say Hello: The Psychology of Human Destiny*, London: Corgi (originally published 1972).

Clarkson, P. (in press) *Transactional Analysis-An Integrative Approach to Psychotherapy*, London: Routledge.

Goulding, M.M. and Goulding, R.L. (1979) *Changing Lives Through Redecision Therapy*, New York: Brunner Mazel.

James, M. and Jongeward, D. (1971/1973) *Born to Win: Transactional Analysis with Gestalt Experiments*, Reading, Mass: Addison-Wesley.

Schiff, J.L., Schiff, A.W., Mellor, K., Schiff, E., Schiff, S., Richman, D., Fishman, J., Wolz, L., Fishman, C. and Momb, D. (1975) *Cathexis Reader: Transactional Analysis Treatment of Psychosis*, New York: Harper & Row.

Stewart, I. and Joines, V. (1987) *TA Today: A New Introduction to Transactional Analysis*, Nottingham: Lifespace Publishing.

11

Cognitive therapy

STIRLING MOOREY

Historical context and development in Britain

Historical context

During the middle years of this century psychology was dominated by the twin edifices of behaviourism and psychoanalysis. For one the individual's internal world was unimportant and his or her actions were determined by environmental events. For the other the internal world was all important, but its workings were unconscious and accessible only with the help of a trained guide. The thoughts which most people regarded as central to their experience of everyday life were seen by both schools as peripheral. There were, however, some lone voices which defended the individual as a conscious agent. Kelly (1955) emphasized the way in which the person seeks to give meaning to the world, and suggested that each of us constructs our own view of reality through a process of experimentation. Ellis (1962) drew attention to the role of irrational beliefs in neurotic disorders, and developed rational-emotive therapy (RET) to change these beliefs systematically. The study of the mental processes which intervene between stimulus and response is termed 'cognitive psychology'. This includes a wide range of activities such as thinking, remembering and perceiving. It was not until the 1970s that psychology began to undergo a 'cognitive revolution' (see Mahoney and Arnkoff 1978) which led to a greater interest in the relevance of cognitive processes to therapy.

This revolution came in part from within behaviourism. Starting from a learning theory perspective, some behavioural psychologists began to investigate how cognitions could be treated as behaviours in their own right, and so might be conditioned or deconditioned (Cautela 1973). Others considered the person's contribution to the management of his or her own behaviour (Kanfer and Karoly 1972); this led to a theory of self-regulation known as self-control theory. Cognitive theory started to break away from Skinnerian and Pavlovian learning theory with the work of Bandura. He showed that it was possible to understand the phenomenon of modelling from a cognitive rather than strictly behaviourist perspective (Bandura 1977; Rosenthal and Bandura 1978). An even more radical step was taken when Mahoney drew attention to the significance of cognitive processes such as expectation and attribution in conditioning (Mahoney and Arnkoff 1978). Clinical psychology now pays considerable attention to factors that in the past would have been considered far too mentalistic (Brewin 1988).

This increasing interest in cognition has led to the development of various cognitive-behavioural therapies. Although they all have slightly different theoretical perspectives they share common assumptions and it is often difficult to distinguish them in terms of the techniques used in clinical practice. Mahoney (1987) has recently listed seventeen current cognitive therapies. Of these the most influential are Ellis's rational-emotive therapy, Meichenbaum's cognitive-behaviour modification and Beck's cognitive therapy. Ellis aims through therapy to make the client aware of his or her irrational beliefs and the way in which they lead to maladaptive emotional states. His emphasis is on cognitive processes that are evaluative rather than inferential. If, for example, a client reported that she felt depressed when a friend ignored her in the street, rather than asking her if there were any alternative explanation (e.g. her friend was preoccupied and did not notice her) Ellis would initially home in on the evaluative belief underlying her reaction ('I must be liked by people'). Although RET has had a consistent following in the USA it has never become widely practised in Britain. Meichenbaum's approach differs from Ellis in the emphasis it places on the role of cognitive processes in coping. Meichenbaum (1985) has studied the use of self-instructions as a means of coping with stressful situations. This has led to a therapy which he has called 'Stress Inoculation Training'. This model has had considerable influence on cognitive-behaviour therapy in general and on stress management in particular, but few therapists would see themselves as using Meichenbaum's approach exclusively.

There would, however, be a larger number of clinicians in Britain who see their practice as a form of Beck's cognitive therapy. This is probably the most intensively researched form of cognitive-behaviour therapy (Beck *et al.* 1979; Beck and Emery 1985). Beck, like Ellis, was originally an analyst who became disillusioned with the orthodox Freudian tradition of the 1950s. His research into depression led him to believe that this condition was associated with a form of 'thought disorder' (Beck 1963; 1964), in which the depressed person distorted incoming information in a negative way. The therapy that arose from Beck's cognitive model focused on teaching patients to learn to identify and modify their dysfunctional thought processes. In 1977 Beck's group published the first outcome study comparing cognitive therapy with pharmacotherapy in depressed patients (Rush *et al.* 1977). This generated great interest, first, because previous studies had shown psychotherapy to be less effective than drug treatment with this group of patients, and second, because psychologists were already becoming interested in cognitive approaches. From its origins in the USA cognitive therapy has become increasingly popular in Europe, particularly Britain and Scandinavia.

Development in Britain

Cognitive therapy became known in Britain largely through the pioneer work of British researchers who sought to evaluate the treatment in the British Isles. Dr

Ivy Blackburn carried out an outcome study in Edinburgh (Blackburn *et al.* 1981), while Dr John Teasdale and Dr Melanie Fennell carried out similar work in Oxford (Teasdale *et al.* 1984). These studies showed cognitive therapy to be as effective as anti-depressants with depressed patients, and also proved that the treatment could be applied outside American private practice in a National Health Service setting. In keeping with the empirical nature of the therapy (see below) British cognitive therapists have been committed to research. From the work carried out with depression in the early 1980s cognitive therapy in Britain has broadened to encompass generalized anxiety, panic disorders (Clark 1986), eating disorders (Fairburn 1985) and hypochondriasis (Salkovskis and Warwick 1986).

Theoretical assumptions

The image of the person

This chapter will concern itself with Beck's cognitive therapy, but many of the theoretical and clinical points described are shared with other forms of cognitive-behaviour therapy. Cognitive therapy makes a number of assumptions about the nature of the human individual:

1 The person is seen as an active agent who interacts with his or her world.
2 This interaction takes place through the interpretations, inferences and evaluations the person makes about his or her environment.
3 The results of these 'cognitive' processes are thought to be accessible to consciousness in the form of thoughts and images, and so the person has the potential to change them.

Emotions and behaviour are mediated by cognitive processes. This distinguishes cognitive therapy from strict behaviour therapy which sees the organism as a black box: what goes on inside the box is of little consequence. It also distinguishes it from psychoanalysis, which gives prime importance to unconscious rather than conscious meanings. According to Beck

> The specific content of the interpretation of an event leads to a specific emotional response . . . depending on the kind of interpretation a person makes, he will feel glad, sad, scared, or angry – or he may have no particular emotional reaction at all.
>
> (Beck 1976: 51–2)

The behavioural response will also depend upon the interpretation made: if a situation is perceived as threatening the person may try to escape, if it is perceived as an insult the person may take aggressive action. An important concept in Beck's view of normal and abnormal behaviour is the idea of the 'personal domain'. The personal domain is the conglomeration of real and abstract things which are important to us: our family, possessions, health, status, values and goals. Each of us has a different set of items in our personal domain; the more an event impinges on our domain the stronger our emotional reaction is likely to be.

Since Beck's model has been concerned largely with explaining emotional disturbance, particularly anxiety and depression, he has not developed a comprehensive theory of personality or normal functioning, although there is an assumption of continuity between normal and abnormal mood states. This has disadvantages when trying to make sense of human social behaviour outside of the clinical setting, but it has a major advantage in keeping the theory focused on its original locus of explanation.

Conceptualization of psychological disturbance and health

In the cognitive model, psychological disturbance is seen as a result of some malfunction in the process of interpreting and evaluating experience. Most of the time we are capable of processing information in an accurate or even a slightly positively biased fashion (as evidenced by studies demonstrating that non-depressed subjects make internal attributions for success but external attributions for failure: Alloy and Ahrens 1987; Bradley 1978). In emotional disturbance information processing is biased, usually in a negative distorted way.

Beck suggests that we are all capable of functioning as rational problem-solvers at least some of the time. Psychological health requires us to be able to use the skills of reality-testing to solve personal problems as they occur. For instance, an adaptive way of dealing with a failure experience such as being turned down for a job would involve thinking about the interview, assessing one's performance, taking responsibility for any faults or weaknesses which might have contributed to the failure and looking for ways to prevent it happening in the future. In psychological disturbance people revert to more primitive thinking which prevents them functioning as effective problem-solvers (Beck *et al.* 1979: 15). This thinking tends to be global, absolute and judgemental. So a depressed person who is not successful at a job interview would label herself as a total failure, would conclude that it was entirely her own fault that she did not get the job, and would ruminate about the interview, focusing on all the things that went wrong without thinking about any of the positive factors.

Faulty and adaptive information-processing

When this primitive thinking is in operation information-processing is biased or distorted. Beck (1976) identifies 'logical errors' which characterize the thinking in emotional disorders. Table 11.1 summarizes some of the common logical errors. The tendency to distort information repeatedly in a maladaptive way is one of the factors which distinguishes psychologically healthy from psychologically disturbed individuals. Psychological health is seen as a state where the individual is able to make relatively accurate interpretations and evaluations of events, but this does not imply that psychologically healthy people will always think and act rationally. There is no definition of mental health in the cognitive model because it was developed to explain emotional disorder and so an absolute definition of adaptive information-processing is not possible.

The conditions in which this theory has been tested are depression and anxiety. Beck (1976) suggests that in depression there is a negative view of the self, the world and the future. (See Brewin 1988 for a review of the growing evidence that depressed patients do indeed distort information in a negative way.) In anxiety the cognitive distortions involve a perception of major physical or social threat

Table 11.1   Cognitive distortions

---

1 *Arbitrary inference* refers to the process of drawing a specific conclusion in the absence of evidence to support the conclusion or when the evidence is contrary to the conclusion.
2 *Selective abstraction* consists of focusing on a detail taken out of context, ignoring other more salient features of the situation and conceptualizing the whole experience on the basis of this fragment.
3 *Overgeneralization* refers to the pattern of drawing a general rule or conclusion on the basis of one or more isolated incidents and applying the concept across the board to related and unrelated situations.
4 *Magnification and minimization* are reflected in errors in evaluating the significance or magnitude of an event that are so gross as to constitute a distortion.
5 *Personalization* refers to the patient's proclivity to relate external events to himself when there is no basis for making such a connection.
6 *Absolutistic, dichotomous thinking* is manifested in the tendency to place all experiences in one of two opposite categories; e.g. flawless or defective, immaculate or filthy, saint or sinner. In describing himself, the patient selects the extreme negative categorization.

(From Beck *et al.* 1979)

together with an underestimation of the individual's ability to cope with the threat. There is evidence that anxious patients selectively attend to cues which represent threat (Mathews and MacLeod 1985; MacLeod *et al.* 1986).

Negative automatic thoughts
People with psychological disorders differ from the non-distressed in the content as well as the form of their thinking. They are prone to frequent, disruptive thoughts known as 'negative automatic thoughts'. These are spontaneous thoughts or images which are plausible when the patient experiences them, but are in fact unrealistic. For instance, an anxious person may repeatedly think 'I can't cope. There's nothing I can do about my problems. Something terrible is going to happen. What if I'm going mad?' and may have images of collapsing, or going berserk. A depressed person may ruminate about his failures, thinking 'I'm useless, I never do anything right, I'm just a fraud'. We all experience these thoughts at times, but they are much more frequent in people with emotional disorders.

The cognitive schema
The disturbance in the *content* of a person's thinking (automatic thoughts) and in the way she processes information (cognitive distortions) is explained in terms of an underlying cognitive structure or schema which determines the perception and interpretation of events (Kovacs and Beck 1978). This cognitive schema is like a template which makes sense of the world. Life is too short to attend to every aspect of experience and commit it to memory. Schemata help us to decide what to attend to and what to screen out. In areas we know well we have well-developed schemata (e.g. schemata for driving a car, or how to behave at a social gathering), whereas in new situations schemata will be less well developed. In psychological

disturbance these structures are rigid and inflexible, and instead of allowing the person to attend to the salient features of a situation they so bias the perception of the situation that normal functioning may be suspended. In depression there is a negative cognitive triad which produces a negative bias about the self, the world and the future. In anxiety states the schema causes selective attention to danger signals in the environment while safety or rescue factors are filtered out. In addition to acting as a filter the schema also integrates and organizes the individual's behavioural responses.

Acquisition of psychological disturbance

Beck considers that there are many factors which predispose an individual to emotional disturbance. He has considered these factors both for depression (Beck 1987) and anxiety (Beck and Emery 1985). He attempts to integrate cognitive factors with other factors to develop a multifactorial theory of psychological disorder. Table 11.2 shows some of the long-term (predisposing) and short-term (precipitating) factors which may be associated with anxiety or depression in adult life.

This suggests a much more complex aetiology for emotional disorders than the simplistic notion that cognitions cause emotions. Beck very clearly asserts that

> the primary pathology or dysfunction during a depression or an anxiety disorder is in the cognitive apparatus. However, it is quite different from the notion that cognition causes these syndromes – a notion that is just as illogical as an assertion that hallucinations cause schizophrenia.
>
> (Beck and Emery 1985: 85)

The aetiological factors described above can all be seen as operating on the 'cognitive apparatus' in one way or another.

Table 11.2   Long-term and short-term vulnerability factors

Predisposing factors
1 Genetic predisposition.
2 Physical disease (e.g. hypothyroidism and depression, hyperthyroidism and anxiety).
3 Developmental traumas which lead to specific vulnerabilities (e.g. loss of a parent in childhood may be associated with depression in adult life).
4 Personal experiences too inadequate to provide adequate coping mechanisms (e.g. parents who provide poor models of how to cope with rejection).
5 Counter-productive cognitive patterns, unrealistic goals, unreasonable values and assumptions learned from significant others.

Precipitating factors
1 Physical disease.
2 Severe external stress (e.g. exposure to physical danger may precipitate anxiety, loss of a partner may induce depression).
3 Chronic insidious external stress (e.g. continuous subtle disapproval from significant others).
4 Specific external stress (which acts on a psychological vulnerability).

(Adapted from Beck and Emery 1985: 83)

Underlying assumptions

Early learning experiences, traumas and chronic stresses can all lead to idiosyncratic beliefs and attitudes which make a person vulnerable to psychological disturbance. For instance, someone who endures long periods of illness as a child and
is overprotected by his parents may develop a belief that he is frail and vulnerable
and needs to be supported by others in order to survive. Someone who is continually criticized for making even small mistakes may elaborate the belief that she
must get everything she does completely right. Continuing our view of the person
as an active construing agent, we can conceptualize these beliefs as a way the person makes sense of the world by developing ideas about how the world does, or
should, operate. The more rigid, judgemental and absolute these beliefs become,
the more likely they are to cause problems. Examples of beliefs which predispose to
anxiety include:

> 'Any strange situation should be regarded as dangerous.'
> 'My safety depends on always being prepared for possible danger.'
> 'I have to be in control of myself at all times.'

Examples of beliefs which predispose to depression include:

> 'I can only be happy if I am totally successful.'
> 'I need to be loved in order to be happy.'
> 'I must never make a mistake.'

These assumptions may remain relatively quiescent until an event occurs which is
of particular relevance to them. This causes them to be activated and to become
the primary mode for construing situations. For instance, because of early
childhood experiences a woman may believe that she needs to be loved in order to
survive. While she is in a relationship this belief will not be salient, unless she
thinks that she might lose the love of the person concerned. But if she is rejected by
her lover it is likely to be activated. It acts as a premise to a syllogism:

> 'I need to be loved in order to survive.'
> 'X has left me.'
> 'Therefore I cannot survive.'

These underlying assumptions become less obvious again when the person
recovers from the depression. But they remain dormant as a potential source of
vulnerability. Cognitive therapy therefore aims not only to correct faulty information processing but also to modify assumptions and so reduce vulnerability to
further psychological disturbance.

Perpetuation of psychological disturbance

The concept of biased information processing readily explains how information
which is contrary to the client's cognitive schema is filtered out or manipulated in
such a way that it is made consistent with her belief system. This is commonly seen
in depression, where positive information (e.g. past achievement) is repeatedly
disqualified. The depressed person will say that past successes do not count
because they were due to luck, or to people helping. As Beck remarks,

even though the depressive may be reasonably accurate in a cognitive appraisal (for example, 'They seem to like me'), the overall meaning is still a negative one: 'If they knew how worthless I was, they would not like me.'

(Beck 1987: 12)

External factors can also help to perpetuate psychological disturbance. Real-life problems such as unemployment or bereavement make it difficult for depressed people to believe that there is a future, or to believe that they are of value. Similarly chronic stress, or social rejection can contribute to the continuation of anxiety states. The influence of close personal relationships can be very important in this respect. Hooley *et al.* (1986) have shown that a relationship in which the partner makes frequent negative comments predicts relapse in depression. The more negative the external environment the more difficult it is to challenge negative thinking.

Change

At present the cognitive model has not been developed to explain changes in emotional state that are not due to psychological intervention. It is possible to accept that the special techniques which will be described later can help a person out of a profound depression or anxiety state, but if the schema shuts out information which is inconsistent with the negative self-image how can a spontaneous remission occur? This is a question which the cognitive model has not yet been able to answer. It may be that over time a succession of positive experiences slowly break down the depressive style. In some instances it seems that a single important event can produce cognitive change. For instance, a woman who believes that she can be happy only if she is in a relationship might experience an improvement in mood if she finds a new boyfriend. Alternatively it may be that other factors, perhaps even biological ones, are responsible for recovery.

Practice

Goals of therapy

Cognitive therapy has three main goals:

1 to relieve symptoms and to resolve problems
2 to help the client to acquire coping strategies
3 to help the client to modify underlying cognitive structures in order to prevent relapse.

Unlike other forms of psychotherapy which sometimes lose sight of the patient's presenting complaint, cognitive therapy is problem-oriented. Whether the complaints are symptoms of psychiatric illness like anxiety and depression, behavioural problems like addiction or bulimia, or interpersonal ones like social anxiety, the primary goal is always to help clients solve the problems which they have targeted for change. In the first session the therapist helps to clarify the problems as the patient sees them and to establish priorities. The therapist tries to target symptoms or problems which are both important to the client and are amenable to therapeutic intervention.

The whole course of cognitive therapy can be seen as a learning exercise in which the client acquires and practises coping skills. The aim is to teach skills which can be used to deal with the current episode of distress, but can also be employed if problems recur. Many clients find that the methods of cognitive therapy can be generalized to other situations beyond the initial focus of therapy. This goal of therapy is 'to help patients uncover their dysfunctional and irrational thinking, reality test their thinking and behaviour, and build more adaptive and functional techniques for responding both inter- and intrapersonally' (Freeman 1983: 2). While cognitive therapy seeks to relieve distress it does not set out to change the personality completely. Learning how to navigate the squalls of life in our own battered vessel is often a more realistic objective than trying to rebuild it to someone else's specification as an ocean liner.

The final goal of therapy is the modification of maladaptive underlying assumptions. The intention is not to restructure all of a person's irrational beliefs, but only those which are causing problems. Beliefs which are rigid, global and self-referent (e.g. I can be happy only if I'm successful at everything I do; I need a close relationship to survive) predispose the individual to future emotional disturbance. If these beliefs can be made more flexible then specific vulnerability to psychological disturbance will be reduced.

Selection criteria

Which patients?

Psychotherapy research is showing increasingly that a variety of therapies are effective with people in emotional distress; research has not yet determined which clients respond best to which type of treatment. The criteria which therapists employ in the selection of clients for therapy are therefore usually based on clinical experience rather than scientific evidence. The possible exception to this is in the field of depression, where some data are available from outcome studies to guide the clinician (see Moorey 1988 for a review of factors predicting outcome in cognitive therapy of depression). Cognitive therapy has been found to be as effective or more effective than anti-depressants in the treatment of depressed outpatients (Rush et al. 1977; Blackburn et al. 1981; Murphy et al. 1984). One can predict that patients who fit the criteria used in these studies will be good candidates for cognitive therapy. Thus depressed outpatients who do not show symptoms such as delusions and hallucinations or psychomotor retardation are likely to respond well. As with most treatments the more chronic the problem the more difficult it is to produce change. What does seem clear from these studies is that within the normal range the level of intelligence does not correlate with outcome, neither does education or social class, so this therapy does not have to be restricted to socially privileged groups. Less severe forms of depression as encountered in patients attending a general practitioner may respond even better (Blackburn et al. 1981; Teasdale et al. 1984). Insufficient studies exist to make judgements about cognitive therapy with depressed inpatients, but a cognitive-behavioural approach seems promising.

Clinical experience suggests that what applies to depression also applies to other disorders. As a self-help therapy cognitive therapy is limited by the client's capacity to engage in self-help strategies. The more severe the disorder, whether it is severe anxiety, depression, obsessive compulsive disorder, and so on, the more difficult it is to carry out homework assignments and challenge dysfunctional thinking. Another factor which may interfere with this self-directed component of therapy is the personality of the client. People with major difficulties in the way they relate to others often bring these difficulties into the therapy session, so a dependent person may want to rely too much on the therapist or an obsessional person may get so bogged down in recording thoughts that he or she makes no progress. While it is possible to treat patients with personality disorders, and work in this area is currently being carried out by Beck and co-workers at the Center for Cognitive Therapy in Philadelphia and by Jeffrey Young in New York, this may require significant modifications in the therapy (Young, personal communication).

Another factor which seems to affect outcome is the extent to which the client understands and accepts the cognitive model. Fennell and Teasdale (1987) have suggested that those who accept the rationale for therapy and find their first homework assignment a success are more likely to do well. The implications of this are that if clients do not respond to the idea that their thoughts might have some relevance to the problem during the initial sessions then cognitive therapy may not be the right approach. There are some people who are just not 'psychologically minded', and who find it extremely difficult to introspect even to the extent that cognitive therapy requires.

Individual or group therapy?
Studies have shown that group cognitive therapy is effective in depression, but the effects are not as strong as with individual therapy (Rush and Watkins 1981). For this reason therapists reserve group work for the less severely disturbed patient. Some problems, however, lend themselves to a group approach. Social anxiety and other problems which contain a significant interpersonal element may be well suited to group therapy, since it allows a degree of in-session testing out of maladaptive beliefs about other people. Another consideration in choosing clients for group therapy is the extent to which the group can help in modelling appropriate coping behaviour. Simon Jakes, working with people with tinnitus at the Royal Throat, Nose and Ear Hospital in London, has (personal communication) successfully used a group cognitive therapy approach, and here it seems that one of the important components is the opportunity to share the experience of the illness with others who are in a similar situation.

Behavioural marital therapists are becoming more cognitive in their approach (Epstein 1983), and techniques exist for treating couples with cognitive behaviour therapy. Although therapists using Beck's model have usually worked in an individual or group format cognitive therapy for couples is now developing in its own right (Beck 1989).

Some patients may initially require individual therapy when they are most distressed but can then go on to a group as their mood improves. This can be particularly helpful if interpersonal factors (e.g. lack of assertiveness or fear of disapproval) are considered to be relevant to future relapse. Young (personal communication) describes a combination of group and individual therapy in the treatment of patients with personality disorders. The group provides a 'laboratory' where the client can test out maladaptive beliefs in relative safety.

A rather different use of groups is the utilization of more than one therapist (Moorey and Burns 1983). This is an effective training procedure but can also be of help to the patient. When therapy gets stuck it may be helpful to bring another therapist into the session, who will then provide a new perspective on the case. Burns (personal communication) is using multiple therapy with difficult clients at his clinic in Philadelphia.

Qualities of effective therapists

First and foremost cognitive therapists need to have good general interpersonal skills. Although the therapy sometimes appears to place a strong emphasis on cognitive and behavioural techniques these are deemed to be effective only if they are used within the context of a good therapeutic relationship. Warmth, genuineness and empathy are vital components of this relationship:

> We believe that these characteristics in themselves are necessary but not sufficient to produce an optimum therapeutic effect. However, to the degree that the therapist is able to demonstrate these qualities, he is helping to develop a milieu in which the specific cognitive change techniques can be applied most efficiently.
>
> (Beck *et al.* 1979: 45–6)

Cognitive therapists need to have good listening skills, to be able to reflect accurately the cognitive and emotional components of the client's communication, and to demonstrate an active and warm interest in the client. If this is not done there is a real danger that attempts to challenge distorted thinking will be perceived by the client as insensitive or even persecutory. Good therapists seem to be able to get inside the client's cognitive world and empathize while at the same time retaining objectivity.

Many would see the qualities described above as essential to any form of psychotherapy. It is more difficult to specify qualities which make someone a good cognitive therapist rather than a good psychotherapist in general. Perhaps one of the most important factors is the extent to which the therapist can accept the cognitive model. The therapist has to be prepared to work in a problem-oriented way without continually looking for unconscious motives in the patient's self-defeating thinking and behaviour. He or she must be able to blend the interpersonal skills described in the last paragraph with a directive approach which involves a great deal of structure and focus. While specific cognitive therapy skills can be learned the therapist still needs to accept the basic rationale for doing therapy in this way. No published data exist on factors which predict how well someone will function as a cognitive therapist, although it has been shown that competency in the therapy improves with training (Shaw 1984). The impression from my own experience of training cognitive therapists is that people with more clinical experience do better than those without, people with a background in behaviour therapy do better than those with a psychodynamic background, and people who take to the model enthusiastically do better than those who are less committed.

Therapeutic style

The aim of cognitive therapy is to teach the client to monitor thought processes and to reality-test them. Rather than assume that the client's view of the situation is distorted or correct, the cognitive therapist treats every statement about the problem as a hypothesis. Therapy is *empirical* in the sense that it is continually setting up and testing out hypotheses. Client and therapist *collaborate* together like scientists testing a theory. For instance, a depressed person may believe that there is no point in doing anything because there is no pleasure in life anymore.

> *Hypothesis*
> If I visit my friend tomorrow I will get no pleasure from it.
> *Experiment*
> Arrange to visit friend from 3 pm to 4 pm, and immediately after rate the amount of pleasure I get on a 0–10 scale.

Most depressed people find they get at least some enjoyment out of activities which they used to find pleasurable. Experiments like this can gradually erode the belief that it is not worth doing anything by providing evidence that there is still some pleasure open to them and so increase the person's motivation.

Teaching the client to be a 'personal scientist' is done through *collaboration* rather than prescription. Wherever possible the therapist will encourage the client to choose problems, set priorities and think of experiments. This collaboration is the hallmark of cognitive therapy and there are a number of reasons for including the client in the problem-solving process as much as possible.

1 Collaboration gives the client a say in the therapy process and so reduces conflict.
2 Collaboration fosters a sense of self-efficacy by giving the client an active role.
3 Collaboration encourages the learning of self-help techniques which can be continued when therapy is ended.
4 Collaboration allows an active input from the person who knows most about the problem.

Cognitive therapy sees the therapist and client as partners in the process of problem-solving. This does not prevent the therapist being very active and directive at times, but it always gives space for the client to contribute and give feedback on what the therapist is doing. With more severely depressed clients there is often a need for a lot of direction at first, but as the mood improves and the client learns the principles of cognitive therapy the relationship becomes more collaborative. Ideally by the end of therapy the client is doing most of the work and thinking up his or her own strategies for change. When the therapist is most directive at the beginning of treatment he or she must also be most empathic in order to establish rapport.

Another characteristic feature of cognitive therapy is the way in which the session is structured. At the beginning of each session an agenda is set, with the client and therapist both contributing to this. Usually the agenda will include a brief review of the last session, developments in the last week and the results of homework assignments. The work then goes on to the major topic for the session. Anyone listening to a cognitive therapy session will also be struck by two further features: the use of summaries and feedback. Two or three times through a session the client or therapist will summarize what has been going on so far. This helps to keep the client on track, particularly important if anxiety or depression impairs concentration. Asking the client to summarize also reveals whether or not the therapist has got a point across clearly. The therapist regularly asks for feedback about his or her behaviour, the effects of cognitive interventions, and so on.

Major therapeutic strategies and techniques

Emery (in Beck and Emery 1985) describes a four-step process of problem-solving in cognitive therapy:

1 conceptualize the patient's problems
2 choose a strategy
3 choose a tactic or technique
4 assess the effectiveness of the technique.

Conceptualization

Cognitive therapy is based on a coherent theory of emotional disturbance, and this theory can be used to conceptualize the patient's problems. The clearer the conceptualization the easier it becomes to develop strategies (i.e. general methods for solving the patient's problems) and techniques (specific interventions). For instance, a woman presented with complaints of fatigue and memory problems, but did not have any physical cause for these symptoms. The initial formulation was that the symptoms were stress-related, and over the course of two assessment interviews the therapist was able to construct a clearer picture of the problem using the cognitive model. The client had a very poor self-image and was in a difficult marriage where her husband was very critical. She described a constant stream of thoughts criticizing herself which occurred whenever she needed to make decisions. She was also able to identify negative thoughts about the marriage ('It's hopeless, I'm trapped'). The cognitive formulation explained her memory problems as a natural result of only partly attending to anything: she was distracted by the running commentary she gave on her actions. Her fatigue probably resulted from the frequent negative thoughts she was having about herself and her marriage. Because she had a belief that there was nothing she could do about her marital problems she tended to put these thoughts to the back of her mind using 'cognitive avoidance', and selectively focused on the physical symptoms. This in turn led to a further set of negative thoughts – 'Is there something wrong with my brain? Am I going senile?' This formulation allowed the therapist to develop a comprehensive treatment strategy.

Therapeutic strategies

Each therapist has a particular way of formulating a case, and strategies are tailored to the individual personality of the client. The following list tries to cover the strategies most commonly used in cognitive therapy. For different coverage of this issue see Beck and Emery (1985: 180–6) and Guidano and Liotti (1983).

Distancing and distraction   These strategies are aimed at helping the client to get some distance from the constant flow of maladaptive thinking. Distancing the client from the automatic thoughts helps to reduce the strength of the negative emotional response. Techniques that help the client to act as a more objective observer of his or her own thoughts are usually helpful here. Counting negative thoughts, explaining the rationale and defining problems all help to achieve some distance and perspective. Distraction reduces the frequency of automatic thoughts. This can be done by getting the client to engage in mental or physical activity which moves the attention from the negative thoughts to something else.

Challenging automatic thoughts   This strategy aims to change the client's thinking by challenging the validity of the cognitions. Techniques can be behavioural, e.g. setting up an experiment, or cognitive, e.g. looking for the evidence in favour and against a maladaptive belief.

Challenging underlying assumptions   This strategy challenges the rules that guide the client's maladaptive behaviour. A broad range of cognitive and behavioural techniques are needed to achieve this. For instance, the advantages and disadvantages of an assumption can be explored, reasoning used to challenge the assumption and a behavioural experiment arranged to test it out.

Building skills   Not all problems are caused by inappropriate thoughts. Some of the difficulties the client experiences will be due to real problems, and cognitive therapy then employs problem-solving techniques. This often requires the teaching of particular skills, e.g. through assertiveness training, social skills training and time management.

Major cognitive techniques
In this section I will describe some of the cognitive and behavioural techniques which are commonly used in cognitive therapy. There is considerable overlap between all of these methods and the distinctions made here are somewhat arbitrary. In challenging a particular cognition a therapist might employ several cognitive and behavioural techniques.

Socratic questioning   Cognitive therapy helps clients to identify and then modify their maladaptive thoughts. This is achieved by using the approach of collaborative empiricism described earlier. The client and therapist are co-investigators trying to uncover the interpretations and evaluations which might be contributing to the client's problems. This is an inductive process of guided discovery. Wherever possible the therapist asks questions to elicit the idiosyncratic meanings which give rise to the client's distress and to look for the evidence supporting or refuting the client's beliefs. This use of questioning to reveal the self-defeating nature of the client's automatic thoughts has been termed 'Socratic questioning'.

Identifying negative automatic thoughts   The therapist teaches the client to observe and record negative automatic thoughts. Initially the concept of an automatic thought is explained: it is a thought or image that comes to mind automatically and seems plausible, but on inspection is often distorted or unrealistic. Thoughts the client has during the session can be used to illustrate this, e.g. in the first session a depressed client may be thinking 'I don't know why I've come, there's nothing anyone can do for me'. Written material such as the leaflet 'Coping with depression' (Beck and Greenberg 1974) is also used to explain the basic features of therapy. The client is then given the homework task of collecting and recording negative automatic thoughts. The exact format of this will depend on the problem. A depressed client will be asked to monitor depressed mood, recording the situation which triggered a worsening of depression, and the thoughts associated with it. Someone with an alcohol problem would monitor cravings for drink, and again record the situations in which they occurred and the thoughts which precipitated them. This phase of identifying thoughts helps clients to start making the link:

Event $\longrightarrow$ negative automatic $\longrightarrow$ disturbed
thought   emotion or
                                        behaviour

Identifying thoughts may also be therapeutic in its own right since just recording negative thoughts sometimes reduces their frequency. Clients should try to record their thoughts as soon after the stressful event as possible, since it will then be fresh in their mind.

Modifying negative automatic thoughts   When the client has learned to identify the maladaptive thinking the next step is to learn how to challenge the negative thoughts. Through a process of Socratic questioning the therapist shows the client how to change his or her thinking. This cognitive restructuring by the therapist usually brings relief in the session, but it takes longer for the client to practise challenging thoughts outside the therapy session. The therapy session becomes a situation where the therapist models the process of cognitive restructuring and gives the client feedback on his or her success at the task. Clients are encouraged to use a form to record and challenge their automatic thoughts (see p. 230) to help them internalize the process of identifying and modifying negative automatic thoughts. There are a number of methods the therapist can use to help a client modify negative thinking:

1 *Reality testing*   This is probably the most common method of cognitive restructuring. The client is taught to question the evidence for the automatic thoughts. For example, you hear that your 5-year-old son has hit another child at school. You immediately think 'He's a bully. I'm a useless parent' and feel depressed. What is the evidence that your son is a bully? Has he done this sort of thing before? Is this unusual behaviour for a 5-year-old child? Bullying implies an unprovoked attack. Could he have been provoked? What is the evidence that you are a useless parent? Have you been told by anyone in your family that you are doing a bad job? Is a single instance of bad behaviour in a 5-year-old child proof that you are a bad parent?

2 *Looking for alternatives*   People who are in emotional crisis, especially if they are depressed, find it difficult to examine the options which are open to them. They get into a blinkered view of their situation. Looking for alternatives is a way of helping them out of this mental set. The therapist gently asks for alternative explanations or solutions and continues until as many as possible are generated. At first these will probably all be negative but after a little while the client will start to come up with more constructive alternatives.

3 *Reattribution*   A more specialized form of the search for alternatives involves reattributing the cause of, or responsibility for, an event. A client who experiences panic attacks may believe that the physical sensations of dizziness and a pounding heart are signs of an impending heart attack. The therapist, through education, questioning and experimentation, helps the client to reattribute the cause of these experiences to the natural bodily sensations of extreme anxiety. For example, the client who attributes her son's behaviour to her failure as a mother can be taught to change the focus of responsibility; many factors contribute to a child's behaviour, and a parent does not have control of all of them.

4 *Decatastrophizing*   This has been termed the 'What if' technique (Freeman 1987). The client is taught to ask what would be the worst thing that could happen in the situation. In many cases when the fear is confronted it becomes clear that it is not so terrible after all. For example, you are preparing to visit a friend for the weekend, and do not have much time to pack. You think, 'I can't decide what to pack. I mustn't forget anything.' You get into more and more of a panic trying to remember everything in time. What would be so awful if you did forget something? Would it be the end of the world if you turned up without a toothbrush?

5 *Advantages and disadvantages*   This is a very helpful technique to enable clients to get things into perspective. If a difficult decision has to be made or if it seems difficult to give up a habitual but maladaptive behaviour, the client can list the advantages and disadvantages of a particular course of action.

Behavioural techniques

Freeman (1987) considers the behavioural techniques in cognitive therapy to serve two purposes: first, they work to change behaviour through a broad range of methods, and second, they serve as short-term interventions in the service of longer-term cognitive change. This second goal differentiates the behavioural tasks used in cognitive therapy from those used in more conventional behaviour therapy. These tasks are set within a cognitive conceptualization of the problem and they are used to produce cognitive change. Seen in its simplest form behavioural work changes cognitions by

1 distracting clients from automatic thoughts.
2 challenging maladaptive beliefs through experimentation.

Behavioural methods are often used at the beginning of therapy when the client is most distressed and so less able to use cognitive techniques.

Activity scheduling   This is a technique which is particularly useful with depressed clients but can be applied with other problems too. The rationale for scheduling time centres on the proposition that when they are depressed clients reduce their level of activity and spend time ruminating on negative thoughts. The schedule is an hour-by-hour plan of what the client will do. As with all the procedures in cognitive therapy this needs to be explained in some detail and a clear rationale given. It is often set up as an experiment to see if certain activities will improve mood. The therapist stresses that few people accomplish everything they plan, and the aim is not to get all the items done but to find out if planning and structuring time can be helpful. Initially the aim may just be to monitor tasks together with the thoughts and feelings which accompany them. The emphasis is usually on engaging in particular behaviours in a certain time period rather than the amount achieved. For instance, a client would be encouraged to decide to do some decorating between 10am and 11am on a certain day, rather than plan to decorate a whole room over a weekend. These tasks are set up as homework assignments and the results discussed at the beginning of the next session.

Mastery and pleasure ratings   This is a technique which can be used in conjunction with activity scheduling. Clients rate how much mastery (feelings of success, achievement or control) or pleasure they get out of a task (on a 0–10 scale). Since depressed clients often avoid engaging in pleasant activities, this method allows the therapist to establish which activities might be enjoyable for clients and to encourage them to engage in them with greater frequency. It also challenges all-or-nothing thinking, by showing that there is a continuum of pleasure and mastery, rather than experiences which (1) are totally enjoyable or unenjoyable and (2) yield complete success or failure.

Graded task assignments   All-or-nothing thinking can also be challenged using graded task assignments. Many clients think, 'I have to be able to do everything I set myself, or I have failed'. The therapist begins by setting small homework tasks which gradually build up in complexity and difficulty. The patient is encouraged to set goals that can be realistically achieved, so that he or she completes a series of successful assignments.

Behavioural experiments   We have already seen how behavioural experiments are an important component of cognitive therapy. Hypotheses are continually generated and put to the test. This will usually involve a negative prediction of some form. For instance, an anxious client may state that he is too anxious even to read. An experiment can be set up in the therapy session where the client reads a short paragraph from a newspaper, thus disproving the absolutism of this statement. The client can then go on to read articles of increasing length over the following week. Experiments are often set as homework. For instance, a depressed client who firmly believes that she is unable to go shopping could go shopping with her husband. Even if the client is not able to carry out the assignment the experiment is not a failure because it provides valuable information about what might be the blocks to the activity.

Relaxation   Relaxation is a useful procedure for patients with anxiety-related problems. There are several methods of relaxation training which can be used successfully – graded muscle relaxation, breath control, visualization of pleasant scenes, meditation, etc. These can be taught in the session or the client can take away a relaxation tape. Relaxation serves the following purposes in cognitive therapy:

1 promoting self-awareness and monitoring of bodily states
2 providing a coping technique for reducing anxiety
3 providing a coping technique to facilitate the execution of behavioural experiments
4 promoting a feeling of mastery over symptoms.

Other behavioural techniques Cognitive therapy employs a variety of other behavioural techniques where appropriate. Cognitive and behavioural rehearsal is frequently used during the session in preparation for a difficult homework assignment. Role-play can be a very effective cognitive change technique. When clients have practical problems that need to be solved behavioural techniques based on a skills training model are especially useful. This will usually involve forms of assertiveness training or social skills training for people who have deficits in interpersonal skills.

The change process in therapy

It is difficult to summarize a typical course of cognitive therapy since strategy and technique depend on the individual client and the problems being treated. There is, however, generally a progression through therapy. At the beginning of therapy the emphasis is on conceptualizing the client's problems, teaching the cognitive model and producing early symptom relief. Techniques aimed at symptom relief in the early stages of therapy tend to be more behavioural. As therapy progresses the client learns to monitor and challenge automatic thoughts and this forms the major focus in therapy. As the client's problems reach some resolution the emphasis shifts to identifying and challenging underlying assumptions, and work on relapse prevention. Change occurs through the modification of cognitive structures as evidence accumulates to refute the distorted view of the world which the client holds. This process is not always smooth. The client may come with very different expectations of treatment than the therapist. For instance, a client with a hypochondriacal preoccupation will believe that there is a physical cause for his or her problems and will be reluctant to accept the cognitive model. In the early sessions with this type of client the therapist tries to engage the client in the therapy, perhaps examining the evidence for the client's explanation of the symptoms, and getting his or her agreement to try the new approach on an experimental basis. Some people find it difficult to understand the concept of negative automatic thoughts. It may take longer to explain and demonstrate their nature. Others are frightened to record them because they make them feel worse. This may require more time to spend examining the possible gains from exposing themselves to short-term distress in order to achieve long-term benefit. With clients with personality problems maladaptive patterns of relating to others will be brought into the session and these need to be addressed as part of therapy, for example dependent clients may fail to carry out homework assignments because they hope that the therapist will support and help them without the difficult learning of self-reliance. These patterns often act as blocks to therapy and must be openly discussed with the client.

Limitations of the approach

Many of the limitations of cognitive therapy are the same as those that apply to any form of psychotherapy. People with very severe mental disturbances cannot be treated with talking treatments. This applies particularly to those who suffer from delusions and hallucinations. Motivation to change is an important construct that is not always assessable until therapy is underway. The emphasis placed on homework and self-help can be a limitation for some clients. One study of cognitive therapy for depression found that people who endorsed ideas about self-control did well with cognitive therapy, whereas those who did not responded better to drugs (Simons *et al.* 1986). As we have seen already the question of acceptance of the theoretical model, and the ability and willingness to carry out self-help assignments must be taken into account when considering clients for therapy. The more clearly difficulties can be defined as problems the easier it is to do cognitive therapy. With vague characterological flaws which manifest themselves as problems in interpersonal relationships it is sometimes very hard to find a focus. With these clients the form of therapy described here may not be adequate. One major advantage that cognitive therapy has over some other forms of therapy is its commitment to the scientific method. It is being applied to a widening field of disorders, and as long as its practitioners continue to evaluate its efficacy the next ten years should provide answers to the question: what are the areas of application and the limits of this approach?

Case example

The client

Philippa was a 45-year-old librarian who came for help because of problems with tension and anxiety. She had attended a relaxation class but was so wound up that she found it impossible to use the methods. She had always been a nervous person, but things had been getting worse over the last four years and had now reached the point where she was frequently irritable, had problems sleeping and was in a state of constant bodily tension which left her exhausted.

She had married another librarian in middle age and had no children. Her father was dead but her mother was still alive and there were considerable problems in their relationships. At assessment Philippa said that she thought this was at the root of her problems. The mother was highly critical of her, had wanted a boy and had always seen the daughter as failure. Her mother thought that Philippa was not successful enough, was second rate because she was only a librarian, and would never amount to anything in life. Her brother was a successful businessman who could do nothing wrong in the mother's eyes. Intellectually Philippa was aware that her mother's criticism was unfair, but at a gut level she still believed it.

The therapy

Session 1

The main problems were elicited at the first session and the client's background history taken. Philippa seemed to be suffering from a chronic state of generalized anxiety associated with low self-esteem. She was intelligent, highly motivated and had already done much of the work in defining the problems herself. The therapist hypothesized that her acceptance of her mother's criticism on a gut level contributed to her poor self-image. She described frequent self-critical automatic thoughts, and was continually matching her own performance against her mother's expectations. The tension and anxiety seemed to stem from her fear that at any moment she would get things wrong and prove what a failure she really was. The automatic thoughts which were elicited supported this conceptualization:

> 'I've got to get things right.'
> 'I'm not a person of any consequence.'
> 'I'll never amount to anything.'

Underlying these thoughts was a schema which she used to judge all her actions:

> 'I have to be a success in my mother's eyes in order to have any value as a person.'

Therapist and client agreed on ten sessions of therapy in the first instance to be reviewed, with the possibility of further sessions if necessary. It was stressed that this was a short-term therapy which would not eradicate her problems but give her effective methods to use in the long-term process of working on them herself. The therapist explained the rationale of cognitive therapy, showing how the frequent self-critical and self-defeating thoughts interfered with her performance, made her feel tense and depressed, and tired her out. The initial strategy was to help her achieve some distance from these thoughts. Explaining the rationale of cognitive therapy, that is that her distorted thinking contributed to her distress, helped her to see that her emotional reactions were not inevitable. The first homework assignment was also designed to promote distancing. The therapist asked her to get more information about the nature of these thoughts by recording when they occurred and how she felt in response to them.

Sessions 2 and 3

Philippa did well at monitoring situations and the negative automatic thoughts associated with them. She was surprised to find that anger, rather than anxiety or depression, was the commonest unpleasant emotion which she recorded. The strategy was changed from distancing to actually challenging the negative thoughts. She was soon able to see how many of her reactions were misinterpretations of events, and that she jumped to the conclusion that the behaviour of others, particularly her husband, was a sign that they were critical of her. Table 11.3 shows the daily record of negative automatic thoughts for the second week of treatment.

Table 11.3 Daily record of negative automatic thoughts

Emotion(s)	Situation	Negative automatic thoughts	Rational responses
Anxiety 40%	Cashcard transaction failed	Surely I got the number right; I can't be wrong 100%	The machine was at fault; a re-attempt succeeded instantly; my fear that I had made a mistake was unfounded 100%
Panic 100%	Losing cashcard	My husband will kill me 100%	No he won't; he is never as upset at my mistakes as I am 35%
Anger/ Humiliation 100%	Dispute over what we put in the rubbish bin	He's always blaming me; he shouldn't treat me like this 70%	I accept 50% of the blame, but he is in the wrong too; he's not really trying to put me down – he just does not think when he starts arguing
Rejection 50%	Not being invited to a colleague's leaving party	They're deliberately leaving me out; I'm not important 80%	If I hadn't been told about it, I would not have known anyway; we didn't get on anyway, so why pretend; there are plenty of things to suggest my real friends at work do appreciate me 80%

Sessions 4 and 5

Therapy continued with her practising recording and challenging negative automatic thoughts both in the session and in real life. She began to handle difficult situations without losing control and flying off the handle. Empathizing with her husband's point of view helped her to see that his behaviour was not necessarily critical of her. It seemed that when she believed that she was unimportant she felt depressed, but when her self-esteem rose a little she saw any slight criticism as a threat to her self-esteem and reacted angrily. In these sessions we also explored the relationship with her mother in more detail, and she was able to break down and cry when thinking about the way her mother treated her. This ventilation proved quite helpful since it gave her some relief from the constant feeling of tension and holding herself together. The therapist suggested that she look at her own goals in life and compare them with the goals of her mother. What she wanted out of life was the complete opposite of what her mother saw as success. Philippa's goals were more to do with personal development e.g. playing the violin, learning to be more appropriately assertive, rather than worldly success.

Session 6

This proved to be a key session. Philippa came into the room in a very distressed state. She said she was feeling at rock bottom because of a disastrous weekend in which her dinner party had proved unsuccessful because one guest did not arrive and some of her cooking went badly. She also felt that her husband was taking her for granted. Her negative self-schema was so strongly activated that she came out with a plethora of negative automatic thoughts:

'I won't get anywhere or do anything in life.'
'Everything I do is wrong.'
'I really don't matter.'

She believed this last thought 75 per cent. The therapist challenged it by asking her to look for evidence for and against this belief.

Evidence for	*Evidence against*
1 There is good evidence that the library is not supportive of me.	1 I am a good listener and valued by friends because of this.
2 My brother seldom contacts me.	2 Another friend recently told me that I am just like one of the family.
3 My next-door neighbours don't even ask me when they repair our joint fence.	3 People were very considerate when I was ill recently.
	4 Although my husband is sometimes inconsiderate he sometimes does things that show he cares.

Following this discussion she was able to see that her idea that she didn't matter was completely erroneous, and went on to challenge the other negative automatic thoughts herself. This proved a useful success experience and further weakened her negative self-image.

Sessions 7, 8 and 9
In these three sessions we focused on Philippa's relationship with her mother. At this stage the strategic intervention was aimed at challenging underlying assumptions which she had developed as a result of her mother's criticism. Further beliefs were elicited:

> 'If I don't marry a successful man that means I am not successful.'
> 'You can measure people's success by their status in an organization.'
> 'If parents put in a lot of time and energy to their children's education the children must do well to repay them.'
> 'Good daughters are loyal to their mothers at all times.'

She challenged these beliefs during the session, and as homework began writing down her own criteria for success to demonstrate how these were broader and more realistic than her mother's.

Session 10
The previous nine sessions brought about an improvement in Philippa's self-esteem. The feelings of tension were reduced, but she still felt stressed and her habitual over-reactions had not improved to the extent that she hoped they would. At this point it was decided collaboratively that since most of the emotional reactions now occurring were in the setting of the relationship with her husband it would be appropriate to bring him into the therapy. He proved to be a pleasant, rather shy and extremely unemotional man. He intellectualized the situation, finding it very difficult to empathize with his wife's feelings of being criticized and taken for granted; he saw her reactions as irrational and that was that. He was, however, prepared to come to therapy, and it seemed appropriate to change from individual therapy to couples work. Over the next five sessions he made a little progress in tempering his own reactions to his wife's emotional upsets. Although he did not admit that the therapy was of any use he did learn to change his behaviour and became more overtly supportive of her. At the end of treatment their problems were by no means ended, but Philippa's distress was significantly reduced and she felt less in a state of constant tension.

This illustrates how the course of individual therapy can change as new information accumulates. The therapist changed his initial conceptualization as the extent of the marital problem became clear. There was a need to balance the gains possible from individual therapy against those from marital work. The decision to move into couples work was determined by the evidence that the husband's behaviour was feeding into the client's negative cognitive system. Philippa's feelings of tension would probably not have changed more rapidly if the husband had been included in therapy from the first session, because she had to learn self-control skills on her own before she could make use of couples work.

Philippa's tension was not completely eradicated, nor were her angry outbursts, but they were substantially reduced. She learned self-control techniques to temper her reactions, and there was a definite shift in her attitudes towards her mother.

She decided that trying to change her mother or attempting to get her approval was just a waste of time. Moreover, her belief in her own inadequacy and her tendency to judge herself by her mother's standards were also reduced. These gains were moderate, and as frequently occurs in people with long-standing emotional problems were less than those achieved with acute anxiety and depression, but Philippa felt that individual cognitive therapy helped her considerably with problems that had been troubling her all her life.

Cognitive therapy is not a panacea, but it does provide a way of understanding and working with clients that is applicable across a wide range of problems. It is a coherent, comprehensible and practical therapy which I believe will become increasingly popular with both therapists and clients.

Acknowledgement

I should like to thank my colleague Mrs Ruth Williams for her helpful advice in the preparation of this chapter.

References

Alloy, L.B. and Ahrens, A.H. (1987) Depression and pessimism for the future: biased use of statistically relevant information in predictions for self versus others, *Journal of Personality and Social Psychology* 53: 366–78.

Bandura, A. (1977) *Social Learning Theory*, Englewood Cliffs, NJ: Prentice-Hall.

Beck, A.T. (1963) Thinking and depression: 1. Idiosyncratic content and cognitive distortions, *Archives of General Psychiatry* 9: 324–33.

—— (1964) Thinking and depression: 2. Theory and therapy, *Archives of General Psychiatry* 10: 561–71.

—— (1976) *Cognitive Therapy and the Emotional Disorders*, New York: International Universities Press Inc.

—— (1987) Cognitive models of depression, *Journal of Cognitive Psychotherapy: An International Quarterly* 1: 5–39.

—— (1989) *Love is Never Enough*, London: Viking Penguin.

Beck, A.T. and Emery, G. with Greenberg, R.L. (1985) *Anxiety Disorders and Phobias: A Cognitive Perspective*, New York: Basic Books.

Beck, A.T. and Greenberg, R.L. (1974) *Coping with Depression*, New York: Institute for Rational Living.

Beck, A.T., Rush, A.J., Shaw, B.E. and Emery, G. (1979) *The Cognitive Therapy of Depression*, New York: Guilford.

Blackburn, I.M., Bishop, S., Glen, A.I.M., Whalley, L.J. and Christie, J.E. (1981) The efficacy of cognitive therapy in depression: a treatment trial using cognitive therapy and pharmacotherapy, each alone and in combination, *British Journal of Psychiatry* 139: 181–9.

Bradley, G.W. (1978) Self-serving biases in the attribution process: a re-examination of the fact or fiction question, *Journal of Personality and Social Psychology* 36: 56–71.

Brewin, C.R. (1988) *Cognitive Foundations of Clinical Psychology*, London: Lawrence Erlbaum Associates.

Cautela, J.R. (1973) Covert processes and behavior modification, *Journal of Nervous and Mental Diseases* 157: 27–36.

Clark, D.M. (1986) A cognitive approach to panic, *Behaviour Research and Therapy* 24, 461–70.

Ellis, A. (1962) *Reason and Emotion in Psychotherapy*, Secaucus, NJ: Lyle Stuart.

Epstein, N. (1983) Cognitive therapy with couples, in A. Freeman (ed.) *Cognitive Therapy with Couples and Groups*, New York: Plenum Press.

Fairburn, C.G. (1985) Cognitive-behavioural treatment for bulimia, in D.M. Garner and P.L. Garfinkel (eds) *Handbook of Psychotherapy for Anorexia Nervosa and Bulimia*, New York: Guilford Press.

Fennell, M.J.V. and Teasdale, J.D. (1987) Cognitive therapy for depression: individual differences and the process of change, *Cognitive Therapy and Research* 11: 253–71.

Freeman, A. (1983) Cognitive therapy: an overview, in A. Freeman (ed.) *Cognitive Therapy with Couples and Groups*, New York: Plenum Press.

—— (1987) Cognitive therapy: an overview, in A. Freeman and V. Greenwood (eds) *Cognitive Therapy: Applications in Psychiatric and Medical Settings*, New York: Human Sciences Press.

Guidano, V.F. and Liotti, G. (1983) *Cognitive Processes and Emotional Disorders: A Structural Approach to Psychotherapy*, New York: Guilford.

Hooley, J.M., Orley, J. and Teasdale, J.D. (1986) Levels of expressed emotion and relapse in depressed patients, *British Journal of Psychiatry* 148: 642–7.

Kanfer, F.H. and Karoly, P. (1972) Self-control: a behavioristic excursion into the lion's den, *Behavior Therapy* 3: 378–416.

Kelly, G. (1955) *The Psychology of Personal Constructs*, Vols 1 and 2, New York: Norton.

Kovacs, M. and Beck, A.T. (1978) Maladaptive cognitive structures in depression, *American Journal of Psychiatry* 135: 525–7.

MacLeod, C., Mathews, A. and Tata, P. (1986) Attentional bias in emotional disorders, *Journal of Abnormal Psychology* 95: 15–20.

Mahoney, M.J. (1987) Psychotherapy and the cognitive sciences: an evolving alliance, *Journal of Cognitive Psychotherapy: An International Quarterly* 1: 39–59.

Mahoney, M.J. and Arnkoff, D.B. (1978) Cognitive and self-control therapies, in S.L. Garfield and A.E. Bergin (eds) *Handbook of Psychotherapy and Behavior Change*, 2nd edn, New York: Wiley.

Mathews, A. and MacLeod, C. (1985) Selective processing of threat cues in anxiety states, *Behaviour Research Therapy* 23: 563–9.

Meichenbaum, D. (1985) *Stress Inoculation Training*, New York: Pergamon Press.

Moorey, S. (1988) Cognitive therapy with depressed outpatients: patient factors associated with outcome, in W. Dryden and P. Trower (eds) *Cognitive Psychotherapy: Stasis and Change*, London: Cassell.

Moorey, S. and Burns, D.D. (1983) The apprenticeship model: training in cognitive therapy by participation, in A. Freeman (ed.) *Cognitive Therapy with Couples and Groups*, New York: Plenum Press.

Murphy, G.E., Simons, A.D., Wetzel, R.D. and Lustman, P.J. (1984) Cognitive therapy and pharmacotherapy singly and together in the treatment of depression, *Archives of General Psychiatry* 41: 33–41.

Rosenthal, T.L. and Bandura, A. (1978) Psychological modeling: theory and practice, in S.L. Garfield and A.E. Bergin (eds) *Handbook of Psychotherapy and Behavior Change*, 2nd edn, New York: Wiley.

Rush, A.J. and Watkins, J.T. (1981) Group versus individual cognitive therapy: a pilot study, *Cognitive Therapy and Research* 5: 95–103.

Rush, A.J., Beck, A.T., Kovacs, M. and Hollon, S. (1977) Comparative efficacy of cognitive therapy and imipramine in the treatment of depressed outpatients, *Cognitive Therapy and Research* 1: 17–37.

Salkovskis, P.M. and Warwick H.M.C. (1986) Morbid preoccupations, health anxiety and reassurance: a cognitive-behavioural approach to hypochondriasis, *Behaviour Research and Therapy* 24: 597–602.

Shaw, B.F. (1984) Specification of the training and evaluation of cognitive therapists for outcome studies, in J. Williams and R.L. Spitzer (eds) *Psychotherapy Research: Where are We and Where should We Go?*, New York: Guilford Press.

Simons, A.D., Murphy, G.E., Levine, J.L. and Wetzel, R.D. (1986) Cognitive therapy and pharmacotherapy for depression, *Archives of General Psychiatry* 43: 43–8.

Teasdale, J.D., Fennell M.J.V., Hibbert, G.A. and Amies, P.L. (1984) Cognitive therapy for major depressive disorder in primary care, *British Journal of Psychiatry* 144: 400–6.

Suggested further reading

Beck, A.T. (1976) *Cognitive Therapy and the Emotional Disorders*, New York: International Universities Press Inc.

Beck, A.T. and Emery, G. with Greenberg, R.L. (1985) *Anxiety Disorders and Phobias: A Cognitive Perspective*, New York: Basic Books.

Beck, A.T., Rush, A.J., Shaw, B.F. and Emery, G. (1979) *The Cognitive Therapy of Depression*, New York: Guilford.

Brewin, C.R. (1988) *Cognitive Foundations of Clinical Psychology*, London: Lawrence Erlbaum Associates.

Scott, J., Williams, J.M.G. and Beck, A.T. (eds) (1989) *Cognitive Therapy in Clinical Practice*, London: Croom Helm.

12

Behaviour therapy

GERALDINE O'SULLIVAN

Historical context and development in Britain

Historical context

The term 'behaviour therapy' was coined by Skinner in the early 1950s and was reintroduced and made popular by Lazarus in 1958. Behaviour therapy includes a variety of techniques which bring about observable and measurable changes in human behaviour. The basic therapeutic principles have been in use for centuries as shown by examples of its application in literature spanning the ages. Locke (1693) outlined the exposure principle which now forms the basis of a behavioural intervention for decreasing anxiety. He advised that

> if your child shrieks and runs away at the sight of a frog, let another catch it and lay it down at a good distance from him; at first accustom him to look upon it; when he can do that to come nearer to it and see it leap without emotion; then to touch it lightly, when it is held fast in another's hand; and so on, until he can come to handle it as confidently as a butterfly or sparrow.
>
> (Locke 1693: 481–2)

Even Freud (1919: 165–6) acknowledged the importance of exposure to the feared situation. He wrote:

> One can hardly master a phobia if one waits till the patient lets the analysis influence him to give it up. . . . One succeeds only when one can induce them by the influence of the analysis to go and to struggle with the anxiety while they make the attempts.

In the 1800s a captain in the Royal Navy controlled the behaviour of prisoners on an island in the Pacific by using the technique of contingency rewards (Pitts 1976). In the early 1900s Janet (1925) observed that ritualizers who entered certain institutions (the Army or the Church) often improved with the discipline imposed by institutional practices. This is reminiscent of the technique of response prevention, which is now used in combination with exposure in treating obsessive-compulsive disorder. The variety of early literature reports indicate that in many respects behaviour therapy is based on common sense but its routine application in clinical practice has been developed and systematized only within the last twenty-five years.

Originally, behaviour was viewed as being explicable in terms of the principles of learning theory. During the early 1900s learning theory was undergoing development. The concept of classical conditioning was formulated by Pavlov (1927) based on experiments with animals. In his famous experiment, Pavlov paired presentation of food with the sound of a bell. After a series of such presentations, eventually the bell alone elicited salivation. The essential feature of classical conditioning is that an unconditioned stimulus (food), which leads automatically to an unconditioned response (salivation), when presented repeatedly with a conditioned stimulus (bell), causes the conditioned stimulus to be sufficient in itself to produce a conditioned response (salivation). About that time operant conditioning was also undergoing development. Thorndike (1911) studied animals using a wooden box with a door which could be opened by pulling a loop. When a cat was placed within the box generally it made a number of ineffectual movements but eventually it accidentally pulled the loop and escaped. Gradually the animal decreased the length of time it took to pull the loop and escape. Instrumental or operant conditioning states that behaviour is largely determined by its consequences. Favourable consequences (escape) reinforce a particular piece of behaviour (pulling the loop) and if reinforcement is discontinued, then that piece of behaviour is likely to cease gradually (extinction).

A series of applications of these new learning models followed in human case experiments. Maladaptive behaviour was produced and abolished in humans (usually children) using learning principles. The most infamous case was that of little Albert, who was subjected to repeated presentations of a white rat paired with a loud noise (Watson and Rayner 1920). After a number of such pairings the infant reacted with fear to the white rat. This fearful response generalized to other similar stimuli, e.g. a fur coat. On the basis of this experiment Watson and Rayner (1920) concluded that phobias are conditioned emotional responses. Watson's conviction of the power of learning theory to explain human behaviour was so great that he claimed that through conditioning he could make an infant into a thief, a lawyer or a doctor.

Wolpe (1958) proposed a hypothesis of neurosis in terms of Pavlovian learning principles. Within this theory behaviour was viewed as being under direct stimulus control. Wolpe (1958) attempted to incorporate learning principles in the treatment of neurotic disorders. He advocated the pairing of relaxation, which is antagonistic to anxiety, with contact with conditioned stimuli. The client was trained to relax and relaxation was paired with imaginal contact with the feared object or situation, the assumption being that relaxation reciprocally inhibits the anxiety response leading to a weakening of the association between the stimuli and anxiety. This technique was termed systematic desensitization and was used for many years in the treatment of phobic and obsessive-compulsive disorders.

Development in Britain

Wolpe spent some time at the Maudsley Hospital; British psychologists such as Hans Eysenck and Jack Rachman and psychiatrists such as Isaac Marks and Michael Gelder were interested in behaviour therapy. They played significant roles in the development and the systematic therapeutic application of behavioural techniques. Eysenck and Rachman (1965) wrote an influential book entitled *Causes and Cures of Neurosis*. Since that time the Maudsley has continued to play a significant role in the development and refinement of behaviour therapy. In 1971 the British Association for Behavioural Psychotherapy was formed by the Maudsley group to foster basic research and exchange of information and to promote behaviour therapy in Britain. Over the years modifications have arisen, including incorporation of cognitive components in an attempt to improve outcome further. Cognitive therapies focus on modifying distorted thoughts and then to use the new cognitive skills to aid exposure to feared situations. In addition, cognitive therapies focus on internal cues such as somatic manifestations of autonomic arousal and catastrophic thoughts. This represents a change from the external cues which behaviour therapy has traditionally focused on. However, all cognitive approaches also include exposure to external cues.

Within Britain two schools have developed: one adheres to the behavioural approach and does not focus on cognitions in therapy, and the other cognitive-behavioural group focuses on cognitions first and then behaviour. A disadvantage of cognitive therapy is that it is more time-consuming than behaviour therapy. In the latter the role of the therapist is reduced to that of assessor, monitor and coach as the majority of patients carry out between-session homework. In addition it is believed that attitude change automatically arises as a result of change in behaviour and cognitions do not need to be formally addressed in therapy. On the other hand, the cognitive-behavioural group argue that outcome is improved in the long term as a result of changing the way the individual responds on encountering stressful situations, so breaking the vicious circle in which symptoms cause worry and worry leads to more symptoms (Gelder 1986). The reluctance to adopt the cognitive approach reflects the lack of current evidence from controlled trials indicating a superiority of the cognitive-behaviour approach. The area remains controversial. It can be resolved only by comparing the two approaches in a controlled study, ensuring the validity of each treatment, measuring change in the various components and examining outcome in the short term and the long term. Such a trial is being planned.

Behaviour therapy has evolved into the study of the application of therapeutic interventions in clinical phenomena. Accompanying this empirical investigation has been the growth in behavioural literature. A substantial number of journals on the treatment of anxiety disorders has arisen both in the USA and in Britain over the last two decades.

In Britain the clinical demand for treatment has led to the training of many other mental health professionals in behavioural psychotherapy. Today, behaviour therapy is a well-established treatment modality and is a safe, effective intervention in disorders that were previously untreatable. However, advances in

treating anxiety disorders have not been accompanied by a corresponding understanding of the mechanisms of treatment.

Theoretical assumptions

Image of the person

According to the behavioural approach people's behaviour is a reflection of their
overall state of well-being. Human functioning can be enhanced by influencing
behaviour. Self-control and mastery of the environment allow people to achieve
their goals.

Learning theory
According to the traditional behavioural model all human behaviour, both normal
and abnormal, is determined by learning: classical and operant conditioning.
Symptoms are viewed as discrete pieces of behaviour which have arisen through
faulty learning. A disordered stimulus–response link leads to an inappropriate
response to neutral stimulus, this response being maintained by its consequences.
There are individual variations in conditionability, with some individuals
showing greater arousal and autonomic lability. However, just as normal
behaviour can be modified, maladaptive behaviour can be altered by means of
unlearning.

Objectivity
This is a central theme of behaviourism. It focuses on overt behaviour and the
environment rather than subjective experiences or the internal forces that are
assumed to underlie the problem. It has emphasized the empirical approach and
insists that alteration of human behaviour is quantifiable.

Cognitive theory
Dissatisfaction with the stimulus–response explanations of behaviour led Lazarus
(1971) to appeal for a more eclectic view of human behaviour in *Behavior Therapy
and Beyond*. As traditional behaviour therapy neglected internal mediating
concepts, the cognition-based approach emphasizes the causal role of private
thoughts, beliefs, irrational ideas and assumptions in the production and
maintenance of abnormal behaviour. It stresses the importance of each
individual's perception of external events rather than the direct influences of the
environment itself. In turn, modification of these abnormal assumptions and
perceptions can aid alterations of problematic behaviour.

Conceptualization of psychological disturbance and health

Maladjusted vs well-adjusted
The pattern of behaviour which predominates in a society determines the norms.
Behaviour that violates social norms is deemed pathological and is labelled
'deviant' and maladjusted. One's ability to behave competently, sometimes even

in the face of adversity, influences one's general adjustment in many aspects of life. Many anxious individuals are maladjusted in important areas such as social, interpersonal, work, sexual and leisure activities. Their abnormal behaviour precludes achievement of mastery in these areas. In contrast the well-adjusted individual moves competently in these areas which in turn leads to more positive social reinforcements.

Fear of fear vs stoicism
Fear of anxiety, panic and even the somatic manifestations of these is a common theme amongst anxious individuals. Avoidance can rapidly ensue after just one panic. The somatic manifestations of anxiety (e.g. increased heart-rate) are selectively attended to and sometimes normal activities which elicit these can also be avoided (e.g. exercise). All of us experience stress, anxiety and fear regularly, but despite this we continue to face the situations associated with these, i.e. there is an acceptance and ability to cope with stress and anxiety.

Passivity-avoidance vs assertion
The individual who continuously retires in the face of discomfort will not recognize a relationship between his or her actions and environmental circumstances which are amenable to change. In contrast the individual who manipulates the environment will elicit favourable responses leading to a high rate of positive reinforcement.

Learned helplessness vs self-efficacy
An individual's behaviour is an index of his or her perceptions of self-competence or self-efficacy (Bandura 1977). The healthy individual perceives oneself as having the ability to cope with daily stress and even threatening situations. It is closely related to the individual perception of control over his or her life. In learned helplessness (Seligman 1975) the individual perceives his or her responses as futile, leading to failure to initiate coping responses, i.e. there is a perceived lack of personal competence.

Psychological health
The behavioural model views psychological well-being in terms of control over one's environment and good adjustment in social, interpersonal, work, sexual and leisure activities. The healthy individual elicits a high rate of positive reinforcement from the environment and has the ability to evaluate events and situations appropriately based on a realistic appraisal of the evidence.

Acquisition of psychological disturbance

There is a tendency to make inferences about the aetiology of a disorder based on effective interventions but this can lead to incorrect conclusions. A variety of different causes can lead to the same end-result. It is now known that depression may be caused by a number of factors, including an inherited biological predisposition, endocrine abnormalities and adverse life events. Within an individual, factors interact in complicated ways to produce illness. Similarly behaviour disorders are not explicable in terms of one specific aetiological factor; instead it is likely that they are the end-results of a series of complicated interactions involving many factors. Some factors implicated in causation and perpetuation will be considered. It should be noted that these interact in complicated ways within the individual sufferer.

First, our predisposition to experience fear/anxiety in specific ways and to react to these with predictable patterns of behaviour are partly determined by inherited biological factors. In evolutionary terms, defensive adaptations against threat were necessary to ensure survival and have been incorporated into our genetic make-up (Marks 1987). Survival requires a search for hostile factors within the environment so that evasive action can be taken. Evolutionary factors may be invoked to explain the limited range of phobias that commonly arise in people. Because of evolutionary pressures, certain aspects of the environment may be attended to more readily and therefore are more likely to produce fear/anxiety responses. In addition, specific responses may be associated with certain environmental cues. There are certain fears which can be considered as being innate as they are observed prior to any sensitizing contact with these stimuli. Examples include heights (as shown by avoidance of a 'visual cliff' by young children: Gibson and Walk 1960), loud noises, sudden movements (e.g. writhing movements of snakes) and the separation anxiety observed in children when contact with a familiar figure is threatened. Being in an unfamiliar environment automatically leads to increased vigilance. Agoraphobia (fear of public places) can be viewed as venturing beyond one's familiar home territory to a more threatening and hostile one, where increased vigilance is necessary. However, with continued contact with that unfamiliar environment the appraisal of it as threatening wanes. This is equivalent to the way *exposure therapy* improves phobias that are seen in clinical practice. Phobias and rituals commonly involve situations (snakes, spiders, open spaces, checking) that are potentially threatening (or potentially protective) to pre-technological humans (De Silva *et al.* 1976).

Genetic studies have shown that anxiety neuroses occur more frequently among relatives of sufferers. Family studies have found a prevalence of approximately 20 per cent among relatives, with females being at twice the risk compared with males. However, to date adoption studies are lacking so the existing studies have failed to separate hereditary from environmental factors. These are necessary to determine the extent of the contribution of vicarious factors, that is children observing the behaviour of neurotic parents and using this as a model for their own future behaviour, as opposed to a purely genetic contribution.

Socio-cultural factors are also important in the neuroses. Within our society it is easier for women to show fear and be fearful. In western countries the majority of agoraphobics are female (75 per cent) as opposed to India, where the reverse applies with a preponderance of male agoraphobics. The feminist view is that traditionally 'a woman's place is in the home' and, within a patriarchal society, sex-role stereotyping promotes the display of fear and the development of phobias in women. On the other hand, typically men are supposed to be fearless, macho and the traditional breadwinners. They are more likely to be coerced through social pressure to face up to and endure their anxiety, which is the basic component of exposure therapy. An interaction between genetic and social factors can be postulated leading to the likelihood of women showing neurotic disorder at a lower genetic loading than men because of sex-role stereotyping.

An organic-biological theory of anxiety has been advocated (Klein 1967). It is claimed that panic is caused by a biological dysfunction, independent of psychological and situational factors, leading eventually to agoraphobia. Such a circumscribed hypothesis seems insufficient to explain the origin of such a complex disorder. Moreover, proponents of this theory infer that because of the biological aetiology, only a physical method of treatment is indicated. Empirical evaluation of panic disorder or agoraphobia suggests that avoidance can sometimes precede panic (Lelliott *et al.* 1989). In addition, results of numerous controlled trials of exposure therapy and pharmacotherapy, individually and in combination, indicate that exposure therapy is superior to drugs and leads to lasting improvement (Marks and O'Sullivan 1988). There is no doubt that at some stage anxiety/panic are mediated at a biological level but so far the evidence suggests that this is a manifestation of anxiety rather than a cause.

Most people develop fears and rituals at some time, but in the majority these do not develop into major handicaps. Phobias and rituals may be caused by failed extinction rather than acquisition (Marks 1982). This may be part of a generalized failure in coping. Goldstein and Chambless (1978) found that agoraphobics lacked assertiveness compared with other groups. Perhaps those who develop major disorders are the ones who tend to retreat in the face of discomfort and are less likely to face their fears. During exposure therapy they are taught to face their fears leading to a general increase in self-mastery. Results of many follow-up studies in phobics and obsessive-compulsives demonstrate that there tends to be a generalization of gains from the main problem to other areas over the months and years after treatment.

In summary, a comprehensive view of the aetiology of anxiety disorders is a complex one embracing several factors interacting in different ways and modifying the expression of emotion within each individual sufferer. These include evolutionary, genetic, cognitive, socio-cultural, past experience and vicarious factors.

Similar aetiological factors apply with regard to 'appetitive' disorders. All forms of behaviour can be viewed as being on a continuum, with abnormal behaviour being at one end, that is differing quantitatively rather than qualitatively. This variation may be of constitutional and genetic origin or alternatively may be acquired through faulty learning. Whatever the precise cause of 'deviations' from norms, there is no doubt that sociological factors largely determine the criteria used to define 'deviance'. Behaviour that falls outside the normal pattern is considered 'deviant'. The sociological concept of deviance is related to laws, mores and behaviour (Bancroft 1974). Most forms of deviance violate these factors.

In the eating disorders social factors have again been implicated in causation. Pressure on females to be thin in order to be considered attractive has led to the rigorous pursuit of thinness. Reports of anorexia nervosa are rare in the early literature, when being thin was not the norm. Cases are unusual in developing countries, where to be fat is regarded favourably as it symbolizes wealth.

Perpetuation of psychological disturbance

Once a fear of a particular object or situation has not been extinguished but has become established, the thought of approaching or coming in contact with the feared stimulus elicits intense anxiety and as a result approaching the stimulus becomes very difficult and avoidance often ensues. The reduction in anxiety that results because of avoidance promotes further avoidance. A vicious cycle of fear and avoidance ensues, each perpetuating the other. Catastrophic thoughts about the situation or the associated physical consequences of anxiety are common. Examples include fears of dying or doing something uncontrolled when anxious and panicky. Others focus on the physical components and may fear vomiting, shaking or blushing in public, and so on. In effect, fear of fear and a spiral of anti-cipatory anxiety occur and avoidance of fear-evoking situations perpetuates the problem. At the time of presentation for treatment, the mean duration of the problem is on average eight to ten years for most phobic and obsessive-compulsive patients. Learning theory fails to explain the perpetuation of neurosis. A central argument of operant conditioning is that unreinforced conditioned reactions extinguish fairly rapidly. Mowrer (1950) wrote:

> Common sense holds that a normal, sensible man or even a beast will weigh and balance the consequences of his acts; if the net effect is favorable, the action producing it will be perpetuated, and if the net effect is unfavorable, the action producing it will be inhibited, abandoned. In neurosis, however, one sees actions which are predominantly unfavorable consequences, yet they persist over a period of months, years or a lifetime.
>
> (Mowrer 1950: 127)

Therefore, the conditioning theory of neurosis does not explain the chronic course of such disorders. However, operant conditioning is useful in explaining the continuation of 'appetitive' behaviour. The positive reinforcement obtained from engaging in the behaviour leads to its perpetuation.

Certain aspects of the environment may promote perpetuation of the problem. Alcohol and minor tranquillizers may be used as a means of reducing anxiety, but once their effect begins to wear off, more needs to be taken to reinstate the effect, leading to the risk of dependence. Indeed, many male phobics may be presenting at Alcohol Dependence Units rather than seeking help for their phobias. Inter-personal factors may facilitate continuation of the problem. The phobic individual, in particular the agoraphobic, often has impaired ability to work and socialize and to carry out everyday tasks. Some may be so incapacitated that they become housebound, leading to dependence on others to fulfil their basic needs. It has been speculated that spouses of agoraphobics have chosen timid, dependent partners because this fulfils a particular need in themselves and they may resist changes in their partner, thereby perpetuating the problem. In turn, spouses have difficulty adjusting to and accepting a more independent, self-sufficient partner once the sufferer has been successfully treated with exposure. In general this pattern does not overtly apply but occasionally a morbidly jealous spouse may welcome a housebound partner and may resist any attempts towards change.

In the eating disorders, characteristically, subjects have cognitive distortions with regard to food, weight and body image. These distortions serve to maintain the problem. In the behavioural excesses the positive reinforcement obtained by engaging in the behaviour maintains it.

Change

Some individuals naturally overcome their phobias and fears in the early stages of their development because avoidance of the fear-eliciting object or situation may not be feasible. They are thus exposed to the phobic object/situation, leading to habituation. Social circumstances can sometimes alter so that approaching one's fears becomes inevitable. For those who engage in behavioural excess, the environmental contingencies associated with it can occasionally change so that the negative consequences of the behaviour increase and the rewards diminish, that is positive reinforcement decreases leading to a reduction in the behaviour. An example is the transvestite who marries and whose spouse threatens to leave if the behaviour persists.

It is likely that individuals lacking specific skills may acquire them through vicarious factors. Timid individuals may model the behaviour of those who are more assertive and thereby increase their own assertive skills. These examples of change are naturally occurring applications of the techniques used in behaviour therapy.

Practice

Goals of therapy

Behavioural psychotherapy consists of a range of therapeutic methods whose goal is to change behaviour directly. It focuses on the main problem without attempting to uncover unconscious processes. It is problem oriented, structured, directive, empirically based and short term. The problem may be a behavioural deficit (e.g. phobic avoidance, social skills deficit, erectile failure, etc.) or excess (compulsive rituals, sexual deviation, habit disorders, etc.) which lead to severe handicap. Initially the principal goal is to *alter behaviour* which restricts the clients' day-to-day activities, thus improving the quality of life; later in the treatment process, other areas can be focused on. The aim is *not* to abolish anxiety totally, as this is generally impossible, but rather to help individuals to put their anxiety in perspective so that incapacitation is reduced. Individuals are taught to face the situations that lead to anxiety and learn to deal with this.

Selection criteria

Certain criteria aid the identification of patients likely to benefit from behaviour therapy. First, the problem should be defined in terms of observable behaviour, for example, the persistent avoidance of certain situations that trigger discomfort. Second, the problem needs to be current and predictable, that is there are consistently identifiable triggers. Anxiety is situational as opposed to free-floating or generalized. Third, the patient, with the aid of the therapist, should be able to specify clearly definable behavioural goals. This is crucial to treatment. Nebulous statements like 'I want to live a normal life' are not adequately precise. Both patient and therapist must agree on specific goals. Fourth, patient co-operation is essential. The patient cannot be treated against his or her wishes and must be willing to invest a lot of time and effort to overcome the problem. The individual must set aside adequate time each day for several weeks to carry out homework tasks. In addition, patients often have to endure considerable discomfort during the programme, so motivation to overcome the problem in order to achieve worthwhile change is essential. A family member who acts as a co-therapist is helpful in the treatment process in that he or she can readily provide encouragement to carry out tasks and praise for achievements made. This can be valuable in maintaining motivation and co-operation. Fifth, major physical or mental complications are contra-indications to behaviour therapy. Serious physical diseases such as cardiac, respiratory and gastro-intestinal disorders make high levels of anxiety undesirable. In these conditions rapid exposure is not advisable and if behaviour therapy is to be carried out at all, it needs to be graded to avoid extreme anxiety. Major psychiatric disorders such as acute psychotic illnesses, severe depression and mania are contra-indications. Sixth, otherwise suitable patients who take quantities of alcohol to the point of being drunk or large doses of sedative drugs (e.g. benzodiazepines) daily are unlikely to benefit from exposure therapy. These substances produce state-dependent learning leading to loss of any treatment gains once the effect of alcohol or drugs wears off. Sometimes patients are willing to reduce alcohol or drugs and a withdrawal regime may need to be worked out with them. During the treatment the maximum permissible amount of alcohol is two units daily or diazepam 10 mgs daily (or the equivalent thereof). Anti-depressants do not interfere with behaviour therapy and indeed can be indicated in those obsessive-compulsive and agoraphobic patients who intermittently develop depressive episodes.

Definite clinical indications for behaviour therapy include phobic, obsessive-compulsive and sexual disorders (including sexual dysfunctions and deviations), social skill deficits, habit disorders such as hair pulling, stammering, certain childhood problems such as enuresis, school phobia and conduct disorders. Behavioural intervention has been shown to be beneficial and can be used as an adjunct to treatment in eating disorders (anorexia nervosa, bulimia, obesity), morbid grief, hypochondriasis, nightmares, psychosomatic disorders and mental subnormality. The majority of patients fulfilling these selection criteria respond well to exposure therapy provided they comply with treatment. A small percentage fail to habituate despite compliance. Attempts have been made to identify these but to date no reliable pre-treatment markers have been found to pin-point non-responders. However, after treatment has begun, those who fail to make gains within a few weeks of adequate exposure have a less favourable prognosis. In addition, those who tend to remain demoralized and depressed despite some improvement in main phobic or obsessive-compulsive handicap are more likely to do less well in the long-run (Hand 1988). The whole area of non-responders to exposure therapy needs further examination.

As behaviour therapy is tailored for each individual patient, it is usually carried out on an individual basis. However, it can also be carried out in groups. There are no specific indicators for individual as opposed to group therapy; the approach is the same in both. Behavioural group therapy can be useful for patients who have similar problems. In general, outcome is similar for both but behavioural group therapy is particularly helpful in patients with social skills deficits where they can use the group setting for role-play and modelling; furthermore they can obtain feedback from the other group members. There is no evidence to suggest that those who fail to respond to individual behaviour therapy are likely to respond to group-based treatment.

Qualities of effective therapists

It is a misconception that special expertise is required to be a behaviour therapist, nor is profound background knowledge of learning theory required. Originally, behaviour therapy fell within the realm of psychologists and doctors, but now many nurses and other mental health professionals have been trained as behaviour therapists and are successfully treating a large number of sufferers. The degree of therapist input required varies from patient to patient. Some patients need basic assessment and instructions and are largely self-sufficient, while others require much therapist guidance and coaching including modelling, pacing and en-couragement. In behavioural psychotherapy it is the systematic application of intervention techniques which is viewed as being responsible for change. It is a doing and not just a talking process. It analyses discrete behaviours provided they can be specified in quantifiable terms and empirically validated techniques are applied to these. Traditionally, less scientific approaches have been shunned and little attention has been paid to non-specific aspects of the treatment process including the patient–therapist relationship. More recently, the patient–therapist relationship is being viewed as an important component in the treatment process. A good therapeutic relationship is advantageous for many reasons. First, therapist and client need to agree on the aims and goals of therapy. Targets have to be set and altered at regular intervals. In addition, a good therapeutic relationship may hinder patient drop-out, particularly during the early phases of treatment when discomfort is often at its greatest. Lastly, it may also aid patient co-operation and compliance and so improve the outcome. As in any therapeutic interaction a warm empathic therapist is preferable. However, in behaviour therapy the therapist must also be directive, as setting targets and pacing the rate of treatment are essential components. Therefore the combination of qualities of warmth and the ability to be directive is often found in the most effective therapists.

In summary, in behavioural psychotherapy the patient–therapist relationship is not viewed as central to the treatment process as ultimately it is the methodology which is essential, but a good therapeutic relationship is likely to aid the treatment process and so influence the outcome.

Therapeutic style

The behavioural psychotherapist is not cold and aloof but is actively involved in the treatment process, often forming a warm, empathic relationship with the patient. Even though the therapist focuses on the target problem he/she takes note of the various aspects of the patient's environment, interpersonal relationships and mood during treatment.

Having gathered all the relevant information the therapist designs a realistic treatment programme which is tailored to the needs of the individual patient. Negotiation of goals is a central feature of the approach. Flexibility on the part of the therapist thereby allowing individual variations in the pace of treatment and the rate of progress is an inherent element of the therapeutic style. The therapist guides the patient through the treatment by explaining and teaching behavioural strategies and helping the patient to overcome obstacles to treatment. Monitoring improvement and the provision of praise, encouragement and feedback about progress are essential components of the therapeutic style.

Major therapeutic strategies and techniques

Behavioural analysis

When a patient who fulfils the selection criteria presents for treatment the first step is the behavioural analysis. This allows the therapist to gain a detailed picture of the problems and therefore to formulate therapeutic strategies that are individually tailored. This involves obtaining precise information about the nature, predictability and impact of the problem. First, the *nature* of the problem needs to be ascertained in detail. This involves several components. The behavioural consequences of the occurrence of the fear need to be determined; does fear lead to avoidance, escape, reassurance, seeking, engaging in excesses (checking), and so on? The physical/autonomic manifestations of the fear should be inquired about: what happens physically in the feared situation, for example palpitations, sweating, diarrhoea, trembling? Some patients are very frightened by certain physical components. This is particularly true with regard to panics, which are sudden surges in the level of anxiety accompanied by a variety of somatic symptoms. Some patients fear they may die during one of these panic attacks. Explanation to patients that panic is a variant of anxiety and that people don't die during panics often brings immense relief. What precise feelings and thoughts are evoked by the fear: 'I will make a fool of myself', or 'Everybody is watching me', or 'I am going to lose control'. What were the antecedents of the episode? Was there anticipatory anxiety and catastrophic thoughts? It is important to determine the precise nature of all the situations that elicit fear, and each should be rated for the degree of distress aroused allowing the formation of a hierarchy of the various fear-evoking situations. The aftermath is also important; is there immediate relief or discomfort for several hours? Information about the onset of the problem can sometimes be obtained by asking the patient to describe the first episode, as many can recall this accurately. Some report adverse life events or interpersonal problems preceding onset. The course since onset can vary considerably with some patients describing some fluctuations in the course of the condition, including exacerbations and temporary remissions while others describe a gradual, continuous deterioration. Aggravation of symptoms is sometimes reported by female patients pre-menstrually. In these circumstances attempts to ameliorate pre-menstrual tension can be helpful. The presence of modifying factors should also be inquired about. Some patients' distress is temporarily reduced by alcohol or the presence of a trusted companion. In particular, some agoraphobics use a pushchair when venturing out of home, which acts as a 'safety signal'. Careful questioning along these lines provides information about the behavioural, psychological, cognitive and physical components of the problem, along with its onset and course. The next step in the behavioural analysis is to determine the current *predictability* of the problem. This incorporates the frequency, duration, severity and all the situational features of the episodes. Lastly, the *impact* of the problem on the individual's life is important. In what ways and to what degree is the individual's life-style impaired? Are work, social and leisure activities affected and if so, to what extent? What effect does it have on other family members? Careful collection of this information will give the therapist a comprehensive picture of the patient's avoidance profile and therefore an appropriate treatment plan can be drawn up.

The precise behavioural strategy used to treat an individual patient depends on the presenting problem. Therapeutic approaches can be divided into three main categories. First, a reduction in *anxiety-linked behaviour* (phobias, rituals, ruminations, sexual dysfunction) may be the goal of therapy. The techniques used in this case will be different from those required to reduce *appetitive behaviour* (obesity, bulimia, sexual deviation) and from those which are useful in the *development of new behaviour* (social skills deficits). Each of these three categories will be discussed.

Anxiety-linked behaviour
The central component in achieving anxiety reduction for a fear-eliciting stimulus is *exposure* to that situation and the resultant discomfort endured until it diminishes. Most techniques used to overcome anxiety-linked behaviour contain the exposure ingredient. The principal techniques include exposure *in vivo* (real-life exposure) and occasionally imaginal exposure (fantasized exposure). Others include audio-tape techniques which involve repeated listening to a taped distressing ruminative thought. Response prevention is the obstruction of discrete neutralizing behaviours that diminish discomfort following exposure to the eliciting cue, for example preventing handwashing following contact with a door handle. The deliberate exaggeration of fears is occasionally used and this is termed paradoxical intention. It is sometimes claimed that relaxation therapy effectively improves situational anxiety, but this has not been shown in controlled studies. However, relaxation techniques applied as coping tactics during exposure may be beneficial in some patients but the systematic use of reciprocal inhibition, that is alternating relaxation with exposure, does not yield optimal results and may retard the rate at which gains are made.

The exposure principle   In clinical practice the majority of patients who present for treatment suffer from phobic or obsessive-compulsive disorders. Exposure therapy is now the most widely used behavioural intervention in phobic and obsessive-compulsive disorders. Exposure is better when carried out with *real* rather than fantasized fear cues. Real-life exposure leads to more discomfort in the course of treatment than imaginal but generally leads to greater improvement and more rapid gains. The latter can be resorted to when exposure *in vivo* is difficult to arrange as for example in flight phobias. In planning an exposure programme it should be remembered that long periods of exposure reduce fear more than shorter ones. Stern and Marks (1973) found that two hours of continuous exposure was more effective than four half-hour sessions. With continued exposure to the frightening situation panic commonly begins to reduce within 30–40 minutes of the start of exposure, even in phobias that have been present for many years. Occasionally, several hours may be needed before anxiety begins to fall. The crucial factor is to continue exposure until this happens. Exposure treatment can be *therapist-aided*, in which the therapist accompanies the patient into the phobic situation, or *self-exposure*, when the patient enters the phobic situations alone. The rate at which exposure is carried out can vary, but more rapid exposure yields faster clinical gains. Ultimately the pace is governed by what the sufferer is able to do. Rapid real-life exposure to the most feared stimulus in the fear hierarchy is termed *flooding*. In clinical practice a more graded approach is generally used, beginning with the less fearful cues and gradually working up the hierarchy. Exposure can vary from being an easy task in some cases to being complicated in others and the amount of therapist input necessary varies considerably from patient to patient. Some execute their own programme with the aid of self-help manuals and homework diaries while others require much therapist input, involving grading and alteration of tasks, attention to all fear cues, pacing and therapist-aided exposure.

Discomfort may be particularly high during the early stages of treatment and the urge to escape will be strong, but gradually as treatment progresses the level of anxiety will fall and eventually situations which were previously avoided can be approached without undue discomfort. Between therapist sessions homework exposure activities will be required to be carried out, with the patient setting aside at least two hours daily for homework and all activities should be recorded in a homework diary. A self-help manual such as *Living with Fear* (Marks 1978) which sets out guidelines for an exposure programme can be used by the patient. Each week targets are set, which are reviewed and altered as treatment progresses. Targets are specific pieces of behaviour which are currently absent from the individual's behavioural repertoire but would be of value to the individual and are frequently repeatable within the individual's daily life-style. An inherent part of behavioural treatment is the repeated measurement of levels of anxiety and avoidance. This will provide objective information about progress. Relatives can reduce therapist input by acting as co-therapists, accompanying the patient into phobic situations. They can also monitor the homework programme and provide praise for gains that are made.

Illness phobics, hypochondriacs and obsessive-compulsive patients seek reassurance repeatedly, usually from family members. It is counter-productive to reassure those who ritualistically seek reassurance. The illness phobic and hypochondriac will seek reassurance that they don't have a specific illness or are not ill. The provision of reassurance leads to a temporary reduction in anxiety but anxiety quickly returns. Similarly obsessional patients may seek reassurance that they have not harmed someone or become contaminated. Family members must be taught not to respond to requests for reassurance. The therapist may need to get them to rehearse an appropriate response to requests for reassurance, such as 'Hospital instructions are that I don't answer that question'. Illness phobics and hypochondriacs may seek reassurance behaviourally from their general practitioners by requesting frequent physical examinations and blood tests. In these circumstances the primary care physician needs to be accurately informed about the treatment process and requested not to provide any further reassurance in form of unnecessary investigations and examinations.

An aspect of obsessive-compulsive disorder which has proven resistant to behavioural interventions is the obsessional rumination. Techniques such as thought stopping and prolonged exposure have not proven very effective. More recently, case reports indicate that the technique of listening to an audio-tape of the ruminative thought and its unfavourable consequences can be effective (Headland and McDonald 1987). This is currently being evaluated further in a series of ruminators.

An exposure approach is helpful in some cases of morbid grief. In guided mourning it is assumed that avoidance of feelings and situations associated with a deceased loved one maintains the morbid grief. The subject is exposed to memories and situations, both in real-life and in imagination, which are associated with the deceased.

Appetitive behaviour

To achieve a reduction in appetitive behaviour any combination of techniques can be applied. Self-monitoring and self-regulation involve diary-keeping and the recording of both internal and external cues that induce the problematic behaviour. These aid the therapist and the patient to examine the particular problem and the circumstances in which it occurs. Substitution of a normal behaviour pattern is attempted by prescribing the normal behaviour at regular set intervals along with the use of stimulus-control measures. This approach is useful in obesity and bulimia. Confining eating to one room; eating food prepared and placed on a plate; limiting 'danger' foods; drawing up and adhering to a shopping list are examples of stimulus-control measures. In addition, alternative activities are encouraged as these can substitute for the problematic behaviour and thereby reduce the likelihood of its occurrence. These behavioural techniques are frequently used in conjunction with a cognitive approach during which the individual's attitudes and thoughts about the problematic behaviour are explored.

In the sexual deviations aversion therapy was originally used. This is the pairing of a noxious stimulus such as an electric shock or an emetic with the overt or imagined deviant act. A series of such pairings leads to reduction and eventual extinction of the problem. But despite the efficacy of aversion therapy it remained unpopular because of its unpleasantness. Today 'covert sensitization' devised by Cautela (1966) is the technique applied most regularly in the sexual deviations. Instead of physical aversions unpleasant mental images (appropriately chosen for each individual) are employed and are paired with the deviant behaviour. This is practised regularly. The next stage is to increase arousal to an individually chosen normal scene by pairing arousal by masturbation with a normal fantasy.

Other techniques which can be employed to reduce appetitive behaviours include response cost (engaging in the activity carries a negative consequence, e.g. contributing a fixed sum of money to one's most hated organization) and satiation (the repeated practising of the behaviour for hours until the individual becomes fed up with it).

Development of new behaviour
Social skills training is a step-wise training in how to show appropriate emotional expression in social circumstances by use of voice, eyes, posture, gesture and key phrases. It aims to teach new forms of social behaviour beginning with the simplest. Active components are goal setting, role-play, modelling rehearsal, problem-solving, feedback, graded real-life practice, homework, assignments and evaluation. It is often conducted in groups because of the opportunity they provide for modelling, peer feedback and real-life practice. It is usually considered important for all group members to have roughly similar levels of skills to avoid the danger of some being left behind. Social skills training groups are generally closed and time limited, usually comprising six to ten members which meet weekly for approximately ten or twelve sessions. Often training begins with simple behaviours, such as exchange greetings and maintaining eye contact and gradually moving on to more complex situations such as conversing with strangers. Between sessions, individuals are asked to record performance and feelings.

In sexual skills training, education, improving communication, regular graded practice allowing adequate time and privacy for sex and diary-keeping are used. Contingent reward may be particularly useful in children or mentally handicapped individuals, the basic principle being that positive consequences depend on the individual's engaging in the appropriate activity. Response cost and time-out may be helpful in reducing undesirable, discrete behaviours.

Depression With the advent of behavioural/cognitive models of depression, psychological interventions using behavioural/cognitive strategies have been developed and used either independently or as adjuncts to physical methods of treatment. One view advocated by Lewinsohn (1974) was that depressives did not engage or engaged less often in positively reinforcing activities, that is he viewed depression along the stimulus–response paradigm. In treatment the aim is to improve social skills and to reinstate reinforcing activities which have decreased. This involves identifying events which were enjoyed in the past and then setting goals of increased involvement in these activities. Seligman (1975) proposed that the depressed-prone individual has a lifelong history of failure in exercising control over reinforcers in the environment and is characterized by passivity, helplessness and inability to be assertive. In treatment various techniques such as self-control therapy, self-monitoring, self-evaluation, self-reinforcement, assertiveness training and pleasant event therapy can be used. While not formally addressing distorted cognitions, the behavioural approach utilizes some cognitive techniques including self-observation, self-monitoring and self-control. In this respect there is more overlap between the behavioural and cognitive approaches in the management of depression.

Beck's cognitive model not only emphasizes the depressed invididuals' feelings of helplessness and hopelessness but also focuses on cognitive distortions involving negative view of self, current circumstances and the future (Beck 1963). In cognitive therapy the aim is to identify these negative thoughts by getting the individual to keep a written record of moods and associated thoughts during everyday life. Then these negative thoughts are answered by examining the evidence for and against each belief, so the individual becomes aware of cognitive errors and thereby corrects them leading ultimately to altered cognitions. As well as these verbal tests, 'behavioural tasks' are assigned between sessions to aid 'learning from experience'.

In summary the majority of patients requiring behavioural treatment can be managed on an outpatient basis. A minority (approximately 5 per cent) require admission. Certain individuals may need admission to withdraw from alcohol or drugs, or because of distances involved. In these circumstances, a relative may also need to be admitted so that co-therapy can proceed following discharge.

The change process in therapy

To achieve habituation the individual must experience fear while attending to fear-relevant information. With continued contact with the fear-evoking stimulus a new 'non-fear structure' is formed leading to emotional change. Patients who improve with treatment first show physiological responses which correspond with their self-reports of anxiety. These two responses both change with continued contact with the feared object or situation. With repeated exposures the original fear response decreases. Habituation of autonomic responses with continued exposure may aid attitudinal change in the individual regarding the persistence of anxiety. In this way, behaviour therapy leads to modification of attitude. Overall three stages are observable in the modification of fear; the activation of anxiety, its diminution during sessions and its waning across sessions. These stages correspond with treatment outcome (Foa and Kozak 1985). The length of exposure required for habituation varies; the more intense the fear, the longer the duration of exposure is needed. Habituation occurs more quickly in simple phobics compared with agoraphobics and obsessive-compulsives (Foa and Kozak 1985). In appetitive disorders the individual's behaviour is controlled first in the therapeutic setting and with homework this generalizes to the individual's natural environment. A reduction in the unwanted behaviour is usually accompanied by an increase in alternative, more appropriate behaviours, i.e. there is a change in the probability of performing a particular response. This new behaviour is incorporated as the normal response pattern within the natural environment. In behavioural deficits, new behaviour is practised in a controlled setting following role-play. Observational learning may aid the acquisition of these new skills. The modelled behaviour is encoded imaginally which the individual draws on later to perform the appropriate response. With repeated practices the response is incorporated as part of the normal behavioural repertoire within the natural environment.

In summary, in the anxiety disorders change involves activation of fear and the formation of a new set of information to modify it; in behavioural deficits, new skills are observed and practised and then incorporated; in the behavioural excesses, appropriate behaviours replace inappropriate ones. In the long term modification in general beliefs and attitudes occurs leading to general changes in self-efficacy and improved coping abilities.

Limitations of the approach

Overall, behavioural psychotherapy is beneficial for approximately 25 per cent of all neurotic patients and for 10 per cent of adult psychiatric patients as the main therapeutic intervention (Marks 1982). One of the drawbacks of exposure is the discomfort the individual must endure to overcome the problem. Approximately 25 per cent of patients either refuse the offer of treatment or drop out soon after it has begun. For those who comply with the treatment programme the majority make substantial gains but few lose all traces of anxiety. Many experience a sufficient amelioration in anxiety or rituals in the presence of provoking stimuli, to allow them to lead a normal life-style. A minority of patients fail to respond despite compliance and these need to be studied further in the future. These non-responders are generally also resistant to other interventions such as anti-depressants. As noted earlier, behaviour therapy has focused on external cues, but hopefully with increasing attention to internal cues, the exposure principle can also be successfully applied to the other anxiety disorders which do not possess specific external triggering factors.

Case example

The client

Mrs B is a 27-year-old university graduate, married with no children, who presented complaining of anxiety, panics and avoidance of a range of situations. She felt anxious all the time and her anxiety peaked into panics several times daily. During a typical panic, she developed palpitations, breathlessness, sweating, tingling of her fingers, tremor, felt unreal and feared that she might lose control. A variety of cues triggered panics, including minor events such as the telephone or door-bell ringing. She generally avoided a large range of situations including supermarkets, shopping precincts, queues, crossing roads, all forms of public transport, long car journeys, motorways, restaurants and crowded places such as cinemas and theatres. Social anxiety was also problematic and interaction with others caused distress. She avoided speaking on the telephone, meeting new people, answering the front door, eating, speaking and writing in front of others. She rarely socialized and avoided visiting friends and members of her family. She was unable to leave her home unless she had taken alcohol. For many years she had used alcohol as an anxiolytic and gradually the quantity ingested increased to approximately one-quarter to one-third of a bottle of vodka daily, the precise daily quantity depending on the amount of time she had to spend outside her home. She had stopped working six months prior to presentation. In summary, the problems were a combination of agoraphobia, social phobia with generalized anxiety and panic attacks, complicated by heavy alcohol consumption. In the past she had always been shy and sensitive but had coped normally until her teens. She recalled her first panic as arising at the age of 15 years while in the school canteen. She had experienced some prodromal discomfort in the canteen for a few months previously. During that panic she had shaken uncontrollably and thereafter she avoided eating in public places. However, panics continued to arise intermittently in a variety of social and public places and over the years avoidance had gradually increased. The problem had become incapacitating over the eighteen months prior to presentation. She lived with her husband to whom she had not disclosed the full extent of her problem and had also managed to conceal the extent of her alcohol abuse. Their relationship was otherwise stable.

Treatment

When the patient was assessed she was timid, blushed easily and would not readily make eye contact. She was willing to undergo treatment once the exposure rationale had been explained to her. She agreed to reduce alcohol intake to a quantity not greater than one or two units daily and managed to stop completely for two weeks prior to commencing treatment. Her husband agreed to act as a co-therapist but due to the demands of work, he was generally able to accompany her only over weekends. At the outset the following goals were agreed upon: being able to use buses freely; socialize including eating in crowded restaurants; walk long distances from home along main roads; shop in crowded supermarkets; travel long distances from home along large open motorways.

Prior to treatment, these activities were not within her behavioural repertoire. We agreed that she would require at least eight weeks of exposure therapy. For the first two sessions I accompanied her on her outings. During the first two-hour session we walked along a series of busy streets for sixty minutes, crossing them several times, until she became reasonably comfortable in this setting. I encouraged her to take note of her surroundings, so that dissociation would not occur and thereby impede habituation. We next visited a large supermarket and again stayed there until she habituated to the surroundings. Homework instructions for the week included walking to her local shopping centre, entering her garden and with the aid of her husband to go on a bus journey. I requested her to spend at least two hours daily carrying out one or more of these tasks. She was advised to plan exactly at the outset which target she was going to achieve and to set aside enough time to reach the target. At the end of each session she recorded her achievements in diaries including the target activity, date and time spent and whether she was alone or accompanied, so that this could be reviewed at the next session.

By the second session, one week later, she had carried out thirteen hours of exposure homework. Panics had increased in frequency but she was coping. Overall she was pleased with her progress. In the second session we went on a long bus journey to central London which was followed by entry into large stores while I waited at a designated exit. Again she habituated gradually. New targets were set for the following week with the targets gradually becoming more difficult, that is progressing along the hierarchy of feared situations. Over the course of the following six weeks, she required only six one-hour sessions with me, my role being reduced to that of simply monitoring her progress, coaching and providing encouragement and praise. She habituated well to the specific cues which she exposed herself to. At the end of eight weeks of daily exposure (most of which was self-exposure), she no longer avoided the original goals. She socialized regularly and overall the quality of her life had improved substantially. She experienced some discomfort in certain situations but she was able to endure this. She stated that her husband had difficulty adjusting to the more assertive, outgoing person she had become. However, their relationship remained stable.

Three months post-treatment, gains had all been maintained and anxiety and panics had virtually disappeared. However, she felt it was still too early to resume work. At six months there had been some deterioration arising during a holiday abroad with her husband, when anxiety and panics recurred. On return from holiday, she felt anxious and tended to avoid socializing. She was instructed to resume exposure for these activities. She successfully did this and improved subsequently. At the last follow-up improvement had remained stable.

References

Bancroft, J. (1974) *Deviant Sexual Behaviour: Modification and Assessment*, Oxford: Clarendon Press.

Bandura, A. (1977) Self-efficacy toward a unifying theory of behavioral change, *Psychological Review* 84: 191–215.

Beck, A.T. (1963) Thinking and depression, *Archives of General Psychiatry* 9: 324–33.

Cautela, J.R. (1966) Treatment of compulsive behavior by covert sensitization, *Psychological Research* 16: 33–41.

De Silva, P., Rachman, S. and Seligman, M. (1976) Prepared phobias and obsessions, *Behaviour Research and Therapy* 15: 65–77.

Eysenck, H.J. and Rachman, S. (1965) *Causes and Cures of Neurosis*, London: Routledge & Kegan Paul.

Foa, E.B. and Kozak, M.J. (1985) Treatment of anxiety disorders: implications for psychopathology, in A.H. Tuma and J.D. Maser (eds) *Anxiety and the Anxiety Disorders*, London: Lawrence Erlbaum Associates.

Freud, S. (1919) Turnings in the ways of psychoanalytic therapy, in *Collected Papers, Vol. 2*, London: Hogarth Press & Institute of Psychoanalysis.

Gelder, M.G. (1986) Psychological treatment for anxiety disorders: a review, *Journal of the Royal Society of Medicine* 79: 230–3.

Gibson, E.J. and Walk, R.D. (1960) The 'visual cliff', *Scientific American* 202: 64–71.

Goldstein, A.J. and Chambless, D.L. (1978) A reanalysis of agoraphobia, *Behavior Therapy* 9: 47–59.

Hand, I. (1988) Long-term follow-up in behaviour therapy. Paper given at the World Congress on Behaviour Therapy, Edinburgh, 8 September.

Headland, K. and McDonald, B. (1987) Rapid audio-tape treatment of obsessional ruminations: a case report, *Behavioural Psychotherapy* 15: 188–92.

Janet, P. (1925) *Psychological Healing*, New York: Macmillan.

Klein, D.F. (1967) Importance of psychiatric diagnosis in prediction of clinical effects, *Archives of General Psychiatry*, 16: 118–26.

Lazarus, A.A. (1971) *Behavior Therapy and Beyond*, New York: McGraw-Hill.

Lelliott, P., Marks, I.M. and McNamee, G. (1989) The onset of panic and agoraphobia, *Archives of General Psychiatry* 46: 1000–4.

Lewinsohn, P.M. (1974) A behavioral approach to depression, in R.M. Friedman and M.M. Katz (eds) *Psychology of Depression: Contemporary Theory and Research*, New York: Wiley.

Locke, J. (1693) *Some Thoughts Concerning Education*, London: Ward Lock.

Marks, I.M. (1978) *Living with Fear*, New York: McGraw-Hill.

—— (1982) *Cure and Care of Neuroses: Theory and Practice of Behavioural Psychotherapy*, New York: Wiley.

—— (1987) *Fear, Phobias and Rituals*, New York: Oxford University Press.

Marks, I.M. and O'Sullivan, G. (1988) Drugs and psychological treatments for agoraphobia/panic and obsessive compulsive disorders: a review, *British Journal of Psychiatry* 15: 650–8.

Mowrer, O.H. (1950) *Learning Theory and Personality Dynamics*, New York: Arnold.

Pavlov, I.P. (1927) *Conditioned Reflexes*, London: Oxford University Press.

Pitts, C.E. (1976) Behavior modification, *Journal of Applied Behavior Analysis* 9: 146.

Seligman, M.E.P. (1975) *Helplessness*, San Francisco, Calif: Freeman.

Stern, R.S. and Marks, I.M. (1973) Brief and prolonged flooding: a comparison in agoraphobic patients, *Archives of General Psychiatry* 28: 270–6.

Thorndike, E.L. (1911) *Animal Intelligence*, New York: Macmillan.

Watson, J.B. and Rayner, R. (1920) Conditioned emotional reactions, *Journal of Experimental Psychology* 3: 1–14.

Wolpe, J. (1958) *Psychotherapy by Reciprocal Inhibition*, Stanford, Calif: Stanford University press.

Suggested further reading

Agras, W.S. (1978) *Behavior Modification: Principles and Clinical Applications*, Boston, Mass: Little, Brown.

Curran, J.P. and Monti, P.M. (eds) (1982) *Social Skills Training: A Practical Handbook for Assessment and Treatment*, New York: Guilford.

Kazdin, A.E. (1978) *History of Behavior Modification: Experimental Foundations of Contemporary Research*, Baltimore, Md: University Park Press.

Marks, I.M. (1982) *Cure and Care of Neuroses: Theory and Practice of Behavioural Psychotherapy*, New York: Wiley.

Rehm, L.P. (ed.) (1981) *Behavior Therapy for Depression: Present Status and Future Directions*, New York: Academic Press.

13

Approaches to individual therapy:
some comparative reflections

WINDY DRYDEN

To attempt a thorough-going comparative analysis of eleven different approaches to psychotherapy may well be an impossible task. Anyone foolhardy enough to undertake such an exercise would require at least a book to do justice to the enterprise. Even then the person would run the risk of attracting the criticism that he or she had not adequately represented the approaches to therapy under consideration. For it is probably true that different therapists of a particular approach have differing views on that approach.

However, if I were not to attempt some comparative reflections on the eleven approaches, I would consider that I would be shirking my editorial responsibility as well as disappointing many readers who are themselves interested in the similarities and differences among therapeutic approaches and expect to find some comparative remarks in a book of this nature.

The therapeutic alliance as a framework for comparison

After much deliberation, I decided to employ a reformulation of the therapeutic alliance concept as a framework for comparing the eleven different approaches to individual therapy covered in this book. This reformulation was first put forward by Ed Bordin (1979) who argued that the therapeutic alliance comprises three components: bonds, goals and tasks. I want to stress at the outset that this is only one possible comparative framework and readers may well wish to employ others in conducting their own comparative analysis.

My reflections throughout this chapter are based on interviews that I conducted with the authors of chapters 2–12. While I have attempted to stick closely to the words they used during these interviews I take full responsibility for the accuracy of the views expressed in this chapter.

Bonds

The therapeutic bond – or the interpersonal relationship between therapist and client – has several different factors. Three such factors emerged from my interviews with the eleven authors.

The first factor relates to the degree of *interpersonal equality* between therapist and client. Several authors referred to terms such as mutuality (Brian Thorne – person-centred therapy); phenomenological equality (Malcolm Parlett – Gestalt therapy), an Adult–adult contract (Petrūska Clarkson – Transactional Analysis); a collaborative relationship (Stirling Moorey – cognitive therapy); a dialogue between equals (Richard Carvalho – Jungian therapy) and equality (Jenny Clifford – Adlerian therapy) to express the idea that therapist and client are on an equal footing in the therapeutic relationship.

Other authors, while recognizing that therapist and client are equal as human beings, did stress that they are also unequal in certain ways, especially with respect to differences in expertise, skills and knowledge. These differences were often expressed by the authors in terms of reciprocal role relationships between therapist and client. Emmy van Deurzen-Smith (existential therapy), for example, remarked that the relationship between therapist and client approximated to that between tutor and pupil where the two are equal in humanness but where the therapist (tutor) has greater expertise in the philosophy of living than the client (pupil). Fay Fransella considered the therapist–client relationship in personal construct therapy to be similar to that between a Ph.D supervisor and her Ph.D. student. The supervisor knows more about the pitfalls of research than the student, who, in turn, knows more about the subject matter of his research than the supervisor. Similarly, in personal construct therapy the client knows more about the subject in question, namely himself, whereas the therapist knows more about psychological change and its pitfalls than the client. The client does the work of change while the therapist acts as a kind of guide, encouraging the client to develop alternative ways of looking at questions and issues.

Stirling Moorey also evoked the teacher–pupil model (albeit a collaborative one) in describing the therapeutic relationship in cognitive therapy, but in different terms from Emmy van Deurzen-Smith. In cognitive therapy the emphasis is more on the *technical* expertise of the therapist–teacher, whereas in existential therapy the greater expertise of the therapist with respect to the client reflects a greater wisdom, a greater expertise in the philosophy of living. The technical expertise of the therapist was also alluded to by Geraldine O'Sullivan (behaviour therapy), who viewed the behaviour therapist as a coach (with greater expertise in the psychology of behaviour change) with the client as someone who actively practises outside therapy sessions what he learns from the therapist-coach inside therapy.

Interestingly, neither David Smith (representing Freudian therapy) nor Cassie Cooper (representing Kleinian therapy) alluded to the concept of therapist–client equality or inequality in their descriptions of the therapeutic relationship. What they did emphasize however, could be placed under the heading of the second bond factor-degree of *interpersonal closeness* between therapist and client.

David Smith emphasized that in the Freudian approach, the therapist adopts a neutral stance and operates according to the rules of anonymity (where the therapist gives the client minimal cues about herself and observes what sense the client makes of this) and abstinence (where the therapist refuses to gratify the client in an everyday social sense). The Freudian therapist is thus a participant observer and in order to make use of this the client needs to be able to tolerate this situation which by ordinary standards is very frustrating. Cassie Cooper also emphasized that Kleinian therapists operated according to the rules of abstinence and anonymity but claimed that Kleinians were less neutral and more confrontative than their Freudian counterparts.

In stark contrast to the neutral participant observer stance of Freudian and Kleinian therapists are person-centred therapists who strive to be genuine or congruent in the therapeutic encounter and who would regard the detached stance of these other therapists as anti-therapeutic. Person-centred therapists strive to develop and maintain a real I–Thou therapeutic relationship with their clients who need to be willing to develop trust in their therapists and in the therapeutic process in order to benefit from this approach.

Close to Freudian and Kleinian therapists on the interpersonal closeness factor would be Jungian therapists, who also strive to be participant observers, adhere to the rule of abstinence and do not engage in self-disclosure. To the extent that Jungian therapists 'use their self' in the therapeutic relationship, albeit in a restrained, non-pretending way, they would seem to be less anonymous than Freudians and Kleinians. They also feel freer to intervene in the therapeutic process than do these latter therapists.

Also closer to Freudian and Kleinian therapists than to person-centred therapists on this factor are existential therapists who, while varying their degree of warmth according to the needs of different clients, engage little in self-disclosure and disclose little of their feelings about their clients to the clients.

Quite a few of the other approaches (personal construct therapy, Adlerian therapy, Gestalt therapy, Transactional Analysis (TA), cognitive therapy and behaviour therapy) recognize the importance of establishing a therapeutic relationship based on the core conditions of empathy, genuineness and respect (or some variant of these) emphasized by person-centred therapists. Where they would differ from the latter would be in the latter's assertion that such conditions are necessary and sufficient for therapeutic change. Rather the position of these aforementioned therapists is that such conditions are often important but rarely necessary or sufficient for client change. Particularly in behaviour therapy and to some degree in cognitive therapy, the core conditions provide the base from which clients are enabled to implement powerful cognitive and behaviour change methods.

The third bond factor and one emphasized in particular by Petrūska Clarkson (TA) and Malcolm Parlett (Gestalt therapy) concerns *interpersonal flexibility* where the therapist varies her interpersonal style according to the therapeutic needs of the client. Indeed, Clarkson stated that TA theory allows for about sixty-eight such variations! Gestalt therapists often vary their interpersonal style in order to, in Parlett's words, 'interrupt the client's interruptions of being in contact with self and others'.

While it is possible or even probable that therapists from other approaches also vary their interpersonal style according to the dictates of the therapeutic situation, this did not feature in their representatives' descriptions of salient features of the therapeutic bond.

General issues

According to Bordin (1979), effective therapy is more likely to occur when therapist and client form a productive working bond. While we are far from understanding those factors which constitute a well-matched therapeutic pairing, one salient variable is likely to be client expectations and the extent to which therapists meet or modify these. Thus a client who anticipates and hopes to find a therapist who will be interactive and a real presence in the relationship will be more likely to work productively with a person-centred therapist than with a Freudian therapist. Thus, it is important to remember that no matter what kind of therapeutic bond therapists from particular approaches seek to establish with their clients, successful therapy may well depend, in part, on the extent to which these clients can make productive use of the bond offered.

Goals

Psychotherapy is a purposeful activity with a direction – broadly to relieve clients' psychological distress and/or to promote healthy client functioning (Mahrer 1967). The eleven approaches to therapy described in this book differ concerning the stance that they take on client goal setting.

The three psychodynamic approaches to therapy herein represented are unstructured, open-ended and do not emphasize the explicit setting of goals. For example, David Smith argued that in Freudian therapy, clients are neither encouraged nor discouraged from setting goals. While they may note their clients' goals, Freudian therapists, however, do not do anything different whether or not clients explicitly set their own goals.

On the other hand, Adlerian, TA, cognitive and behaviour therapists do adopt a more explicit goal-oriented stance. Adlerians encourage their clients to set short-term (specific) and long-term (more general) goals. In TA there is a contractual approach to goal setting. Petrūska Clarkson noted that TA therapists distinguish between contracts for behavioural change and contracts for script cure (see Chapter 10). In behaviour change contracts, goals are simple to understand, specific and observable by self and others and the emphasis is on what the client will do. In script cure contracts, goals are more vague (even metaphysical) and are based on the concept of autonomy. Here the client is helped to 'get a new show on the road'. The link between the two is that behavioural goals are stage posts on the path to script cure.

In both cognitive therapy and behaviour therapy, goals are set by both therapist and client and are specific, overt and measurable. In behaviour therapy the goals are usually behavioural, while in cognitive therapy, the goals can be affective, behavioural or cognitive depending on the nature of the problem.

By contrast, in existential therapy, when goals are set the emphasis is on broad life goals (e.g. 'to be a wiser person') that are vague rather than specific. If a client does have a specific goal, the existential therapist would attempt to broaden the discussion in order to shed a different and wider perspective on the problem.

Later, if the client still wishes to retain a specific goal-oriented focus he or she would be referred to a therapist from a different school who would be prepared to work with the client in this specific manner.

The other three approaches to therapy so far not mentioned in this section are less easy to group, either with those approaches already discussed or with each other. However, there is a similarity between Gestalt therapy and personal construct therapy in that both display scepticism towards clients' stated goals. Gestalt therapists are concerned not to accept uncritically clients' stated goals because these goals are seen as representing only one part of the person. These therapists assume that when clients state goals, they also have a part of themselves that wants the opposite. Thus Gestalt therapists do not see themselves as change agents with respect to helping clients to achieve goals but rather they see their task is to help clients increase awareness of both the 'want to change' part and the 'stay as I am' part of themselves. Gestalt therapists' primary task, then, is to help their clients to integrate all the different parts of themselves and thus to integrate their different goals.

Fay Fransella, speaking for personal construct therapy, noted that clients often set goals (e.g. 'I have a problem and I want to get rid of it'). However, personal construct therapists know that such goals are unlikely to be attained in the way they are phrased (i.e. the disappearance of the symptoms). It is this scepticism (often unexpressed at the outset of therapy) that is reminiscent of Gestalt therapy. However, rather than attempt to help clients to achieve greater awareness and integrate different parts of themselves as in Gestalt therapy, personal construct therapists consider that their goal is to help their clients to get 'unstuck' and psychologically get moving again rather than to achieve something specific. '*Movement*' is deemed to be more important than *achievement* in personal construct therapy. Therapists from this approach also believe that more meaningful client goals are likely to emerge using the therapeutic process than those expressed at its outset. When specific goals are set and pursued in personal construct therapy, this is done according to client need but again such goals are set to promote psychological movement rather than goal achievement.

Brian Thorne argued that goals always feature in person-centred therapy but are not necessarily overtly expressed. More specifically, the person-centred stance on goals is that goals are set according to client need. Goals, when set, can be specific or general but almost always emerge from the client's frame of reference and rarely, if ever, emanate entirely from the therapist. Because person-centred therapists strive to be genuine in the therapeutic relationship, they would challenge their clients' stated goals if they experienced ongoing concern that these goals were potentially harmful to the personal development of these clients. Person-centred therapists also stress that clients' goals often change during the therapeutic process. As such, much of their activity in the goal domain of the alliance involves clarifying clients' half-expressed goals so that they can be explored more fully.

General issues

Bordin (1979) noted that effective therapy in the goal domain of the alliance is most likely to occur when client and therapist agree to pursue the client's goals and when these goals enhance the client's personal development. Effective therapy can occur when therapist and client implicitly agree to pursue the client's vaguely stated goals as well as when they explicitly agree to pursue the client's specifically stated goals. Problems in the alliance occur, for example, when the therapist wishes to be explicit and specific about the client's goals, but when the latter is not ready for that degree of explicitness and specificity (e.g. a behaviour therapist working with a client who would be more suited to one of the psychodynamic approaches). Conversely, as noted by Emmy van Deurzen-Smith, therapy would stall when the client wishes to work towards specific goals and when the therapist prefers to work towards broad band goals.

Tasks

Tasks are therapeutic activities undertaken by both therapist and client which are designed to help the client to achieve his or her goals, however broadly or specifically these are defined. These activities may be viewed as occurring both within therapy sessions or outside these sessions (e.g. 'homework' assignments). In considering the eleven approaches detailed in this book, tasks can be seen to serve three main aims: to facilitate *awareness*, *understanding* and *behaviour change*. While it may be said that, to some degree, all eleven approaches seek to facilitate each aim, they differ both in the emphasis they place on each aim and certainly in terms of how they pursue the aim(s) emphasized.

Gestalt therapy is the approach that places most emphasis on therapist and client tasks which are designed to help both stay with present awareness. Clients are encouraged to attend to 'here and now' thoughts, feelings, bodily sensations, fantasies, images, gestures and actions. Therapists encourage their clients to communicate what is happening with them on a moment-to-moment basis and, in addition, attempt to set up experiments to explore clients' reality in the present as they experience what is *not* here and *not* present. Malcolm Parlett acknowledges that there is less emphasis on specific tasks in Gestalt therapy these days, although tasks such as two-chair dialogues are still employed.

Person-centred therapists also strive to encourage awareness in their clients although the language they employ is different. They encourage their clients to experience, explore and listen to themselves in the context of a facilitative relationship. Here, person-centred therapists' major task is to create the kind of relationship in which clients can listen to themselves. As such, in the terminology of therapeutic alliance theory the major therapeutic *task* in this approach is the establishment and maintenance of a facilitative *bond*.

TA therapists also strive to facilitate client awareness particularly at those times when clients are operating according to script and when they are in particular ego states (see Chapter 10). However, TA therapists also seek to facilitate understanding and behaviour change and utilize many therapeutic tasks in the service of these three aims.

The majority of the therapeutic approaches in this book seek to facilitate client understanding but employ different tasks in operationalizing this aim. The psychodynamic approaches of Freud and Klein, for example, make use of clarification, confrontation and interpretation in helping clients to understand their unconscious distortions that are expressed in the transference relationship with their therapists. In order for this to occur, clients are called upon to play their part. They are to turn up reliably to sessions, engage in the tasks of free association (Freudian therapy) or reminiscence (Kleinian therapy) and also to share the fantasies they have of their therapists. Kleinians are perhaps more confrontative and interpretative than Freudians (and according to Cassie Cooper more active and more lively!), whereas the latter pay strict attention to the maintenance of the therapeutic environment so that the analytic process can work. Here meticulous attention is paid to ensuring privacy, confidentiality and reliability where sessions occur at a fixed time in a fixed place and for a fixed duration.

Jungian therapists also use clarification and interpretation in the service of facilitating client understanding as well as drawing attention to what the client is saying (including making appropriate links). However, free association is not as actively encouraged by Jungians as it is by other psychodynamic therapists. Jungians pay much attention to exploring the imagery that clients bring in as this is expressed in dreams or fantasies. This is done in order to discern the archetypal material which needs to be understood and which points to the resolution of neurosis.

Adlerian therapists adopt more of an active-directive therapeutic style than psychodynamic therapists in helping clients to reveal and challenge their mistaken ideas and mistaken goals, that prevent them from living effectively. They also encourage their clients to carry out behavioural assignments which are designed to challenge and revise these mistaken ideas and goals. There is less emphasis than in the psychodynamic approaches on helping clients reveal and understand unconscious material. In all these respects Adlerian therapists are most similar to cognitive therapists who talk of negative automatic thoughts and maladaptive assumptions rather than mistaken goals and ideas. Nevertheless, both approaches encourage their clients to monitor, challenge and change self-defeating thought patterns through the use of cognitive and behavioural techniques.

Similar to Adlerian and cognitive therapists are personal construct therapists, whose major task is to help their clients to reconstrue. This involves therapists in: first, eliciting and subsuming clients' construct system (here techniques specific to personal construct therapy are used, e.g. repertory grids, laddering and pyramiding – see Chapter 7); second, helping clients to find alternative ways of looking at the problem or issue; and third, encouraging clients to experiment with these alternatives outside therapy in order to find out what may be acceptable to clients and what may help them to become 'unstuck' and move forward. In addition, the therapist acts to identify pitfalls in the reconstruing process preferably in advance of the client.

Although the concepts used by Adlerian, cognitive and personal construct therapists may be seen as different by advocates of these approaches, at a broader level there are similarities among these approaches. They all attempt to encourage clients to change the way they view themselves, other people and the world and to encourage clients to act differently in the world in order to change existing meaning systems and to test out the utility of alternative systems.

In existential therapy there is less focus on challenging assumptions or on carrying out experiments to test out new ways of construing. Rather the therapist strives to clarify with the client hidden possibilities within their experience and to help him to develop these possibilities. In doing so the existential therapist helps her client to develop his own framework rather than use the theoretical framework of the therapy itself. Although the value of between session work is implied in existential therapy it is not an ongoing explicit part of the approach.

This brings us to the final aim, that of explicitly facilitating behaviour change. Obviously behaviour therapy emphasizes this aim. The behaviour therapist carries out a rigorous behavioural analysis of the client's problems, helps the client to set goals and to monitor salient and observable features of the problems. Then the therapist (or coach) models and teaches appropriate skills and encourages the client to practise these between sessions and gives praise when gains are made. The client's major task is to comply with the therapist's instructions and to carry out homework assignments.

I have already noted that personal construct therapy, Adlerian therapy and cognitive therapy all emphasize the execution of explicit tasks or experiments between sessions. However, while in these three approaches behaviour change is intended to facilitate change in clients' construing, mistaken ideas and maladaptive assumptions respectively, behaviour therapy emphasizes behaviour change as a *direct* way of helping clients to rid themselves of disabling symptoms and does not suggest that change in behaviour mediates any other kind of change.

TA does emphasize the facilitation of behaviour change but not over and above the facilitation of awareness and understanding. As noted earlier, TA sees behaviour change as stage posts to script cure and thus, in this respect, it is quite similar to Adlerian therapy, personal construct therapy and cognitive therapy.

All the other approaches not so far mentioned in this section do not ignore behaviour change but do not attempt to facilitate it explicitly although person-centred therapists will do so if the suggestion comes from the client.

General issues

I have argued elsewhere (Dryden 1989) that effective therapy in the task domain is most likely to occur under the following conditions:

1 When clients understand the nature of the therapeutic tasks that they are called upon to execute.
2 When clients see the instrumental value of carrying out their tasks, that is when they can see that executing those tasks will help them to achieve their goals.
3 When clients have the ability and the confidence to carry out the therapeutic tasks required of them.
4 When clients understand the nature of the therapist's tasks and see how these relate to their own tasks and how they are relevant to their goals.
5 When the therapist has the necessary skill in carrying out her tasks.
6 When the tasks of both therapist and client have sufficient therapeutic potency to facilitate goal achievement.

While there are, no doubt, a number of other ways of comparing the approaches described in this book, I hope that the framework used here has provided readers with some food for thought and will stimulate further discussion and comparison.

References

Bordin, E.S. (1979) The generalizability of the psychoanalytic concept of the working alliance, *Psychotherapy: Theory, Research and Practice* 16, 3: 252–60.

Dryden, W. (1989) The therapeutic alliance as an integrating framework, in W. Dryden (ed.) *Key Issues for Counselling in Action*, London: Sage.

Mahrer, A.R. (Ed.) (1967) *The Goals of Psychotherapy*, New York: Appleton-Century-Crofts.

14

Research in individual therapy

MICHAEL BARKHAM

Introduction

The preceding chapters have documented a wide range of approaches to the practice of individual psychotherapy currently being implemented in Britain. While interest in the practice of psychotherapy has never been greater, there exists a considerable gap between psychotherapy practice and research. This gap is long-standing and has repeatedly been documented in the psychotherapy literature (Barlow *et al.* 1984). Frustration about the existence of this gap arises because ultimately the role of psychotherapy research is to inform practice. In reality, however, it has tended to be the opposite, with clinical insights and experiences guiding research. This situation is largely attributable to researchers and clinicians having different priorities. Researchers employ large-scale studies and focus on differences between group means, with the assumption of the 'average' client. In contrast, practitioners work with individual and specific clients. Often, it is difficult for practitioners to see the relevance of research findings to the clients they see. This concern of making psychotherapy research more relevant to the practitioner will become apparent throughout this chapter.

Initially, research can make evaluative statements as to the effectiveness, or not, of particular procedures: this has traditionally been termed 'outcome' research. Additionally, and perhaps more interestingly, research can attempt to explain why improvement or deterioration occurs: this has traditionally been termed 'process' research. The knowledge that a particular therapy is effective (outcome) together with knowing what makes it effective (process) can then inform practitioners, thereby enhancing the delivery of the psychotherapeutic mode. Against this background, the purpose of this chapter is twofold. First, to provide an overview of current research findings in individual psychotherapy which are relevant to everyday therapeutic practice, and second, to provide an overview of individual psychotherapy research in Britain.

The art of psychotherapy research

At the outset, it is important to understand that, much like psychotherapeutic practice itself, research varies considerably in quality. In the same way that practitioners aim to learn and integrate into their practice those ingredients which enhance the effectiveness of psychotherapy, so researchers seek to adopt those methods and procedures which lead to good research. This parallel between practice and research is being made, initially, so the reader can appreciate similarities between being a 'practitioner' (i.e. a therapist) and a 'scientist' (i.e. a researcher). The two are not mutually exclusive and the reader is encouraged to view these two aspects as *integral* components to any therapeutic endeavour. This integration is one means of achieving a closer approximation to the ideal of the scientist-practitioner (Barlow *et al.* 1984).

Accordingly, while this chapter provides the interested reader with a review of current findings of psychotherapy research, an equally important aim is to present the reader with a 'feel' for the activity of psychotherapy research. Therefore, this chapter places a central focus on the *method* of psychotherapy research as much as on the *outcome*. The skill of the psychotherapy researcher is reflected in the design and method employed: it is not the outcome *per se* which is important.

Psychotherapy: a framework for theory, research and practice

In attempting to provide an overview of psychotherapy research which has value to the interested reader, it is necessary to present it within a structure, or plan, which has an immediate relevance to the practical setting. To achieve this aim, the structure adopted in this chapter is derived from a model of psychotherapy which has been advocated by Orlinsky and Howard (1987). These authors proposed three sequential phases (input, process and outcome) which encompass all relevant aspects of psychotherapeutic practice across major schools of therapy. Briefly, the *input* phase incorporates those components which exist prior to, or are brought to, the session (e.g. client and therapist characteristics). The *process* phase, which is probably the most important for practitioners, comprises those aspects which take place during the session (e.g. the interventions made by the therapist, the development of the relationship between client and therapist, and the therapeutic realizations made by the client). The *output* phase, or outcome, comprises the changes resulting from therapy which occur over a period of time (e.g. immediately, medium term and long term).

Although these three phases presented in this order reflect the progress of each client through therapy from 'beginning' to 'end', it is probably more helpful to address these three phases in reverse order. Accordingly, the first section will address *outcome* findings, while the second section will focus on *linking outcome and process*; the third section will address *process* findings, and the fourth section will summarize various *precursors* to psychotherapy.

The outcomes of individual psychotherapy

This section addresses a series of questions concerning the general effectiveness of psychotherapy. For example, 'Is it effective?', 'Do the effects last?', 'Are some therapies better than others?', 'Are some therapists better than others?', 'Are some problems better treated with certain therapies?', 'How much psychotherapy do people need?', and 'Is individual psychotherapy cost-effective?' This section presents current research findings drawn from the international literature appropriate to these questions.

Is individual psychotherapy effective?

The general effectiveness of psychotherapy has been summarized as follows: 'There is now little doubt . . . that psychological treatments are, overall and in general, beneficial, although it remains equally true that not everyone benefits to a satisfactory degree' (Lambert *et al.* 1986: 158). This statement has been arrived at on the basis of research studies focusing on three types of groups, each of which will be reviewed briefly.

The first form of comparison is achieved by randomly allocating clients either to a treatment or a *'no-treatment control'* group. In the latter condition, by definition, no formal therapy is provided. The purpose of assigning clients to a no-treatment condition, often referred to as a control group, is to evaluate the effect of clients' improvement over time without the aid of formal therapy. Improvement occurring under these conditions is termed 'spontaneous remission'. In effect, it is the improvement which would occur regardless of therapy and it is obviously important when evaluting specific therapies to know how much improvement is occurring due to spontaneous remission. Critics of the effectiveness of psychotherapy, most notably Eysenck (1952) and Rachman (Rachman and Wilson 1980), argued that two-thirds of neurotic clients improved in a two-year period irrespective of receiving therapy. However, there are considerable shortcomings in the data used to derive this estimate, and more recent and considered work based upon thirteen studies found the median percentage of clients showing spontaneous improvement to be 43 per cent (Lambert 1976). Generally, it has been found that after therapy the average treated client is better than 80 to 85 per cent of untreated (i.e. control) clients (Shapiro and Shapiro 1982: Smith *et al.* 1980).

The second form of comparison involves assigning clients randomly either to a treatment or to a *placebo* group in which, although no formal therapy has been offered, clients have received the components associated with the knowledge that they are in treatment (i.e. attention, hope, etc.) together with some treatment rationale. Findings attest to the superiority of treatment over placebo groups (Smith *et al.* 1980). However, the use of placebo controls is problematic in psychotherapy research as, unlike drug trials, it is often difficult to provide a feasible placebo rationale (i.e. which incorporates the components of therapy which the researcher wishes to control for) which is also acceptable to the client (i.e. the client is not disappointed in some way with the placebo treatment). Studies comparing the results of improvement rates for clients used in no-treatment and placebo control groups have established the superiority of placebo over no-treatment groups. It has been estimated that the average client in a placebo group will be better than 70 per cent of no-treatment clients after completion (Smith *et al.* 1980). Lambert (1986) has estimated from the literature that approximately 15 per cent of improvement in clients is attributable to placebo (i.e. expectancy) effects.

The third comparison which has been made involves randomly allocating clients to one of two psychological therapies. This is termed a *comparative* outcome study in which researchers focus on the difference between two or more therapies. Rather than asking whether therapy is effective or not, these studies seek to identify the effect of specific treatment techniques. Interestingly, the comparative outcome design makes the use of a placebo control unnecessary as each group is receiving the 'common factors' incorporated within each therapy. Accordingly, they effectively cancel each other out although the contribution of these factors to each therapy would be closely evaluated. The results of comparative studies of psychotherapy are addressed in a later section. Lambert (1986) has estimated that approximately 30 per cent of improvement is accounted for by 'common factors' (e.g. empathy, warmth, acceptance, encouragement, etc.) and 15 per cent by specific treatment techniques (e.g. systematic desensitization biofeedback). The above comparisons, therefore, provide overwhelming evidence of a differential effectiveness favouring treatment over placebo, and placebo over no-treatment controls.

The results presented above derive from findings using a procedure termed *meta-analysis* (Smith and Glass 1977: Smith *et al.* 1980). As its name implies, it involves analysing data of already published studies at a more superordinate level. For example, Smith and Glass (1977) used data from 375 controlled outcome studies in their comparison of different therapies. Meta-analytic procedures have enabled statements to be made about the size of treatment effects (known as an 'effect size'). Hence, rather than simply saying that one treatment is better than another, we are now able to say *how* much better it is. Briefly, an effect size is the mean difference between the pre- and post-outcome scores divided by the standard deviation of the control group. Accordingly, the effect size is a standardized way of expressing how much improvement, in standard deviation units, has been made by the treatment group relative to the control group. The use of these procedures has enabled researchers to progress from asking the question 'Is psychotherapy effective?' to addressing the question of the size of treatment effects for differing psychotherapies.

Do the effects of therapy last?

Whatever percentage of clients show improvement immediately after treatment, a more socially meaningful evaluation of outcome can be ascertained by improvement rates at some time after therapy has finished, anytime from one month to five years or more. This form of evaluation is known as a 'follow-up' assessment. Nicholson and Berman concluded that 'despite considerable theoretical discussion to the contrary, gains achieved during therapy appear to be maintained over time' (1983: 273). Thus, outcome at post-treatment is highly correlated with outcome at follow-up. This finding obtains irrespective of the length of the follow-up interval, and also applies to differences between treatments. Obviously, caution should be taken due to the possibility of alternative explanations. Some competing explanations might be that clients received further therapy from other agencies, or were influenced by informal social networks. Consideration also needs to be given to the nature of the dysfunction as, in the case of depression for example, improvements over a longer time period can be due to the cyclical nature of the disorder.

Are some therapies more effective than others?

Research has consistently found a rather surprising answer to this question which has considerable bearing upon the practices described in the previous chapters. Despite the extensive diversity of content in differing therapies (e.g. DeRubeis *et al.* 1982), there is a general equivalence of outcome (Smith *et al.* 1980). While some outcome differences *do* occur, they are slight when considered against the widely divergent techniques employed. The NIMH Collaborative Study of Depression (Elkin *et al.* 1985) in which four treatments were compared (imipramine plus clinical management, cognitive therapy, interpersonal therapy, and a placebo plus clinical management) found no evidence at the group level of greater effectiveness for one treatment compared with others. However, when each active treatment was compared alone with the placebo, the placebo was found to be least effective. Results also showed a different *course* of improvement in response to the different treatments so that the imipramine group showed superior improvement after eight weeks compared with the other treatments but this was equivalent at sixteen weeks. In addition, the most severely depressed clients responded better with the imipramine treatment (Elkin *et al.*, in press).

The results of meta-analytic studies suggest a slight advantage for cognitive and behavioural methods over verbal psychotherapies. However, these findings can be challenged on various methodological grounds. In particular, issues of sampling (e.g. employing student rather than clinical samples) and extrinsic validity (e.g. using cases, such as a spider or snake phobia, which are unrepresentative of clinical cases usually seen for psychotherapy). Indeed, when student samples are excluded, the advantages to cognitive and behavioural therapies disappear. Lambert *et al.* (1986) argue that there are reasons 'to believe in both the theory of equal effects of therapies and the notion of superior effects of cognitive and behaviour therapies' (1986: 166). Another possible weakness in the methodology stems from strategies used to measure therapy outcome. For example, the advantage to behavioural techniques may be a function of using more 'reactive' measures. In effect, this concerns the potential for self-report measures by clients or therapists, or interviewers who are not blind to the treatment, unintentionally biasing the results. In a sense, the report of outcome is being 'mediated' by a person's perceptions and this must have an effect on the result. This effect contrasts with the use of, for example, more physiological outcome data. Ideally, at least one non-reactive measure should be used, together with general and theoretically specific measures. For example, dynamically oriented therapies may be more appropriately assessed by measures tapping gains in insight and interpersonal relationships. Therefore, therapy-specific outcome measures could add a richness and clarity to the debate about the equivalence of divergent therapeutic techniques.

Are some therapists more effective than others?

Surprisingly, comparatively little work has been carried out on therapist effectiveness. Lambert *et al.* (1986) concluded that 'It is possible that outcome statistics in general are deflated by the use of practitioners who are conducting only a mere semblance of psychotherapy' (1986: 179). In general, little attention has been paid to therapist effects, largely because of the sensitive nature of this issue. It is a personally challenging task for therapists to evaluate their own performance and address the hypothesis that poorer client outcomes may be associated with less effective therapists. Lafferty *et al.* (1989) found less effective trainee psychotherapists to display lower levels of empathic understanding, to rate their clients as more involved in therapy, and to rate themselves as more supportive than the more effective therapists. It is very likely that when therapist effects *are* systematically studied, they will show larger differences than those obtained between competing therapies.

Are certain problems more appropriately addressed in specific therapies?

Consistent with the increasing emphasis on specificity rather than uniformity within psychotherapy research, it is appropriate to ask whether there is any evidence that particular problems can be best addressed by particular modes of therapy. Shapiro (1985), drawing on findings from two large meta-analytic studies (Smith *et al.* 1980; Shapiro and Shapiro 1982) considered the effects of three therapeutic schools (behavioural, cognitive, and dynamic/humanistic) on clients with neurotic, phobic, and emotional/somatic diagnoses. He concluded that no clear pattern emerged except for the inferiority of dynamic/humanistic approaches. However, such findings are at a relatively gross level and research remains to be done in this area. More specifically, Miller and Berman (1983) compared findings from studies in which depression, anxiety, and somatic disorders were treated with cognitive therapy. Although the treatment effect was greater for depression than for the other diagnoses, differences were not reliable and the authors concluded: 'the available research evidence . . . does not convincingly demonstrate that specific problems are particularly amenable to this [cognitive] form of treatment' (1983: 46).

How long need therapy be?

The duration of therapy varies considerably. The literature reports a range from a single session (e.g. Bloom 1981) to 1,114 sessions (Weiss and Sampson 1986), and probably upwards. Recently, Howard *et al.* (1986) reported on the percentage of clients that could be expected to show measurable improvement as a function of the number of weekly therapy sessions they received. This relationship, called the dose-effect curve, shows that 14 per cent of clients might be expected to show measurable improvement prior to attending for their initial therapy session. The percentage of clients showing measurable improvement according to the number of weekly therapy sessions received thereafter is as follows: 24 per cent (1 session), 30 per cent (2 sessions), 41 per cent (4 sessions), 53 per cent (8 sessions), 62 per cent (13 sessions), 74 per cent (26 sessions), 83 per cent (52 sessions), and 90 per cent (104 sessions). The shape of the curve after a period of two years is not reported by Howard *et al*. (1986). Accordingly, whether the curve reaches 100 per cent after a further period of time is not known, although there will always be a small percentage of clients receiving psychotherapy who fail to show any measurable improvement. Two points about the dose-effect curve are noteworthy. First, the curve is *accelerating*: that is, the longer clients remain in therapy, the more improvement they are likely to report. Second, and perhaps more importantly, the curve has a *negative* function: that is, there is a disproportionate amount of improvement during the early sessions, but as therapy proceeds, the degree of improvement becomes less and less.

In short, this negatively accelerating curve shows that there are diminishing returns from therapy after a certain point in time. Thus, while Howard *et al*.'s (1986) findings suggest that more clients improve the longer therapy continues, there is a very clear implication that this is not cost-efficient. This curve, derived from fifteen studies spanning thirty years, provides much incentive for those practitioners committed to briefer forms of psychotherapy. However, caution is advised against over-interpreting the dose-effect curve. The figures, particularly those for the earlier phases in therapy, are extrapolations based upon improvement rates reported later in therapy. What is needed are more studies of the exact relationship between a *planned* duration of therapy and outcome.

Is individual psychotherapy cost-effective?

A related and an increasingly pertinent question concerns the cost-effectiveness of psychotherapy. Establishing the efficacy of a particular therapy is not the same as determining whether it is cost-effective. Theoretically, Newman and Howard (1986) have identified three components of 'therapeutic effort' (i.e. the cost of providing a therapeutic delivery service): dosage (i.e. the amount of therapy received), restrictiveness of treatment (i.e. the degree to which personal freedom is restricted: for example, outpatient vs hospitalization), and the cost of resources invested in treatment. Newman and Howard (1986) argue that the concept of therapeutic effort should be used in research designs, either as a dependent measure in order to discover optimal treatments for clients, or as an independent variable in order to evaluate the cost of obtaining a desired outcome.

While researchers have been slow to incorporate economic variables in their evaluation of psychotherapy, some attempts have been made. For example, Piper *et al*. (1984) compared and costed four forms of psychotherapy: short-term and long-term individual therapy (STI and LTI), and short-term and long-term group therapy (STG and LTG). Interestingly, it was the particular form of the therapy which was important rather than either the type (individual or group) or duration (short or long) of therapy. The best outcomes were obtained with STI and LTG while the worst outcome occurred with STG therapy. When cost was evaluated in terms of therapist time, STI was five times as expensive as STG (which was shown to have the worst outcome) but one-quarter the cost of LTI. For the client, STI was one-quarter the cost of LTI. The authors concluded that, when considering outcome *and* cost-effectiveness, results favoured either short-term individual therapy or long-term group therapy.

Overall, this section has considered a range of questions pertaining to the outcome of individual psychotherapy. The question of effectiveness is becoming one of *cost*-effectiveness, and with an increasing role played by political and economic factors, this is likely to be a feature of outcome research in the 1990s. In turn, this could provide the incentive for pursuing questions of therapist effectiveness and treatment-specific models of therapy for particular presenting problems.

Linking outcome and process

Evaluating change

The findings presented above are predicated upon assumptions about how change is monitored. It is important for the reader to have some understanding of the key issues involved in obtaining outcome findings, and to be aware of other issues concerning the evaluation of the psychotherapy process. Accordingly, this section aims to review certain areas of this literature focusing first on outcome, and then on process.

A critical issue in psychotherapy research focuses on measures and measurement. Central to this issue is the recognition that change is a multidimensional process. If we are to tap the variety of processes involved, we need to adopt a multidimensional approach to measurement: the outcome of psychotherapy cannot be summarized by any single instrument alone. Psychotherapy researchers need to adopt a core battery of measures, thereby enabling both a comprehensive description of change and an effective basis for comparisons between different researchers. In addition, the measures used should be clinically realistic; that is they should tap psychological constructs which are amenable to change.

A further consideration in evaluating change is to use reliable measures and use them often. Research using only pre- and post-therapy measures does not allow researchers to evaluate the effects of time, life events, or the delayed effects of other factors. Accordingly, in addition to using standard outcome measures, Barlow *et al.* (1984) recommend using one measure that can be employed repeatedly across time. This is partly because tracking change across the duration of therapy by multiple data points enables the use of time-series analysis, a technique little utilized but increasingly recommended for the analysis of change. Multiple data points increase the dependability of the data and make it practical for clinicians to analyse their cases.

A consistent criticism of psychotherapy research has been the irrelevance of statistical significance to clinical outcome. In short, statistically significant findings say little about clinical improvement. Statistically significant results are statements about the probability that any change which has occurred due to an intervention was due to the experimental manipulation and not to chance. For example, suppose a group of obese people receive treatment to reduce their weight and achieve a mean reduction in weight of one stone from eighteen stone to seventeen stone. Compared with a control group who achieve no weight loss, the weight loss of the treated group may be statistically significant. However, a loss of one stone, considering their absolute weight, will do little to alleviate the subjects' vulnerability to heart attacks. In other words, no *real* difference in subjects' clinical states has occurred. For their part, researchers have been slow to adopt ways of making results relevant to clinicians. Importantly, clinicians want to know whether a particular client has improved: statistical improvement, acceptable in scientific circles, has little currency with clinicians.

Jacobson and Revenstorf (1988) have suggested two approaches for enhancing the clinical significance of research findings. The first requires the client to move from the dysfunctional to the functional population. This requires normative data on the change measure so that comparisons can be made between the dysfunctional group (i.e. clients) and data derived from a normal population. This form of 'social' comparison (e.g. Nietzel *et al.* 1987) enables researchers to evaluate how a treated group of clients compare after therapy with data from people within the normal population. However, normative data are often not available. In such cases, a second approach determines whether the difference between a pre- and post-measure score reliably exceeds the measurement error of the difference between the two scores on a particular instrument as well as moving two standard deviations beyond the intake mean. For many purposes, however, improvement to one standard deviation might suffice in terms of obtaining clinical improvement. These procedures reflect a growing concern among researchers to tackle the issue of clinical significance which, it is hoped, will be universally adopted.

From outcome to process

Having considered various methods for evaluating outcome which have more clinical relevance, we can continue this approach by viewing methods for evaluating psychotherapy process. Underpinning psychotherapy research lie a variety of strategies for studying psychotherapy process which can be viewed as roughly equivalent to the therapeutic 'techniques' developed and implemented by practitioners within particular theoretical models. The assumptions underlying psychotherapy process-outcome research have recently been questioned (Stiles and Shapiro 1989), and there has been a movement towards the adoption of new styles of research aimed at investigating the 'change process' (Greenberg 1986) together with new paradigms of psychotherapy research. One part of this movement can be summarized as follows: 'the process of therapy can . . . be seen as a chain of patient states or *suboutcomes* that are linked together on a pathway toward *ultimate outcome*' (Safran *et al.* 1988: 5). Consistent with this movement is the notion of specificity hypotheses which reflect the findings that processes ebb and flow both within and across sessions. Specific episodes within therapy sessions may prove to be a more profitable way of establishing process-outcome links than correlating a single process measure with outcome.

This view has led to what had been termed the 'events' paradigm of research. Essentially, this paradigm acknowledges that in order to study the change process, the intensive study of significant moments occurring during therapy are more informative than the aggregating process of traditional therapy whereby considerable 'noise' is included in the data. It is also a substantially better informed strategy than the sampling of random segments of therapy sessions. The events paradigm emphasizes the experiences and perceptions of participating clients and therapists and focuses on significant change events which are studied intensely. The events are usually derived from a variant of a procedure termed interpersonal process recall (IPR). This procedure requires the client, following a therapy session, to identify with an assessor a significant event which occurred during the session. This event then becomes the focus of subsequent intense analysis (including the client and therapist's perceptions of various aspects of the event). This procedure has been described in detail elsewhere (Elliott and Shapiro 1988). This methodology, while theoretically congruent with the process of change in psychotherapy has, to date, been implemented by only a few researchers. This may be attributable to the fact that despite its having a low financial cost and high clinical relevance, it is relatively labour-intensive.

A further innovation in process research concerns task analysis (Greenberg 1983). Task analysis is uniquely suited to the analysis of the psychotherapeutic change process. It attempts to explicate a model of the information-processing activities which the client and therapist perform across time and which lead to the resolution of particular cognitive-affective tasks. The preliminary model can be developed by rational/theoretical speculations and then its 'goodness of fit' verified against empirical examples of psychotherapy change processes. It has been suggested that there should be a process of cycling back and forth between the rational model and the empirical phenomenon, evaluating and refining the model at each stage. This type of model will potentially provide clinicians with information about the type of client operations (e.g. that the client becomes less self-critical) necessary for a therapeutic intervention to be effective or for a good outcome to be achieved. In addition, the development of such models have clear implications for training and the manualization of therapies.

The process of individual psychotherapy

The second major component within the generic model pertains to the *process* of psychotherapy. In effect, this refers to what actually happens between client and therapist in the course of therapy sessions. While 'input' components play their part, particularly perhaps in the realm of non-specific effects, research has attempted to establish the contribution of therapist and client behaviours in the therapeutic session (i.e. process) to outcome. Areas considered in the generic model include, amongst others, the therapeutic contract, therapeutic interventions, the therapeutic bond, and therapeutic realizations.

The therapeutic contract

Psychotherapy contracts differ largely according to whether or not they are time-limited. Orlinsky and Howard (1986) reported findings from seven studies, only one of which supported a significant disadvantage to time-limited therapy. Both clinical pragmatism as well as increasing awareness of manualized therapies, are leading clinicians to adopt time-limited therapy contracts as a norm. A corollary of this concerns session frequency. Orlinsky and Howard (1986) found approaching three-quarters of studies reviewed, showed no significant difference in efficacy between once-weekly or more frequent sessions. Johnson and Gelso (1980) argued that, initially at least, sessions should be weekly. Moreover, they argued for the inclusion of a standard follow-up session in contracting any model of therapy.

A component of the therapeutic contract which has been found to be a good predictor of outcome, and yet has rarely been implemented by clinicians, is role-preparation. In a review of the literature, Orlinsky and Howard (1986) could find no evidence suggesting that role preparation was significantly associated with poorer outcome. In contrast, more than half the studies reviewed showed a significantly positive association. It remains an anomaly that while therapists believe themselves to benefit in their role from training, the same rationale is not applied to clients, particularly in the light of the research findings attesting to its relative effectiveness.

Therapeutic interventions

In order to establish the relative contribution of particular therapist interventions, psychotherapy researchers have employed various taxonomies of verbal response modes (i.e. therapist interventions). A comparison of six taxonomies found general agreement on six therapist interventions: interpretation, reflection, question, advisement, information, and self-disclosure (Elliott *et al.* 1987). Although relatively time-consuming to collect and code reliably, verbal response modes have provided psychotherapy researchers with a much needed behaviourally based unit of analysis with which to study psychotherapy process. In addition, they have also enabled researchers to ascertain, in what are termed manipulation checks, that therapists are delivering the particular therapy in a style consistent with the theory.

In studies linking process with outcome, Marziali (1984) found a significant relationship between the frequency of interpretations and outcome, a finding not replicated in a later and more sophisticated study (Piper *et al.* 1986). Recently, Luborsky and his colleagues have investigated the impact of interpretations using a theoretically derived model called the Core Conflictual Relationship Theme (CCRT: Luborsky 1984). A recent study (Crits-Christoph *et al.* 1988) found high correlations between the accuracy of interpretations (according to the CCRT) and outcome. This result obtained even after the effects of general errors in treatment techniques and the quality of the helping alliance had been controlled for. These findings provide some promise that specific intervention techniques may be directly related with client improvement.

Findings from studies focusing on psychotherapy process have suggested that when compared with judgemental or explanatory interpretations, exploratory interpretations are viewed as more empathic (Barkham and Shapiro 1986) and tentative interpretations as more positive (Jones and Gelso 1988). Therapeutically, interventions based upon a shared frame of reference between client and therapist may be more effective in facilitating change. Confrontations, in which the aim of the therapist is to foster insight and bring about a directly meaningful experience for the client, have been found to be consistently effective (Orlinsky and Howard 1986). This may well be a function of a greater emphasis on the affective component, similar to the more process-orientated interpretations. Interpretations construed predominantly as cognitive interventions are less appropriate.

These findings attest to the relative potency of specific therapist interventions, in some cases against the argument that a single process variable can reliably predict outcome. However, the effectiveness of more active interventions are likely to be moderated by two additional components: therapist skilfulness and interpersonal manner (Schaffer 1982). Effecting change is, as stated earlier, a multidimensional procedure. Accordingly, research on particular interventions needs to consider the skill with which they were delivered (e.g. timing, appropriateness) as well as the interpersonal manner (e.g. empathic, cold, authoritarian). Thus, the effectiveness of, for example, moderately deep interpretations, might be a function of their being delivered empathically and timed correctly. Research has, for too long, pursued the strategy of attempting to find a direct relationship between single process variables and outcome.

Surprisingly, perhaps, relatively little systematic research has been carried out on therapist skilfulness. In a related area, there is increasing interest in standardizing the delivery of therapies through the manualization of therapies and, thereafter, monitoring the delivery of the therapy through checks on the degree to which the therapist adheres to the way in which the treatment should be presented. These procedures ensure the integrity of the treatments presented, thereby enhancing the validity of findings pertaining to the impact of particular therapist interventions. Further, it will enable future studies to be more exacting in addressing issues of therapist technique.

While there has been some research on therapist in-session behaviour, there has been less research in the arena of *client* behaviour. Nevertheless, this is being addressed by new style process research which includes task analysis. Greenberg (1983), for example, developed a three-stage model of conflict resolution in Gestalt 'two-chair' dialogues. By using a variety of measures, he assessed the interaction between the two chairs (representative of parts of the client) in the resolution sequence. Results indicated that the two sides of the conflict go through a stage of opposition and then enter a merging phase, in which the critical side softens its attitude. In the final phase, both sides become more autonomous and affiliative, and negotiate rather than contest each other. Process indicators derived in this way have been found to be successful predictors of outcome.

The therapeutic bond

Considerable research effort has recently been expended on determining the contribution of the therapeutic bond, or alliance, to psychotherapeutic processes and outcomes, and has been summarized by Hartley and Strupp (1983). Bordin (1979) called it the working alliance and identified three features: (1) an agreement on goals, (2) the degree of concordance regarding tasks, and (3) the development of personal bonds. The therapeutic bond is probably the most parsimonious explanation in accounting for therapy outcome and is likely to be a better predictor of outcome than any other single therapy variable. Its importance in both the process and outcome of therapy is apparent from findings showing that cases with more successful outcomes display an increase in alliance scores early in therapy in contrast to less successful cases in which alliance scores display a decrease (Hartley and Strupp 1983). The importance of the early phase of therapy for the development of a therapeutic alliance has also been found by Luborsky (1976). Similarly, in one part of a series of studies, Strupp (1980) found most successful therapy outcomes to be a function of the clients' ability to develop a meaningful relationship with the therapist.

From their review of the literature, Orlinsky and Howard (1986) identified three components of the therapeutic bond: (1) role-investment (i.e. client and therapist commitment to therapy), (2) empathic resonance, and (3) mutual affirmation. For *role-investment*, research findings suggested that client and therapist's active engagement and therapist's credibility both have a significant effect on client outcome. Interestingly, however, therapist genuineness was not strongly associated with positive outcome. For *empathic resonance*, therapist attunement, especially from the client's viewpoint, was strongly associated with positive outcome. Similarly, reciprocal resonance was positively related to outcome, although therapists rated themselves low. The third component, *mutual affirmation*, concerns an interest in and endorsement of the client's well-being. Findings for both client and therapist affirmation showed a consistent relationship with positive outcome.

In the classic Sloane *et al.* (1975) study, clients were asked at four-months' follow-up to respond to components of therapy which they found helpful. The statements included items on technique (both dynamic and behavioural) as well as common factors. Successful clients, irrespective of the therapy they received, identified largely similar items: personality of the therapist, providing understanding of problems, encouragement to face problems and helping them towards greater self-understanding. Interestingly, psychotherapy techniques were not rated as the most important.

Assimilation of problematic experiences (or therapeutic realization)

Ultimately, clients seek to resolve the problematic experiences which led them to seek therapy. One particular theoretical model for understanding the process of change through therapy has recently been developed (Stiles *et al.*, in press). This model presents change along a continuum from unwanted thoughts and the associated affective reaction of the problematic experience being warded off, through awareness and the gaining of insight, to problem solution and the associated affective reaction of the problematic experience being mastered. This model attempts to align therapeutic impacts with their affective reaction in resolving problematic experiences. While the recency of this model means that no research has yet been implemented, it is likely to prove profitable in future years in facilitating attempts to identify the significant points in the process of therapeutic change.

The precursors of psychotherapy

This section provides an overview of research bearing upon those components contributing to the input phase of therapy. While the influences are multitudinal, consideration here will be limited to factors pertaining to the participants: therapist and client characteristics.

Therapist characteristics

In contrast to the contextual components of societal and treatment settings, research on client and therapist characteristics have been more fully documented in the literature. Before doing so, however, it is worth emphasizing the relative complexity of carrying out research in this area. For example, one characteristic which traditionally comes to mind is that of therapist age. This might appear straightforward: is it better to have an older or younger therapist? However, therapist age is most often confounded with therapist experience: older therapists tend to be more experienced. Further, it is not simply the age of the therapist *per se*, but also the age difference between therapist and client which will exert an influence on the therapeutic process. In addition, the age difference will have a differing effect depending on whether it is the client or therapist who is older. Accordingly, the reader is cautioned against seeking too simplistic a finding within the area of client and therapist characteristics.

These difficulties provide one reason for the comparative slow pace of research into client and therapist matching. However, in one of the better designed studies, Karasu *et al*. (1979) found evidence to suggest that matching clients and therapists of similar ages resulted in more productive therapy as compared with those of different ages. In a review of research findings concerning sex and gender, Beutler *et al*. (1986) concluded that female therapists first, and then same-gender therapists second, most facilitated treatment outcome.

It might be assumed that clients seek out therapists with whom they share a common belief system. However, although there is some support to the claim that similarity of academic, intellectual and social values contribute significantly to client outcome (Arizmendi *et al*. 1985), generally there is little evidence to support this assumption. While psychotherapy is an interpersonal activity, research attempting to identify the effect of therapist personality on process and outcome has produced inconclusive results. Indeed, Beutler *et al*. have concluded: 'It is unlikely that any single dimension of [therapist] personality or personality similarity is a major facilitator or inhibitor of therapy benefit' (1986: 271).

As to therapist well-being, somewhat reassuringly Beutler *et al*. (1986), in their review of therapist variables in psychotherapy process and outcome, concluded that findings indicated greater improvement in client symptomatology to occur among clients whose therapists had the lowest levels of emotional disturbance. They also found generally consistent research findings attesting to the influence of therapist competence (i.e. the adequacy or skill of therapist actions). As was mentioned earlier, this has been a relatively recent development arising out of the need for researchers to establish that therapies are being delivered in a manner consistent with theoretical models. However, findings also suggest 'a rather convincing relationship with therapeutic benefit' (Beutler *et al.* 1986: 293). Therapist expectations, when based upon accurate information (i.e. their observations rather than third-party reports) and when open to further ongoing information, have also been found to play a significant role in influencing outcome, as have various social influence attitudes (i.e. expertness, trustworthiness and attractiveness). Of these three attitudes, therapist expertness appears to be the most potent.

From the above, it is apparent that the results providing the most consistent and promising findings derive from research into what has traditionally been called 'common factors'. While the reader may wish to know the influence of specific demographic variables (e.g. age and sex), it is most likely that to the extent that such therapist factors do have an influence, they do so *via* common factors.

Client characteristics

A long-held view has been that older clients have tended to respond less favourably to psychotherapy than younger clients. Although the view that older clients tend to have 'slightly poorer prognosis' has held some currency, a recent reviewer suggests the findings to be more equivocal (Garfield 1986). Similarly, Smith *et al.* (1980) obtained a zero correlation between age and outcome. In his review, Garfield (1986) found support for a relationship between clients remaining in therapy (i.e. as opposed to dropping out) and social class and educational level, but no clear relationship between length of stay in therapy and variables such as age, sex or psychiatric diagnosis. An often-quoted client variable deemed to be important is motivation. While likely that this is indeed an important variable, there is a paucity of well-designed studies in this area. Similarly, while, as Garfield (1986) suggests, many clinicians might prefer to work with 'reasonably intelligent' clients, the jury is still out on whether this is a critical variable affecting outcome. Garfield concluded a review of research into client variables in psychotherapy by stating: 'Although we can state with some degree of assurance that such patient variables as social class, age, and sex do not appear to be predictive of outcome, definitive statements based upon personal qualities are more difficult to formulate' (1986: 246).

Individual psychotherapy research in Britain

Introduction

This section of the chapter provides a representation of past and current work on individual psychotherapy in Britain. Psychotherapy research is carried out at different geographical sites, and there is no overall research plan or strategy. Further, there is very limited funding for psychotherapy research in Britain. As will become apparent, the large-scale, experimentally controlled evaluations of psychotherapy can feasibly be carried out only in research settings, where there is research council funding (e.g. Medical Research Council Units in Edinburgh, Sheffield and Cambridge), regional centres for psychotherapy (e.g. Manchester and Oxford), or teaching hospitals (e.g. United Medical and Dental Schools,

London). While considerable moneys are available to fund research into drug treatments (e.g. by drug companies as well as research councils), psychotherapy research is, economically, a very poor relation.

This situation is important for the reader to appreciate. Invariably, the most effective research designs require considerable resources in subjects, therapists, support staff and facilities. Many projects either do not proceed or are constrained because of shortage of finances. This is one argument for adopting a scientist-practitioner model. This section aims, first, to provide a representation of the range of psychotherapy research carried out in Britain, and, second, to incorporate research issues which are important for the reader to appreciate. It is hoped, therefore, that the reader will understand as much about the problems of designing and implementing psychotherapy research as learn about psychotherapy itself from current research findings.

A history of individual psychotherapy research in Britain

The watershed for psychotherapy research in Britain, as elsewhere, occurred with Hans Eysenck's (1952) critique of the effectiveness of psychotherapy. The legacy left by Eysenck's work, mostly his critique of the effectiveness of psychotherapy, still remains. Eysenck (1952) argued that approximately two-thirds of people with a neurotic disorder improve over a two-year period irrespective of whether or not they receive psychotherapy. Further, he established improvement rates of 64 per cent and 66 per cent respectively from studies of eclectic psychotherapy and psychoanalysis (in the latter cases when early terminators were excluded). These rates were, Eysenck argued, no better than the rate for spontaneous remission. Accordingly he concluded that the efficacy of psychotherapy was not proven.

This rate for spontaneous remission appeared to undermine the efficacy and cost-effectiveness of psychotherapy as a viable treatment mode. However, these results were based upon studies which were methodologically poor. In particular, subjects were not randomly assigned to treatment or no treatment groups. Two studies by David Malan and colleagues based at the Tavistock Clinic attempted to investigate spontaneous remission by studying the improvement in forty-five untreated neurotic clients (Malan *et al*. 1968; Malan *et al*. 1975). Serious questions arise due to the highly selective nature of the sample, which therefore compromises the generalizability of findings. However, Malan and his colleagues found that while one-half (49 per cent) of clients had improved on symptomatic criteria, only one-quarter (24 per cent) had done so on dynamic criteria.

Malan also carried out two series of studies on analytic psychotherapy (1963; 1976). In the first series, Malan (1963) investigated a sample of twenty-one patients. Psychodynamic formulations were devised for all clients based upon disturbances in their social relationships requiring a resolution between the id and the superego. Malan assessed therapy according to whether patients improved their social relations consequent on their symptom improvement. Of the twenty-one patients, five met the criterion for substantial improvement. In the second series, Malan (1976) studied the outcome of a further thirty clients and found significant improvement in five. In particular, he found a significant association between outcome and interpretations linking transference with parent or sibling. In reality, the value of these two studies lies in their attempt to study the material of psychotherapy keeping closely to the clinical material rather than as definitive studies of the effectiveness of psychoanalytic therapy. Accordingly, these early research studies did little to establish the efficacy of psychotherapy.

Interestingly, Rachman and Wilson (1980) reported that at this same time (1972), annual publications in behaviour therapy had, for the first time, matched those for psychoanalysis (1980: 117). With the growth of behavioural therapies during the 1960s, followed by cognitive therapies in the 1970s, attention turned towards deriving statements about the overall effectiveness of these therapies. Investigations of behavioural, and subsequently cognitive, psychotherapy had brought with it more stringent research designs and procedures. Following the impact of the Smith and Glass (1977) meta-analytic review of psychotherapy outcome, there was a heightened awareness of the need to adopt more sophisticated research methods in Britain.

Current status

In order to provide a conceptual framework for reviewing research carried out in Britain, the work has been presented under thematic headings: (1) comparative outcome research; (2) naturalistic studies; (3) psychotherapy process; (4) common factors and integration; (5) cost-effectiveness of psychotherapy; and (6) psychotherapy training, skills and research.

Comparative outcome research

This section presents the results of research carried out evaluating differing modes of therapeutic interventions (pharmacotherapy, cognitive, cognitive-behavioural, cognitive-analytic, interpretative and relationship-oriented therapies). Evaluations of the comparative effectiveness of cognitive therapy with pharmacotherapy have been carried out by Ivy Blackburn and her colleagues at the MRC Brain Metabolism Unit in Edinburgh. This work is significant in that it presents a rigorous attempt to establish the relative potency of drug versus cognitive therapy in the treatment of depression. Findings for hospital clients, although not statistically significant, tended to support the view that combined drug and cognitive therapy was more effective than cognitive therapy alone which was, in turn, more effective than drug treatment alone (e.g. Blackburn *et al.* 1981). However, these authors found that this pattern did not hold for general practice clients. First, clients receiving pharmacotherapy alone did significantly worse than the other two client groups. And second, there was little difference between the combined therapy and the cognitive therapy groups. This suggested that in the general practice group, drug and cognitive therapies failed to have the additive effect which occurred in the hospital client group.

The effectiveness of psychotherapy has also been evaluated against other forms of clinical management. This applied particularly in clients diagnosed with anorexia nervosa or bulimia nervosa. In one study of severe anorexia nervosa, clients were randomly assigned to either twelve sessions of dietary advice or twelve sessions of combined individual and family psychotherapy (Hall and Crisp 1987). At one-year follow-up, the dietary advice group showed significant weight gain. In contrast, while clients receiving the combined psychotherapy did not obtain a statistically significant improvement in weight gain, they did make significant improvements in their sexual and social adjustment. In another study of bulimia nervosa, ninety-two women diagnosed as bulimics were randomly assigned to one of three treatment conditions (cognitive-behavioural, behavioural, and group therapy) while a further twenty women were assigned to a waiting-list control group (Freeman *et al.* 1988). All three treatments were effective compared with the control group. The researchers predicted that cognitive-behavioural therapy would be superior to the other two active treatments. However, where differences did occur, they tended to favour behaviour therapy.

Comparative studies evaluating different modes of therapies have been carried out by David A. Shapiro and colleagues at the MRC/ESRC Social and Applied Psychology Unit in Sheffield (e.g. Shapiro and Firth 1987). A programmatic series of studies has been devised to evaluate both the outcome of these therapies and what is effective (i.e. process) within each therapy. The first Sheffield Psychotherapy Project (Shapiro and Firth 1987) compared eight-session phases of prescriptive (cognitive-behavioural) and exploratory (experiential-psychodynamic) sessions in which forty professional and managerial workers diagnosed as depressed or anxious received either eight sessions of prescriptive followed by eight sessions of exploratory, or the same two therapies in the reverse order. All clients saw the same therapist throughout therapy. Findings suggested a slight advantage to prescriptive therapy as well as an advantage to the initial phase (i.e. first eight sessions) of a sixteen-week therapy. These findings are consistent with results of meta-analytic studies in terms of mode of therapy and with the dose-effect curve in terms of duration of therapy.

Importantly, strenuous attempts to control for extraneous variables, in particular common factors, because clients received the same therapist throughout their treatment, showed that non-equivalent outcomes could be attained through a carefully controlled study. In addition, this study provides an exemplar of cost-effective research in having obtained a huge data bank of process material. Currently, the second Sheffield Psychotherapy Project (Shapiro *et al.* 1990) is in progress with the two therapy modalities, prescriptive and exploratory, being implemented in pure form, together with two therapy durations (eight and sixteen sessions). The design calls for 120 white-collar workers, diagnosed as depressed, being randomly assigned to five therapists. This project will be able to answer questions raised by findings from the first Sheffield Psychotherapy Project as well as addressing questions concerning the modifying effect of, for example, client personality, therapist effects, as well as various components of the client–therapist relationship (Agnew and Shapiro 1988). In addition, a replication of this study is being implemented within NHS settings which, in addition to enhancing the sample size and providing a concurrent replication, will also test the feasibility of carrying out a highly sophisticated research study outside a research setting (Agnew *et al.* 1989).

A major commitment towards the evaluation of time-limited therapies has been undertaken by Anthony Ryle, James Watson, and others based at, or associated with, the United Medical and Dental Schools (UMDS) St Guy's and St Thomas's Hospitals in London. For example, a comparison between more traditional 'interpretative' therapy versus cognitive-analytic therapy has been carried out (Brockman *et al.* 1987). Although the overall findings report no difference, one aim of this study was to evaluate effectiveness carried out by trainees. Accordingly, it could be argued that the finding of no difference is a function of inexperienced therapists rather than similarly effective treatments. It is still valid to conclude that the two treatments are equally effective with trainee therapists. However, as the authors acknowledge, an unequal attrition (i.e. drop-out) rate led to the two groups' differing in severity level at intake. Because the two groups were not equivalent in severity at intake, rigorous comparisons as to the comparative effectiveness of one condition with another is problematic.

The efficacy of cognitive therapy, particularly for depression, has been evaluated by John Teasdale (originally at Oxford and now at the MRC Applied Psychology Unit in Cambridge) and associated colleagues (e.g. Melanie Fennell and Elizabeth Campbell). Teasdale has written extensively on a model of understanding depression within a cognitive – behavioural framework (Teasdale *et al.* 1984). Through both theoretical (Teasdale 1985) and empirical (Fennell and Teasdale 1987) work, Teasdale has developed a model of depression in which 'depression about depression' is a central component. Teasdale (1985) argues that depression about depression is best attacked by helping clients to view it as a problem to be solved rather than evidence of personal inadequacy.

To test out this hypothesis, Fennell and Teasdale (1987) investigated the process of change in outpatients with major depressive disorder. Cognitive therapy was compared to treatment as usual. Cognitive therapy produced marked improvement within the initial two-week period which was maintained through the course of treatment. The study showed that when fast responders were analysed between the two treatment groups (i.e. cognitive therapy vs treatment as usual), only the good responders in the cognitive therapy group maintained their level of improvement. Establishing predictors of improvement is an important aim of psychotherapy research. By detailed session-by-session analysis, Fennell and Teasdale (1987) found the major differentiating factor between high and low responders to be clients' responsiveness to a booklet about depression. Clients who responded positively to the booklet improved most quickly. The authors argued that this was because the booklet addressed the issue of being 'depressed about their depression'. If the client responded positively to this construction of their depression, then improvement occurred more quickly.

Studies of cognitive therapy for anxiety have been carried out at the Warneford Hospital, Oxford. Butler *et al.* (1987a) treated a total of forty-five clients diagnosed as having generalized anxiety disorder. Twenty-two received anxiety management immediately while a further twenty-three received the same treatment after a three-month wait period. The results suggested that clients in the immediate treatment group improved significantly more than the matched group waiting for treatment. When the wait group received treatment, a similar improvement obtained. An important design issue worthy of note is that the delayed treatment group functioned as an effective control group and were not denied treatment.

This is important ethically. Indeed, they acted as a replication for the immediate treatment group.

In a comparative trial carried out in London and Brighton, Blowers *et al.* (1987) studied a sample of sixty-six clients diagnosed as suffering from generalized anxiety. Clients were randomly assigned to one of three conditions: wait list, non-directive counselling, or anxiety management training (combined relaxation and brief cognitive therapy). Surprisingly, perhaps, there were few significant differences in outcome between non-directive counselling and anxiety management training. Blowers *et al.* (1987) summarize their findings as follows: 'A reasonable conclusion would therefore be that anxiety management training is indeed effective, but that its superiority to a less structured and less directive alternative remains to be proven' (1987: 500). However, as Morley (1988) suggests, it can be no surprise that such studies find little differences between anxiety management training and non-directive counselling. These studies are not really evaluating cognitive therapy but rather cognitive components divorced from their behavioural concomitants.

In summary, the above research is broadly consistent with the findings reported in the earlier part of this chapter: that a range of therapies comprising non-equivalent contents result in broadly similar outcomes. This is what has been termed in the psychotherapy literature the 'equivalence paradox' (Stiles *et al.* 1986). A major feature of the above studies is their attempt to combine both internal validity (i.e. the attempt to minimize any possible bias usually through random assignment of clients to particular conditions) and extrinsic validity (i.e. sampling a clinical rather than a student population). Perhaps the best single indicator of such attempts is the use of random allocation of clients to treatment conditions. Often, however, it is not possible to do so either for ethical or practical reasons. When it is not possible to incorporate high components of both forms of validity, researchers face a choice. They must either employ analogue studies (e.g. studying students with test anxiety) in which internal validity is high but which are problematic in generalizing the findings to clinical populations, or use more naturalistic studies (i.e. describing and evaluating clients referred to outpatient settings) which do not permit the researcher to manipulate specific variables. Due to the priority given to studying clinical populations, the next section will consider studies in this latter group.

Naturalistic studies

A study using a naturalistic design and studying inpatients has been carried out by Denford *et al.* (1983). These workers completed a retrospective study of twenty-eight successive admissions for inpatient psychotherapy at the Cassel Hospital, a community using a combination of both individual and community psychotherapeutic methods. Their findings suggested that

> to maximise the proportion of patients who improve, the hospital should be inclined to accept patients who have neurotic rather than borderline or psychotic psychopathology, those who appear considerably depressed, those

with a history of minimal out-patient psychiatric treatment, and possibly those judged to be of superior intelligence.

(Denford *et al*. 1983: 235-6)

An important difference between successful clients when compared with clients rated as failures and drop-outs was that motivation for insight and change was high in 50 per cent of successful cases and lower in both failed (38 per cent) and drop-out clients (13 per cent). Blind ratings of motivation tended to distinguish success and failed groups at triage, a finding consistent with the results obtained by Malan (1963; 1976).

Another retrospective study was carried out by Keller (1984), who investigated the applicability of brief psychotherapeutic methods developed at the Tavistock Clinic in NHS outpatient psychotherapy clinics. Fifteen clients in all were treated and no findings obtained statistical significance. At non-significant levels, however, the results indicated that outcome was better for those clients who experienced high levels of distress subjectively but who functioned well externally. In addition, outcome was better for those clients who had a supportive relationship outside therapy and for whom a psychodynamic focus could be formulated. Keller argued that these findings generally substantiate Malan's (1976) work. Interestingly, this study exemplifies the difficulties of practitioners carrying out research. In their favour, these practitioners set up a workshop to provide a framework for the participating practitioners to adapt their methods to the clients they saw in their own practices as well as providing an environment for research to be implemented and carried out. However, from the researcher's viewpoint it is difficult to have much confidence in the findings: they are non-significant, based on a small sample, and contaminated by other influences (including rater bias). In addition, the finding that more distressed clients fair better (a finding also reported by Denford *et al*. 1983) may be a function of scores regressing to the mean. Scores regressing to the mean refers to the phenomenon where scores at the extreme of the normal distribution (i.e. very high or very low) will, if assessed a second time, tend to be nearer the mean than on the first occasion. Accordingly this phenomenon should always be borne in mind when considering improvement in high scorers.

Psychotherapy process

In the study of the 'psychotherapeutic process', work on psychoanalytic therapy has been, traditionally, the most difficult to carry out. However, there are studies worthy of note. For example, Moran and Fonagy (1987) carried out a non-experimental single-case study of a diabetic teenager who received psychoanalysis five times weekly for three and a half years. They investigated the relationship between psychoanalytic themes and glycosuria (i.e. the presence of sugar in the client's urine). They found that the working through of psychic conflict predicted an improvement in diabetic control, both in the short and in the long term. Of particular importance to the authors were the findings occurring in the short term where, they argued, other common factors could not be viewed as competing explanations. This view appears to counter research evidence attesting to the potency of common factors *irrespective* of time. Importantly, however, one aim of this study was to attempt to apply scientific rigour to psychoanalytic processes. As the authors state: 'the present study is viewed as an initial step towards the increased systematization of the treatment of psychoanalytic data and . . . other workers using similar methodologies may be able to explore psychoanalytic hypotheses which eluded the current authors' (Moran and Fonagy 1987: 370).

In an attempt to ascertain how cognitive therapy works, Fennell (1983) drew together the purported mechanisms of change in cognitive therapy for depression. She asked three questions: How does cognitive therapy achieve its immediate effect? How does cognitive therapy affect depression over the course of the treatment as a whole? How are treatment effects maintained over the longer term? In answer to the first question, Fennell (1983) concluded that active thought modification in itself can bring about significant change. In addition, where the intensity or frequency of depressive thinking is reduced, a reduction in severity of depression occurs. In answer to the second question, Fennell concluded that the most powerful strategy for achieving change is a 'close interweaving' of thought-change and behaviour-change. 'Thought-change allows behaviour-change to occur and behaviour-change in turn provides evidence to further counter distorted negative thinking' (1983: 102). The third question is answered by suggesting that long-term improvement will be most effectively achieved with the widest range of clients by training in generalized coping-skills rather than modifying assumptions. This is due to modification of underlying assumptions being less easy to achieve when depressed.

In a study of clients diagnosed as anxious, Butler *et al.* (1987b) attempted to determine the effective components of anxiety management. These researchers found evidence to suggest that treatment-specific components included the control of anxiety-related cognitions, and the confronting of anxiety-provoking situations (as compared with the previous strategy of avoidance).

The attempt to discover the therapeutic ingredients responsible for the effectiveness of psychotherapy has been undertaken in a series of studies deriving from detailed analyses of the first Sheffield Psychotherapy Project (Shapiro and Firth 1987). Llewelyn *et al.* (1988) investigated client perceptions of helpful impacts occurring in prescriptive and exploratory therapy. The most common impacts reported by clients as helpful at the session and phase level (i.e. after eight sessions) were (1) 'awareness' (the client getting in touch with feelings which may have been previously warded off) and (2) 'problem solution' (possible ways of coping being worked out or rehearsed in the session). Not surprisingly, 'awareness' was largely attributable to exploratory therapy and 'problem solution' to prescriptive therapy. As Llewelyn *et al.* (1988) argue, these findings suggest that clients are achieving the major types of therapeutic realization intended by the two different therapies.

Links between process variables and outcome have also been investigated. For example, Stiles *et al.* (1988) investigated the *impacts* of exploratory and prescriptive sessions. Impacts refer to the participants' evaluations of the immediate effects of the therapy session (e.g. their evaluation of the session, how they feel immediately afterwards, etc.). These authors found these differing therapies to have different impacts. Both therapists and clients rated prescriptive sessions as 'smoother' (i.e. smooth, easy, pleasant, safe) than exploratory sessions. However, while both therapists and clients rated exploratory sessions as 'rougher' (the opposite of smoothness), therapists but not clients rated exploratory sessions as 'deeper' (e.g. deep, valuable, full and special).

Taken together, these results show different therapies to have different impacts. When these findings are combined with the finding that there is a general equivalence of outcome, the most parsimonious explanation is that equivalence 'occurs' *after* the differing therapies have had their impact. That is, there are different routes (i.e. processes) to achieving broadly similar outcomes. This view has been supported in a further study of the change in clients' presenting problems *across* these two contrasting therapies (Barkham *et al.* 1989). This study used data from individualized questionnaires completed by clients three times a week for the duration of therapy, thereby providing a highly reliable (i.e. dependable) source of data. Findings showed a smoother process of change as reflected in the question- naire items when exploratory therapy was followed by prescriptive therapy compared with prescriptive followed by exploratory. In the former ordering of therapies, the change midway through treatment did not lead to any significant difference in the direction of change (i.e. improvement continued). In the latter ordering of therapies, the change in therapy midway through treatment was more disruptive with the questionnaire items from a greater number of cases showing a change in direction (i.e. from improvement to deterioration, or vice versa). It seems likely, therefore, that the most plausible explanation is that different therapies have different processes and that the processes may differ as a function of the different goals of therapy.

Common factors and integration

The above sections have addressed particular therapies which are based upon as- sumptions that they comprise specific techniqès which can, or will, account for ef- fective change. By contrast, research into common factors has provided a vehicle for arguing that the effective ingredients of therapy tend to be shared factors (i.e. relationship, etc.). Murphy *et al.* (1984) asked clients to describe curative factors following individual therapy. Findings showed 'advice' and 'talking to someone interested in my problems' to be elicited from more than half the clients. Further, the study found that 'receiving advice' and 'talking with someone who under- stands' were both moderately correlated with outcome. The relationship of each of these to outcome accounted for approaching 20 per cent of the outcome variance.

In a study of phobic clients, Bennun and Schindler (1988) investigated therapist and client factors operative within behavioural treatments. Ratings on these factors by clients and therapists were positively correlated with outcome, suggesting that interpersonal variables may contribute to treatment outcome. The results showed that the more positive the participants' ratings of each other after the second session, the greater the amount of change achieved at the end of therapy. Bennun and Schindler conclude: 'Researchers and clinicians should not be too preoccupied with technique; favourable interpersonal conditions are also essential for therapeutic change' (1988: 151). In a study of clients' and therapists' views of therapy, Llewelyn (1988) sampled forty therapist–client dyads partic- ipating in psychological therapy in standard British clinical settings. During the course of therapy, the most frequently reported helpful events for clients were 'reassurance' and 'problem solution', while at termination 'problem solution' was the most frequently rated as helpful. By contrast, therapists rated 'insight' as the most common helpful event both during therapy and at termination.

These findings suggest that clients and therapists have quite different perceptions of what is helpful during the course of therapy. Clients appeared to value the common ingredients of reassurance and relief. In contrast, therapists valued both the cognitive and affective insight felt to be attained by their clients during therapy. Of course, if insight 'leads' to problem solution, at least in the sense of preceding it, it may be that clients are focusing on the consequences of their insight while therapists value the more personal and dynamic component of insight itself rather than the action arising from it. In the final analysis, it is to be expected that two differing perspectives on the therapeutic process will provide two differing perceptions.

Anthony Ryle has carried out research spanning some two decades in psychotherapy. Underlying Ryle's work is the aim of establishing an understanding of psychotherapy based within a cognitive framework. This was apparent in his early work using repertory grids. Ryle has developed three important constructs relevant to understanding change (Ryle 1979): 'dilemmas' (i.e. the narrow way in which a client will see the possible alternatives), 'traps' (i.e. patterns of behaviour which are based upon and also serve to reinforce negative assumptions about the self), and 'snags' (i.e. the avoidance of change due to its effects, real or imagined). Ryle (1980) studied fifteen cases in which clients received focused integrated active psychotherapy. The aim was to define therapeutic goals which were specific and individual to clients and yet which referred to underlying cognitive processes as well as to overt symptoms. In general, clients reported improvements both in target complaints as well as in target dilemmas, traps and snags.

Results showed that in clients where a change in target dilemmas in the predicted direction occurred, this change was invariably accompanied by a change in the client's cognitive structure and target problems. This provided support for Ryle's view that, first, a cognitive framework for understanding psychotherapeutic change is both feasible and informative. Further, Ryle argued that his research counterbalances the more narrow approaches to psychotherapy, stating that attending to deeper cognitive structures enables questions to be answered which have long interested dynamic therapists but which have eluded researchers. It is certainly true that psychotherapy research 'should attend with adequate subtlety . . . the fundamental but less easily demonstrated changes aimed for' (Ryle 1980: 481). These findings have led to the formalization of Ryle's cognitive integration of theory and practice (Ryle 1982), and more recently, to the development of a form of brief therapy termed cognitive-analytic therapy (CAT).

Cost-effectiveness of psychotherapy

There is currently considerable interest, both economically and clinically, in evaluating the cost-effectiveness of the psychotherapies. For example, McGrath and Lawson (1987) have argued for the legitimacy of assessing the benefits of psychotherapy from an economic standpoint and conclude that it is possible to justify the provision of psychotherapy within the NHS on economic grounds.

The issue of cost-effectiveness is being addressed in a study of very brief individual psychotherapeutic interventions in which therapies have been modified to be delivered in the form of two sessions one week apart and a third session three months later. This generic model of therapy, termed two-plus-one therapy, has been implemented using cognitive-behavioural (Barkham 1989) and relationship-oriented therapies (Barkham and Shapiro 1990). Significant improvements in clients' reported levels of symptomatology have been obtained following the two-plus-one intervention, and a large comparative outcome trial is currently in progress to evaluate further this model. Uniquely, the two-plus-one model of therapy derives from the research literature, thereby attempting to address the issue of psychotherapy research meeting practitioners' needs. For example, it is informed by the dose-effect curve which would predict 30 per cent of clients to show improvement after two sessions. Interests in cost-effectiveness are therefore focused on identifying, like Fennell and Teasdale (1987), those clients who are able to respond beneficially to such treatment models. This is consistent with attempts to match treatment-specific delivery models with clearly defined presenting problems.

Cost-effectiveness is not synonymous with brevity. For example, while Freeman *et al.* (1988) acknowledged that improvement rate for bulimics in their study (77 per cent) was marginally less than in other studies, they argued that the greater intensity of treatment offered in the other treatments (e.g. being seen several times a week or for half a day at a time) for marginally greater improvement was not necessarily cost-effective. Similarly, Peveler and Fairburn (1989) argued that while their treatment for a case of anorexia nervosa with diabetes mellitus lasted one year, 'the treatment was of relatively low intensity, amounting to just under 40 hours of therapist time in total'. More salient, perhaps, was the fact the diabetes required only routine specialist input and no hospital admission, making the treatment cost-effective when compared with the potential cost of a single hospital admission. In general, the issue of cost-effectiveness will become increasingly central in the coming years.

Psychotherapy training, skills and research

An alternative thrust has focused on attempts to increase the *quality* of therapists' practice. An ongoing programme of psychotherapy teaching and training has been implemented and evaluated in Manchester, largely through the work of David Goldberg, Robert F. Hobson, Frank Margison and colleagues. This work has arisen through its being a regional centre for psychotherapy. Consistent with its teaching priority, there has been considerable research into teaching psycho-therapeutic methods to other care-givers such as the conversational model of psychotherapy, together with a comprehensive teaching programme (Goldberg *et al.* 1984; Maguire *et al.* 1984). The conversational model of therapy has been developed over the past thirty years as a therapeutic method for dealing with people who have experienced difficulties in their interpersonal relationships.

Hobson, in some ways reflecting the impact of Rogers, not only developed the model, but also has been central in advocating its investigation through video-recording and research. This method has been packaged for teaching purposes and has been shown to be transferable to junior doctors (Goldberg *et al.* 1984).

The extension of psychotherapy skills to people in a primary care setting emphasizes not only an increasing adoption of a psychosocial model of presenting problems but also the notion that providing primary care-givers with psycho-therapeutic skills results in an increase in the detection of psychological illness. For example, Gask (Gask and McGrath 1989) has worked extensively on the application of psychotherapeutic skills to general practitioners dealing with issues such as AIDS.

A further centre for psychotherapy research training stems from the MSc course run by John and Marcia Davis at Warwick University. The distinctive feature of this MSc course is its focus on eclectic and integrative psychotherapy as well as on the central role of research skills training. This dialogue between practitioner and researcher is evidenced in ongoing research focusing on therapist difficulties (Davis *et al.* 1987). These authors devised a taxonomy of nine categories in which they were able to classify reliably therapists' difficulties. The three most commonly occurring difficulties were therapists' feeling threatened (the therapist feels a need to protect self against the client), feeling puzzled (the therapist cannot see how best to proceed), and damaging (the therapist feels that he or she may be injuring the client). Most interestingly, therapists showed internal consistency in the patterns of difficulties experienced. This led the authors to argue that these profiles would be highly related to therapists' personalities and consequently might help identify potential counter-transference problems for different therapists.

In a further development of this work, these workers have identified correlates of these therapist difficulties and the coping strategies employed to resolve them (Binns *et al.* 1989). They found the most prevalent difficulties to be those in which therapists felt threatened by their clients. In response to this, the most common coping strategy employed by therapists was to employ therapeutic technique. Not surprisingly, therapists were more likely to feel threatened by clients whose pathology was described as 'borderline', although there was evidence that age and clinical experience have a protective function for therapists experiencing threat.

Towards the future

This chapter, although presenting current findings relating to individual psycho-therapy, has also cautioned the reader against seeking oversimplified answers concerning the processes and outcomes of psychotherapies. Similarly, the reader should be cautioned against asking oversimplified questions. Psychotherapy is a complex and interactive process incorporating processes of intentionality, meaning, and responsiveness. Central to future research should be the recognition that psychotherapy cannot be adequately summarized by either technique or common factors alone. It seems highly probable that while common factors (e.g.

the therapeutic alliance) are extremely potent, they are also shaped and refined by the moment-to-moment interventions of the therapist.

Ultimately, the research route followed is predicated upon the view adopted by the individual researcher. However, there is now a strong call for psychotherapy research to move towards the intensive study of the change process (Greenberg 1986). Although there are still questions concerning psychotherapy outcome to be addressed, the wealth of evidence has resulted in a verdict of 'case proven' beyond reasonable doubt. The task of research now is to provide models for understanding the change process in psychotherapy rather than the simple association of numerous variables. The pursuit and identification of possible change mechanisms is congruent with this aim. It would be an aspiration that such work would enable existing psychotherapies to be modified and enhanced to maximize their impact by using ingredients which are shown to be most effective in bringing about change. Subsequently, this might lead to a further need for comparative studies between these enhanced models of psychotherapy. Accordingly, it might at some future time be found that certain psychotherapies, delivered skilfully and in a standardized way, are more effective with specific client samples than other forms of psychotherapy.

The 1990s are likely to be a time of intense activity for psychotherapy research in Britain. For example, in addition to the annual meeting of the UK Chapter of the Society for Psychotherapy Research (April each year), at least two major international conferences will be sited in Britain which are likely to inspire dialogue between existing and potential researchers (Second International Conference for Client-centred and Experiential Psychotherapy, Stirling, 1991; International Meeting for the Society for Psychotherapy Research, 1994). Such dialogues, leading to possible collaboration between researchers and clinicians, may well provide the basis for enhancing the move towards the investigation of psychotherapeutic change processes.

Acknowledgement

I would like to thank Roxane Agnew for her comments on a previous draft.

References

Agnew, R.M. and Shapiro, D.A. (1988) Client–therapist relationships: the development of a measure, SAPU Memo 785, Department of Psychology, University of Sheffield.
Agnew, R.M., Culverwell, A., Halstead, J., Harrington, V., Barkham, M. and Shapiro, D.A. (1989) The MRC/NHS Collaborative Psychotherapy Project: rationale, design, and pilot outcomes, SAPU Memo 1155, Department of Psychology, University of Sheffield.
Arizmendi, T.G., Beutler, L.E., Shanfield, S., Crago, M. and Hagaman, R. (1985) Client–therapist value similarity and psychotherapy outcome: a microscopic approach, *Psychotherapy* 22: 16–21.
Barkham, M. (1989) Brief prescriptive therapy in two-plus-one sessions: initial cases from the clinic, *Behavioural Psychotherapy* 17: 161–75.
Barkham, M. and Shapiro, D.A. (1986) Counselor verbal response modes and experienced empathy, *Journal of Counseling Psychology* 33: 3–10.

—— (1990) Exploratory therapy in two-plus-one sessions: a research model for studying the process of change, in G. Lietaer, J. Rombauts and R. Van Balen (eds) *Client-Centred and Experiential Psychotherapy in the Nineties*, Leuven: Leuven University Press.

Barkham, M., Shapiro, D.A. and Firth-Cozens, J.A. (1989) Personal questionnaire changes in prescriptive vs exploratory psychotherapy, *British Journal of Clinical Psychology* 28: 97–107.

Barlow, D.H., Hayes, S.C. and Nelson, R.O. (1984) *The Scientist-Practitioner: Research and Accountability in Clinical and Educational Settings*, Oxford: Pergamon Press.

Bennun, I. and Schindler, L. (1988) Therapist and patient factors in the behavioural treatment of phobic patients, *British Journal of Clinical Psychology*, 27: 145–51.

Beutler, L.E., Crago, M. and Arizmendi, T.G. (1986) Therapist variables in psychotherapy process and outcome, in S.L. Garfield and A.E. Bergin (eds) *Handbook of Psychotherapy and Behavior Change: An Empirical Analysis*. (3rd edn), Chichester: Wiley.

Binns, M., Davis, J.D., Davis, M.L., Elliott, R., Francis, V.M., Kelman, J.E. and Schroder, T.A. (1989) Some correlates of therapist difficulties and coping strategies. Paper presented at the 6th Annual Meeting of the Society for Psychotherapy Research (UK), Ravenscar, April.

Blackburn, I.M., Bishop, S., Glen, A.I.M., Whalley, L.J. and Christie, J.E. (1981) The efficacy of cognitive therapy in depression: A treatment trial using cognitive therapy and pharmacotherapy, each alone and in combination, *British Journal of Psychiatry* 139: 181–9.

Bloom, B.L. (1981). Focused single-session therapy: initial development and evaluation, in S.H. Budman (ed.) *Forms of Brief Therapy*, New York: Guilford Press.

Blowers, C., Cobb, J. and Mathews, A. (1987) Generalized anxiety: a controlled treatment study, *Behaviour Research and Therapy* 25: 493–502.

Bordin, E.S. (1979) The generalizability of the psychoanalytic concept of working alliance, *Psychotherapy: Theory, Research and Practice* 16: 252–60.

Brockman, B., Poynton, A., Ryle, A. and Watson, J.P. (1987) Effectiveness of time-limited therapy carried out by trainees: comparison of two methods, *British Journal of Psychiatry* 151: 602–10.

Butler, G., Cullington, A., Hibbert, G., Klimes, I. and Gelder, M. (1987a) Anxiety management for persistent generalized anxiety, *British Journal of Psychiatry* 151: 535–42.

Butler, G., Gelder, M., Hibbert, G., Cullington, A. and Klimes, I. (1987b) Anxiety management: developing effective strategies, *Behaviour Research and Therapy* 25: 517–22.

Crits-Christoph, P., Cooper, A. and Luborsky, L. (1988) The accuracy of therapists' interpretations and the outcome of dynamic psychotherapy, *Journal of Consulting and Clinical Psychology* 56: 490–5.

Davis, J.D., Elliott, R., Davis, M.L., Binns, M., Francis, V.M., Kelman, J.E. and Schroder, T.A. (1987) Development of a taxonomy of therapist difficulties: initial report, *British Journal of Medical Psychology* 60: 109–19.

Denford, J., Schachter, J., Temple, N., Kind, P. and Rosser, R. (1983) Selection and outcome in in-patient psychotherapy, *British Journal of Medical Psychology* 56: 225–43.

DeRubeis, R.J., Hollon, S.D., Evans, M.D. and Bemis, K.M. (1982) Can psychotherapies for depression be discriminated? A systematic investigation of cognitive therapy and interpersonal therapy, *Journal of Consulting and Clinical Psychology* 50: 744–56.

Elkin, I., Parloff, M.B., Hadley, S.W. and Autry, J.H. (1985) NIMH treatment of depression collaborative research program: background and research plan, *Archives of General Psychiatry* 42: 305–16.

Elkin, I., Shea, M.T., Watkins, J.T., Imber, S.D., Sotsky, S.M., Collins, J.F., Glass, D.R., Pilkonis, P.A., Leber, W.R., Docherty, J.P., Fiester, S.J. and Parloff, M.B. (in press) NIMH treatment of depression collaborative research program: 1. General effectiveness of treatments, *Archives of General Psychiatry*.

Elliott, R. and Shapiro, D.A. (1988) Brief structured recall: a more efficient method for studying significant therapy events, *British Journal of Medical Psychology* 61: 141–53.

Elliott, R., Hill, C.E., Stiles, W.B., Friedlander, M.L., Mahrer, A.R. and Margison,

F.R. (1987) Primary therapist response modes: comparison of six rating systems, *Journal of Consulting and Clinical Psychology* 55: 218–23.

Eysenck, H.J. (1952) The effects of psychotherapy: an evaluation, *Journal of Consulting Psychology* 16: 319–24.

Fennell, M.J.V. (1983) Cognitive therapy of depression: the mechanisms of change, *Behavioural Psychotherapy* 11: 97–108.

Fennell, M.J.V. and Teasdale, J.D. (1987) Cognitive therapy for depression: individual differences and the process of change, *Cognitive Therapy and Research* 11: 253–71.

Freeman, C.P.L., Barry, F., Dunkeld-Turnbull, J. and Henderson, A. (1988) Controlled trial of psychotherapy for bulimia nervosa, *British Medical Journal* 296: 521–5.

Garfield, S.L. (1986) Research on client variables in psychotherapy, in S.L. Garfield and A.E. Bergin (eds) *Handbook of Psychotherapy and Behavior Change: An Empirical Analysis*, 3rd edn, Chichester: Wiley.

Gask, L. and McGrath, G. (1989) Psychotherapy and general practice, *British Journal of Psychiatry* 154: 445–53.

Goldberg, D.P., Hobson, R.F., Maguire, G.P., Margison, F.R., O'Dowd, T., Osborn M.S. and Moss, S. (1984) The clarification and assessment of a method of psychotherapy, *British Journal of Psychiatry* 14: 567–75.

Greenberg, L.S. (1983) Towards a task analysis of conflict resolution in Gestalt therapy, *Psychotherapy: Theory, Research and Practice* 20: 190–201.

—— (1986) Change process research, *Journal of Consulting and Clinical Psychology* 54: 4–9.

Hall, A. and Crisp, A.H. (1987) Brief psychotherapy in the treatment of anorexia nervosa: outcome at one year, *British Journal of Psychiatry* 151: 185–91.

Hartley, D.E. and Strupp, H.H. (1983) The therapeutic alliance: its relationship to outcome in brief psychotherapy, in J. Masling (ed.) *Empirical Studies of Psychoanalytic Theories*, vol. 1, Hillsdale, NJ: Analytic Press.

Howard, K.I., Kopta, S.M., Krause, M.S. and Orlinsky, D.E. (1986) The dose–response relationship in psychotherapy, *American Psychologist* 41: 159–64.

Jacobson, N.S. and Revenstorf, D. (1988) Clinical significance and outcome research: methods for reporting variability and evaluating clinical significance, *Behavioral Assessment* 10: 133–45.

Johnson, D.H. and Gelso, C.J. (1980) The effectiveness of time limits in counseling and psychotherapy: a critical review, *The Counseling Psychologist* 9: 70–83.

Jones, A.S. and Gelso, C.J. (1988) Differential effects of style of interpretation: another look, *Journal of Counseling Psychology* 35: 363–9.

Karasu, T., Stein, S.P. and Charles, E. (1979) Age factors in patient–therapist relationship, *Journal of Nervous and Mental Disease* 167: 100–4.

Keller, A. (1984) Planned brief psychotherapy in clinical practice, *British Journal of Medical Psychology* 57: 347–61.

Lafferty, P., Beutler, L.E. and Crago, M. (1989) Differences between more and less effective psychotherapists: a study of select therapist variables, *Journal of Consulting and Clinical Psychology* 57: 76–80.

Lambert, M.J. (1976) Spontaneous remission in adult neurotic disorders: a revision and summary, *Psychological Bulletin* 83: 107–19.

—— (1986). Implications of psychotherapy outcome research for eclectic psychotherapy, in J.C. Norcross (ed.) *Handbook of Eclectic Psychotherapy*, New York: Brunner Mazel.

Lambert, M.J., Shapiro, D.A. and Bergin, A.E. (1986) The effectiveness of psychotherapy, in S.L. Garfield and A.E. Bergin (eds) *Handbook of Psychotherapy and Behavior Change*, 3rd edn, Chichester: Wiley.

Llewelyn, S.P. (1988) Psychological therapy as viewed by clients and therapists, *British Journal of Clinical Psychology* 27: 223–37.

Llewelyn, S.P., Elliott, R.K., Shapiro, D.A., Firth-Cozens, J.A. and Hardy, G.E. (1988) Client perceptions of significant events in prescriptive and exploratory phases of individual therapy, *British Journal of Clinical Psychology* 27: 105–14.

Luborsky, L. (1976) Helping alliance in psychotherapy, in J.L. Claghorn (ed.) *Successful Psychotherapy*, New York: Brunner Mazel.

—— (1984) Principles of Psychoanalytic Psychotherapy: A Manual for Supportive-Expressive Treatment, New York: Basic Books.

Luborsky, L., Woody, G.E., McLellan, A.T., O'Brien, C.P., and Rosenzweig, J. (1982) Can independent judges recognise different psychotherapies? An experience with manual-guided therapies, *Journal of Consulting and Clinical Psychology* 49: 49–62.

McGrath, G. and Lawson, K. (1987) Assessing the benefits of psychotherapy: the economic approach, *British Journal of Psychiatry* 150: 65–71.

Maguire, G.P., Goldberg, D.P., Hobson, R.F., Margison, F.R., Moss, S. and O'Dowd, T. (1984) Evaluating the teaching of a method of psychotherapy, *British Journal of Psychiatry* 144: 576–80.

Malan, D.H. (1963) *A study of Brief Psychotherapy*, New York: Plenum Press.

—— (1976) *Toward the Validation of Dynamic Psychotherapy: A Replication*, New York: Plenum Press.

Malan, D.H., Bacal, H.A., Heath, E.S. and Balfour, F.H.G. (1968) A study of psychodynamic changes in untreated neurotic patients: I. Improvements that are questionable on dynamic criteria, *British Journal of Psychiatry* 114: 525–51.

Malan, D.H., Heath, E.S., Bacal, H.A. and Balfour, F.H.G. (1975) Psychodynamic changes in untreated neurotic patients: II. Apparently genuine improvements, *Archives of General Psychiatry* 32: 110–26.

Marziali, E. (1984) Prediction of outcome of brief psychotherapy from therapist interpretive interventions, *Archives of General Psychiatry* 41: 301–4.

Miller, R.C. and Berman, J.S. (1983) The efficacy of cognitive behaviour therapies: a quantitative review of the research evidence, *Psychological Bulletin* 94: 39–53.

Moran, G.S. and Fonagy, P. (1987) Psychoanalysis and diabetic control: a single case study, *British Journal of Medical Psychology* 60: 357–72.

Morley, S. (1988) Status of cognitive therapies, *Current Opinion in Psychiatry* 1: 725–8.

Murphy, P.M., Cramer, D. and Lillie, F.J. (1984) The relationship between curative factors perceived by patients in their psychotherapy and treatment outcome: an exploratory study, *British Journal of Medical Psychology* 57: 187–92.

Newman, F.L. and Howard, K.I. (1986) Therapeutic effort, treatment outcome, and national health policy, *American Psychologist* 41: 181–7.

Nicholson, R.A. and Berman, J.S. (1983) Is follow-up necessary in evaluating psychotherapy?, *Psychological Bulletin* 93: 261–78.

Nietzel, M.T., Russell, R.L., Hemmings, K.A. and Gretter, M.L. (1987) Clinical significance of psychotherapy for unipolar depression: a meta-analytic approach to social comparison, *Journal of Consulting and Clinical Psychology* 55: 156–61.

Orlinsky, D.E. and Howard, K.I. (1986) Process and outcome in psychotherapy, in S.L. Garfield and A.E. Bergin (eds) *Handbook of Psychotherapy and Behavior Change*, 3rd edn, Chichester: Wiley.

—— (1987) A generic model of psychotherapy, *Journal of Integrative and Eclectic Psychotherapy* 6: 6–27.

Peveler, R.C. and Fairburn, C.G. (1989) Anorexia nervosa in association with diabetes mellitus: a cognitive-behavioural approach to treatment. *Behaviour Research and Therapy* 27: 95–9.

Piper, W.E., Debbane, E.G., Bienvenu, J.P. and Garant, J. (1984) A comparative study of four forms of psychotherapy, *Journal of Consulting and Clinical Psychology* 52: 268–79.

Piper, W.E., Debbane, E.G., Bienvenu, J.P., de Carufel, F. and Garant, J. (1986) Relationships between the object focus of therapist interpretations and outcome in short-term individual psychotherapy, *British Journal of Medical Psychology* 59: 1–11.

Rachman, S. and Wilson, G.T. (1980) *The Effects of Psychological Therapy*, 2nd edn, New York: Pergamon Press.

Ryle, A. (1979) Focus in brief interpretive psychotherapy: dilemmas, traps, and snags as target problems, *British Journal of Psychiatry* 134: 46–54.

—— (1980) Some measures of goal attainment in focussed integrated active psychotherapy: a study of fifteen cases, *British Journal of Psychiatry* 137: 475–86.

—— (1982) *Psychotherapy: A Cognitive Integration of Theory and Practice*, London: Academic Press.

Safran, J.D., Greenberg, L.S. and Rice, L.N. (1988) Integrating psychotherapy research and practice: modeling the change process, *Psychotherapy* 25: 1–17.

Schaffer, N.D. (1982) Multidimensional measures of therapist behavior as predictors of outcome, *Psychological Bulletin* 92: 670–81.

Shapiro, D.A. (1990) Recent applications of meta-analysis in clinical research, *Clinical Psychology Review* 5: 13–34.

Shapiro, D.A. and Firth, J.A. (1987) Prescriptive vs. exploratory psychotherapy: outcomes of the Sheffield Psychotherapy Project, *British Journal of Psychiatry* 151: 790–9.

Shapiro, D.A. and Shapiro, D. (1982) Meta-analysis of comparative therapy outcome studies: a replication and refinement, *Psychological Bulletin* 92: 581–604.

Shapiro, D.A., Barkham, M., Hardy, G.E. and Morrison, L.A. (in press) The Second Sheffield Psychotherapy Project: design, rationale, and preliminary outcome, *British Journal of Medical Psychology* 63: 97–108.

Sloane, R.B., Staples, F.R., Cristol, A.H., Yorkston, N.J. and Whipple, K. (1975) *Psychotherapy Versus Behavior Therapy*, Cambridge, Mass: Harvard University Press.

Smith, M.L. and Glass, G.V. (1977) Meta-analysis of psychotherapy outcome studies, *American Psychologist* 32: 752–60.

Smith, M.L., Glass, G.V. and Miller, T.I. (1980) *The Benefits of Psychotherapy*, Baltimore, Md: Johns Hopkins University Press.

Stiles, W.B. and Shapiro, D.A. (1989) Abuse of the drug metaphor in psychotherapy process-outcome research, *Clinical Psychology Review* 9: 521–43.

Stiles, W.B., Shapiro, D.A. and Elliott, R.K. (1986) Are all psychotherapies equivalent?, *American Psychologist* 41: 165–80.

Stiles, W.B., Shapiro, D.A. and Firth-Cozens, J.A. (1988) Do sessions of different treatments have different impacts?, *Journal of Counseling Psychology* 35: 391–6.

Stiles, W.B., Elliott, R.K., Llewelyn, S.P., Firth-Cozens, J.A., Margison, F.R., Shapiro, D.A. and Hardy, G. (in press) Assimilation of problematic experiences by clients in psychotherapy, *Psychotherapy*.

Strupp, H.H. (1980) Success and failure in time-limited psychotherapy, *Archives of General Psychiatry* 37: 595–603.

Teasdale, J.D. (1985) Psychological treatments for depression: how do they work? *Behaviour Research and Therapy* 23: 157–65.

Teasdale, J.D., Fennell, M.J.V., Hibbert, G.A. and Amies, P.L. (1984) Cognitive therapy for major depressive disorder in primary care, *British Journal of Psychiatry* 144: 400–6.

Weiss, J. and Sampson, H. (1986) *The Psychoanalytic Process: Theory, Clinical Observations, and Empirical Research*, New York: Guilford Press.

15

The training and supervision of individual therapists

MARK AVELINE

The purpose of training in psychotherapy is to facilitate the exercise of natural abilities and acquired skills to best effect. This statement which is based on my experience as a trainer in psychotherapy in the National Health Service asserts two propositions, each of which is central to this chapter. First, that therapists bring to their work a greater or lesser degree of natural talent for psychotherapy. Two subsidiary propositions are that the possession of talent is an essential foundation on which expertise can be built in training and that the talent is not a unitary predisposition; the talent may be for one of the individual therapies or for some other form such as group or family therapy. Second, that psychotherapy is a purposeful activity in which trainees and trainers share a professional and ethical commitment to evaluate and refine their work. Thoughtful therapists will ask themselves three questions again and again: what in the therapy and this person's life actually helped the patient, could the end have been achieved more expeditiously, and was anything done that was to the patient's ultimate detriment? (In this chapter 'the patient' is a generic term for someone who suffers and is seeking help.)

In this chapter, it is impossible to do justice to the fine detail of training in each of the many forms of individual therapy. Instead, attention is drawn to important issues in each area of training. After the introduction, I present a checklist of training objectives, then proceed to discuss motivating factors in therapists and selection for training before considering the sometimes neglected but universally important dimensions of counter-transference and the abuse of power. The three cardinal elements of theoretical learning, supervised clinical work, and personal therapy are discussed in turn. Supportive therapy and the need for continued education is, then, considered. A section on registration of psychotherapists completes the overview.

Introduction

'In what is called "individual psychotherapy", two people meet and talk to each other with the intention and hope that one will learn to live more fruitfully'. This deceptively simple statement by Lomas (1981: 5) encompasses the central dimensions in psychotherapy practice – meeting, talking (I prefer the form 'talking with' rather than 'talking to') in a hopeful spirit and the purposeful intention of achieving more fruitful living in the patient's everyday life. The statement sets out in ordinary language the parameters of a kind of psychotherapy with which I can identify, a rather ordinary encounter between two people but one of exceptional promise. However, as is so often the case, the results of our intentions frequently do not measure up to our hopes. Training is intended to enhance the competence of the therapist but in itself is no guarantee of success. Please note that trainings which emphasize the apparent substantial difference in form between therapies may obscure underlying, powerful similarities.

Luborsky *et al.* (1975) in a survey of the effectiveness of different approaches to psychotherapy subtitled 'Is it true that "everyone has won and all must have prizes"?' calls attention to the fact that all the psychotherapies are similarly effective and none pre-eminent, a sobering conclusion for partisans of their school or faction. In other words, what effective therapies across schools have in common is more important than what divides them, a theme I return to later. This is not to say that certain therapies are not particularly suitable for a given person or problem, nor that a therapist will not function especially well in the approach that he or she finds most congenial. What are the best applications of the different therapies is a matter for research, while the natural affinity of a trainee for particular approaches is a key aspect to be identified in training.

The findings of Luborsky and other researchers certainly have not stilled debate about who is or is not a psychotherapist or which theoretical system if any contains the most truth. Or can one variant, for example psychoanalysis and psycho-analytic psychotherapy which share so many features, consistently and with enhanced therapeutic effect be distinguished from the other? Sandler (1988), a distinguished psychoanalyst, thinks not. In such debates, questions of power, prestige and authenticity lurk in the shadows and threaten to upstage the essential questions of how appropriate and effective are the approaches with which patients and what problems. All the warring tribes in the psychotherapy nation have a vested interest in promoting their ascendancy over competitors and, within their own ranks, in stilling dissident voices; in such struggles, the pursuit of truth may be neglected. In selecting a training programme, trainees need to bear these points in mind.

Given the wide range of approaches that may be gathered under the generic title of individual psychotherapy and the partisanship that goes with differences that are often more apparent than real, I am mindful of the hazard of this chapter being dismissed by adherents of one approach on the grounds of irrelevance to their practice, ignorance of what they do or believe, and partiality to my own bias. In contrast, my intention is to address important issues for trainees *and* trainers which I hope will be heard across the spectrum. But first I must state what is central to my approach for two reasons. I will be declaring my bias and setting out a synthesis, derived from my experience as a therapist, with which the reader may compare their own conclusions.

Psychotherapy attends both to the vital feelings of hope, despair, envy, hate, self-doubt, love and loss that exist between humans and to the repeated pattern of relationships that a person forms; in particular, to those aspects of the patterns for which that person has responsibility and over which they can come to exercise choice. As a therapist, I encourage my patients to take personally significant action in the form of new ways of relating both in the consulting room and in their relationships outside that, once succeeded in, will begin to rewrite the cramped fiction of their lives. This therapeutic action challenges the determining myths that individuals have learnt or evolved to explain their actions; commonly, these myths are restrictive and self-limiting. I work with the psychological view that people take of themselves, their situation and the possibilities open to them; essentially, this is the view that has been taken of them by important others and by them of themselves in the past and which will go on being the determining view unless some corrective emotional experience occurs (Aveline 1986). What is the view that individuals take of themselves is illuminated by the relationship patterns that form between patients and the people in their lives and me; jointly, the patient and I examine the meaning of the patterns. Importantly, it is change in the external world of the patient, rather than inferred intrapsychic change, against which I judge the success of our mutual endeavour. Lest this sound too demanding, let me balance the statement by the recognition that many with deep problems of self-doubt and negative world view need sustained care in order to gather the courage to change.

On one level, I make no distinction between enlightened analytic and behaviour therapy that both recognizes and utilizes the therapeutic factors they have in common; they both offer encouragement, the one covertly, the other overtly. In the former, intrapsychic terrors are faced and the treatment proceeds by analogy; if a new end to the old sad story can be written in the relationship with the therapist, the same new chapter can be written in the natural relationships outside the consulting room. In the latter, direct action is taken, perhaps after a period of rehearsal, often undertaken with the therapist. What characterizes good psychotherapy of any sort is a sustained, affirmative stance on the part of an imaginative, seasoned therapist who respects and does not exploit (Schafer 1983). I hope that my relationship with the patient is both passionate and ethical, for both these elements are necessary if personal change is to occur. In the interplay of therapy, I influence and am influenced by what passes between us. It is the other person's journey in life, but it is a journey for us both and one in which I may expect to change as well as the patient. It is a journey and not an aimless ramble; though the ultimate destination may be unknown, the way-stations are known and aimed for; the therapist has expertise in guiding the other through terrain which is novel for them. It is, also, a journey in which I do not expect to be the guide for the whole way; someone may enter therapy for a while, gain what they require to get their life moving, go away to try their modified approach and return later if they need; in this, I am a minimalist. I do not aim, even if it were possible as early psychoanalysts hoped, to exhaust through the therapy the patient's potential for neurosis or, necessarily, to place the locus of change wholly in the relationship with me.

I have presented my conclusions in summary form. The constraint of space means that I cannot spell out the significance of each point, but I offer my conclusions as a personal point of reference for the following discussion of the elements in training. Let us begin by recognizing the formidable task that awaits the trainee therapist.

What the individual therapist has to learn

Despite the plethora of texts and manualized procedures whose purpose is to lend assistance to both experienced and novice therapists, the practice of psychotherapy is challenging in its elusive complexity, ambiguity and frustratingly slow pace of change. Even in the more procedure-dominated cognitive and behavioural therapies, the ambiguous, uncertain reality of practice is disconcerting to those (and this includes many with medical, nursing and psychology backgrounds) who are used to the predictable clarity in the physical sciences of structure, intervention and consistent outcome. Furthermore what happens between therapist and patient is complicated by the often unrecognized involvement of the therapist in the patient's self-limiting fiction and by the arousal in the therapist of unresolved personal conflicts; this phenomenon of transference and counter-transference has the central place in the analytic therapies (and, of course, is fostered by their techniques) but to a greater or lesser extent is, also, part of any human interaction and, certainly, of any therapy where the participants have a close relationship. Yet, I trust, for readers of this volume the struggle to become proficient as therapists is worthwhile not least because psychotherapy is a fundamentally important activity in our technological and materialistic age; it attends to individual and shared experience and meaning and it attests to the ability of people to support and help each other. But this practical discipline and creative art is not easily learnt.

What a therapist has to learn depends on the level and intensity at which she has to practise, be it at the level of beginners gaining a limited appreciation of what psychotherapy is or of qualified professionals who as generalists need psychotherapeutic skills as part of their work or of career psychotherapists and future trainers of therapists. The caveat to this is that, at all levels, the same lessons are repeated again and again. The individual therapies vary substantially in theory, focus and technique and there is much to be learnt. However, the trainee who quite appropriately immerses herself in one approach risks being ignorant of other approaches. It is, thus, tempting when faced with such variety to attempt to learn simultaneously two dissonant approaches but trainee confusion and trainer alienation may result. Yet not to look widely at the therapy spectrum during the formative period of training is to risk premature closure in thinking and mental ossification.

General objectives for the trainee therapist

1 To make progress towards the optimal use of natural ability and acquired skills.
2 To identify the type(s) of therapy and range of patient problem and personality with which the therapist can work effectively.

Specific objectives (in approximate order of priority)

1 To learn to listen to what is said and not said by patients and to develop with them shared languages of personal meaning.
2 To develop the capacity to keep in contact with patients in their pain and anger-filled explorations.
3 In interaction with patients, to learn to move between participation and observation. To get a sense of when and when not to intervene.
4 To gain a coherent conceptual frame with which to understand what happens and is intended to happen in therapy.
5 To study human development, the process of learning, and the functioning of naturally occurring personal relationships between friends, couples and in families and the artificial, constructed relationships in psychotherapy where strangers are brought together.
6 To understand and bring to bear both the therapeutic factors that types of therapy have in common (these, which are often referred to as non-specific factors, are detailed in the section on theoretical learning) and those that are approach-specific.
7 To gain confidence in the practice of the preferred type of therapy. To make full use of one's own emotional responses, theoretical constructs and techniques in resolving the patients' problems.
8 To increase one's own level of self-awareness and to work towards the resolution of personal conflicts which may interfere with the process of therapy.
9 To come to know personal limitations and be able to obtain and use supervision.
10 To know the features of major psychiatric illness and the indications and contra-indications for psychotropic medication.
11 To make valid diagnostic assessments psychiatrically, psychologically and dynamically (Malan 1979: chs 17–22).
12 To be sufficiently knowledgeable about other types of therapy so as to match optimally, by referring on, patient and approach (and therapist).
13 To consider ethical dilemmas and internalize high ethical standards.
14 To cultivate humility, compassion and modesty as well as a proper degree of self-confidence.
15 To be familiar with the chosen theoretical system and aware of its areas of greatest utility and its limitations. To appreciate the significance of cultural and social factors and to adjust therapy accordingly.
16 To evaluate critically what is enduring truth and what is mere habit or unsubstantiated dogma in the practice of psychotherapy through the experience of clinical practice, being supervised and studying the research literature.
17 At the level of career psychotherapist, to acquire that professional identity.

Objectives for the trainer

1 To assess accurately both the stage at which trainees are in their development as therapists and their strengths and weaknesses. At different stages, this may involve the normative functions of selection for training and evaluation for graduation. (In educational terms, 'normative' refers to entry/exit, pass/fail criteria, whereas 'formative' refers to non-examined elements that enrich the educational experience of training.)
2 To help trainees secure the formative learning experiences which will clarify and develop their natural affinity for particular types of therapy and problem.
3 To hold the balance of interest between the learning needs of trainee therapists and the clinical needs of their patients until such time as the trainee therapists can do this for themselves.

This long list is not intended to be intimidating but it does serve to underline the seriousness of embarking on training to be a therapist. It provides a framework with which to assess training needs, progress and the suitability of the training programme for a particular trainee.

Training has no end point or single path. An individual's training over time is the result of personal and occupational choices. The choices may mark a progression from the expertise needed by a generalist with an interest in the subject to that required by a career psychotherapist, and within psychotherapy from one type to another as the trainee's interest changes. Just as therapy should meet the needs of the patient, so should training meet the requirements of the therapist's practice, both those that stem from the type of therapy and the work setting. Thus, what a therapist working in brief therapy in a clinic with a long waiting list needs to know is very different from one specializing in long-term therapy in independent practice who takes on new work only when she has a vacancy.

The reader at this point may be eager to plunge into the detail of the three cardinal elements of training, namely theoretical learning, supervised clinical work, and personal therapy. To accede to this wish would be premature. It would collude with the view that proficiency in psychotherapy is a simple acquired skill. Instead, I argue that the wish to train in psychotherapy arises from events in the trainee's personal history and their consequent effect on character structure. The reflective therapist will want to take stock of what she brings from her inheritance and experience of life to this work before she becomes deeply committed to it. Two things are certain. In the work of psychotherapy, whatever the type, the personal, unique reactions of the therapist will complicate and illuminate the relationship that she and the patient has, and, being a therapist, will expose her to the temptation of abusing that powerful position. What I mean by these strong statements is spelt out in the next four sections which deal with motivating factors in the therapist, the selection of therapists for training, counter-transference and the abuse of power.

Motivating factors in the therapist

The trainee therapist has been long in the making before he or she formally enters training. Family circumstance, life events, gender, race and culture combine with inherited predisposition to form a unique individual who may or may not be suited to the practice of some or all of the psychotherapies. Individual potential therapists will be special in their values, expectations and sensitivities; each will have natural ability in different measure for the work and natural affinity for particular types of therapies and patient problems.

Being a psychotherapist has many satisfactions: the opportunity to develop a unique personal style of practice with a substantial degree of professional independence, to share at close hand an endless variety of human activities far beyond that generally encountered in the therapist's own life, to satisfy the desire to help others, to be intellectually stimulated, to gain in emotional growth, . . . and to have prestige and be paid! (Bugental 1964; Burton 1975; Greben 1975; Farber and Heifetz 1981; Farber 1983).

Guy (1987) distinguishes between functional and dysfunctional motivators. In fact, his items encompass both motivating factors and functional attributes of effective therapists. Functional motivators include a natural interest in people, the ability to listen and talk, the psychological-mindedness of being disposed to enter empathically into the world of meaning and motivation of others, and the capacities of facilitating and tolerating the expression of feelings, being emotionally insightful, introspective and capable of self-denial, as well as being tolerant of ambiguity and intimacy and capable of warmth, caring and laughter (see also Greben's six functional attributes on p. 321).

Dysfunctional motivators draw people to the role of therapist and *may* prove to be functional but when present to excess subvert the process for the therapist's own ends. There is a well-established tradition in dynamic psychotherapy, clearly articulated by Jung, that only the wounded healer can heal. Thus, Storr (1979) writes 'Psychotherapists often have some personal knowledge of what it is like to feel insulted and injured, a kind of knowledge which they might rather be without, but which actually extends the range of their compassion' (1979: 173). Guy (1987) lists six dysfunctional motivators of which the first is the most common:

1 emotional distress, where therapists may seek – and gain – self-healing through their work; the crucial question is one of magnitude. Some acquaintance with emotional pain is essential; an over-preoccupation with unresolved personal needs hinders the therapist from giving full attention to the patient;
2 vicarious coping as a life-style which imparts a voyeuristic quality to the therapy relationship;
3 conducting psychotherapy as a means of compensating for an inner sense of loneliness and isolation: this is self-defeating as it is life lived at one remove;
4 fulfilling the desire for power and fostering a false sense of omnipotence and omniscience (Marmor 1953; Guggenbuhl-Craig 1979);
5 a messianic need to provide succour; one positive aspect of psychotherapy is that it is an acceptable way for people to show their love and tenderness, but this becomes dysfunctional when it is carried to excess;

6 psychotherapy as a relatively safe way of expressing underlying rebellious feelings in the therapist through getting the patient to act them out.

These dysfunctional motivators give rise to counter-transference problems which are considered later. (Counter-transference means distortions derived from unresolved conflicts in the therapist's life which she unconsciously introduces into the therapy relationship.)

The prevalence of dysfunctional motivators among psychotherapists is not known. In a major survey of 4,000 American psychotherapists (Henry 1977), most reported good relationships with their families though in 39 per cent their parents' marriage was not good. Childhood separations, deaths and incidence of mental illness were similar to that of other college-educated populations. These global statistics doubtless conceal much individual variation . Thus Storr's (1979) impression may be true that many therapists (and here he means dynamically oriented therapists) have had depressed mothers to whose feelings they may have developed a special sensitivity, together with an urge not to upset or distress; their childhood experiences may well have prompted them to seek out in adult life the role of therapist. In Kleinian terminology, the need to make reparation will be great in these therapists; they may be especially adept in making contact with timid and fearful patients. There is some evidence that within the occupation of psychotherapy a history of personal conflicts and a greater experience of mental illness in their family of origin inclines practitioners more towards dynamic rather than behavioural orientations (Rosin and Knudson 1986). I know of no research that distinguishes between the personal backgrounds of therapists choosing to work in individual therapy and those choosing family and group therapy.

These factors and attributes constitute the natural ability for which selection has to be made and which is built on in training.

The selection of therapists for training

Trainers have a dual responsibility in selecting their trainees. The responsibility to the trainee is to help that person to avoid taking on work for which she is not suitable *and* to the patients, from whom she will learn, to ensure that they have optimal care.

Selection is a matter for both the trainee and the trainer; the trainee will want to test out what is on offer and the trainer will test the trainee's readiness for each level of training. Introductory trainings offer the trainee through workshops and brief courses the opportunity to try different types of therapies and to discover the ones for which she has natural affinity. Little or no attempt is made to select at this level. Another formative route into formal psychotherapy training is to be supervised by therapists whose style and orientation vary and, either before or as a supplement to this, to be in personal therapy; both experiences form and clarify aptitude. With advancing level, selection procedures become correspondingly complex. Commonly, for analytic training, candidates will have to complete an autobiographical questionnaire and undergo two extended interviews with different assessors, one more factual and the other explorative in the analytic style;

the results will be considered by a panel of assessors so as to reduce individual bias (a detailed explication of the process and criteria used in one institute can be found in Fleming 1987: chs 3 and 7). Later, the candidate's progress will have to be approved before entry to each further stage of training is allowed.

Sadly, the correlation between training and effectiveness as a therapist is low (Auerbach and Johnson 1977); this finding may reflect deficiencies in research methodology but is, also, a function of the overwhelming importance in promoting personal change of pre-existing personality factors such as decency, a respectful, empathic concern with others, neutrality, persistence and optimism. To continue this diversion into research, effectiveness as a therapist over the years of her career often follows a U-curve and is a function of different attributes; early on, patients benefit especially from the therapist's energy and enthusiasm and later from her acquired wisdom and skill as a therapist. In the middle phase, as therapists become more self-conscious and aware of the complexity of the subject, performance may decline temporarily. Trainees should not feel dismayed by feeling de-skilled when they enter the next level of training, and may with justice on their side ask the training organizers what help they propose to provide with this common reaction.

The above should not be taken to imply that putting effort into selection is worthless. Personality is all-important. 'The greatest technical skill can offer no substitute for nor will obviate the pre-eminent need for integrity, honesty, and dedication on the part of the therapist' (Strupp 1960). As a selector, I look for the functional motivators listed by Guy (1987) but, also, the six qualities identified by Greben (1984): empathic concern, respectfulness, realistic hopefulness, self-awareness, reliability and strength; for these are the qualities that are necessary if the therapist is to win the patient's trust; they give him the sense of being tended to and valued. Women often seem to have these qualities in greater abundance than men. It must be stressed that no one is perfect; what is required for this work is a sufficiency of these qualities. In addition, I look for two markers of maturity in life; first, that the trainee has struggled with some personal emotional conflict and achieved a degree of resolution and, second, has enjoyed and sustained over years a loving, intimate relationship. The first may bring in its wake humility and compassion, the second an active commitment to and capacity for good relationships, so well-summed-up in Fairbairn's (1954) concept of mature dependence. I am wary of aspiring therapists who have a scornful, rejecting or persecutory cast to their nature or who are not emotionally generous in their interaction.

My impression is that therapists who prefer to work in individual therapy rather than in, for example, group therapy have a number of identifying characteristics. They seem to have a greater interest in the vertical or historical axis of there-and-then exploration into the childhood origins of adult problems and their recreation within the therapy relationship as opposed to the horizontal axis of here-and-now interactions which is central to the focus of the group therapist (and increasingly of the modern psychodynamic therapist). They are more interested in fantasy, prefer to take a passive role and like the immediacy of the one-to-one relationship and the scope to work in depth. These impressions may help the trainee in the choice of which type of therapy to train in though other factors will, also, be influential. The high patient demand for individual therapy and its greater economic viability in private practice may powerfully reinforce natural affinity for the dyadic way of working.

A controversial issue concerns whether or not a trainee therapist should have as a prerequisite for being a psychotherapist a qualification in one of the core health care professions; these are generally taken to be medicine, psychology and social work, all degree occupations, but should also include nursing and occupational therapy and, perhaps, the new categories of art and drama therapy. Talent as a psychotherapist is not the exclusive preserve of any profession. However, the possession of a core qualification indicates that the trainee has a certain level of intelligence and ensures familiarity with the symptoms and signs of major psychiatric illness. It will also have offered the trainee the opportunity to internalize high ethical standards and, through membership of a professional organization, ensures that he or she will be subject to disciplinary procedures which help maintain good practice. Qualifications in literature, philosophy and religion are relevant but trainees with these backgrounds will need special training in the features of major psychiatric illness and what may be gained from pharmacological treatment, especially if they intend to practise independently. I shall return to this question in the sections on theoretical learning, supervised practice, and registration.

In the foregoing two sections I have written at some length about the personal qualities and qualifications that a trainee therapist brings to the work. In order to bring out two important consequences that stem from the intensity of the closed, asymmetrical personal relationship between patient and therapist that lies at the heart of individual therapy, the next two sections deal with the importance of counter-transference reactions and the temptation for therapists to abuse their power in *all* types of psychotherapy.

Counter-transference

Unconsciously mediated transference and counter-transference reactions inevitably feature in any relationship and especially in the intimate, prolonged relationship of individual therapy. Even in the symptom-oriented, individual cognitive and behaviour therapies, these powerful distortions are present. However, many behavioural training programmes pay scant attention to these processes, a deficiency shared by some more psychodynamically based individual therapies. Trainees are advised to check that attention is given in the training to this aspect of the therapy relationship.

Individual therapists need to be as fully aware as possible of how these distorting processes are operating, what they may mean and what implications they may have for the work. Let us illustrate this with the consequence of a positive transference reaction in two types of individual therapy; in this reaction, the patient may transfer on to the therapist idealized, dependent feelings which derive from the relationship with his parents, but which may also signify an unresolved, intrapsychic conflict and a dependent style in relationships. In a supportive psychotherapy in which, by definition, deep probing of mental defences and conflicts is avoided, the consequence of understanding what was happening might be not to address and try to resolve the transference but simply to bear in mind the hazard of fostering unnecessary dependence and make use of the transference in mobilizing the patient's sense of hope and expectation of benefit from the therapy. In behaviour therapy, the passive compliance that signifies that a person may not have mastered the maturational task of separation and individuation would be understood for what it means, probably not addressed on the level of its historical significance but circumvented by encouraging the patient to take the initiative in devising behavioural tasks. Of course in the analytic therapies, directly examining these reactions and counter-reactions is *the* focus of the work.

The term counter-transference is used in two senses; it may refer both to feelings that are the counterpart of the patient's feelings and to feelings that are counteractions to the patient's transference (Greenson 1967). Counterpart feelings are part of empathy; they provide valuable information about the other as when the therapist feels in herself the disowned, hidden sadness or anger of the other (for a discussion of projective identification, see Chapter 3). Thus the therapist's unconscious mind understands that of her patient (Heimann 1950). Counteractions are situations where the patient's communications stir up unresolved problems of the therapist. An example would be a therapist who fears her own aggression and placates the patient whenever the therapist detects hostile feelings towards her. In addition, the patient, through some combination of age, gender or other characteristics, may be a transference figure for the therapist; examples would be as parent or rival. Furthermore, the dependence and intimacy of the role relationship of therapist and patient will have a personal meaning for the therapist based on past and childhood experiences of psychologically similar situations.

Consider the following list of counter-transference reactions and their consequences (Bernstein and Bernstein 1980) and see how each limits the therapeutic potential of the encounter.

1 Do I require sympathy, protection and warmth so much myself that I err by being too sympathetic, too protective toward the patient?
2 Do I fear closeness so much that I err by being indifferent, rejecting, cold?
3 Do I need to feel important and therefore keep patients dependent on me, precluding their independence and assuming responsibility for their own welfare?
4 Do I cover feelings of inferiority with a front of superiority, thereby rejecting patients' need for acceptance?
5 Is my need to be liked so great that I become angry when a patient is rude, unappreciative or uncooperative?
6 Do I react to patients as individual human beings or do I label them with the stereotype of a group? Are my prejudices justified?
7 Am I competing with other authority figures in the patient's life when I offer advice contrary to that of another health professional?
8 Does the patient remind me too much of my own problems when I find myself being overly ready with pseudo-optimism and facile reassurance?
9 Do I give uncalled-for advice as a means of appearing all-wise?

10 Do I talk more than listen to patients in an effort to impress them with my
   knowledge?

Counter-transference problems are signalled by intensifications or departures
from the therapist's usual practice. At the time, they seem plausible, even justifiable; yet, when considered in supervision or in the routine self-scrutiny that is the
mark of responsible psychotherapy, their obstructive nature becomes apparent.
Menninger (1958) lists among the items that he has 'probably experienced':
repeatedly experiencing erotic feelings towards the patient, carelessness in regard
to appointment arrangements, sadistic unnecessary sharpness in formulating
interpretations, getting conscious satisfaction from the patient's praise or affection
and sudden increase or decrease in interest in a certain case.

Items like the above can serve as a checklist to help identify counter-transference
problems that arise from conflicts in the therapist's unconscious mind. This is
different from the equally problematic feelings that are manifestations of the
therapist's involvement in the patient's determining fiction or, in the language of
psychoanalysis, the transference and transference neurosis; one example would be
the way in which a patient who has been brought up in a persecutory environment
expects others to persecute him, perceives the therapist as being persecutory
(transference) and prompts the therapist to actually act in a persecutory way
(transference neurosis), another example would be when the therapist finds herself
not respecting the boundaries of a patient whose boundaries as a child have been
breached by a parent in incestuous acts. A golden route for promoting change lies
in identifying these involvements, exploring their meaning and disentangling both
therapist and patient from them. Both sets of involvements are encompassed
within a new taxonomy of therapist difficulty devised by Davis *et al.* (1987). This
allows therapists to compile their own distinctive profile of difficulty on nine
categories. Trainees might benefit from plotting their profile and using this to
highlight to them their idiosyncracies which could then be focused on in training.

The abuse of power

A particularly common form of noxious therapy relationship results from the
abuse of power. Individual therapists are all too easily seduced into abusing the
therapy relationship. When this occurs, the relationship is no longer therapeutic.
During training, trainees need to learn how to recognize when abuse is likely to
happen and is happening and take corrective action. In this respect, the work that
is done in supervision is crucial. How does the abuse of power come about? It
results from the conjunction of the patient's transference wishes and dysfunctional
motivators in the therapist; it is encouraged by the inequality of power between the
two.

The arena in which individual therapy takes place is constructed essentially by
the therapist. Though subject to negotiation, the therapist decides the duration,
frequency and form of the therapy. Ultimately, beginning and ending is in her
hands, the latter being a powerful threat to the patient who is dependent or not-
coping. With rare exception, the meetings take place on the therapist's territory.
The therapist, whether trainee or trained, is held to be expert in what goes on in

the arena, certainly by the patient, who is relatively a novice in this setting. What procedures the therapist propounds, the patient is predisposed to accept. Because the sessions takes place in private, the therapy is not subject to the natural regulation of the scepticism and even incredulity of outsiders. All this gives therapists great power and, consequently, exposes them to great temptation.

Ideological conversion through a process analagous to brainwashing is one hazard. When Scientology was investigated (Foster 1971), their practices of 'auditing' and 'processing' were seen to be so dangerous that statutory regulation of psychotherapy was called for (see pp. 336–7). More commonly, eccentric, unsubstantiated beliefs are peddled as truths and clung on to by vulnerable, uncertain people who deserve better.

Another hazard for the patient is the conjunction of the patient's need for an ideal parent who will protect, guide and succour with the therapist's wish to be idealized. What Ernest Jones (1913) termed the 'God complex' lies in wait for the unwary (Marmor 1953). The therapist's ego is boosted by transference admiration; this seductive pitfall is compounded by the common tendency in psychotherapy and especially in individual therapy for therapists to mystify the process through the use of esoteric jargon and the adoption of an aloof, all-knowing stance. Therapists run the risk of coming to feel superior, free from the struggles, conflicts and defeats of their patients. From a detached position which may be bolstered by viewing all the patient's communications as manifestations of transference and, as such, needing only to be put back to the patient for his sole consideration, the therapist is tempted to be a bystander on life, vicariously involved but spared the pain and puffed up by the patient's dependent approval. Progress towards separation and individuation is obstructed. In the artificial, time-limited world of the therapy session, the therapist may have the pretence of having all the answers.

Guggenbuhl-Craig (1979) asserts that within us all is the archetype of the patient and healer. In order to reduce ambivalence, the archetype may be split and either polarity projected on to others. But both are necessary for healing. The sick man needs an external healer but, also, needs to find the healer in himself; otherwise he becomes passive through handing over his healing ability to the other. This is obviously antithetical to the spirit of good psychotherapy. For the healer, the danger is to locate the polarity of the 'patient in himself' in her patients and not recognize it in herself. Then she will come to see herself more and more as the strong healer for whom weakness, illness and wounds do not exist. As a healer without wounds, she will be unable to engage the healing factor in her patients. Traditional medical education can reinforce the division (Bennet 1987).

The therapist who locates weakness in others becomes powerful through their failure. In Jungian language, the charlatan shadow of the therapist has been constellated. Guggenbuhl-Craig (1979) doubts that personal therapy or case discussion is sufficient to reduce the split in the archetype. The analytic shield carefully acquired in training is too effective, the risk of loss of self-esteem or prestige too great, the need to maintain one's allegiance to a school of therapy against outside attack too pressing. In some therapists, the split in the archetype is minimal; their patients' problems illuminate their own and are consciously worked on; they remain a patient as well as a healer. The best way of reducing the split is through involvement in ordinary life in un-analytic, symmetrical relationships which have the power to touch deeply and to throw off-balance, relationships which are quite different from the asymmetrical ones of therapy. Friendships – loving, forceful encounters with equals – develop the therapist as a whole person. What the therapist advocates for others is good for him or herself.

Not surprisingly given the intensity and privacy of individual therapy, some therapists become sexually involved with their patients. It is hard to conceive of circumstances when this is not abusive in its impact or when it is not a dereliction of the responsibilities of being a therapist. One can understand how it happens but it should not be condoned. Many more male therapists have sexual involvements with female patients than do female therapists with male patients but all combinations do occur, including with the same sex. Eroticized transferences and counter-transferences are common in therapy and may be acted out (Holroyd and Brodsky 1977). In the transference, the patient may be looking for a loving parent. This wish may connect with the therapist's need to be a helping figure but subsequent sexual action represents a confusing of childhood wishes, albeit expressed in adult language, with mature intent; sexual action disregards the boundaries that are necessary if the therapy arena is to be psychologically safe.

Lust is a relatively straightforward motivation in acting out; its intensity depends on the urgency of the therapist's biological drive, age, state of health, recency of drive satisfaction, general satisfaction with personal life and, of course, the attractiveness of the patient. Darker motivations such as unconscious hostility towards women or reaction-formations against feared homosexuality or gender inadequacy may be present (Marmor 1972). Sexual action may be rationalized as being for the patient's benefit but this self-deception should not survive the monitoring of self-scrutiny, supervision and personal therapy.

Occasionally, therapist and patient fall in love and form a long-term relationship. Though one may wonder about the basis of a personal relationship founded in the strange circumstances of the therapy room, when the two are in love, the ethically correct action is to suspend the therapy and arrange for it to be continued by a colleague if necessary.

Cardinal elements in training

Theoretical learning, supervised clinical practice and personal therapy are the cardinal elements in training. It is difficult to discuss one without making an artificial distinction from the others as the three are so interrelated. Thus the section on each should be read with the others in mind. The reader is, also, invited to refer back to the section on what the individual therapist has to learn. The order of discussion reflects my priority. Many analytic therapists might wish to give primacy to personal therapy; many cognitive-behaviourists might dispute its relevance to their work. Academic courses awarding Certificates, Diplomas and Masters are likely to emphasize theory and research. Many of the points made here are also relevant to training in other modalities of psychotherapy such as group therapy (Aveline 1988a).

Theoretical learning

Purpose and content

The purpose of training is to facilitate the exercise of natural abilities and acquired skills. To do this therapists need to gain extensive experience in the type(s) of therapy that is required for their practice and for which affinity has been shown, in this case individual therapy. But to begin with, a conceptual framework of what therapy is about, how people mature and learn, and the role of the therapist is necessary. Later in training, theory will be critically examined to discover its areas of greatest applicability and limitations. Studying theory means that therapists do not re-invent the wheel.

Learning theory is part of a broad educational process in which, in enlightened trainings, the development of informed, critical thinking is being encouraged. Theory tends to be taught in an approach-specific way but general, overlapping and complementary perspective also ought to be studied. Both specific and general learning need to be presented in the quantity and level which is appropriate to the trainee's need and ability. Ideally, theoretical learning would encompass the following:

1 *Theory and techniques specific to the therapy approach being learnt* In most trainings, this is the major component but, as has been indicated, the well-educated therapist needs to consider other aspects.
2 *The common therapeutic factors* Frank (1973) has argued strongly that in all effective therapies six influential factors are operative. The therapy provides (1) an exploratory rationale and (2) facilitates the exploration of traumas and conflictual issues in a state of emotional arousal. The effect is strengthened (3) when the therapist is sanctioned as a healer by the society. Responding to the patient's request for help (4) encourages that person to be hopeful about himself and counters the demoralization which typifies most patients' state. Therapy provides or prompts (5) success experiences. Finally psychotherapy provides (6) an intense confiding relationship with a helping person. These factors have a much greater influence on outcome than the contribution made by approach-specific theory and technique (Lambert 1986).
3 *The necessary conditions* Rogers (1957) proposed research studies to support his proposition that three therapist conditions were *necessary and sufficient* for personality change: genuineness, unconditional positive regard and accurate empathy. That these conditions are sufficient in themselves, are always helpful, and should be taken as absolutes has been much investigated and caveats placed on the original proposition. However, a sufficiency of each constitutes the basis of a helpful relationship. In passing, it should be noted that Freud took it as read that the analyst would be a decent, understanding, non-judgemental, respectful and neutral person. These qualities formed the basis of the therapeutic alliance and gave in Ferenczi's words stability (*Tragfestigheit*) to the relationship (Strupp 1977).
4 *The evolution of psychotherapy ideas* How the concepts of psychoanalysis, analytical psychology, individual psychology, existentialism, humanism, Gestalt psychology, psychodrama, learning and systems theory have developed, their

interrelationship and the implications for practice. In the analytic tradition, how an instinct-based theory has evolved to ego-psychology and then to self-psychology with the increasing emphasis on object-relations (human relations) and especially in North America on cultural and interpersonal aspects.

5 *Human development*   How individuals develop over the lifespan with particular reference to maturational tasks, attachment theory, and the elements that contribute to being able, in Freud's definition of maturity, to love and to work.

6 *Mental mechanisms, character structure and the concept of conflict*   How to make a dynamic formulation of the origin and meaning of the patient's problems. The meaning and significance in clinical practice of the technical terms: process, content, therapeutic alliance, transference, counter-transference and resistance. When and how to make effective interpretations and other interventions. Good examples of the practical application of these concepts may be found in Malan (1979) and Casement (1985).

7 *Learning and systems theory*   The role of shaping, modelling, generalization and *in vivo* learning and cognitions in determining human behaviour. The importance of problem definition and behavioural analysis in making a diagnostic assessment. How behavioural, system and dynamic processes operate in marriage and in families and result in disturbed functioning. The contribution of psychological theory on cognitive dissonance, attribution theory and crisis theory to the understanding of change and resistance to change.

8 *Ways in which therapists need to take account of linguistics, philosophy, religion and ethics in formulating a comprehensive model of human aspirations and functioning.*

9 *Cultural relativity with special reference to race, gender and age*   The specific contribution made to twentieth-century understanding of role relationships and psychology by Feminist psychology.

10 *Physical disease presenting as psychological disorder*   Also the trainee will need to know the signs and symptoms of major psychiatric illness, the likely benefits and side-effects of psychotropic medication and when and to whom to refer on. As a counterpart to this medical knowledge, the ways in which the sociological concepts of stigma and labelling further our understanding of alienation and isolation.

11 *Indications and contra-indications for different kinds of therapies.*

12 *The vital role of support in therapy.*

13 *Preparation for therapy and patient–therapist matching*   How negative effects arise through therapy and may be minimized.

14 *Research methodology and classic studies*   How to evaluate the research literature and derive implications for clinical practice.

Format

Theory orders the great mass of clinical information and helps orientate the therapist in finding a way forward. This useful function should not curtail curiosity and the spirit of inquiry that is necessary for the development of the professional *and* the profession. Theory should always be relevant and, dependent on the level at which the training is pitched, comprehensive in coverage.

How theory is presented varies greatly. Commonly the span of knowledge to be studied is set by the training organizers, a stance that has the virtue of making it clear what is to be learnt. Then, there may be set readings either by author or topic, an approach which specifies the route of study and makes it easy for trainer or trainee to spot omissions. However, it may have the negative effect of not engaging the student's active participation. An alternative, as in the South Trent Training in Dynamic Psychotherapy with which I am involved, is to have a planning event each year where the trainees and seminar leaders jointly decide what is to be studied and how this is to be done. Instead of the conventional study of topics and authors, the question may be posed: What do I need to know in order to understand a specified psychotherapy process or problem? This is the approach of researching into a topic rather than simply reading someone else's selection of what is relevant. At the advanced level when many topics will have to be studied, teacher enthusiasm may be retained by offering a menu of courses in the teachers' areas of expertise which may be selected from by the trainee, with the Training Committee having the responsibility of ensuring that a balanced choice has been made.

Theory is not just to be found in textbooks. Novels, plays, films and poems portray the human condition more vividly, complexly and, often, more sensitively than do dry texts. Biographies and autobiographies trace individual lives (Holmes 1986). All these should be studied.

Whatever the format, the trainee should return again and again to the fundamental, practical question: What are the implications of this theory or portrayal of life for *my* practice in *my* working environment with the patients that I see?

Supervised clinical practice

Clinical practice

Appropriate supervised practice is the central learning experience in training. The trainee needs to come to know what can be achieved in brief or focal work (8–25 weekly sessions), medium (40–70 sessions) and long-term therapy (upwards of two or three years). Weekly therapy is the most common mode in NHS psychotherapy and in many other settings; this has its own rhythm and intensity and is quite different from more frequent therapy whose intensity may accelerate the process of change or be necessary in order to contain major personal disturbance. Weekly therapy tends to be more reality-oriented; two, three or five times a week therapy affords greater scope for exploration and regression. The two ends of the spectrum present different learning experiences and need to be sampled.

The supervisor has a key role in ensuring that patients with a wide range of problems and character structure are seen during the training period. Both breadth and depth of experience are important for the development of trainees. Breadth develops flexibility and highlights to the trainee problematic counter-transferences and personal limitations that need either to be addressed in supervision, further experience and personal therapy or avoided. Depth fosters stamina, the ability to contain intense feelings and to have the patience to move at the pace of someone whose sense of basic trust and confident autonomy is poorly developed; often this will mean enduring feeling powerless and helpless as the reality of the patient's inner world is engaged (Adler 1972).

The same principle of breadth and depth in practice applies to supervision. To gain alternative perspectives against which the trainee's own view may develop, several supervisors need to be worked with for a year at a time. In order for the trainee to know one perspective in depth and to feel safe enough to explore certain doubts and conflicts, one main supervisor needs to be engaged with over two or three years. The choice of main supervisor is clearly a matter of great import.

What is judged to be an adequate training in terms of duration, frequency and amount of clinical practice varies between the psychotherapies. At the level of career psychotherapy, it is hard to see that fewer than 1,000 hours of face-to-face individual therapy over three to four years at a rate of not less than 8 hours a week plus 325 hours of supervision divided between one main and two subsidiary supervisors could be sufficient, and this would need to be built on a foundation of less intensive, preliminary training in psychotherapy over two or more years.

In addition, trainees who are not qualified in one of the core mental health care professions need to gain through clinical placements sufficient acquaintance with major psychiatric illnesses in order to be able to recognize their presence; knowledge of the effects and likely benefits of pharmacological and physical treatment is, also, necessary. One example of why therapists need to be familiar with such matters is the high risk of suicide and depressive homicide in severe depressive illness; in such cases, anti-depressants or ECT can be life-saving measures which restore normal functioning. Psychotherapists should not persist in interpreting psychopathology when a speedier and more effective biological remedy is at hand (Aveline 1988b). When patients are once more accessible to verbal interaction and the risk of harm to themselves and their families has receded, then the precipitants and psychological vulnerabilities can be explored in psychotherapy, with the benefit of increased self-understanding and reduced likelihood of recurrence.

The role of the supervisor

The supervisor has a privileged, responsible position of mentor, guide and, often, assessor. From the advantageous position of hearing about therapy at second hand and generally after the event, the supervisor places his accumulated experience and knowledge at the service of the trainee. He helps the trainee work out with the patient the meaning and significance of the patient's communications, the nature of the patient's conflicts and, certainly in the more dynamic therapies, brings into sharp focus the way in which patient and therapist engage and how this may be turned to good account. In the beginning, the trainee will feel an ambivalent mixture of excitement and dread in taking on a new role. During this time of insecurity and fearing being inadequate, she will need the support of the supervisor. As training progresses, the supervisor has to encourage the trainee to let go of the early, perhaps necessary, idealization of the supervisor so that identification can be replaced by an internalization of professional skills (Gosling 1978). In successful trainings, the trainee moves through the stages of inception, skills development and consolidation to mutuality of expertise with the trainer (Hess 1986).

When patient and therapist concur in their appreciation of the aims of therapy and also there is clarity in understanding accurately the structure of the conflicts and the process of the session, two major contributions have been made to the success of the endeavour. Many psychotherapy centres use a pre-assessment interview questionnaire to help clarify the purpose of the therapy; in Nottingham, this has questions on what the problems are, how people think they have come about and in what ways they have been shaped in their life, their self-concept, the characteristic form of their relationships and what has prompted them to seek help now. Of course, in cognitive-behaviour therapy, goal definition and objectification of problem severity as a baseline for therapy is an integral part of the approach. In whatever type of individual therapy, a formulation of the underlying dynamics is beneficial and, I would argue, necessary. Though different approaches will use their own vocabulary, schemas for the content are to be found in Aveline (1980), Cleghorn *et al*. (1983), Perry *et al*. (1987) and Friedman and Lister (1987). I now favour an interpersonal formula which, in Strupp and Binder's (1984) approach, identifies a personally characteristic, recurrent narrative of acts of self, expectations of others, acts of others and introjects; though derived from analytic and cognitive approaches, the formula is atheoretical and may be used by all.

Whichever conceptual schema is used, the supervisor helps the supervisee to make fuller use of the session and, crucially in my view, to see how she is getting caught up in the self-limiting relationship patterns of the patient. Getting caught up is inevitable; the skill in psychotherapy is in recognizing what is happening and using it constructively (Aveline 1989). In the phenomenon called 'negative fit', therapists act in ways that fit the patient's negative preconceptions which have been formed by how important people in his past have responded to him. Thus, Luborsky and Singer (1974) demonstrated two major patterns of negative fit when the tape recordings of experienced therapists were studied. One pattern was confirming the patient's fear of rejection by being critical, disapproving, cold, detached and indifferent, and the other was confirming the patient's fear of being made weak by being too directive, controlling and domineering. Clearly every effort should be made in supervision to identify these two patterns and to turn the potentially negative impact to therapeutic effect. Often the supervisor will be able to guide the trainee in selecting suitable patients for the particular stage in training. In this situation, the supervisor may consider selecting pairings that promise well as when the therapist has resolved in her life a similar conflict to the patient's or avoiding pairings where the therapist seems likely only to reinforce the patient's pattern (Aveline 1987).

Ways of supervising

Pedder (1986) sees supervision in three ways: as being analogous to gardening, that is as a process of promoting growth, as a place for play in the Winnicottian sense, and as being like therapy in that it provides a regular time and place for taking a second look at what happened in the therapy session. (Winnicott derived many of his ideas from his work with children. He saw psychotherapy taking place in the overlap of two playing areas, that of the patient and that of the therapist. The therapist's job is to help the patient move from a state of not being able to play into one of being able to play. Playing is a specially creative, intensely real activity which allows new syntheses to emerge.) Supervision aims to bring to the fore the creative potential of the therapist. It should be noted that supervision is not the same as therapy, though at times the distinction may become blurred.

Broadly speaking, the focus of supervisory interest can be on one of three areas: the process and content of the patient's concerns and communications, transference and counter-transference reactions between therapist and patient, and the trainee–supervisor relationship. The focus on the last is justified by Doehrman's (1976) classic study which demonstrated the re-creation in the trainee–supervisor relationship of the dynamics between patient and therapist and, at least theoretically, supports the view that, if the dynamics in supervision can be comprehended and resolved, blocks in the therapy relationship will be undone (for an example, see Caligor 1984). In practice, all these foci are useful though, in my practice, I incline towards the first as it is the patient's life that is my primary concern.

Much debate rages in psychotherapy circles about how the supervisory material should be presented. Classically in psychoanalytic training, a free-flowing account of the session is given with much attention being paid to what is said and not said and the elucidation of .counter-transferences and associations as ways of illuminating unconscious processes. This is listening with the third ear (Reik 1949). That the report may factually correspond poorly to the observable events of the session is held to be of little importance; indeed some supervisors argue that factually precise reporting both misses the point and may positively obscure it. I cannot accept this position. All ways of capturing the facts and essence of what went on are useful. Aids to supervision are just that: servants, not masters. They can be adapted to meet the needs of the moment.

After each session, trainees will write notes detailing content, process and feeling issues. It is advantageous to have audio or video-recordings of the session, which may be viewed from the beginning or at a point of difficulty or interest or . . . not at all. Such recordings document the actual sequence of events and bring the dimensions of non-verbal and paralinguistic communication and change in emotional tone into the arena of supervision. Other means may be utilized. Transcripts allow the leisurely study of process and form of verbal intervention; as a semi-research exercise, the method of Brief Structured Recall (Elliott and Shapiro 1988) may be used to go over with the patient what were the most significant events in a session; the significant events are identified by the patient immediately after the session, then therapist and patient listen to the tape just before, during and after the event, and amplify through discussion the associated feelings, meaning and impact of that segment of interaction. Live supervision from behind a screen with either telephone contact or a 'bug in the ear' may also be employed, though such measures reduce the scope for the therapist to grapple on her own as a person with the patient's issues. There is more to be said for the supervisor leading the way in openness by occasionally putting his own tapes forward for discussion.

Being supervised is supposed to be helpful, but it can be persecutory (Bruzzone *et al.* 1985) and intrusive (Betcher and Zinberg 1988). The trainee's self-esteem is vulnerable; there needs to be room in the training for privacy and for mistakes to be able to be made and discussed without dire penalty or excessive shame.

Counter-transference reactions on the part of the supervisor must not be forgotten. The trainee may represent the coming generation who may equal or overtake the supervisor in skill and knowledge. Rivalry and the struggle for power may constitute a subtext for the supervisory meetings and, if not resolved, prove detrimental to professional development. A forum for supervisors to discuss problems in supervision is beneficial. In the training, it is also sensible and desirable in its own right to have group supervision as well as individual supervision, as the former provides multiple perspectives, peer support and the morale-enhancing opportunity of being of assistance to colleagues.

Skills development

While I favour weekly supervision over months and years as the best complement to the work of individual therapy, workshops and role-plays quickly lead to the acquisition of fundamental skills. Without risking any harm to the patient, difficult situations that therapists commonly face can be practised, the effects of different interventions observed and the model presented by more experienced therapists evaluated. Micro-counselling training courses first described at the end of the 1960s have retained their promise for the relatively inexperienced trainee; they provide structured, focused learning over periods of one, two or three days with a strong emphasis on skills-acquisition through role-play. At the more advanced, approach-specific level, the use of detailed treatment manuals for such diverse approaches as supportive-expressive psychoanalytic psychotherapy, cognitive and interpersonal therapy of depression and short-term therapy is an interesting, effective, new method of skill development (Matarazzo and Patterson 1986).

Personal therapy

'The therapist can only go as far with the patient as he can go himself', so the maxim runs. What therapists can bear to hear in themselves, they can hear in their patients. What therapists can find in themselves, they can recognize in others. Thus in addition to the resistance made by patients to dismantling defensive, outmoded but originally adaptive patterns, therapists contribute a resistance of their own to free exploration. The therapist's resistance may take the form of avoidance or over-interest; the former limits the opening up of areas of concern for the patient, the latter diverts the focus of the discourse to the therapist's own conflictual issues; these processes largely takes place out of consciousness. Examples have been given in the sections on counter-transference and the abuse of power of some common personal conflicts which may limit or adversely distort the engagement of the therapist. All therapies at some stage confront reflective therapists with the dilemmas in their own lives and the partial solutions that they have adopted. An overlap of conflictual issue between therapist and patient often results in a blocked therapy, but may generate a particularly fruitful dyad when the therapist's conflict is not too great and the overlap enhances empathic contact.

Life experience and the practice of psychotherapy educate therapists about themselves. Self-scrutiny takes the learning about conflicts and their resolution one step further but the therapist's own internal security measures operate to maintain blind spots and protect self-esteem from sobering self-realizations; these defences limit what can be done alone. Personal therapy offers the therapist the same opportunity as the patient has to explore, understand and resolve inner conflicts. It brings together theoretical learning and psychotherapy practice in an experience that makes personal sense of the two. At a practical level, personal therapy provides a means through which sufficient self-understanding can be gained for therapists to recognize how their personality and life experience affect their ability to be objective and to reduce their tendency to impose their own solutions on the life problems of their patients (JCHPT 1987). The nature of the conflicts that interfere with therapists' work predicate their requirements for therapy in terms of type, duration and frequency and the achievement of sufficient resolution in order to work more effectively indicates the end-point of personal therapy on the practical level. At the next level, therapy aims to enhance therapists' abilities to relate, empathically and creatively, to their patients. One element in this is knowing at first hand what it is like to be a patient, another is the loosening through therapy of the self-limiting grip of personal conflicts. Beyond that, as was detailed in the section on motivating factors in the therapist, therapy offers an opportunity for therapists to heal themselves, an unmet need which may have been of prime importance in the selection by the trainee therapist of this kind of work. At a sociological level, personal therapy has the function of a rite of passage, forming and affirming their identity as a psychotherapist and as a member of their professional group.

Perhaps the most compelling argument in favour of personal therapy is that every therapist, like every patient, sees the world through the perspective of their guiding fictions and is impelled to impose that order and those patterns on others. Thus, the more that therapists are aware of what are their personal, determining fictions, the more likely they will be able to engage with the reality of the other.

Personal therapy in varying intensity and duration is a required component of most formal, advanced trainings in psychotherapy; in psychoanalysis, full personal analysis is mandatory. In psychoanalysis, the sequence of engagement in training is being in therapy, then theory seminars and finally conducting analyses. In Henry's (1977) survey of 4,000 North American psychotherapists 74 per cent had been in personal therapy and nearly 50 per cent had re-entered therapy for two to four periods; conversely, 36 per cent had chosen not to pursue that course. Despite the consensus in favour of personal therapy especially at the psychodynamic end of the spectrum, there is little published evidence of its efficacy in enhancing therapeutic ability. Surveys of the literature by Greenberg and Staller (1981) and Macaskill (1988) conclude that first, 15–33 per cent of trainees have unsatisfactory personal therapy experiences, e.g. damage to marriage, destructive acting-out and excessive withdrawal from the outside world, second, therapy early in the therapist's career may have deleterious effects on work with patients, and third, there is no positive correlation between either the fact of having been in therapy or its duration on outcome of the therapist's professional work. The level of reported dissatisfaction is in line with that generally expected for negative effects in psychotherapy, and, as such, emphasizes the importance of the trainee making a sage choice of therapist.

When personal therapy is decided upon, its intensity and duration should parallel the form of psychotherapy that the therapist is going to practise.

Generally, this will be one or more times a week for three or more years. It is important that the therapist enters therapy not only because the training requires it but also to resolve personal conflicts or difficulty that are being encountered in his or her work and life. Advice on whom to consult should be sought from an experienced adviser who can steer the trainee away from pairings that are less than optimal and towards those of greater promise (Coltart 1987). Exploratory sessions should be held with several potential therapists before the choice is made. This counsel of perfection could well apply to patients if ever they were in the position of being able to choose whom to see.

Evaluation

During training, there should be opportunities for evaluation, both formatively and normatively. It will be recalled that, in educational terms, 'formative' evaluation refers to non-examined elements that enrich the educational experience of training, whereas 'normative' refers to entry/exit, pass/fail criteria. The aims of the training should be clearly stated and be attainable within the learning experiences of the scheme. A system for monitoring progress both by self-assessment and by the trainers is necessary, as is the giving of feedback so as to help trainees improve the quality of their psychotherapy. Individual and psychometric assessment of severity of patient problem can form a baseline for the evaluation of the success of therapy. Case books recording progress and any alteration in formulation document the range of therapy experience and the lessons to be learnt not from books but from actual practice. Detailed written case accounts of one or more psychotherapies carried out by the trainee demonstrate the degree of the trainee's development and bring into focus how difficulties have been encountered and struggled with. Personal tutors have a key role as adviser and appraiser to trainees finding their way through the training. Ultimately, evaluation should address the question of therapist competence: how effective is this therapist in aiding the quest of his or her patients towards more fruitful living? The methodology to assess this does not yet exist. Only partial progress has been made towards the subsidiary but important question of what has this training added to the therapist's ability; one example is the quantification of the improvement in interviewing skills acquired through micro-counselling courses (Matarazzo and Patterson 1986).

Supportive psychotherapy

The rhetoric of psychotherapy is towards fundamental change in people's feelings, attitudes and interactions; this has been the type of individual therapy for which training has been described in this chapter. The trainee therapist in her enthusiasm and inexperience of the struggle to survive that many patients face may be tempted to press for a pace and depth of change for which her patient is not ready. Fundamental change will not be possible or desirable for all or, if possible, no authorization may have been given by the patient for deep exploration which may profoundly challenge his view of himself. This situation has to be explicitly respected and the value of support recognized and taught in training. All therapy has to have in it a sufficiently supportive element in order to help the patient contend with the upheaval of change: most therapies will move between challenging and supportive phases. Furthermore, supportive psychotherapy is a subject in its own right. It is indicated for the many individuals who need sustained support in order to return them to their optimal level of adjustment and maintain them there. It has its own complex skills and needs to be learnt by even the most therapeutically ambitious therapist.

Registration

At present, anyone in Britain may practise as a psychotherapist and advertise their services as such. Unlike North America and many European countries, psychotherapy is not a regulated profession. No formal training or subscription to a code of ethics is required. Within institutions such as the NHS, universities and polytechnics, the consumer of psychotherapy has the protection of knowing that for the most part the therapist will have been appointed in open competition with other applicants, and has the sanction of being able to initiate an official complaint. Membership of professions that are regulated by statutory bodies as for example is medicine by the General Medical Council or of training institutes with regulatory powers afford some assurance that the standards of the therapist are adequate and will be maintained. But in the private sector, members of the public have little protection against the misinformed or unethical therapist. This is bad for the consumer and bad for the profession.

The Foster Report (1971), a government-appointed inquiry, recommended that the profession of psychotherapy be regulated by statute. Seven years later, the Sieghart Report (1978) proposed the establishment of a council which would draw up and enforce a code of professional ethics and approve training courses. Registration of individuals as psychotherapists would be indicative rather than functional, that is on the basis of titles associated with various forms of psychotherapy. The desirable goal of registration as some guarantee of integrity and competence has since not made much progress. A Private Member's Bill in Parliament failed and the core professions have not been able to agree on a common position. For several years, a talking shop of psychotherapy organizations has been held each year in Rugby (the 'Rugby Conference'), initially under the auspices of the British Association for Counselling. The participating organizations have with some difficulty grouped into six sections: analyst, analytical, behavioural, family/marital/sexual, and humanistic and integrative psychotherapy plus hypnotherapy and neuro-linguistic programming. In 1989 the Conference adopted a formal constitution. It is possible that this body may become *de facto* a registering body. Whether this occurs or not, some form of registration and, for that matter, re-registration is likely to come into being.

Implicit in the above is the proposition that continued attention to competence is part of the professional attitude of the psychotherapist. This is particularly important for the individual therapist as that person tends to work in relative or absolute isolation and, in the absence of challenging opportunities for further learning, may develop poor working practices. Feedback from colleagues in peer-group supervision of actual clinical work is especially helpful.

Conclusion

The current practice of psychotherapy distils out what is known about human healing. In its practice, it is both an art and a science; both elements need to be born in mind in training. Training may occur in phases but is a lifelong commitment. Competence is achievable but there is always more for the therapist to learn. No end point has been reached in the development of individual therapy as an agent of personal change. Further refinement in theory, scope and practice can be expected, especially if the practitioners of the different individual psychotherapies learn to speak with one another in pursuit of the common goal of assisting patients to lead more fruitful lives.

References

Adler, G. (1972) Helplessness in the helpers, *British Journal of Medical Psychology* 45: 315–25.
Auerbach, A.A. and Johnson, M. (1977) Research on the therapist's level of experience, in A.S. Gurman and A.M. Razin (eds) *Effective Psychotherapy*, Oxford: Pergamon Press.
Aveline, M.O. (1980) Making a psychodynamic formulation, *Bulletin of the Royal College of Psychiatrists* 4: 192–3.
—— (1986) The corrective emotional experience, a fundamental unifying concept in psychotherapy. Paper presented at the Annual Conference of the Society for Psychotherapy Research, Wellesley College, Massachusetts, June.
—— (1987) Parameters of danger: interactive elements in the therapy dyad. Paper presented at the First Tavistock Symposium on The Anxiety of Beginnings, London.
—— (1988a) Issues in the training of group therapists, in M. Aveline and W. Dryden (eds) *Group Therapy in Britain*, Milton Keynes: Open University Press.
—— (1988b) The relationship of drug therapy and psychotherapy, *Current Opinion in Psychiatry* 1: 309–13.
—— (1989) The provision of illusion in psychotherapy, *Midland Journal of Psychotherapy*.
Bennet, G. (1987) *The Wound and the Doctor*, London: Secker & Warburg.
Bernstein, L. and Bernstein, R.S. (1980) *Interviewing: A Guide for Health Professionals*, New York: Appleton-Century-Crofts.
Betcher, R.W. and Zinberg, N.E. (1988) Supervision and privacy in psychotherapy training, *American Journal of Psychiatry* 145: 796–803.
Bruzzone, M., Casaula, E., Jimenz, J.P. and Jordan, J.F. (1985) Regression and persecution in analytic training: reflections on experience, *International Review of Psycho-Analysis* 12: 411–15.
Bugental, J.F.T. (1964) The person who is the psychotherapist, *Journal of Counseling Psychology* 28: 272–7.
Burton, A. (1975) Therapist satisfaction, *American Journal of Psychoanalysis* 35: 115–22.
Caligor, L. (1984) Parallel and reciprocal processes in psychoanalytic supervision, in L. Caligor, P.M. Bromberg and J.D. Meltzer (eds) *Clinical Perspectives on the Supervision of Psychoanalysis and Psychotherapy*, New York: Plenum Press.
Casement, P. (1985) *On Learning from the Patient*, London: Tavistock.

Cleghorn, J.M., Bellissimo, A. and Will, D. (1983) Teaching some principles of individual psychodynamics through an introductory guide to formulations, *Canadian Journal of Psychiatry* 28: 162–72.

Coltart, N. (1987) Diagnosis and assessment for suitability for psycho-analytical psychotherapy, *British Journal of Psychotherapy* 4: 127–34.

Davis, J.D., Elliott, R., Davis, M.L., Binns, M., Francis, V.M., Kelman, J.E. and Schroder, T.A. (1987) Development of a taxonomy of therapist difficulties: initial report, *British Journal of Medical Psychology* 60: 109–19.

Doehrman, M.J.G. (1976) Parallel processes in supervision and psychotherapy, *Bulletin of the Menninger Clinic* 40: 1–104.

Elliott, R. and Shapiro, D.A. (1988) Brief structured recall: a more efficient method for studying significant therapy moments, *British Journal of Medical Psychology* 61: 141–53.

Fairbairn, W.R.D. (1954) *An Object-Relations Theory of the Personality*, New York: Basic Books.

Farber, B.A. (1983) The effects of psychotherapeutic practice upon psychotherapists, *Psychotherapy: Theory, Research and Practice* 20: 174–82.

Farber, B.A. and Heifetz, L.J. (1981) The satisfactions and stresses of psychotherapy work: a factor analytic study, *Professional Psychology* 12: 621–30.

Fleming, J. (1987) *The Teaching and Learning of Psychoanalysis*, New York: Guilford Press.

Foster, J.G. (1971) *Enquiry into the Practice and Effects of Scientology*, London: HMSO.

Frank, J.D. (1973) *Persuasion and Healing*, 2nd edn, New York: Schocken Books.

Friedman, R.S. and Lister, P. (1987) The current status of the psychodynamic formulation, *Psychiatry* 50: 126–41.

Gosling, R. (1978) Internalization of the trainer's behaviour in professional training, *British Journal of Medical Psychology* 51: 35–40.

Greben, S.E. (1975) Some difficulties and satisfactions inherent in the practice of psycho-analysis, *International Journal of Psycho-Analysis* 56: 427–33.

—— (1984) *Love's Labor*, New York: Schocken Books.

Greenberg, R.P. and Staller, J. (1981) Personal therapy for therapists, *American Journal of Psychiatry* 138,1: 467–71.

Greenson, R.R. (1967) *The Technique and Practice of Psychoanalysis*, vol. 1, New York: International Universities Press.

Guggenbuhl-Craig, A. (1979) *Power in the Helping Professions*, Irving, Tex: Spring Publications.

Guy, J.D. (1987) *The Personal Life of the Psychotherapist*, New York: Wiley.

Heimann, P. (1950) On counter-transference, *International Journal of Psychoanalysis* 31: 81–4.

Henry, W.A. (1977) Personal and social identities of psychotherapists, in A.S. Gurman and A.M. Razin (eds) *Effective Psychotherapy*, Oxford: Pergamon Press.

Hess, A.K. (1986) Growth in supervision: stages of supervisee and supervisor development, in F.W. Kaslow (ed.) *Supervision and Training: Models, Dilemmas, Challenges*, New York: Haworth Press.

Holmes, J. (1986) Teaching the psychotherapeutic method: some literary parallels, *British Journal of Medical Psychology* 59: 113–21.

Holroyd, J.C. and Brodsky, A.M. (1977) Psychologists' attitudes and practices regarding erotic and non-erotic physical contact with patients, *American Psychologist* 32: 843–9.

JCHPT (Joint Committee on Higher Psychiatric Training) (1987) Requirements for specialist training in psychotherapy, London: Royal College of Psychiatrists.

Jones, E. (1913) The God complex, *Essays in Applied Psychoanalysis*, vol. 2, London: Hogarth Press.

Lambert, M.J. (1986) Implications of psychotherapy outcome research for eclectic psycho-therapy, in J.C. Norcross (ed.) *Handbook of Eclectic Psychotherapy*, New York: Brunner Mazel.

Lomas, P. (1981) *The Case for a Personal Psychotherapy*, Oxford: Oxford University Press.

Luborsky, L. and Singer, B. (1974) The fit of therapists' behavior into patients' negative expectations: a study of transference-countertransference contagion, unpublished manuscript, University of Pennsylvania.

Luborsky, L., Singer, B. and Luborsky, L. (1975) Comparative studies of psycho-therapies: is it true that 'Everyone has won and all must have prizes?', *Archives of General Psychiatry* 32: 995–1008.

Macaskill, N.D. (1988) Personal therapy in the training of the psychotherapist: is it effective?, *British Journal of Psychotherapy* 4: 219–26.

Malan, D. (1979) *Individual Psychotherapy and the Science of Psychodynamics*, London: Butterworths.

Marmor, J. (1953) The feeling of superiority: an occupational hazard in the practice of psychotherapy, *American Journal of Psychiatry* 110: 370–3.

—— (1972) Sexual acting-out in psychotherapy, *American Journal of Psycho-analysis* 22: 3–8.

Matarazzo, R.G. and Patterson, D.R. (1986) Methods of teaching therapeutic skill, in S.L. Garfield and A.L. Bergin (eds) *Handbook of Psychotherapy and Behavior Change*, 3rd edn, New York: Wiley.

Menninger, K. (1958) *Theory of Psychoanalytic Technique*, New York: Basic Books.

Pedder, J. (1986) Reflections on the theory and practice of supervision, *Psychoanalytic Psychotherapy* 2: 1–12.

Perry, S., Cooper, A.M. and Michels, R. (1987) The psychodynamic formulation: its purpose, structure, and clinical application, *American Journal of Psychiatry* 144: 543–50.

Reik, T. (1949) *Listening with the Third Ear*, New York: Farrer, Straus.

Rogers, C.R. (1957) The necessary and sufficient conditions of therapeutic personality change, *Journal of Consulting Psychology* 21: 95–103.

Rosin, S.A. and Knudson, R.M. (1986) Perceived influence of life experiences on clinical psychologists' selection and development of theoretical orientations, *Psychotherapy* 23: 357–63.

Sandler, J. (1988) Psychoanalysis and psychoanalytic psychotherapy: problems of differentiation. Paper read at Conference on Psychoanalysis and Psychoanalytic Psychotherapy (Association of Psychoanalytic Psychotherapy in the NHS) London, 22–23 April 1988.

Schafer, R. (1983) *The Analytic Attitude*, London: Hogarth Press.

Sieghart, P. (1978) *Statutory Registration of Psychotherapists*, London: Tavistock Clinic.

Storr, A (1979) *The Art of Psychotherapy*, London: Secker & Warburg.

Strupp, H.H. (1960) *Psychotherapists in Action*, New York: Grune & Stratton.

—— (1977) A reformulation of the dynamics of the therapist's contribution, in A.S. Gurman and A.M. Razin (eds) *Effective Psychotherapy*, Oxford: Pergamon Press.

Strupp, H.H. and Binder, J.L. (1984) *A Guide to Time-Limited Dynamic Psychotherapy*, New York: Basic Books.

Appendix 1

Chapter structure
(for authors of chapters 2-12)

1   Historical context and development in Britain (1,000 words)

1.1 Historical context

Your aim here should be briefly to acquaint the reader unfamiliar with your approach with its *historical context*. Examine its historical origins, its intellectual roots and explain why it is called what it is.

1.2 Development in Britain

Your aim here should be to treat briefly the development of the approach in Britain (where this is different from 1.1) up to the time of writing.

2   Theoretical assumptions (2,500 words)

2.1 Image of the person

Outline the basic assumptions made by the approach about the person and human nature.

2.2 Conceptualization of psychological disturbance and health

Outline how the approach conceptualizes both psychological disturbance and psychological health. Explain in detail the *major concepts* utilized by the approach in accounting for psychological disturbance and health.

2.3 Acquisition of psychological disturbance

Explain the approach's views on how psychological disturbance is acquired.

2.4 Perpetuation of psychological disturbance

Explain the approach's position on how psychological disturbance is perpetuated. What *intrapersonal mechanisms* are utilized by individuals to perpetuate their own psychological disturbance; what *interpersonal mechanisms* are recognized as important in the perpetuation process; what is the role of the *environment* on the perpetuation process?

2.5 Change

You should use this section to outline briefly the approach's views on how humans change with respect to movement from psychological disturbance to psychological health. This section should orient the reader to what follows under 'Practice' but should not be limited to the change process in therapy (i.e. it should not duplicate section 3.6). Thus it should both complete the 'Acquisition-Perpetuation-Change' cycle and orient the reader to what follows.

3 Practice (5,000 words)

3.1 Goals of therapy

Your aim here is to set out the goals of the approach.

3.2 Selection criteria

What selection criteria are used to determine whether or not clients will benefit from the approach in its *individual therapy format*? There are two issues here: first, what clients (if any) are deemed unsuitable for the particular approach under consideration (refer back to 3.1 here where relevant), and second, what criteria are employed in deciding whether or not clients who are suitable for the approach would benefit from individual therapy (as opposed to couples, family and group therapy) at the outset. What criteria are employed when decisions concerning transfer from one modality (e.g. individual therapy) to another (e.g. group therapy) become salient? Indeed when do these issues become salient? What are the approach's views on the use of concurrent therapeutic modalities (e.g. where the client is seen in both individual and group therapy)?

3.3 Qualities of effective therapists

From the point of view of the approach under consideration, what qualities do effective therapists have? Focus on both personal qualities and skill variables. In writing this section what is the relative importance of personal characteristics vs skill factors here?

3.4 Therapeutic style

Here you should characterize the interactive style of the therapist in the conduct of the approach in action. (While you will no doubt use your own dimensions the following might be kept in mind: active–passive; formal–informal; self-disclosing–non-self-disclosing; humorous–serious). How does the interactive style of the therapist change during the therapeutic process?

3.5 Major therapeutic strategies and techniques

List and describe the major strategies and techniques advocated as therapeutic by the approach. According to Marvin Goldfried strategies lie at a level of abstraction between theory and techniques, so techniques are more *specific* than strategies. Please use this formulation in preparing this section and list the strategies first, showing how the techniques are specific ways of operationalizing the strategies. I am quite aware that some approaches cannot easily be described in these terms. Contact me if this is the case and we'll discuss how best to write this section.

3.6 The change process in therapy

Here outline the process of therapeutic change from beginning to end. What reliable patterns of change can be discerned in successful cases? Outline the major sources of lack of therapeutic progress and how these are addressed in the approach.

3.7 Limitations of the approach

Here describe the limitations of the approach. Where is there room for improvement? How should the approach develop in the future to rectify such deficiencies?

4   Case example (1,500 words)

Fully describe a case (a British client) which shows the approach in action, referring whenever possible to the above framework and dividing the section thus:

4.1 The client

Briefly describe the client and his/her presenting concerns.

4.2 The therapy

Here the emphasis should be on describing the process of change (i.e. how the therapy unfolded over time). Speculate on the sources of therapeutic change. What, with hindsight, might you have done differently?

Please resist the temptation to select a 'brilliant success'. Choose a case that readers can relate to, i.e. one that had its difficulties and where the client had a realistic (not an idealistic) outcome.

NB: Those of you who contributed a chapter to *Individual Therapy in Britain* should present a NEW case.

Appendix 2

Useful addresses

Contributors were asked to provide not more than two addresses for those wishing information on therapy services and training opportunities in a particular approach. The organizations listed will often give details of others not detailed here.

Psychodynamic therapy: the Freudian approach

Therapy

London Centre for Psychotherapy
19 Fitzjohn's Avenue
London NW3 5JY

Training

British Association for Psychotherapy
121 Hendon Lane
London NW3 3PR

Psychodynamic therapy: the Kleinian approach

Therapy and training

Institute of Psycho-Analysis
63 New Cavendish Street
London W1M 7RD

Psychodynamic therapy: the Jungian approach

Therapy and training

Society of Analytical Psychology
1 Daleham Gardens
London NW3 5BY

Association of Jungian Analysts
Flat 3
7 Eton Avenue
London NW3 3EL

Adlerian therapy

Therapy

Adlerian Society for Individual Psychology
161 Charlton Church Lane
London SE7 7AA

Training

Institute for Individual Psychology
161 Charlton Church Lane
London SE7 7AA

Person-centred therapy

Therapy

Norwich Centre for Personal and Professional Development
7 Earlham Road
Norwich NR2 3RA

Training

Facilitator Development Institute
Norwich Centre for Personal and Professional Development
7 Earlham Road
Norwich NR2 3RA

Personal construct therapy

Therapy and training

Centre for Personal Construct Psychology
132 Warwick Way
London SW1V 4JD

Existential therapy

Therapy and training

Society for Existential Analysis
Psychology Department
Regent's College
Inner Circle
Regent's Park
London NW1 4NS

Gestalt therapy

Therapy and training

The Gestalt Centre, London
Administrator
64 Warwick Road
St Albans
Hertfordshire AL1 4DL

The Gestalt Psychotherapy Training Institute UK
P.O. Box 620
Bristol
BS99 7DL

Transactional Analysis

Therapy and training

Institute of Transactional Analysis
BM Box 4104
London WC1 3XX

Cognitive therapy

Therapy

Referral to local Department of Clinical Psychology via general practitioner

Training

Ruth Williams
Institute of Psychiatry
De Crespigny Park
London SE5 8AF

Behaviour therapy

Therapy and training

Psychological Treatment Unit
Maudsley Hospital
London SE5

Further information

In addition, useful referral and training directories are available from

British Association for Counselling
37A Sheep Street
Rugby
Warwickshire CV21 3BX

Feedback

The editor welcomes feedback on the present volume;
Correspondence should be addressed to

Windy Dryden
Department of Psychology
Goldsmiths' College
New Cross
London SE14 6NW

Index

dysfunctional motivators of therapists, 319–20

eating problems, 63, 64, 67, 258–9, 260, 261, 266, 298–9, 306
eclecticism, 9–10, 11, 13–14
Eder, David, 19
effectiveness of therapy, 284–5
effort, therapeutic, 288
'ego', 21, 43, 74
ego states, 202–5, 214–15, 216–17, 218, 222, 223
Ellis, Albert, 226, 227
Emery, G., 231, 238
empathy from therapist, 95, 97, 112, 117–18, 120, 123, 294
empiricism, 8
empty chair technique *see* two-chair technique
'encouraged individuals', 90
environment
    influence on health/disturbance, 26, 60–1, 93, 112, 154, 155–6, 183, 233
    therapeutic, 30, 31
envy, 47
Enwright, J., 179
equality
    between client and therapist, 94, 95, 96, 99, 187–8, 213, 274
    feeling of, 89, 90, 98, 99
'equivalence paradox', 301
errors, therapeutic, 33, 118
Erskine, R.G., 208
ethical standards, 322
evaluation
    as cognitive process, 227
    of change, 289–90
    of therapists, 335
'events' paradigm of research, 290–1
evolution, personal, 183–5
existential therapy, 149–72, 274, 275, 276–7, 279–80
    acquisition of disturbance in, 154–5
    case example of, 166–72
    change in, 156–7, 164–5
    conceptualization of health/disturbance in, 153–4
    development in Britain, 151–2
    goals of therapy in, 157

historical context of, 149–51
image of the person in, 152–3
limitations of, 165–6
perpetuation of disturbance in, 155–6
qualities of effective therapists in, 159–60
selection criteria in, 158
therapeutic strategies/techniques in, 161–4
therapeutic style in, 160–1
existentialism, 201
expectations/anticipations, 123, 130, 134
experience, living in, 109, 115, 120–1
'experience corollary', 133
experimentation, 188, 191, 196
    behaviour as, 131–2, 134, 135, 146, 237, 242
exposure principle/therapy, 252, 257, 258, 261, 264–6, 269, 270–1
extraversion, 74
Eysenck, Hans, 7–8, 9, 11, 254, 284, 297

Facilitator Development Institute, 107
Fairbairn, W.R.D., 321
Fairburn, C.G., 306
family
    constellation, 92, 96–7, 100, 101
    therapy, 77, 94, 114–15, 135–6
fantasy, 47–8, 52, 75, 79, 82, 83, 182–3
Farrell, B.J., 61
feelings, getting in touch with, 164, 189–90
Fennell, Melanie, 228, 235, 300, 303
Ferenczi, Sandor, 40
First World War, 4–5
fixed role therapy, 138, 141.
flexibility of therapist, 160–1, 188, 213, 263, 275–6
'flooding', 265
foetus, 42–3
'follow-up' assessment, 285
Fonagy, P., 302–3
Fordham, Michael, 71, 72–3
Foster Report (1971), 336
Frank, J.D., 327
Frankfurt School, 11
Frankl, V.E., 151
Fransella, F., 142
free-association, 30, 31, 41, 78

Index compiled by Peva Keane